KINGDOM IN CONTEXT
Missiological Interpretation, Genesis 1 and the City

Adam D. Ayers

Foreword
by
Charles Van Engen

Urban Loft Publishers | Skyforest, CA

Kingdom in Context

Missiological Interpretation, Genesis 1 and the City

Copyright © 2020 Adam D. Ayers

All rights reserved. Except for brief quotations in critical publications or reviews, no part of this book may be reproduced in any manner without prior written permission from the publisher. Write: Permissions, Urban Loft Publishers, P.O. Box 6
Skyforest, CA, 92385.

Urban Loft Publishers
P.O. Box 6
Skyforest, CA 92385
www.urbanloftpublishers.com

Senior Editors: Stephen Burris & Kendi Howells Douglas
Copy Editor: Brittnay Parsons
Graphics: Brittnay Parsons
Cover Design: Elizabeth Arnold

Scripture quotations are from various translations and mostly taken from the *Holy Bible*, English Standard Version, copyright © 2001, 2007, 2016 by Good News Publishers. Used by permission of Good News Publishers, Wheaton, Illinois 60187. All rights reserved.

ISBN-13: 978-1-949625-08-0

Made in the U.S

With love and highest regards, this work is dedicated to pastor Wes Davis, a true brother and example of kingdom service.

Table of Contents

TABLE OF CONTENTS 4

TABLE OF FIGURES 7

Preface 9
Foreword 11
Introduction 17
Acknowledgements 29

Part I 31

Chapter 1: ***Missiological Interpretation*** 31
    Getting the Text 36
    Discerning the Text's Mission 38
    Mission Oriented Reading 39
    Mission, Missional, and Missiological Hermeneutics 40
    Mission and Missiology 45
    The State of Missiological Hermeneutics 51
    Missiology and the Academic Division of Labor 58

Chapter 2: ***Missiological Distinctives*** 65
    Discourse and Purpose 66
    Discourse and Context 67
    Missiological Reference Points 71
    Interpretive Intersections 83

Chapter 3: ***Kingdom and Context: Divine and Human Authorship*** 113
    Kingdom: Interpreting in Light of God's Metanarrative 113
    Context: Reading for Combined Purposes 122

Chapter 4: ***Kingdom and Context: Horizons, Time and Groups*** 137
    Kingdom Context: The Notion of "Gap" 137
    Kingdom Context: Group and Time Horizons 147
    Kingdom Contexts: Varied Readerships 152

    Green's "Behind," "In," and "In Front" Model 154
    Summary 161

PART II 163

    Chapter 5: *Missiological Method: Text as Topography* 163
        Models For Missiological Reading 164
        Topographic Reading as Missiological Reading 167
        Topographic Theory 172
        From Topographic Model to Missiological Method 186
    Chapter 6: **Missiological Method: Text as Product, Ground and Tool** 193
        Bible as a Product of Mission 194
        Bible as a Ground for Mission 198
        Bible as a Tool within Mission 207
    Chapter 7: **Reading the Genesis 1 Creation Account** 217
        Topographic Analysis of Genesis 1 218
        Product, Ground and Tool 243
        Checking Results 267
    Chapter 8: **Missiological Interpretation of the City** 271
        Toward a Missiological Understanding of "Urban": the *missio urbis* 274
        The City as a Thing of Missio 278
        The City as a Joint Composition 284
        Subordinate and Contributive Missios 287
        Category and Particularity 299
        Missio Dei and *Missio Urbis* 305
        Urban Dynamics 310
    Chapter 9: **The City and Genesis 1** 323
        Juxtaposing the City and Genesis 1 323
        Provision and the Urban Horizon 329

PART IV 343

    Chapter 10: **Missiological Consideration of the City and Genesis 1** 343
        The City through Creation Eyes 345
        The City through Kingdom Eyes 355
        The City through Mission Eyes 367

Chapter 11: ***Missio-Urban Concerns*** 373
    Urban Mission Concerns 374
    Ideal States and Experienced States 375
    Urban Frustration and Suffering 379
    Human Rights and Social Justice 387
    Male and Female 396
    Reframing Missio-Urban Concerns 401

Chapter 12: ***Mission in the Urban Context*** 403
    Challenges and Practices 404
    Secular-Religious Relations 412
    Image-based Evaluation and Decision-making 415
    Globalization 418
    Summary 422
    Conclusion 423

Index 425

Works Cited 437

Table of Figures

Figure 1. Hiebert's diagram of "The Modern Worldview" showing the "Excluded Middle" 76

Figure 2. Societal, institutional and personal purposes in knowledge production. 127

Figure 3. Text as a combined production of knowledge. 128

Figure 4. Complex purpose relations within knowledge and texts. 129

Figure 5. God's purposes as a contributing influence. 133

Figure 6. The missio Dei and complex purpose relations. 134

Figure 7. Expanding "We" and "Now" of mission horizons in the first reading event. 151

Figure 8. Mission purposes "for" and "through" the "Behind," "In" and "In Front." 156

Figure 9. Multiple-context relations at the "in Front of" stage. 158

Figure 10. Multiple potential contexts and uses. 160

Figure 11. Resistance and Yield. 174

Preface

This book is in many ways a public invitation to ongoing conversations about mission, biblical interpretation, and the city that have taken place over the last few years between Chuck Van Engen, Joel Green, Jude Tiersma-Watson, Stephen Burris, Paul Hertig and myself. During the course of these conversations, a few key points kept recurring. One point was that there is no time like the present to talk deeply about missiological interpretation. Another was that there was a significant need for a demonstration of missiological method that students and scholars could access without extensive understanding of hermeneutics or mission-based studies. A third point was that missiological interpretation needed to connect biblical reading to the realities of contemporary society, especially to the urban context.

With much gratitude to those who already have shaped the ideas presented here, I want to welcome you in the name of the Lord to join our conversation, and let you know at the outset that you, the reader, already have been in my prayers and in the prayers of the editors at Urban Loft who have made this discussion available. May the Lord grant you a fruitful journey into missiological interpretation, and from missiological interpretation, a fruitful journey outward into the world.

Foreword

With this volume, Adam Ayers has done a special service for all of us who think, teach, write, and research in the discipline we know as "Missiology." Although there were some important Protestant precursors like Hadrianus Saravia (1531-1612), Gisbertus Voetius (1587-1651), and Johannes Hoornbeeck, (1617-1666) Missiology, or "the science of missions" as a recognized academic discipline in its own right is rather recent. Gustav Warneck (1834-1910) the German, nineteenth century pastor and theologian is considered the founder of modern missiology.[1] The best summary of the history of Missiology as a discipline in relation to other areas of theological scholarship is the one compiled forty years ago by Johannes Verkuyl (1908-2001) which he summarized in the first three chapters of his *Contemporary Missiology: an Introduction.*

In that volume, Verkuyl defined Missiology as follows:

> Missiology is the study of the salvation activities of the Father, Son, and Holy Spirit throughout the world geared toward bringing the kingdom of God into existence.

Seen in this perspective, missiology is the study of the worldwide church's divine mandate to be ready to serve this God who is aiming his saving acts toward this world. In dependence on the Holy Spirit and by word and deed, the church is to communicate the total gospel and the total divine law to all (hu)mankind.

---

[1] An excellent resource concerning Gustav Warneck can be found in http://www.bu.edu/missiology/missionary-biography/w-x-y-z/warneck-gustav-1834-1910. See also David Bosch. *Transforming Mission: Paradigm Shifts in the Theology of Mission.* Maryknoll: Orbis, 244; and Gerald Anderson, edit. "Gustav Warneck," *Biographical Dictionary of Christian Missions.* N.Y.: Macmillan, 718.

Missiology's task is in every age to investigate scientifically and critically the presuppositions, motives, structures, methods, patterns of cooperation, and leadership which the churches bring to their mandate. In addition, missiology must examine every other type of human activity which combats the various evils to see if it fits the criteria and goals of God's kingdom which has both already come and is yet coming.

Today students of this discipline are increasingly being referred to as missiologists. Usually, these people have logged some time in the area of practical experience and thus can prevent their scholarly work from turning into arid theorizing. A majority of missiologists concurrently serve as advisors to missionary service and developmental agencies. We missiologists are called to do our work on the threshold of the third millennium after Christ's birth, amid the giant changes and shifts in the world situation.

Missiology may never become a substitute for action and participation. God calls for participants and volunteers in his mission. In part, missiology's goal is to become a "service station" along the way. If study does not lead to participation, whether at home or abroad, missiology has lost her humble calling.[2]

What has been the relationship of Missiology to the other theological disciplines? Since Friedrich Schleiermacher (1768-1834), theological scholarship has been increasingly compartmentalized into specializations: biblical languages, biblical exegetical studies, church history, systematic theology, Christian Education, ethics, and practical or pastoral theology. More recently, other disciplines like "world religions" and "phenomenology of religion" have been added. In relationship to that piecemeal structure, Missiology has struggled to find its place. In this book, professor Ayers seeks to create a place—a space—for Missiology to converse

---

[2] Johannes Verkuyl. *Contemporary Mission: An Introduction*. G.R.: Eerdmans, 1978, 5-6

freely and constructively with other theological disciplines, particularly with biblical studies.

Ten years ago, Wilbert Shenk wrote about the emergence of Anglo-American mission theory. "It is axiomatic," he wrote, "that a science requires a supporting theory. In other words, an activity cannot properly be regarded as scientific if it does not have a supporting theoretical framework." [3] Sadly, the construction of a solid, cohesive, and coherent theoretical framework for Missiology as a "science of missions" has not yet been done. Shenk concludes that,

> Several observations concerning the place of theory in Anglo-American missions since 1800 bring this survey to a close. First, the role of mission theory has been ambiguous and erratic. As a concept it had largely disappeared from missiological thought by 1960. Second, this has left missions without a clear framework and a sense of the mission process as a whole, a basis for accountability. Furthermore, much of the writing on mission theory has been partial and parochial. The decline of theory has contributed to conceptual confusion. Thus, missions have failed to develop clear criteria for evaluating the evangelizing process. Instead, there has been uncritical dependence on the methods and techniques of modernity.[4]

What Shenk observes with regard to Anglo-American theory has been true globally, although there have been some notable recent attempts to rectify this situation, especially in the area of missiological hermeneutics.[5] How does Missiology provide us a particular reading of the Bible? How can we

---

[3] Wilbert Shenk. *Changing Frontiers of Mission*. Maryknoll: Orbis, 1999, 38.
[4] *Ibid*, 47.
[5] It is not possible in this brief Foreword to mention the numerous scholars who have offered us new approaches, methodologies and insights in terms of Missiology and missiological hermeneutics. I invite the reader to examine Charles Van Engen, edit. *The State of Missiology Today: Global Innovations in Christian Witness*(Downers Grove: IVP, 2016) to get an idea of some folks who are working and thinking about these issues.

read the Bible so that the Bible itself will critique, reshape, and transform our mission theory and practice? We are all indebted to the work of scholars like Donald Senior and Carroll Stuhlmueller, David Bosch, Christopher Wright, and Michael Goheen. It is important to note, however, that these colleagues were and are biblical scholars. Few missiologists with long-term cross-cultural, pastoral and missionary experience have dedicated time and effort to developing the theory, methodology, and practice of a missiological reading of the Bible. Pastor Adam Ayers builds on the work of Arthur Glasser, Shawn Redford, and others whom he mentions in this volume and then goes on to offer us new ideas, new approaches, new methods, and new questions.

Twenty-seven years ago, David Bosch challenged all of us to consider thirteen "elements of an emerging ecumenical missionary paradigm". I have long viewed that twelfth chapter in his book, *Transforming Mission Paradigm Shifts in Theology of Mission* as a kind of assignment in the construction of mission theory for all of us who want to think missiologically. In a similar way, Adam Ayers challenges the reader of this volume to construct a deeper, broader, and more complete theory and methodology in a thoroughly biblical missiological hermeneutics that interfaces with, challenges, and transforms all areas of theological reflection. Andrew Kirk said it this way:

> It is impossible to conceive of theology apart from mission. All true theology is, by definition, missionary theology, for it has as its object the study of the ways of a God who is by nature missionary and a foundation text written by and for missionaries. Mission as a discipline is not, then, the roof of a building that completes the whole structure, already constructed by blocks that stand on their own, but both the foundation and the mortar in the joints, which cements together everything else. Theology should not be pursued as a set of isolated disciplines. It assumes a model of cross-cultural

communication, for its subject matter both stands over against culture and relates closely to it. Therefore, it must be interdisciplinary and interactive.[6]

With this work, Dr. Ayers has moved the theory and discussion about Missiology and missiological hermeneutics a giant step forward. This is the case especially in terms of methodological considerations. He has given us tools to be able to better analyze and learn how Missiology can provide us with a new reading of the Bible and how the Bible itself can teach and guide us to more fully understand God's intention, God's mission, and the church's mission today.

Charles Van Engen

---

[6] J. Andrew Kirk. *The Mission of Theology and Theology as Mission*. Valley Forge: Trinity Press, 1997, 50-51.

Introduction

One of the beautiful aspects of contemporary academic discourse is its openness to a variety of voices. This openness, combined with an increasing awareness that human beings need to be engaged actively as custodians of our physical and social worlds, has created fertile ground for the growing discipline of missiology. Books and articles that integrate the idea of mission are now beginning to abound in non-religious environments, and "mission" has become a term of open consideration across a spectrum that ranges from business to art, education, politics, and sports.

As mission is no longer considered an exclusively religious endeavor, perhaps more than ever before it is poised to bridge between secular and non-secular conversations, and between academic and non-academic fields. The concepts that missiology uses and the work that it has already done have something special to offer discourses that may not have not been very involved with religious work to date. And, with the idea of "mission" trending, missiology has a better chance of being heard with fewer misunderstandings.

Missiological Location

In some ways, this presents a two-edged sword. On one hand, it is encouraging to see mission receiving well-deserved attention in mainstream discourse. On another, the breadth of publication that has adopted mission language has stretched the domain of the term *mission* to a degree that qualifying explanations are frequently necessary. I will unpack the terms mission, missional, and missiological more fully in the first section, but at this point I want to be explicit that this work is a *missiological* examination. By missiological, I mean that it addresses the idea of mission with self-awareness, in a manner that integrates formal academic understandings and methods of inquiry. In other words, this is an academic work from a specific academic field, even though it is designed to open conversation between multiple academic fields and be used by non-academic readers in non-academic ways.

Proposing Method

One of the key academic points of this work is to present and demonstrate a missiological angle on interpretive method. Since the book is intended for both academic and non-academic readers, I want non-academic readers to know in advance that proposing method can be a point of contention in academic circles. Because method can be a volatile topic, I will spend some extra space explaining, and, in certain moments, defending methodological agenda, especially toward the beginning of the book.

My overall hope is to lend energy to some of the conversations in which missiology is engaged by openly laying on the table a few of the commitments that inform missiological inquiry. The goal is not to define missiological interpretation, or to propose how it "should" be done. Rather, the main goal is to sketch outlines of one way in which fruitful missiological interpretation can be performed using very fundamental aspects of missiology's disciplinary agenda. Secondarily, the aim is to do this kind of interpretation in a way that is meaningful to other disciplines, especially biblical studies, urban studies, theology and the social sciences.

As is the case with many mission endeavors, this volume is an overture, the offering of an invitation to communicate. It asks you, the reader, to hear a few words from an individual voice that will attempt to represent others who have similar commitments. The point is to self-declare a bit of what missiologists are up to and to extend a hand, seeking interaction with others who are doing related work from different locations. While mission history clearly reveals that liabilities attend such overtures, I believe that the potential benefits make the attempt worthwhile. After all, that is what mission does. It makes attempts in the hope of accomplishing something good.

Agenda for This Book and the Kingdom in Context Series

Kingdom in Context series. This volume has been conceived as a preliminary step to future explorations. Because it is a foundational treatment, much of its space is used to present supporting theory. Because it seeks common ground for future conversation, it also moves beyond theory into concrete applications that serve both as examples and as resources for discussions involving theology and praxis.

Since the work seeks to do two tasks in one volume, the discussions are necessarily limited in all of its sections. Thankfully, the editors at Urban Loft have a vision for offering a series of multi-author works that can follow and delve more deeply into these and related topics, released under the title: *Kingdom in Context: Mission in the Universal and Local.* The aim for following volumes will be to engage in interdisciplinary conversations about contemporary issues at the intersection of mission and society. These dialogs will feature contributors from varied fields in conversation with missiological authors who will be presenting missiological perspectives.

Intended audience. This first book is primarily aimed at a mission-oriented audience. It assumes that the reader will have at least some degree of familiarity with mission practice(s) or with ideas that are commonly addressed within mission studies. This audience includes students of intercultural studies and missiology, especially where those intersect with urban studies, as well as mission workers and pastors. To a lesser extent, it is also directed toward students of religion and the social sciences, and to theologians and biblical scholars.

The general tone and terminology will be most familiar to readers versed in intercultural studies. However, care has been taken not to discriminate between intercultural agents and mission workers who work within their home cultures. Consideration also has been given to include a broader readership of those who are generally interested in mission and the human dilemma, especially readers interested in the intersection of mission theology and urban studies.

The first half of this volume updates and refines work that I did during my PhD studies at Fuller Theological Seminary's School of Intercultural Studies. There, the focus was to map the meta-theoretical and theoretical domain(s) that missiological hermeneutics occupied in relation to other hermeneutic approaches, and to propose a strategy for missiological reading that other interpretive studies could relate to. This book takes a next step by making that theoretical work accessible to non-academic audiences and by applying it both to a biblical text and to the socio-spatial phenomenon of the city. The chapters on theory rely heavily on material that is discussed more thoroughly in my (2011) dissertation, while the chapters on method use material from mission studies courses that I have taught at Fuller Theological Seminary (Ayers, 2012). In both sections those shared contents have been refocused and restyled for the current audience.

Uses for this work. The material here has been designed to serve two purposes. One purpose is to be a supporting text for classroom instruction in intercultural studies and missiology, theology, interpretive methods, and urban studies. Its second, equally important purpose is to function as a resource text for field workers, especially those who are working in urban contexts. As a resource for field workers, the goal is to offer methodological support for those who wish to conduct biblical and social interpretation from missiological perspectives. From either of these angles, this book can be a resource for researchers who are exploring missiological treatment of biblical texts, especially the Genesis origin accounts, or for researchers who are seeking missiological sources that address human existence and society.

Academic Features

Learning outcomes (for educators). Readers who complete this book can expect to be familiar with the foundational commitments that inform missiological interpretation and with the primary approaches that missiologists have used. By the conclusion, readers will recognize the concept of missio and understand how that concept can be used as an instrument for analysis of texts and the socio-spatial phenomenon of the city. They also will know how to interpret biblical texts using "Topographic Analysis" and "Product, Ground and Tool" hermeneutic strategies. Lastly, the reader will be able to compare points of missiological interpretation of Genesis 1 to points of missiological interpretation of the city, and relate those points to mission concerns, issues and practices.

Academic level. The goal in this work is not to debate points of interpretive method as much as it is to explain and to apply mission-oriented approaches. Basic citations have been provided throughout the work in order to meet ordinary standards of academic rigor. However, because this volume is intended to be read by students, fieldworkers, and non-specialists, academic debate and citation has been held to a minimum wherever possible, with greater place being given to explanation, illustration, and reasoning. This is most noticeable in the second half of the book, where the intended goal is to apply a method rather than to survey and compare research.

In order to keep usability central, the format, vocabulary and content have been structured to be accessible to general readers who have entered upper division undergraduate education while being rigorous enough to have value for graduate studies and research. I have tried to include guidepost citations that can assist readers at points where there may be significant disagreement among missiologists or interpretive scholars, but for deeper debates on theory and meta-theory, I refer the reader to my earlier dissertation, *In Search of the Contours of a Missiological Hermeneutic* (2011).

Voice and style. My hope is that you will encounter this work as a conversation. In order to accomplish this, the book has a style and tone that is more conversational than what the reader will find in many traditional academic journals or monographs.

However, this is not a conversation about trivialities in order to enjoy the free interplay of ideas; it is an earnest conversation about very valuable topics. On one side, we are talking about *humankind*, who are valuable beyond description. On the other side, we are talking about *mission*, the presence and activity of the God who is supremely valuable, beyond comparison. In the mix, we find *the city*, home to most of the world's inhabitants, the sacred center of ancient Israel, and the biblical metaphor for both the people of God and the perfection of the eschaton (Rev. 21:1-4), perhaps the most influential socio-spatial construction ever seen.

With such high values involved, I have chosen to present material from an advocacy position instead of attempting a posture of neutrality. I believe that this is academically responsible in light of postmodern observations about the influence of personal location upon knowledge, and I prefer to be explicit about my commitments so that the reader may evaluate freely, without having to read behind the lines for sources of bias.

As an educator, I also have found that knowledge is often formed powerfully amid the pressures of dialectic conflict. Therefore, my goal has been to engage the Genesis text and the city with methodological honesty and consistency, even if the results end up being quite challenging. This is my attempt to explore biblical understandings about people and God responsibly, and an invitation for the reader to engage with me in transparent discourse. My intention is to do this with respect and goodwill. At points where the reader may disagree, I ask you to hear me as a conversational partner in collaborative knowledge-seeking rather than as an opponent.

Commitments. The most influential commitment undergirding this work is my Christian faith. As a Christian, I hold the Hebrew scriptures to be authoritative and foundational for matters of faith and practice, and I approach those texts as my own religious heritage. As a result, the reader will find that the discussion is recognizably Christian, even when working with the sacred texts of ancient Israel. A second commitment that pervades the work is my dedication to mission. I firmly believe in the positive value of mission work and mission studies, and I am an advocate of missiology as an academic discipline. I stand convinced that God is at work in this world, that he reigns as king, that he reveals himself to people and that he transforms lives through encounter with Jesus Christ. My agenda is that the reader would be influenced toward these ends by reading this book.

Interdisciplinary Character

Missiologists often have described missiology as an interdisciplinary discipline (see below, Chapter 1), and, historically, missiology has drawn from multiple cognate fields as it pursues its own inquiries. Currently, as increasing numbers of missiological researchers produce missiological works, the outlines of where missiology stands relative to traditional fields are beginning to show a bit more clearly. This has revealed that, while missiology displays unique disciplinary perspectives, the academic domain in which it operates continues to overlap the boundaries of multiple, previously-established disciplines. This lends missiological examination a unique, blended character, since missiology simultaneously stands upon other disciplines while standing among them. In some sense, missiological treatments offer back to other disciplines the fruits of their own labors, reworked and viewed through mission lenses. This work is no exception to that trend. Even though it is a missiological examination, it draws upon the works of biblical scholars, theologians, linguistic philosophers, anthropologists, sociologists and urban scholars, setting those works into conversation with missiological authors.

Although this kind of interdisciplinary work has much to offer, the vocabulary available for use at the places where biblical, social and missional inquiries intersect is rather small, and it has been charged by separate debates within philosophy, theology, biblical studies, literary studies, the human sciences, and missiology. In order to bridge between these discussions, I often have elected to use generic terms that have not been fully captured by any single discipline. I have chosen these terms deliberately because they are able to make contact between multiple disciplines simultaneously, even if it means that sometimes a degree of imprecision remains at play. My hope is that the ambiguity in turn leaves some space for further conversation.

An interdisciplinary approach also creates what missiologist and anthropologist Paul Hiebert (1994) calls a "bicultural bridge," a unique, hybrid environment that is formed by contact between people groups. As a proposal that has been framed in just such an environment, this work runs the risk of feeling alien to readers who are accustomed to the ways of cognate fields. Depending on the discipline of the reader, some parts may seem too basic or introductory, while other parts may feel too esoteric. As the reader also will see, missiology has its own strategies for making inquiry, and the rules of academic examination will differ at points from the rules that hold sway in other disciplines. Thus, although some names or conversations may be familiar, not all will be, and certain keystone conversations or authors that the reader might expect to be addressed may be omitted. The reader also may find that familiar works are being used in unfamiliar ways in order to elicit unexpected points. That is because the aim here is not merely to transfer conversations from other disciplines into missiology, but to draw upon other disciplines and invite them into a missiological discussion.

In light of this, I ask the reader for two favors that can help to keep the conversation open. First, I ask the reader to extend a patient tolerance when terms or concepts may feel strange or imprecise. Second, I ask that you work with the definitions that are provided, especially when your own expertise may be able to supply more sophisticated nomenclature that is specific to your field. You have my thanks in advance for your graciousness.

Organization

The layout of the book is designed to guide the reader through a natural flow of interpretive process. It demonstrates a complete trajectory that traces from foundations that precede interpretation to grounded proposals that follow from interpretation. This line starts at theory and proceeds through theory into method, interpretive findings and interdisciplinary reflection, finally to end at conclusions and proposals about practice. While each step in this line is linked to the others, in order to aid instructional use, the chapters have been designed as complete discussions whenever possible.

Both the style and the use of sources shift to match each stage as interpretive data is formed and refined. The discussion starts at gathering deep research in order to ground theory and propose method. In the next step, research is replaced by special data as method is applied. After special data is formed, corollary interdisciplinary research is integrated in order to locate and inform those special findings. After interdisciplinary integration, the focus moves toward the development of reflective conclusions that rely upon the data produced from theory, method and interdisciplinary correlation. Those reflections serve as the base for conclusions and proposals.

In order to accomplish this, the book is divided into four parts. Part I introduces missiological interpretation and explores its theoretical foundations. Part II outlines method. Part III applies the principles of missiological interpretation, first to the Genesis 1 account and then to the city, then to both. Part IV develops the findings from these interpretations into discussions about mission, the Genesis text and the city.

Part I is concerned with the underpinnings of missiological interpretation. It locates missiological reading in relation to trends in biblical studies, theology. and missiology, and makes theoretical proposals about how to interpret the Bible missiologically.

Chapters 1-4 work through some of the historical and disciplinary foundations of missiological interpretation. Chapter 1 gives the backgrounds of missiological interpretation and traces where missiological reading stands in relation to more traditional biblical approaches. Chapter 2 looks at the factors that shape missiological reading. It notes some of missiology's key disciplinary commitments and compares those with the commitments of other disciplines in order to reveal how missiological reading relates to non-missiological reading. It grounds a missiological approach in the concept of *missio*, or purpose. Chapter 3 considers the way in which multiple purposes combine to produce joint compositions, paying special attention to metanarratives and the mission of God. Chapter 4 explores readership horizons. It uses the concept of God's kingdom to look at how social and temporal contexts are created and defined.

Part II offers practical approaches. Chapter 5 shifts from theoretical concerns to discuss interpretive method. It introduces two related models and develops the Topographic Analysis model. This model views the text as a construction that produces designed outcomes as it is negotiated by readers. Chapter 6 outlines a complementary model, which views the text in light of joint composition and metanarrative influence. It sees the text from three related angles, as a Product, a Ground, and a Tool of mission.

Part III performs interpretation of the biblical text and the city. Chapter 7 applies the models of Topographic Analysis and Product, Ground and Tool to Genesis 1, looking for insights about creation, humankind, and human purpose. Chapter 8 uses the foundational concept of missio to analyze the phenomenon of "the city" in missiological terms. It frames urban phenomena in missional ways so that they can be compared with missiological reading of the Genesis account. Chapter 9 then juxtaposes the missiological readings of the city and Genesis 1 in order to reveal points of similarity and difference.

Part IV integrates the findings of preceding chapters in a series of exploratory discussions about mission, creation and the city. Chapter 10 considers the missiological implications of points that come into view when the city and Genesis 1 are juxtaposed. It examines the city, creation, the kingdom and mission in light of each other. Chapter 11 refines the exploration of Chapter 10 by focusing on key missio-urban concerns and issues. Chapter 12 concludes the exploratory discussion by focusing on potential missio-urban challenges and practices. Chapter 13 provides a summary review, along with concluding remarks.

Acknowledgements

There are many people who have contributed directly and indirectly to this work. As editor, architect and fellow laborer in mission, Stephen Burris has been the primary catalyst to move the conversation from coffee-talk to print; this book would not have come into being without his urging, vision and patience. Thanks goes out as well to Kendi Howells Douglas for carrying this project to completion through so many layers and to the stable of scholars at Urban Loft for their inspiration and accountability.

I will always owe a debt of ongoing gratitude to Chuck Van Engen for walking me into the field of missiological hermeneutics. I thank Chuck, along with others, especially Chuck Kraft, Joel Green, Paul Hertig, and Betsy Glanville for being so generous with their scholarly excellence, their advice, their encouragement, and their constant willingness to engage in dialog. Also, since I cannot catalog or cite the many, many treasures that I have gained from Jerry Camery-Hoggatt, I must simply say, "Thank you, Jerry"

My wife Wendy has borne the weight of our lives throughout the preparation of this manuscript; she has given extensive feedbacks while listening to more versions of its chapters than any person should bear. She and our daughter Kimberly have brought light to my eyes and strength to my heart when it was needed most, and they deserve credit for anything accomplished here. Thanks also go to Faith Worship Community, and mahalo nui loa to the ohana of Kaua'i Christian Fellowship for so much understanding and gracious support. While these partners all have added significantly to this work, any flaws to be found in it are certainly my own.

Part I

Chapter 1: Missiological Interpretation

At its very heart, this book is a proposal about how to understand things from the viewpoint of mission. The two main things that we are hoping to understand this way are the biblical text of Genesis 1 and the sociospatial phenomenon of the city. The final aim for doing so is that by understanding those two things missiologically we can gain insight into mission, the kingdom of God and our human context.

Although it might save time to jump straight into discussing the creation account and the city, we first need to talk about why using a mission viewpoint matters, and how it works. This will accomplish two things. It will satisfy academic standards for inquiry and grant others access to missiological process. The formal name for both the description of the process and the process itself is *missiological hermeneutics*, or *missiological interpretation*. This is a discipline that stands under the umbrella of missiology, yet interacts with biblical studies and other related interpretive fields.

As we will see, missiological interpretation can be a tricky endeavor. It takes a very special angle of view within a broad, diverse, and deeply explored enterprise. As a result, missiology's approach sometimes runs counter to strongly held positions within traditional interpretation. This is only to be expected, since interpretation has a long history that has seen many controversies, while the distinct field of missiological hermeneutics is comparatively young and in a stage of emergence.

Because missiological hermeneutics is specialized, it will require a bit of background explanation for the proposals here to make sense. Therefore, prior to performing interpretive work we will have a few academic discussions about the forces that have shaped missiological reading and about the disciplinary commitments that give missiological interpretation its unique flavor. This naturally involves some theoretical conversation about how the process of reading works. As we talk about these things, I want to urge you to keep in mind that this is primarily a missiological proposal. In other words, the goal here is not to argue about what has been said in the various conversations about interpretation, or to describe what's being done in related fields. It is simply to open a doorway to missiological understanding and to offer enough supporting material to empower interpreters to enter that door with confidence.

As already mentioned, missiological reading is different. It has been birthed from mission concerns and it stands on foundations in the field of *mission*, which only partially draws upon biblical and theological studies. It has a distinctive character, and it yields unique results that sometimes can feel foreign to people who are accustomed to other interpretive traditions. And, as is the case with any new skill, missiological reading is not quickly or simply acquired. Its unfamiliar processes usually require time, mental flexibility, focus and investment of effort from the interpreter in order to understand them and use them with facility.

However, missiological interpretation is also quite fun, and a bit refreshing, since it often yields unexpected results from familiar objects. And, since it is rooted in the missionary tradition, missiological interpretation can be deeply satisfying for people who want to discover new things about the Bible, people, and the world, with an eye toward sacred service. It is an approach that fits well with interpreters who are committed to sacred inspiration and with those who wish to wed biblical understanding to action in the world on behalf of God and his kingdom. Like mission, missiological interpretation is an adventure, and it is sometimes one that can feel strange, disorienting, or even perilous, yet those who pursue it are sure to find that the task is worth the investment.

Orienting the Questions

Before we jump into discussions about missiological theory and method, I think that it would be good to read a joke. This one comes from comedian Steven Wright (2013):

> I went to a place to eat. It said, 'breakfast at any time.' So I ordered French Toast during the Renaissance.

Now, let me explain the joke to you:

> This joke exploits complexities within the semantic range of the term, "time." Time may indicate an era or epoch, but it also may indicate the progression of hours and minutes in the daily cycle. It also may mean a moment in a work or business day. Some businesses use the phrase, "at any time" to say, "all moments within business hours."
>
> In North American culture, it is common for certain foods to be served only during certain times of the day. Breakfast menus are most notable for this. Breakfast service often concludes during mid-morning at restaurants, so it is common for restaurants to advertise when they continue to serve breakfast foods throughout their business hours. This is called, "serving breakfast at any time."
>
> Steven Wright's joke creates cognitive tension over the phrase "at any time" as he reframes the meaning of "any time" to indicate "any era or epoch" instead of "during all business hours." Because Wright's opening phrase references "a place to eat," the hearer of his joke will proceed under the impression that in this case "time" indicates business hours. That hearer is pleasantly surprised when she finds the "time" in Wright's order instead to be "the Renaissance," since it would be impossible for the restaurant to serve food during a past historical era.

As Wright makes his impossible menu choice, the hearer experiences a form of insider's joy to see the restaurant's claim defeated, especially since Wright appears to be acting out of naiveté. Strategically, Wright chooses "French Toast" as his breakfast. This appeals to latent connotative associations in the hearer that connect France with the Renaissance. It also heightens the effect of the joke since French toast is a food that is served almost exclusively at breakfast and ordinarily excluded from midday or evening menus. With that in mind, please read the joke again:

> I went to a place to eat. It said, 'breakfast at any time.' So I ordered French Toast during the Renaissance.

As a third step, I would like to propose a question. If you are willing, it would help if you pause your reading and take the time to frame a one sentence answer. It would be best if you try to write out your response.

Here's the question:

What is the *meaning* of the joke?

There are crucial choices to be made here. For, if the meaning of the joke is that you would understand its structures, grammar, literary strategies, and social implications, your orientation toward the joke will be one that prioritizes *comprehension*. From this orientation, you will be more satisfied when I explain the joke than when you simply read it.

Hopefully, we could appreciate the joke from this angle, but we have to admit that my explanation isn't very funny, and we would probably not laugh very much. This is especially true if I explain the joke to you *before* you read it.

If, however, the meaning of the joke is related to being *humorous*, that is, if the meaning is that you would laugh and have some enjoyment, then you will have a different orientation toward the joke. Coming from this angle, you would expect me *not* to explain the joke in advance, or to spend too much time outlining its mechanics afterward, because explaining the joke would spoil the fun and "ruin" it for you.

These two orientations, one aimed at *comprehending* the joke and the other at *experiencing* the joke, tend to compete with each other. Except for those aficionados who are well versed in the art of humor, it is difficult to engage both orientations fully, and even humorists would find it nearly impossible to do both at the same time.

The tension between these two competing senses leaves you, the joke reader, with a decision to make about your reading agenda. If you want to *comprehend* the joke, you are forced to suspend at least some of your *experience* of the joke. On the flip side, if you wish to experience the joke, you must release some of your critical attention *about* the joke.

Now, let's change the question:

When is the joke *fulfilled?*

This question is much easier to answer than the question about the joke's "meaning" because it takes into account what we already know about the *purpose* of jokes. We know that jokes have a deliberate design that aims at eliciting humor, laughter, and pleasure. We also know enough about human experience to be able to discern when humor happens and when it doesn't.

Our knowledge about the purpose of jokes gives us a crucial factor that can help us get beyond ambiguities that surround the term "meaning." We know what the expected outcome is; we can recognize that outcome in ourselves and others, and we can compare the outcomes that happen as the joke is told or read in light of the purpose of the joke. When all of those factors line-up, we can say that someone "gets" the joke. He has heard it "well." When all of those factors fail to line-up, we can say that someone does not "get" the joke. Something has gone wrong and the hearer was not able to hear it well.

In common parlance, we could say that the joke is *fulfilled* when someone "gets" the joke. That is, the joke is fulfilled when the reader laughs or feels humor. We can also say that when that happens the joke's *purpose* is satisfied. That fulfillment of purpose holds true whether or not the one who "gets" it can describe exactly why she has had a humorous experience, whether or not she can define exactly what humor is, and whether or not she can describe the structures of the joke.

Getting the Text

By now, you may realize that I am using the joke as an analogy for the biblical text. Although the Bible is not a joke, the dynamics of reading run parallel, for it is one thing to "get" a biblical text because one has experienced it or responded to it, and another thing to comprehend a biblical text as an object that is understood or analyzed.

Very possibly, getting a text, whether it is a joke, this book or the Bible, is a more central goal than comprehending a text on cognitive levels. For, when one gets the joke, one can make a solid claim that one truly *knows* the joke, even if one cannot explain exactly why one gets it. Yet, even if one can explain the joke's structures and strategies in minute detail, if one has never experienced the joke's humor there is not much ground to claim that one truly knows the meaning of the joke.

A quote popularly attributed to the impressionist master Claude Monet talks about "getting" art in a similar way. He says:

People discuss my art and pretend to understand, as if it were necessary to understand, when it's simply necessary to love.[7]

For Monet, the purpose of art is to evoke love and appreciation. He contrasts that outcome with comprehension. The epistle of James talks about "getting" God's word using almost the same distinction. James exhorts, "But be doers of the word, and not hearers only, deceiving yourselves" (Jas. 1:22, ESV)[8]. Like Monet, James prioritizes response over mental reception. He even goes so far as to characterize comprehension without response as self-

---

[7] This is the English version (claude-monet.com) (2018). There are variants in French sources: *"Je ne comprends pas pourquoi tout le monde discute de mon art et fait semblant de comprendre, comme si il était nécessaire de comprendre, quand il est simplement nécessaire de l'aimer."*(Grace) and, *"Tout le monde discute de mon art et prétend comprendre, comme s'il était nécessaire de comprendre, quand il est simplement nécessaire d'aimer"* (BrainyQuote)

[8] ESV (*The English Standard Version Bible - containing the Old and New Testaments with Apocrypha*, 2009)

deception. This parallels Jesus' focus on the hearer's ability to "understand with [the] heart." As Jesus prepares to explain his parable of the sower, he quotes Isaiah, explaining that the problem is not hearing, per se, but unresponsiveness:

> For this people's heart has grown dull, and with their ears they can barely hear, and their eyes they have closed, lest they should see with their eyes and hear with their ears and understand with their heart and turn, and I would heal them. (Matt. 13:15, ESV)

Jesus, James, and Monet seem to agree that hearing in its fullest sense is more about response to a message than it is about mental access or perception. Whether it's the hearing of a joke, the viewing of a painting, or the hearing of the sacred word, the core factor in meaning appears to be the outcome that results from the interaction between a hearer and a message. When we focus on the outcomes that are supposed to happen, we are doing reading that emphasizes the text's *mission*. This is a crucial dimension of concern when we are dealing with sacred texts, and it is the center point of the discussions that will follow in this book.

The primary aim of this first section is to explore what reading for designed outcomes, that is, for *purpose*, looks like and how it can be done in a way that does not exclude divine messages. Missiology is a discipline that is concerned with how things get done, and it follows that missiological interpretation would pay close heed to what it is about texts that enables them to get things done. For missiology, the kind of understanding that arises as a response to the text's design differs in quality from other kinds of understanding. Mission is all about engagement, and from its viewpoint, an orientation that gains the outcome of the text's design holds a stronger claim to the meaning of the text than an orientation that fails to regard the text's purpose.

Even more, missiology is concerned with what God wants to get done, and how people are to be responsive to him. It follows that missiological interpretation would look for how texts can get *divine* things done. This is of prime importance when looking at the biblical text, since we assume that sacred texts can be divinely aimed at spiritual responses. In other words, while discerning what the text *says*, or can say, is important, in a missiological view the real trick is to discover what the text *does*, especially when it is doing something according to divine purpose.

This does not mean that missiological interpretation excludes comprehension. It simply means that missiological reading gives first attention to outcomes and it includes God's purpose(s) as a formative factor for those outcomes. Put in a more formal way, we could say that missiological inquiry prioritizes the productive dimension of texts along with textual capacity for divine communication. That is, missiological interpretation deliberately looks at the full range of responsive outcomes that the Bible produces, including spiritual outcomes, and it considers that full range of response to be central to the text's meaning. This proposes that, by design, the biblical text, like a joke, yields the better part of its meaning when its reader is moved than when its reader analyzes. It also proposes that eliciting outcomes constitutes the purpose, or mission, of the text, and that this can be divine communication.

Discerning the Text's Mission

Why should missiology have such concern for textual design? At the risk of stating the obvious, missiology is concerned with the nature and performance of *Mission* (with a capital "M") and with the various "little m" *missions* that contribute to it. It follows then that missiological reading strategies place critical attention on the mission of the text, looking for how the "little m" mission of the text integrates with the "big M" of Mission.

Looking from this angle, discerning what the text *does* can reveal the text's *mission*, which exposes the essential ground for the text's existence. Thus, discovery of the text's core purpose is a concern that lies at the very center of mission-oriented reading. And, while there is no consensus yet on the topic among missiologists, discovering the biblical text's mission may be the defining orientation that makes missiological reading a distinct and fruitful endeavor.

We will unpack this more fully throughout this section, but for now suffice it to say that missiological readers approach the text distinctly because they read the text through the lens of a concern to perform something in the world. And, crucially, missiological interpreters seek to coordinate their own lives, actions, and concerns with what the biblical text is designed to accomplish. Another way of putting this is that missiological readers seek to align what they hope to do in the world with what the text is designed to do. Thus, for the missiological interpreter, a doing-based knowledge of the text, which focuses on the text's fulfillment can take priority over a comprehending-based knowledge that seeks perception.

Mission Oriented Reading

Christian mission has been a long project. It has a tremendously colorful, and at times, conflicted, history. This is especially true where the Bible is concerned. It should come as no surprise then, that at the time of this publication the field of mission studies is not homogeneous and that its lack of homogeneity is reflected in the small sub-field of missiological hermeneutics.

There also is not much consensus about mission or mission studies in the academic world. Even though mission has experienced many successive waves of popular appeal, those ebbs and flows have not translated into missiology's place among the academic disciplines. Within the academy, mission and mission related studies have had stormy relationships with traditional fields and the history of mission-oriented Bible reading is particularly fraught with differences.

Because of these factors, before we can explore practices, we will need to take a step back and get a larger view, so that the reader first can understand more about what mission-oriented reading is, how it developed, and where the practice of mission-grounded interpretation stands today. In other words, we will need to be able to take into account some of the issues that are in play around missiological hermeneutics and we'll need to develop some common understandings about mission-oriented approaches, so that the rest of what we talk about can be heard clearly and provide full benefits.

For those readers who are only now dipping their feet in the academic waters of missiology, I urge you simply to try to get the basic lay of the land from what follows in this chapter. That will be enough to enable you to finish this book with a functional comprehension. For those readers who are already familiar with mission studies, this will be more of a review from which you may be able to glean an unexpected nugget or two about the special topic of missiological hermeneutics. In the first part of the chapter we will examine some key terms, then follow with a survey of academic conversation about missiological interpretation.

Mission, Missional, and Missiological Hermeneutics

As a first step, we will need to establish a few working definitions. These will serve as controls against the "terminological imprecision" that Michael Barram notes to be an ongoing challenge for our field. In order to do this, I will distinguish between three terms that often are used interchangeably, which I categorize into three types of mission-related hermeneutics. These are "mission," "missional," and "missiological" hermeneutics.[9] I want the reader to understand that this is an external categorization, and that the authors and works listed below are given as examples, in order to show the general character of the groups. The authors do not use the terms in precisely the same ways that I am using them, and they do not use them uniformly, so I refer the reader to my earlier work, *In Search of the Contours of a Missiological Hermeneutic* (2011), for a more in-depth survey of various authors and their approaches. For this work, by

---

[9] H. Beeby understands "mission" to concern "praxis," "missional" to be "adjectival" and "missiological" to involve "science." He argues for a "missionary hermeneutic" that takes into account "mission to our minds…to the church…[and] to the culture" (2000, pp. 277-278). J. Roxborogh defines "missiology" as "the study of Christian mission and the issues that arise through commitment to it. He sets this in contrast to "mission studies," which is, "the study of Christian mission including its social and cultural effects" (2009, p. 8). My definitions here run roughly parallel to C. Wright's (2004, pp. 104-106).

the first term, "mission hermeneutics," I refer to interpretation that is performed by mission agents as they go about the business of mission. An example of this is what the apostle Paul did when he interpreted existing scripture during the course of his ministry. New Testament scholar Michael Barram (2006) and missiologist Timothy Carriker (1994) look at this kind of hermeneutic. The distinctive for this term is that a "mission hermeneutic" operates under the influence of mission perspectives and objectives, yet it does not *overtly* take into account that it is doing so. This is simply a functional description of what is occurring as a person who is acting in mission interprets. As such, it is an extremely open term.

The second, "missional hermeneutics," refers to a hermeneutic that knowingly takes into account the mission orientation of God, the "people of God," or the Church in the world.[10] This is a term that has come into widespread use in recent years, in large part due to the work of Darrell Guder and the Gospel and Our Culture Network.[11] It also is a hermeneutic orientation that has been associated on popular levels with a variety of church movements who identify themselves as *emergent* and/or *relevant*.[12] One example of missional reading is Christopher Wright's, *The Mission of God*, according to which, "a missional hermeneutic proceeds from the assumption that *the whole Bible renders to us the story of God's mission through God's people in their engagement with God's world for the sake of the whole of God's creation*" (2006, p. 51) [italics in original].[13]

---

[10] See Guder (1998, p. 223) on Hunsberger for this. His brief note on hermeneutics states, "We read the Bible using a missional hermeneutic that enables us to recognize in the Scripture testimony not only to the content of our message but the way in which that message is to be made known. The Bible gives us of the what and the how of missional obedience. The New Testament writings were addressed to communities already in mission; the purpose of the canonical Scriptures was (and is) to enable them to continue that mission. The Scriptures are thus the warrant for the church's mission, instructing and guiding these mission communities engaging their situations, their challenges, and their struggles." Barram (2007) uses "missional" and "missiological" interchangeably, as does Shawn Redford (2007).

[11] See Guder (1998); Beeby (2000) is influenced by this movement's definitions.

[12] (Gibbs & Bolger, 2005, pp. 58-64). Similar examples are Frost and Hirsch (2003, pp. 17-30) and Hirsch (2006, pp. 17-37).

[13] Wright sees a "missional hermeneutic" as being much broader and deeper than just involving the people of God. He sees it as recognizing the full scope of what God is doing in the universe, oriented around the *missio Dei*, one of the products of which is the Bible. He describes

While this book interacts in part with these first two approaches, neither of them are its focus. Here, we will be concentrating on the last term, "missiological hermeneutics." By this, I refer to a hermeneutic that knowingly involves itself with reflective critical practices that examine mission.[14]

There are several parts to this definition that need to be clarified. The first is that missiological hermeneutics entails self-awareness. Like a missional hermeneutic, a missiological hermeneutic is performed by people who are self-consciously mission oriented. Second, missiological interpretation is reflective. It not only consciously proceeds from mission; it also observes itself as it proceeds. Third, missiological interpretation participates in recognized critical practices. This means that missiology does more than self-describe or self-involve in a mission orientation; it also employs analytic thinking that is in some way connected to established critical disciplines. This is not to say that missiology is limited to formal examination, but that it makes rigorous academic assessment a part of its self-observation. It is linked more closely than "missional" hermeneutics to missiology's agenda of integrating interdisciplinary theory (Scherer, 1987).

By way of illustration, consider a person who is on her way to a store to buy ice cream. This person is on a *mission*. She has a known outcome that she wishes to achieve. However, her mission might not be at the forefront of her mind as she proceeds. She might be listening to music or thinking about other concerns as she makes her way to the store. Those activities are not related to her goal; they are incidental, even though she is doing them during her mission activity.

Along the way, our mission agent performs a reading task that is in fact related to her goal. She checks a phone app for reviews about different

---

this in an earlier article: "A missional hermeneutic of the Bible sets out to explore that divine mission and all that lies behind it and flows from it in relation to God himself, God's people and God's world" (2004, p. 105).

[14] See (Bosch, 1991; Nissen, 2002, pp. 73-76; Scherer, 1987, pp. 507-521; C. J. H. Wright, 2004, p. 106)

kinds of ice cream and she uses that information to get coupons. At this point, she is doing a task that is not specifically her mission, since her mission is to "get ice cream," not to "read reviews and get coupons." Yet, her reading is not incidental in the way that listening to music would be; it is *related* to her mission. Her reading contributes to her overall task, and she is doing it with an eye to accomplish her mission. She can perform her mission with or without reviews, but reading the reviews assists her. This is the kind of task that Christian missionaries have most often done when they have read the Bible. They have read the Bible and used the Bible as something that assists them in their mission works. For our consideration, our ice cream missionary is on *mission* and she is doing a *mission* reading of coupons and reviews.

If we change the scenario a bit, our missionary once again is going to buy ice cream. However, this time she is very self-aware about her task. She is thinking about how many times she has gone to get ice cream recently. She is also thinking about the types of ice cream that she has been buying and the way that the reviews she reads have shaped her choices about ice cream. She also is noticing that she has made reading reviews and coupons a part of her ice cream buying routine.

She is now *reflectively* aware and engaged. She is consciously focused on her mission; she is observant about her own actions in that mission, and, by choice, she has integrated her reading of reviews into her own understanding of her overall mission. She reads them knowingly, giving attention to the fact that reading reviews is an integral part of her process. She maintains her mission as the backdrop for her reading and she is aware of the influence that her reading has upon her mission. Using the distinctions that we have developed, she is being *missional* and doing a *missional* reading of her reviews.

Shifting the narrative, we once more find our ice cream missionary going to the store. And, once again, she is aware and reflective about her ice cream mission. However, this time, she is not solely thinking about her own ice cream shopping. This time, she is bringing her thoughts about her own ice cream buying into conscious evaluative interaction with other discourses. She is considering her physician's recent suggestion that she eat ice cream after noting that she is a triathlete who had been charting excessive weight loss. Further, she is juxtaposing her physician's input against advice from her alternative medicine nutritionist, who cautioned her that eating ice cream could cause imbalances. As she weighs these voices, she is considering the ongoing conflicts between traditional and alternative approaches to nutrition. She is self-observing that she has felt and performed better since she started eating ice cream. She also is wondering whether or not her nutritionist and physician eat ice cream, and, if they do, whether or not they would read ice cream reviews and get coupons in the same way that she does.

At this point, our ice cream missionary is taking into account the voices of formal disciplines as she considers her own ice cream shopping, and she is evaluating the inputs from those other voices as she analyzes her own activities. She is on a mission; she is self aware and reflectively engaged in that mission, and she is also engaged with critical disciplines that have something to say about her mission and about the reviews that she reads. Using the criteria that we've outlined here, she is being *missiological* and doing a *missiological* reading of her reviews.

Keeping these distinctions in mind, for the purposes of our discussion, "missiological hermeneutics" means interpretation in which: 1. the interpreter views the text with an anchoring concern for mission; 2. the interpreter is reflectively aware of having mission as a grounding concern and actively applies that concern as an interpretive agenda; 3. the interpreter inquires from the location of academic discourses that examine mission and from that location interacts with cognate academic discourses that intersect with mission studies.

Mission and Missiology

As we make these distinctions, I want to be careful not to give the impression that interacting with the academic dimensions of missiology is a simple step. Missiology is too diverse for that. Under the broad umbrella of "mission study" it draws together an entire constellation of ideas, histories, cultures and outlooks (Verstraelen, 1995). Thus, it can be somewhat misleading to speak collectively for or about "missiology," and attempting to do so runs the risk of totalizing or reduction. Partly, this is due to the fact that missiologists have tended to resist monolithic description of the field. By way of example, Catholic scholar George Soares-Prabhu intentionally prefers a generalized description. He and the prominent South African missiologist David Bosch hold that the field should be considered, "a pluriverse of missiology in a universe of mission" (Bosch, 1991, p. 8; Soares-Prabhu, 1986, p. 87).

Their viewpoint is fairly representative of both missiological sentiments and mission history. Denominations and major mission conferences historically have disputed with each other about mission, and their provisional statements have often shifted to accommodate changing trends in social and theological spheres (Verkuyl, 1978; Verstraelen, 1995). Bosch not only states that there has never been a unified theology of mission, his entire monumental work "traces the contours" of "paradigm shifts" within mission thinking. He contends that, "Ultimately, mission remains undefinable," and he warns against delineating mission "too sharply and too self-confidently," opting to use an "interim" definition of mission, based in "approximations of what mission is all about" (1991, pp. 8-9).

While at first glance it might seem odd that scholars would prefer ambiguity in their field, it is a reasonable state of affairs when the sheer breadth of mission is taken into account. Mission by its very nature must be able to bridge between unlike peoples, cultures, contexts, and worldviews. It follows naturally from this that adaptivity and fluidity of thought would be among its hallmark characteristics; it also follows that these characteristics would stymie attempts to define missiology absolutely or establish its protocols and agenda in final ways. From many angles, missiological literature seems to indicate that missiology's core commitment to engage widely varied cultures and logics has required it to maintain greater openness than is customarily found in conventional western academic pursuits.[15] As a result, despite trends that may have popularized certain versions of the term "mission" for certain seasons, the awkward fact remains that no final consensus exists among missiologists about what is meant by "mission" or by the term, "missiology."[16]

Even though this is understandable, and even though the field still coheres, the absence of clear, consensus self-description presents a significant hurdle for any proposal about missiological reading. For, any proposal about *missiological* hermeneutics must rely in some way upon an understanding of *missiology*, and an understanding of missiology, in turn, must rest upon an understanding of *mission*. The conundrum then arises that if mission remains indefinable, it follows that missiology also remains indefinable,[17] and as a result, so does missiological hermeneutics.

---

[15] On this point, see also Timothy Carriker (1994, p. 18).

[16] In his article, *Missiology as a Discipline and What it Includes*, James Scherer writes, "Let me suggest that each of these diffuse and comprehensive, but also contrasting models of missiological reflection, each embodying its own definition of the central theme of missiology, is excellent and useful as a basis for our own consideration. Careful study of these and other approaches will probably dissuade us from any premature tendency to settle on an agreed definition of 'what missiology is.' They remind us of the current diversity and plurality of approaches; there appears to be more than one valid way of doing missiology, yet the plurality of approaches may sometimes be seen as necessarily complementing or supplementing each other"(1987, p. 513).

Scherer also highlights "the need for standard nomenclature when referring to 'mission,' 'missions,' and 'missiology'" (1987, p. 508). Michael Barram (2007, p. 43) appears to disagree, "There seems to be widespread agreement that 'mission,' biblically understood, is first and foremost about the nature, character, and purposes of God. Whatever else may be said about mission in terms of theology, strategy, or any other aspect of human participation, biblical mission originates with divine, not human, initiative." He roots this in the concept of the *missio Dei*. However, his qualifier, "biblically understood" seriously conditions the observation, while Johannes Nissen (2004b, p. 168[b]) observes, "Biblical scholars and missiologists tend to define 'mission' in different ways." Additionally, Barram follows his initial observation by noting, "a lack of congruity in the relevant literature with regard to terms related to 'mission.'... typical usage of mission language can seem idiosyncratic" (2007, p. 46).

[17] Scherer observes, "No single definition of 'what missiology is' will satisfy all stripes of missiologist in the absence of prior agreement on 'what mission is.'" (1987, p. 519).

In order to get past this obstacle, throughout this book, in general theoretical discussions we will talk about *mission* as the actualization (or reification) of *missio*, which is the aim to accomplish (something). This concept can be applied both to human and divine aims, so we will distinguish between *divine* mission and *human* mission when that distinction is needed. In these conversations, *missions* will refer to any projects that actualize *missio*.

Since there is also the historical phenomenon to account for, when we discuss historical aspects we will talk about *Mission* (or, *mission*) as the overarching project of accomplishing sacred aims throughout time, or as the abstract conceptualization of that overarching project. In those conversations, *missions* will refer to distinct historical projects that fulfill or have fulfilled particular *missios*.

I do not believe that thwarting proposals about missiological subjects is an outcome that Soares-Prabhu, Bosch, or the missiological community ever intended, especially since their point is aimed at inclusion. If we can hear the tenor of what these scholars have said, it appears that the idea is to hold to definitions lightly, rather than to avoid or prohibit them altogether. By using very simple working definitions like the ones above, we will take a middle path; we will not avoid using terms precisely, but as we use them, we will understand them merely to be functional tools for inquiry.

Keeping that in mind, we will start by surveying just a bit of missiology's conversation about itself in order to sketch general, preliminary views of mission and missiology. We will do this in order to gain a sense of where missiological inquiry has come from and where missiological interpretation can proceed from, which will give us the heuristic elements that we need to ground what follows.

What Missiologists Have Said about Missiology

Unlike many of the western disciplines, missiology has only recently achieved a formal place within western academics.[18] Missiology did not arise from one cultural location or disciplinary founder, and it does not enjoy a clear or uniform history. Its formal academic discourse developed as a conglomerate of academic reflections upon existing practices that already had spread across the world, practices which already had been the subject of much consideration and debate. In some ways, then, missiological self-description has had to proceed deductively, following behind historical mission action, thought, and talk. In the process, missiologists have had to apply disciplinary nomenclature retroactively, which has left some ongoing ambiguity at play about the field.

Traditional designations for missiology's work do not offer much help with this. Johannes Verkuyl's survey (1978) notes that historically mission study has never had an established academic location, being placed within practical theology by Friedrich D. Schleiermacher, Abraham Kuyper, and J. H. Bavinck, in church history by Gustav Warneck, John Foster, C. Mirbt, and K. S. Latourette, and within dogmatics by H. Diem.[19] Verkuyl prefers Manfred Linz' designation, as an independent "complementary science" (pp. 8-9), while David Bosch (1991, p. 9) locates missiology as a "branch of Christian theology."[20] In a more "classic" approach, H.D. Beeby (2000, p. 278) describes missiology as a historically-focused "science" that is related to theology.

---

[18] No single, formal starting point for missiology as an independent discipline, (as distinct from mission work, or from theological and pastoral studies), has been established. Scherer's (1987) key article was still pursuing academic definition in the late 1980's. He notes the first use of the term in Webster's dictionary in 1924, but points toward the founding of the ASM and the publication of the journal *Missiology: an International Review*, in the early 1970's as key milestones of disciplinary emergence.

[19] He concludes, "In fact, as is obvious from the above, it is difficult to put missiology exclusively into any of the general categories. Missiology is involved with all the theological disciplines" (1978, p. 8).

[20] Verstraelen, et al., eds. see that missiology "is a branch of theology in the sense that it is bound up with a faith perspective" (1995, p. 3). Their ecumenical perspective is not quite the same as Bosch's emphasis, "a branch of Christian theology" (1991, p. 9).

Lutheran missiologist James Scherer's article, *Missiology as a Discipline and What it Includes* (1987, p. 509) summarizes, "The quest for an agreed definition of *missiology* remains elusive, and neither the ASM, nor the teaching fraternity represented by the APM, has been able to come up with one." He continues, "the most serious [change in trends] for *missiology*... is current indecision, or at least divergence of opinion, about what *mission* fundamentally is."[21] More recently, at the ANZAMS symposium in 2009, John Roxborogh appeared to confirm Scherer's position that missiology's place among the theological disciplines still remains unsettled (2009).[22]

Still, Scherer holds that, "The principal goals of missiology – [are] 'to study the church's mission especially with respect to missionary activity'" (1987, p. 514). He offers what he considers to be a "both/and" definition of "essential" missiology:

> Missiology's primary task is the study of the mission of the Triune God, and within that of the mission of Jesus, the apostles, the church(es), and mission sending bodies. This means that missiology is the study of God's mission everywhere—in all six continents, 'from everywhere to everywhere'... though we cannot here spell out the scope of *Missio Dei*. World mission in today's understanding is global, even cosmic, in scope. (Scherer, 1987, pp. 520-521)

Some missiologists lean toward reduced or qualified definitions, while others open the vistas quite widely. F. J. Verstraelen, A. Camps, L.A. Hoedemaker, and M.R. Spindler, eds., in *Missiology: an Ecumenical Introduction*, define missiology as the study of the movement of Christianity in its attachment to contexts, which is conducted from a committed "authentic" faith perspective (1995, pp. 1-5).[23] Dutch Reformed scholar

---

[21] (APM) Association of Professors of Mission;(ASM) American Society of Missiology.
[22] (ANZAMS) Aotearoa-New Zealand Association for Mission Studies.
[23] They hold definition of what constitutes an authentic faith perspective to be part of missiology's ongoing task, one performed using theologies that are changing and plural (1995, pp. 3-4).

Verkuyl holds that "Missiology is the study of the salvation activities of the Father, Son and Holy Spirit throughout the world geared toward bringing the kingdom of God into existence" (1978, p. 5).

Edgar Elliston uses a broad scale and narrow focus approach. He initially defines missiology as, "the study of the *missio Dei*" which, "involves all that God has done, is doing and intends to do to accomplish his purpose" (2007, p. 9). Yet, for Elliston, missiology's refined "specific focus" concerns "the crossing of barriers for the communication of the good news of what God has done to reconcile humankind to himself."[24] J. Christopher Wright parallels Elliston's breadth to some degree, repeatedly stating that mission is about "'life the universe and everything'"[25](2004, pp. 104, 109). However, he draws a helpful distinction between missional and missiological thought that emphasizes missiology's use of reflective academic examination (2004, p. 106).

Helpfully, Charles Van Engen isolates three major historical emphases in the field, which show key constellations of missiological concern: the view toward "compassion and justice," the "awareness of structural evil," and attention to the "life and health" and growth of the church, especially as that involves evangelism and local congregations. He sees that tensions between these concerns continue to yield uncertainty and questioning within the discipline, and he suggests that any robust missiology to come must be integrative, "draw[ing] from the wells of all three" as missiology heads deeper into the 21st century (2016).

These differences underscore Soares-Prabhu and Bosch's point that the term "missiology" ought to be taken in a general sense, and its use should be understood to be provisional, not definitive or determinative. The main point for our consideration here is that because it is not possible to

---

[24] James Brownson says virtually the same, calling the "barriers" "boundaries"(1998, p. 1).
[25] On p.104 Wright places this phrase in quotes, but makes no citation. At that point he may have been speaking colloquially, since this is a popular fictional title from the "Hitchhiker's Guide to the Galaxy" series (Adams, Douglas. 1982."Life, the Universe, and Everything." UK, Pan Books).

speak finally of any single, overarching "missiology," it is also not possible to propose a single, definitive "missiological hermeneutic" or "the" practice of missiological hermeneutics.

However, we must keep in mind that all of these scholars are talking about something mutually recognizable as mission study when they talk about the blurry boundaries of "missiology." Even if its outlines are fuzzy, missiology remains a field of academic endeavor that has relatively common overall trends and major representative outlooks, which can be observed within its diverse writings. These all relate to religious actors getting something done in the world. Some of these common concerns and commitments will serve as anchors for our discussions in the chapters that follow, but for now, we can begin by noting that even if we cannot lock down the term in final ways, we can start on a path of theoretical exploration by talking about "missiology" as the study of religious actors getting things done in the world. This will allow us to work at the level of Soares-Prabhu's "universe of mission," talking meaningfully about "missiological interpretation" in a general sense, even if we do not rely upon a single missiological description or track the myriad of variations that may exist at the level of his "pluriverse of missiologies."

The State of Missiological Hermeneutics

Having started with the broadest possible description, that missiology studies the doing of things by religious actors, we can narrow the focus to conversations about the discipline's own hermeneutics. As we do so, we should keep in mind that the concept *hermeneutics* itself is somewhat fuzzy, since a hermeneutic can be both a way of understanding and an understanding that itself can be understood. Thus, we could say on one hand that a missiological hermeneutic *describes how* to understand texts from the perspective of getting things done, and on another hand, we could say that it *practices understanding* texts from the perspective of getting things done.

In this book we start with the first focus, looking at how to understand, then we move to performing that understanding and looking at the results. From both of these angles, we are talking about "getting things done" in the sense of an interpretive criterion or lens, that is, as an anchoring concept. This means that when we try to discover what missiology says about hermeneutics we are looking for missiological conversations that talk about how to interpret using the concepts and commitments of mission.

When we make this distinction, the problem immediately arises that missiology hasn't been talking very much about how to interpret. However, this does not mean that missiology has ignored the Bible. It simply shows that missiology's biblical attentions have been directed along avenues that run oblique to hermeneutics, per se, because they have been focused on performing and understanding mission rather than on how to understand things like the Bible from the location of mission.

This is an interesting situation, since the Bible has been a very central thing in mission and in missiology. For centuries, traditional mission efforts, such as the works of Bible societies and evangelistic or educational programs, have spent tremendous energy developing the means to distribute and use biblical texts within mission work across the globe. In support and analysis of such efforts, missiologists like Eugene Nida (1960), Paul Hiebert (1987), Charles Kraft (1983), and R. Daniel Shaw (2003), have produced powerful works on how to transfer textual contents effectively across cultural boundaries.

From another angle, mission theologians such as Charles Van Engen (1996), Arthur Glasser (2003), D. Senior and C. Stuhlmueller (1983), Stephen Bevans and Roger Schroeder (2004), as well as biblical scholars, such as David Bosch (2006) and Johannes Nissen (2004a), have searched the text using missiological concerns in order to find insights about mission and the Bible, and in order to inform mission thought and work. Adding to their works, more recently, scholars such as Christopher Wright (2006), Paul Hertig and Robert Gallagher (2007), Sarita Gallagher (2014), and Pascal Bazzell (2018), have blended biblical studies with mission theology in applied ways, seeking to discern and articulate mission-relevant aspects of the text.

Still, while each of these valuable missiological projects works with the Bible in light of mission concerns, direct focus on the process(es) of interpretation has remained largely out of view. Despite the significant body of missiological literature that has been produced, at the time of this publication only Carriker (1994), Redford (2007, 2012), and Ayers (2011) have addressed missiological hermeneutics directly at length. Further, these explorations have only been performed relatively recently, and they show significant differences in their approaches.

The earliest of these, Timothy Carriker's (1994) dissertation, looks at the mission-based apocalyptic interpretation of Paul. This would qualify more as a missiological study of mission hermeneutics according to the categories that we've been working with. Shawn Redford's work (2007, 2012), however, treats more directly with the current practice of interpretation. He develops a theory of "spiritually-informed" biblical reading that is grounded in missionary experience of cultural meaning, which stands out by advocating the role of transformational spiritual enlightenment as a hermeneutic key. In Redford's proposal, spiritually inspired interpretation reassesses preceding textual material[26] as persons involved in God's mission fulfill his purposes within their contexts. He sees this spiritual reassessment as inextricably involved with the tangible outworking of missional commitment.[27] He advocates for a "biblically-informed" hermeneutic, which reflects the diversity of intertextual hermeneutics that can be observed to be operating within the Bible, along

---

[26] These texts may be oral material, such as covenant promises from God, or scriptures.

[27] "Scripture indicates that a well developed missional hermeneutic is integrated with good missionary practice. As such, we must break through the misconception that missionaries can understand the gospel apart from appropriate mission practice. The two are intertwined" (Redford, 2007, p. 94). This view presents a difficult hermeneutic circle, for it rests hermeneutic validity upon "good" or "appropriate" missionary practice, which is hard to describe without using biblical appeals. His concept of spiritual enlightenment is helpful to contribute clarity to the interpretive scenario, but it seems insufficient to provide an escape from the problem. He balances this to some degree by also bringing into dialog tradition and reading communities.

with contextual approaches that are informed by spiritual disciplines that are conducted during the course of the missionary task.

Redford recently followed upon his earlier work (2016) by outlining five key approaches within missiological hermeneutics. He characterizes these as: spiritual, thematic, scientific, ethno-, and missio-, and proposes that all five should be combined integratively in order to provide the fullest missiological view. Ayers takes a different approach, which focuses on the concept of *missio* itself as the key to interpretation. As noted in the introduction, this book uses and develops that work, so there is little need to outline those materials here.

Encouragingly, within the last few years, missional writers such as George Hunsberger, Greg McKinzie, and Michael Goheen have been partnering with biblical scholars like Joel Green, Richard Bauckham and Craig Bartholomew in order to offer outlines and samples for mission-grounded hermeneutics that span between missiological and missional approaches. Each of these scholars has self-consciously laid out key points of missional pre-understanding or concern that can inform or control the reading task, and they have done so in interaction with overarching missiological conversations. These joint works integrate academic dialogs at a level that would qualify their proposals as missiological in this exploration, and they have moved the field forward significantly by bringing increased clarity and energy to the conversation.

Goheen's (2017) most recent proposal is distinctly missional, although it responds to the work of biblical scholar Michael Barram (2007) by sketching a framework of key "located" elements through which the text can be understood. These are aimed at the missional involvement of the reader, since the text is both a record and a tool to equip God's people. Earlier, Hunsberger (2011, 2016) also sketched four "streams of emphasis" for missional hermeneutics, prioritizing attention to the missio Dei, the missional locatedness of the reader, the text's goal to equip the reader, and the gospel's engagement with culture. Although it also addresses "missional hermeneutics," Greg McKinzie's (2014) fruitful overview also effectively blends missional and missiological agenda as he plots thematic elements and emphases within the overall conversation about mission based interpretation. His modeling provides one of the strongest mission-based integrations to more traditional hermeneutic theory, offering a revision of Grant Osborne's work on the hermeneutic spiral that synthesizes multiple outlooks in a single operational agenda.

The Background Conversation

These very fruitful contributions come on the heels of a slowly paced and somewhat scattered conversation that has been in process for a few decades at the interface between missiology and biblical studies. In that conversation, Barram (2007) traced points of correspondence in missiological method relative to biblical studies, emphasizing the social location that Goheen responded to. He was preceded by Christopher Wright's (2004) development of a missional "matrix" for interpretation and by Johannes Nissen's (2002, 2004b) articles, which correlated mission-interpretation to current New Testament methods. Between them, Terry Muck (2003) interjected a brief proposal that highlighted the articulation of what missiological interpretation "asks."[28]

Before these, H. D. Beeby (2000) explored a canonical approach; James Brownson (1998), developed a "missional hermeneutic" of "coherence," and A. de Groot (1995) looked at interpretation and the Bible in light of catholicity and plurality. Earlier, John Jonsson (1987) proposed what he calls "Retranspositionalization," as a "missiological" alternative to modern "objective" interpretation.

Before that, in a round of discussion that was triggered by the BISAM project,[29] David Bosch (1986) and George Soares-Prabhu (1986) responded to Marc Spindler's conference notes (1979). Bosch protested

---

[28] Muck's proposal deserves mention, but, since it is only two pages long, it offers too brief of a treatment to be considered substantial.

[29] (BISAM) Biblical Studies and Missiology (project)

limiting the project's discussion to the theme of "witness," proposing that missiological interpretation should be organized around a few central themes and that it should involve contemporary as well as historical-critical agenda. This seems to have been the path that most following proposals have taken, although they have seemed also to acknowledge Soares-Prabhu's call for de-centering interpretation from western hegemony.

Slightly before that round, Nicholas Lash (1985) also proposed a break from traditional models, emphasizing that "faithful rendering" yields action that hearkens to the text. Charles Taber (1983) also highlighted fidelity, calling for a responsible integration of existing western methods with emerging non-western approaches. As a preliminary interdisciplinary conversation, these rounds of articles did not produce much in the way of developed proposals about missiological hermeneutics. Their main accomplishment seems to have been that they called attention both to the methodological gap and to the liabilities that might attend attempts to close that gap. In doing so, they laid the groundwork that has sustained current interdisciplinary proposals.

Looking Forward

Notably, at the time of this publication, joint projects involving biblical scholars and missiologists such as Goheen's collection, as well as ongoing compilations on mission theology by Gallagher and Hertig (2017) and Van Engen (2016) that work with interpretive issues have reenergized some older dialogs and opened some exciting vistas. This book takes a step in one of these directions by using earlier (Ayers, 2011) proposals about missiological hermeneutics to model interpretation of both the biblical text and the city. Other forthcoming interdisciplinary explorations featuring biblical scholars like Joel Green and missiologists like Stephen Burris and urban scholar Kendi Howells Douglas also show high promise of treating biblical texts using mission lenses and criteria. At the same time, missiologists Scott Sunquist, Amos Yong, and John Franke appear to be pursuing trajectories in their Missiological Engagements series that may intersect fruitfully with missiological hermeneutics projects. These are encouraging and overdue developments within the field, and the prospect for their projects to produce mission-oriented treatments in the future is highly promising. However, until the fruits of these efforts have been made available, we must work with the information at hand, which remains quite small, since literatures that specifically address the "hows and whys" of missiological interpretation are notably scarce.

In summary, the missiological conversation about hermeneutics reveals that for many years established missiologists have joined with scholars from biblical studies and theology in sounding a call for missiology to be open and clear about its hermeneutic methods. Those methods have only begun to be articulated, without anything close to a prevailing or consensus approach emerging. Thus, the call for missiological method continues to have relevance, especially as missiological works treating biblical texts are beginning to emerge in greater numbers. As missiological work with biblical texts shows an expanding trend, the moment seems ripe for missiology to respond to that call by being as transparent as it can about its interpretive practices.

Interdisciplinary Concerns

As a caveat, it should be noted that every discipline has the right to establish distinct procedures and canons. Thus, without question, missiology is not obliged to give an account for its disciplinary ways or measure itself against the highly evolved interpretive habits of other fields. Still, it should be kept in mind that as missiological authors perform biblical treatments, they tread in fields that have been plowed extensively by others before them, and those others have a just concern to ask about what missiologists are up to.

This is a sensitive conversation from both sides, since missiology's failure to articulate its hermeneutic agenda in the past appears to have undermined its voice with traditional interpretive disciplines. Yet, this is a fruitful conversation to be had, not only because it can assist with mutual understanding, but also because it can spur missiology to greater ambassadorship as it pursues its interdisciplinary project. Missiology seeks to find bridges between academic disciplines just as mission seeks bridges between cultures and peoples. It can only help for missiology to be ready to discuss whatever hermeneutical difference(s) it may have with those cognate disciplines it hopes to engage. In order to support that conversation, we now will take a brief look at missiology's interdisciplinary relations and how they have affected its hermeneutic project.

Missiology and the Academic Division of Labor

For a long time, mission agents have worked with language, and much of that work has involved the Bible. Thus, given mission's experience and needs, it would seem that mission studies would have been predisposed toward exploring hermeneutics. However, this has not been the actual case. Very possibly, this outcome can be attributed to the division of labor scheme that prevailed in earlier academic circles under the influence of modernistic approaches to learning, coupled with the historical fact that in this scheme, mission was viewed more as a delivery activity than as a domain of inquiry (Bosch, 1986; Carriker, 1994). Broadly speaking, in the modern approach, inquiry was territorial, as the scientific project sought to coordinate a number of specialized angles of inquiry upon a common, knowable reality (Vanhoozer, 2006). In this scheme, each discipline was understood to be exerting its unique attention to its own allotted task as a contributing partner in a combined effort to describe a common universe that could be observed objectively (Lyotard, 1993).[30]

During the times when the modern agenda was in full swing, mission was largely conceived to be a work that took place on the margins, at the interfaces between western societies and non-western societies. And, since the western world held that its sciences had advanced further than the

---

[30] Lyotard notes, "In Humboldt's model of the University, each science has its own place in that system crowned by speculation. Any encroachment of one science into another's field can only create confusion, 'noise' in the system. Collaboration can only take place on the level of speculation, in the heads of philosophers" (1993, p. 52).

knowledge traditions of other societies, mission was characterized broadly as an effort to transfer understanding outward from the West's centers of knowledge toward others. Thus, mission was not seen as an activity that took place within the academy, where theology and biblical studies took place. And, even in places where mission study was pursued, that study still was more conceived as part of a wider effort to move knowledge responsibly than as a means to develop new knowledge.

Catholic theologian Nicholas Lash, in his article, *What Might Martyrdom Mean?* portrays this scheme as a "relay race" (1985, pp. 16-17) in which missiology waited upon biblical studies for the fruits of proper exegesis, which it could in turn propagate to the world via mission, or which it could use while framing its own theology of mission. In this arrangement, the disposition held sway that mission workers and, later, missiologists, were expected to perform mission and talk about mission, while the work of biblical interpretation was performed by scholars in biblical studies and theology.

To some degree, this can be chalked up to historical dynamics. As we have already seen, the study of mission (later, missiology) did not enjoy a simple designation within the dominant academic catalogs of the divinities, and, even when it was included, it certainly did not hold a place of key concern. Because of this, mission specialists and workers were not at the center of the academic endeavor, and they were expected to rely upon other traditional western disciplines to establish how the Bible should be read and interpreted appropriately (Lash, 1985).

If, however, mission scholars and workers did not care about reading "appropriately," the alternative remained for them to opt out of the formal work of interpretation altogether. They could limit themselves to non-methodological, inspirational, or devotional readings that could circulate freely within mission's own spheres of practice, without academic recognition. This was not an intentional or oppressive silencing of mission writers; it was simply the way of academic specialization at the time. Still, as it worked under this scheme, mission interpretation took upon itself the manners of the era, and the net result was that missiology did not see it as appropriate or important to develop or put forward interpretive agenda of its own.

As a result, even while most missiological works touch upon Bible in some manner (Taber, 1983), their foci were usually upon mission tasks, such as translation, mission history, or mission theology, not upon hermeneutics. For many years, as missiology was finding its place in the academy, missiologists remained in the undesirable position of having to conduct their interpretations as non-specialists. These readings frequently employed interpretive practices that were considered to be non-standard or sub-standard when compared to other disciplines (Barram, 2007). This has left missiology in a disadvantaged position, perched awkwardly upon the watersheds that divide lay, applied, and critical methods. For, even when recognized hermeneutic tools were borrowed from other disciplines, they tended to have been borrowed selectively and applied in unusual ways, with minimal attention being given to their theoretical foundations or implications (Bosch, 1986; Taber, 1983).

Thus, historically, mission authors produced interpretations without holding the pedigree to establish the processes that they used. Since those readings did not conform to established best practices, mission interpretations gained a fairly marginalized reputation in academic circles, and that legacy repeatedly impacted discussions about missiological reading, both within and without missiological circles. Indeed, much of the challenge facing mission interpretation today involves negotiating the academic rubble left in the wake of conflicts over how missiologists interpreted when they did step out of the division of labor scheme and attempt to perform their own readings. However, missiology should not be characterized as a victim in all of this, for it participated in the division of labor scheme, and, even if that participation was done out of a cooperative spirit, missiologists did elect to take up tools that were forged in other disciplines in ad hoc ways instead of choosing to frame their own.

In the late 1970's, Marc Spindler sounded a strong warning against just such unexamined borrowing of other disciplinary methods, which warrants a citation in full:

> Indeed, the missiological methodology we employ either guarantees or ruins the credibility of missiology as an academic discipline. It is because of the problem of methodology that missiology is threatened as a discipline since it loses its originality and raison d'etre if it shamelessly borrows its methodologies from other disciplines and fails to develop any distinctives of its own. It uses the political methodology when mission is regarded as political, the sociological method when mission is regarded as a sociological phenomenon, etc. Perhaps missiologists need either to develop a 'comprehensive' multidisciplinary methodology (or interdisciplinary), or they need to develop a plurality of 'missiological schools,' distinctive in theological commitment and aggressive in developing consistent methodology. (1979, p. 82)

His point was clear that missiology needed to develop distinctive methods, and, even though his solution remains open-ended, it would seem to support the framing of a distinct subfield for missiology's interpretive inquiry.

It was only a few years later that Lash (1985) forthrightly called for missiology to work out its own hermeneutic questions. Key points in his criticism of the academic relay race were his protest that biblical scholars have not asked the questions of truth that are of chief concern to those concerned with witness, and, more importantly, that they have never seemed to reach the point of actually handing off the biblical "baton" (1985, pp. 16-17) so that missiologists could have access to a reliable, consensus biblical meaning. He further objected that biblical scholars have not provided methodological tools that are pragmatically functional outside of their own academic domain.

Lash's point is well taken. Not only has this hindered missiologists from garnering biblical meaning(s) for use in doing mission work, it also appears to have undermined missiology's place to present distinctive theoretical contributions within the interdisciplinary hermeneutical conversation. This is further highlighted by the fact that writers such as Bosch, Nissen, Senior and Stuhlmueller, and Wright, who are considered to have produced major missiological works, have written on the Bible and mission from the location of persons trained primarily in biblical studies.

However, as Scherer notes,

> [T]he essential questions must be raised again and again in a timely way in the light of both changing modes of mission and changing views of biblical interpretation. If biblical scholars do not normally focus on missiological issues, and if missiologists are not by training equipped to handle hermeneutical matters with depth and expertise, where will the task of correlation be done? Are the members of the missiological fraternity not obliged to seek out and challenge their biblical colleagues? (1987, p. 515)

While I am hesitant to embrace the idea of using a "challenge," approach between disciplines, Scherer's point that the relay race/division of labor model was not sufficient cannot be disputed. As modes and views have indeed changed in both fields, missiology no longer is in a position where it is expected to borrow its interpretations, methods or scholars from other disciplines for the sake of establishing its own legitimacy. Rather, as an interdisciplinary endeavor, which requires it to rely partially upon the works of others, the way is open for missiology to glean among the disciplines for the sake of academic contribution.

In this project, it would be helpful for our borrowing to be done with respect, maintaining integrity to the concepts of others even as we make those significant qualifications that re-frame what we borrow in truly missiological ways. Thus, it is beneficial that Scherer called out the tensions that stood and continue to stand between biblical studies and missiology, but instead of seeking out and challenging biblical colleagues, perhaps a fruitful strategy may be for missiologists to seek for commonly-held theoretic acknowledgements that can serve as crossroads where biblical scholars and missiologists can meet together, along with other cognate disciplines.[31]

Thankfully, although there is much that remains to be resolved, at least the modernist division of labor is no longer taken as absolute, and in some cases, it is not even the dominant state of affairs. This is due to the fact that toward the end of the twentieth century, the modern academic scheme came under challenge from decentralized voices, and the custodianship of interpretation underwent a process of academic democratization that continues to the time of this writing. In the arrangement that is still emerging, the meaning of biblical texts is no longer considered to be an end-product that consists of verifiable knowledge, which results from the application of approved western reading methods as they are conducted by highly skilled specialists (West, 1995) (Taber, 1983). Instead, more contemporary arrangements hold that the production of biblical meaning is open equally to specialists and non-specialists, and that both readerships access the biblical texts from legitimate locations, employing reading strategies that are often highly influenced by social forces.[32]

This shift has proven to be emancipatory for missiology, even though the process has been at times contentious and painful, and even though it presents a kind of double-edged sword. On one hand, missiology does not have to be ashamed if it fails to conduct itself according to the established habits of biblical studies or theology, or literary studies, or any other interpretive discipline. This liberates missiological reading from the

---

[31] Finding theoretical common ground often requires appealing to later twentieth-century scholarship in this study. This is not accidental. In most cases it takes time for works to attain interdisciplinary acknowledgement, and I believe that the broad recognition that major later twentieth century theorists have received provides the interdisciplinary scope that is needed to do what Scherer calls "raising essential questions" in a "timely way" (1987, p. 515)

[32] See discussion below.

burden of having to approach the text under threat of disapproval or while being delegitimized for having done its readings the "wrong" way.

On the other hand, the freedom that missiology enjoys to establish its own interpretive canons also carries with it the responsibility to articulate those commitments clearly if missiology expects to participate in the academic conversation, where peer review is one of the rules of the game. We missiologists may interpret any way that we wish, but if we desire to obtain academic feedback or recognition for our interpretations, we will need to make the processes by which those readings were produced open and available for academic examination. This is a step that is required of all who wish to have a seat at the academic table.

In other words, in the era of decentralized interpretation, each must own its own. It is no longer acceptable for missiology tacitly to default on the difficult task of articulating its own interpretive strategies, especially if it does so by deferring silently to the priority of methods practiced within traditional disciplines. The time has passed in which missiology could defer on its turn to read, claiming, "Yeah, what *they* said."

In part, that is the aim of this book. For, although missiology rightfully may not be focused upon biblical interpretation, it cannot ignore interpretation's place in mission or relegate the task to other disciplines. Missiological tasks involve reading and require that interpretation be performed. The question is not *if* missiological interpretation should or does take place, but only *how*, and according to what canons.

Chapter 2
Missiological Distinctives

In a simplified sense, interpretation results from questions, and questions arise out of concerns. Those concerns in turn arise from certain understandings about the world. As Michel Foucault has shown in *The Archaeology of Knowledge* (1972), knowledge of any given thing relies upon a weave of understanding about other things. Since it is not possible to know all things, particular things always must be selected from among the full range of things that could be known, and meaningful connections must be drawn between them. Based upon those choices, understandings arise, and questions are formed. This is in some sense a self-reinforcing process, since those questions in turn organize data by framing data relative to their own inquiries. The result is that "knowledge" is formed as a "discursive practice."[33]

In Foucault's understanding, "there is no knowledge without a particular discursive practice; and any discursive practice may be defined by the kind of knowledge that it forms" (1972, p. 183). In other words, questions matter. The kind of question that one asks arises from what one already understands, and it determines the kind of information that results. This is the crux of the hermeneutic enterprise. For, whether an interpretation arises from folk culture or the academic disciplines, it still

---

[33] For Foucault, history (in contrast to "History") is a discourse (1972, pp. 3-17). A "discursive formation" results from the connection of statements that are linked through arbitrary rules via the governance of a "general enunciative system." See his summary on discursive formation and statements (1972, pp. 113-117). Discourse itself is a "practice" (1972, p. 46).

must rely upon webs of understanding, which frame and sustain its inquiries. Based upon its discursive foundations, any given hermeneutic will ask distinctive textual questions, and it will organize the available textual data according to those questions. Hermeneutic questions cannot be framed without assumptions and concerns, for a hermeneutic expects to find certain answers, and it only finds those answers that its questions empower it to discern.

Discourse and Purpose

Thus, as any hermeneutic must, a missiological hermeneutic needs to have agenda for its inquiries. In order to be academically viable, its agenda also need to provide criteria of examination that can be understood by others. That is, a hermeneutic must have something distinct to look for, or to see things in light of, and it should be able to tell others what that distinctive might be. For missiological interpretation, then, in order to be truly missiological, the agenda need to have clear connections to the discursive interests of missiology.

I believe that the question of *purpose* can provide a key for discursive inquiry, since the notion of purpose is perhaps missiology's most crucial point of commitment. Notably, many major contributors to missiological discussion refer to the purpose(s) of God in a foundational way (Barram, 2007, pp. 46-47; Bauckham, 2003, p. 11; Elliston, 2007, p. 9; Charles Van Engen, 1996, pp. 35-36; C. J. H. Wright, 2004, p. 137),[34] and the idea is endemic to mission studies, regardless of whether those are "mission," "missional," or "missiological."[35] If we take the idea of *purpose* in a dispositional sense, that is, as an active orientation toward accomplishing

---

[34] Also, see Nissen (2004b, p. 168) on "intentionality and activity."
[35] Michael Barram is a key example of this. He sees interpretive approaches that understand mission "to refer to the church's overall vocation or purpose as defined by the *missio Dei*" as particularly promising (2007, p. 46). He also notes, "linking 'mission' with 'purpose' parallels common usage." He continues, "using mission in a holistic way to invoke the overarching purpose of the church appropriates the recognition that the church's mission is in fact, God's" (2007, p. 46).

an end, the concept can be seen to be central both to the general idea of *missio*[36] and to the special idea of *missio Dei*.

Taken this way, missiology's concern for purpose provides a special kind of what Hans-Georg Gadamer calls "fore-grounding" or "fore-meaning" (2004, pp. 268-273). This corresponds to what Polanyi and Prosch[37] call "subsidiary awareness" (1975, p. 33). When used as fore-grounding, *purpose* can be understood as characteristic quality that can pervade texts, and missiology's special attention to purpose can be understood to enable it to discern purposive quality in a manner and in instances that other disciplines do not. Along this line, missiologists Newbigin (1986)[38] and Bosch (1986), appeal to Polanyi in order to assert that the creation of knowledge rests upon faith commitment.[39] Building upon all of these positions, we can assert that missiology's dedication to fulfilling purposes, especially God's purposes, provides a faith commitment for missiology that can empower the formation of knowledge. For missiology, then, "the kind of knowledge that it forms" in its discourse consistently relates to *missio* in a general sense and to the *missio Dei*, particularly. Both of these are expressions of *purpose*.

Discourse and Context

Essentially, a discourse is a "dot to dot" web of statements, commitments, values, and concepts, which forms an epistemological ground matrix. Within a discourse, the network of relationships between knowledge points serves as a foundation for framing new understandings. Even when

---

[36] The term *missio* generally corresponds to the idea of *mission*, but it is more conceptually abstracted. *Missio Dei* (mission of God) is a term that missiologists frequently use as a reference point in their conversations when referring to all that is encompassed in God's intentions and purpose, There is perhaps no more pervasive phrase in missiological literature. Yet, the very pervasiveness of the phrase *missio Dei*, like mission, makes it hard to describe, and it has been used to support widely varied agenda (Bevans & Schroeder, 2004, pp. 286-304).

[37] Polanyi is the primary authorial source; Harry Prosch is the editing compiler of Polanyi's material. Because of this, subsequent citations will reference Polanyi only.

[38] Newbigin is cited by Bosch as his foundation.

[39] Polanyi argues that all scientific knowledge is ultimately grounded in "personal knowledge," which requires skillful "*personal* judgments" or "art," (1975, pp. 31, 33) and personal acts of integration (1975, pp. 37-38) through attention (1975, pp. 22-45). He qualifies this, "It will appear that all knowledge is intrinsically guided by impersonal standards of valuation set by a self for itself" (1975, p. 42)

related concepts within a discourse are not articulated in the same way, using the same points, they still rely upon the same overall network of common understanding.

Because of this, even though missiology has not defined itself or its hermeneutics, when missiologists start to talk about the Bible (or any related topic), missiological discourse invariably comes out. This means that it is possible to get a sense of how missiology frames up its knowledge by looking at things that are considered to be "givens" across the span of its dialog. These other understandings support and inform the questions of missiological hermeneutics because they are key points in missiology's discursive fabric.

For example, Taber understands the Bible to exhibit, "a deep common theme... the story of God's redemptive purpose and activity in history -- the missiological theme" (1983, p. 231). Commentators Senior and Stuhlmueller talk about the "attempt to fulfill the divine mandate given to the church that humanity reflect God's own life as one people drawn together in love and respect" (1983, p. 3). David Bosch ponders about intrinsic aspects of mission, considering, "The term 'mission' presupposes a sender, a person or persons sent by the sender, those to whom one is sent, and an assignment" (1991, p. 1). More recently, Wright (2004, p. 137) reads biblical material "in light of...God's purpose for his whole creation...God's purpose for human life in general...God's historical election of Israel...the centrality of Jesus of Nazareth...God's calling of the church."

While these samplings have significant differences, common elements can be seen in all: 1) actors, especially God, and, 2) activity, which involves: 3) meaningful intention or sending. This is conducted in 4) multiple contexts. These show through as some of missiology's "fore-meanings," the pre-understandings that undergird its discourse and shape its attentions. Without having to make final definitions, then, and without stretching very far, we can at least note that the missiological discourse frames its knowledge in terms of mission, and that it talks about mission as the purposeful activity of persons in certain contexts. It also sees the Christian mission as involving God-in-Christ in those purposeful, contextual activities.

Purpose and Context

Within the discourse of missiology, then, we find that *purpose* has a significant link to *context* and that both terms intersect the concept of *missio*. As the study of *missio*, missiology looks at purpose itself and at purposeful activity that expresses in contexts. This includes the purposeful activity of God within contexts (the *missio Dei*). These aspects: *purpose* (general), *God's purpose* (special), and *context*, establish a baseline set of factors for missiological examination of texts. As Van Engen asserts:

> We cannot have mission without the Bible, nor can we understand the Bible apart from God's mission. The missio Dei is God's mission. Yet the missio Dei happens in specific places and times in our contexts. Its content, validity and meaning are derived from Scripture, yet its actions, significance and power happen in our midst. (1996, p. 37)

Van Engen makes a serious point. From missiological perspectives, purpose does not exist somewhere "out in space," unattached to real people. Neither do people exist as automatons, lacking purpose. People do things meaningfully. They do meaningful things alone and in society, and they do them for reasons that involve others in real places. When it comes to reading, even biblical reading, people learn to read for real reasons in real places under the influence of real social purposes. They are taught to read for reasons, and they continue to perform their readings for reasons.[40] Those reasons are both personal and social, and they are often complex and variable.[41]

---

[40] "In other words, you teach what you know: such is the expert... In this way the student is introduced to the dialectics of research, or the game of producing scientific knowledge"(Lyotard, 1993, p. 25).

[41] This observation is axiomatic to ideological and social criticisms, such as feminist, postcolonial or Marxist hermeneutics.

The contextual factor is a point that interdisciplinary dialog already has highlighted. For example, Barram calls this an area of disciplinary convergence between missiology and biblical studies about "social location" (2007, pp. 44-45). Similarly, Taber's critique calls missiology to recognize "the contextual rootedness of each of the various traditions and parts of the Bible" (1983, p. 235). He also calls out a point of common ground that is, "at heart all about exactly the same phenomenon: the historical and cultural rootedness of each situation and event, of each person and group, of each set of conceptual categories and system of symbols, and of each human experience" (1983, p. 236).

As we will see below, it appears that just about everyone involved in the hermeneutic conversation, whether missiological or non-missiological, sees context as a core factor. Importantly, the social dimension of context is an aspect widely recognized as providing theoretic grounding and it gives a point of agreement between many disciplines. Therefore, if we can see that the idea of "purpose" is related to the reality of "social location," it is theoretically possible to examine social constructs (such as texts) for the social telltales of their purposes without having to ascribe purpose on solely metaphysical grounds. This can empower us to look for *missio* in a general sense in all social productions.

Further, if we do not allow western worldview biases to exclude *a priori* the possibility of God's involvement as a social actor, it follows that we can look for the *missio Dei* as one among the many purposes that are at play in social contexts. I believe that this is possible, and that the intersection where the social construction of knowledge meets the social dimension of activity is a place where missiological hermeneutics can find traction because of missiology's unique attention to the nature, traits and expressions of purpose. To put it more concisely, mission is all about purpose, but it is about purpose that relates to context. This particular mix, *purpose:context*, gives missiology a distinct agenda that hallmarks its formation of knowledge, and in turn, its hermeneutics.

Even with that hallmark on the table, missiological interpretation has difficult work to do if it is to make itself understood by other disciplines, since the overall landscape of interpretation is deeply fragmented from major theoretical conflicts. Even if missiology had a consensus position from within its own field to hold forth, the fragmentation in non-missiological interpretation makes comparison(s) awkward and the risk of being misunderstood high. This presents missiology with the delicate task of self-articulation in a volatile environment. Still, reference points need to be established in some way if the conversation is to move forward. Granted, one-to-one comparison is not really possible, but the option remains to discern key points from missiological discourse and relate those with non-missiological discourses. This can give us a sufficient sense of where missiological interpretation stands amid the interpretive disciplines.[42]

Missiological Reference Points

While missiology can connect partially with a wide array of approaches, many hermeneutics arise from epistemological locations that missiology is ill-fitted to embrace *in toto*. This is not because missiology has a single, homogeneous worldview. Rather, it is due to the fact that, as a coordinated endeavor, missiology has sought self-consciously to operate among multiple worldviews.

In the quest to find a way for diverse people to join hands, missiologists have spent a considerable amount of time and energy hammering out a sufficient number of shared concerns for missiology to have a recognizable disciplinary profile. While all missiologists may not agree precisely, they have interacted on these points enough to form common ranges of commitment that can serve as the field's conversational intersections, as touch points that stretch its discourse across worldview systems. Although they may not be as intrinsic to the concept of mission as

---

[42] Michael Polanyi asserts that meaning is sufficiently achieved when "understanding" is gained through coherence, rather than "explanation." This is a state of plausibility that entails "relief of puzzlement" as a criterion of satisfaction (1975, p. 53). This is the level and kind of plausibility that I am seeking here.

purpose and context are, these touch points remain discursive places where various missiologists can agree to meet "enough," without having to depart from their own worldviews.

These conversational touch points can serve as auxiliary anchors to the concepts of purpose and context because they form an array of limits, which in turn set some of the parameters for missiological reading. For example, because missiology is committed to a holistic view of reality that includes supernatural and natural dimensions, missiology is not able to meet on common ground with hermeneutics that require *a priori* exclusion of ontology, teleology, transcendence, or the metaphysical. That same commitment prevents missiology from agreeing to treat metaphysical talk as something that refers solely to human perceptive elements or operations. From another angle, missiology is foundationally committed to the concept that God is a being who can be active in creation. Thus, it cannot bracket God from history or historical inquiry, etc.

We will explore more on these points below, and we will revisit the issue of metaphysical exclusion frequently throughout the conversations in later chapters. For now, it is important to note that, similar to many moral and ethical discourses, missiology's discourse points often act as limits against theoretical demands that arise unilaterally from western rational outlooks (Lin, 2016). It would be misleading to treat these limits as assertions that arise from religious ignorance or antagonism to reasonable thinking. Rather, they are the products of missiology's protection of its openness to plurality of worldview. When acknowledged, they prevent the silencing of entire ranges of discourse that are of high value to non-western cultures because they hold at bay the constraints that western rationalism historically has imposed upon academic talk and interpretive practices. In order to see this on functional levels, we will survey just a few of the conversation points below and see how they intersect with some western interpretive conventions.

Distinctive Concerns

Although it may sound tautological, one of the sticky points in this conversation is the reality that disciplinary distinctives are in fact, "distinctive." Missiological themes are often unique to missiology's field of vision. This uniqueness can make missiology's most important points serve poorly as grounds for interdisciplinary dialog, especially in cases when other disciplines might pre-limit or exclude central missiological concerns out of hand. In turn, issues that are of great concern to other disciplines may not appear to exist at all to missiologists.

Particularly, missiology runs afoul of other hermeneutic discourses when it presents readings that are full of talk about "purpose," "intention," "God's work," and "personal presence," because these involve questions of ontology, teleology, and metaphysics, which have become hermeneutically and philosophically suspect topics in the West. Yet, these topics matter significantly both to missiologists and to those with whom mission agents interact. This places missiology on the horns of a dilemma. If it is to connect with prevailing talk in western disciplines, missiology is expected to release its central discursive commitments to these kinds of meta-rational topics. Alternately, if it is to continue to connect with non-western outlooks and maintain its concerns for these points, it must proceed at the cost of western academic regard.

Hopefully, this is a tension resulting from misunderstanding, not prejudice or knowing marginalization. If such is the case, then it would seem fruitful for missiology to make the overture in goodwill of providing some points of explanation before expecting recognition of its methods. In order to place that on the table, for the rest of this chapter, we will look first at some key concerns of missiology and see how those affect its reading, then we will see how those concerns relate to key concerns from other interpretive fields.

Gospel as spiritual and social. Probably the most pervasive issue in missiology during the 20th and 21st centuries has been discerning the nature of the gospel, combined with articulating the nature of mission, itself.[43] Much of this discussion has centered on whether the gospel, and hence, mission, is primarily "this-worldly" and "social" or "other-worldly"[44] and spiritual (Kirk, 2000, p. 59). Marc Spindler calls this issue "a classic debate," tracing it to Hans Schaerer, who in 1944, "divided missiological positions very sharply into two camps," which grounded mission respectively in "nature" or the "supernatural" (1995, p. 124). He understands this to be a "double-grounding," that separates those who hold to "biblical" (supernatural) foundations from those who prefer "natural bases for mission, namely the anthropological, social, historical, economic, and political grounds."

This issue is historically involved, so here I will have to refer the reader to surveys provided by Verkuyl (1978), Van Engen (1996), Bosch (1991), and Bevans and Schroeder (2004), as well as the ecumenical compendium of Verstraelen (1995), et al. (eds.). In summary, during the course of debates that attended 20th century paradigm shifts in epistemology, theology, and mission, an impasse was reached about the fundamental grounding of mission. As it stands today, the overwhelming majority position has come to be that whether or not one prioritizes a certain dimension, it is a false path to separate the two aspects. Missiology's conclusion was that social dimensions carry spiritual reality and spiritual dimensions express in the social realities of culture, context, and praxis.

Missiology wrestled over this issue, in order articulate the natures of mission, witness, and the gospel, not in order to negotiate a hermeneutic problem. Thus, the hermeneutic implications must be teased out in order to be seen clearly. For our discussion, while the debate has not been settled

---

[43] Roxborogh notes that the issue of definition raised by J. Scherer still has not been resolved, even though the centrality of the *missio Dei* has become established (2009, pp. 7-8).
[44] Hiebert's terms (2008, p. 59), see also (2008, pp. 154-155).

finally (and very well may never be), we can at least note that missiology's working consensus so far has been that the gospel is multiform; it is simultaneously this-worldly and social, as well as other-worldly and spiritual.[45]

Paul Hiebert's contribution to missiological theory on the "Flaw of the Excluded Middle" (1982) deserves consideration at this point.[46] In his article, Hiebert contrasts "organic" and "mechanistic" worldviews, observing that the scientific western worldview has imposed separations between "this-worldly" and "other-worldly" realities. He contrasts the western outlook with other worldviews, especially Eastern worldviews, which see a continuum of existence that includes supernatural and natural in a single, unified reality of being. The "Flaw of the Excluded Middle" is the name Hiebert gives for the gap in western understanding that not only overlooks but also excludes the presence of "this worldly," "spiritual" beings and forces, such as magic, which are acknowledged to exist in cultures across the globe (Figure 1).[47]

---

[45] I am borrowing the terms, "This worldly" and "Other worldly" directly from Hiebert (2008, p. 59).
[46] He revisits this concept in many of his works, the most recent treatment is in *Transforming Worldviews* (2008).
[47] This article builds upon Hiebert's experiences with Indian mission, particularly the enduring popular practice of folk magic. In it, he contrasts the western worldview, which divides between "supernatural" and "natural" realities, with majority-world views that do not differentiate between supernatural and natural aspects of reality.
 He proposes analysis of religious systems using "seen" and "unseen" (immanence-transcendence) dimensions, linked to "this worldly" and "other worldly" locating (1982, p. 40). These are examined upon a continuum formed from two analogical lenses: "organic," in which "explanations see the world in terms of living beings in relationship to one another" (1982, p. 41) and "mechanical," in which "things are thought to be inanimate parts of greater mechanical systems" (1982, p. 42). Organic analogies involve relationship, personal action and "ethical considerations," while "(m)echanical analogies are essentially deterministic" and, "are basically amoral in character." Use of this analytic grid reveals a viable place for a "middle level of supernatural but this worldly beings and forces" that is "excluded" when "a western two-tiered view of reality," which reductionistically separates "otherworldly" religion from "this worldly" science, is employed (1982, p. 43).
 Hiebert attributes the dichotomy to western scientific roots in Platonic dualism. He considers questions of the "middle level" to focus on human uncertainty, noting that "transempirical explanations often provide an answer when empirical ones fail" (1982, p. 45). He calls for "missionaries to develop holistic theologies that deal with all areas of life, that avoids the Platonic dualism of the West and takes seriously body and soul" (1982, p. 46), which should include "a theology of God in cosmic history," "a theology of God in human history" and "an awareness of God in natural history," while guarding against a mechanistic view of Christianity as "a new form of magic" (1982, pp. 46-47).

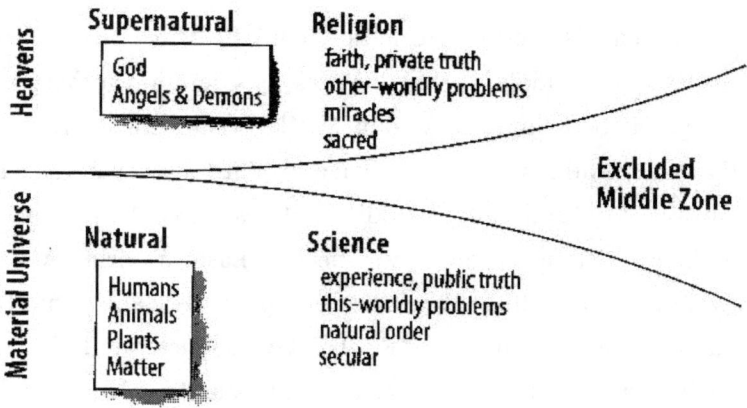

Figure 1. Hiebert's diagram of "The Modern Worldview" showing the "Excluded Middle" Reprinted from *Transforming Worldviews* p.94, by P.G. Hiebert, 2008, Grand Rapids, Baker Academic. Copyright 2008 by Eloise Meneses, Barbara Rowe, and John Hiebert. Reprinted with permission.

Charles Kraft, who acknowledges a significant influence from Hiebert, also soundly rejects western notions of reality that exclude spiritual beings and forces from "natural causality" (2008, pp. 192-201). He protests, "Thus, for western Christians, a constant problem is the strength of the naturalistic conditioning we received in early life" that excludes God's involvement (2008, p. 29).[48] He notes that the majority of the world's

---

[48] He continues, "As a result of that conditioning we learned to look at all of life as if God is not involved in any of it, with the possible exception of some of the things done on Sunday or an occasional miracle when He steps in to overrule some natural rule. We learned such assumptions so early and so strongly and integrated them so thoroughly into our lives at a time when we were aware of no possible alternative perspectives that their ramifications and effects are extremely difficult to ferret out, even when we are strongly committed to doing so" (Kraft, 2008, p. 29).

societies, along with "biblical societies," do not hold to an exclusively natural understanding of cause, and he outlines a variety of alternative worldviews that effectively integrate spiritual reality.[49] Kraft links this blindspot of worldview with interpretation, proposing that the lack of western understanding of spiritual causation "makes it very difficult for us to understand either the Bible or the concerns of non-western peoples in this area" (2008, p. 200).

If we consider Hiebert's and Kraft's points in light of the broad conclusions of 20th century missiology about the nature of the gospel, we can see that missiology as a whole rejects the notion that the gospel must be either supernatural or natural, and it rejects separation between human action and divine action. Missiology does not accept a hard division between human and divine mission, for, from a missiological perspective, there is an irreducible unity of the spiritual and the natural in human existence to which both mission and the gospel are directed. It follows that it is fallacious to dichotomize the gospel or human existence. As Hiebert asserts:

> People are called to respond to God's invitation, and when they do, they are transformed in their lives. Spiritual changes have earthly consequences. Humans cannot be divided, with their spirits functioning independently of their bodies...
>
> Biblical conversion involves real people in their everyday lives. Consequently, it always takes place within the particularities of history. Furthermore, it is both individual and corporate, for people do not exist outside societies and cultures. (2008, p. 307)

For missiology, the unity of existence involves both transcendent and immanent aspects. These realities cannot be dichotomized without doing damage and disservice to the concepts of mission and the gospel. If anything, missiology considers it to be morally and spiritually irresponsible,

---

[49] Hiebert holds that two-thirds of world cultures hold to a concept of a "High God" (2008, p. 59).

even harmful, to attempt to separate them (2007, pp. 126-151).[50] This is a foundational concept within missiology and we will find it recurring from different angles in many later chapters.

With regard to texts, this principle sets a limit because it demands that texts, like all of reality, would be treated as simple wholes, that is, as things that cannot have their natural and supernatural aspects separated. In this view, it would be reductionistic and distortive to think of the Bible solely as a socio-religious or literary text, or to approach it only as a spiritual revelation; it must be both. By the same token, reading itself must be understood as a unified act. It cannot be the case that reading is done *either* spiritually or non-spiritually. The case must be that reading is inextricably a spiritual and material activity that cannot be divided, even when a particular dimension may be emphasized or suppressed.

For missiological hermeneutics, this means that any examination that has only one dimension of inquiry remains insufficient to satisfy missiological concerns, whether that limitation is to a solely metaphysical mode of inquiry or to a solely scientific and material one. It means that both spiritual and natural inquiries into reading or language should be considered (and qualified) as yielding only partial insight and that they each need to be supplemented by examinations that use additional interpretive criteria. Thus, natural readings should be integrated with approaches that use spiritual discernment and spiritual readings should be supplemented with natural discernments.[51]

Witness as Word and Deed

The broad missiological discussion mentioned above also revealed missiology's preference for holism as it examined the relationship between "word" and "deed." As J. Andrew Kirk sums, "Unless God's mission is rooted

---

[50] His point correlates with Soares-Prabhu's (1986) article, if such exclusion was to derive from a position that ascribes normative superiority to the scientism of western hermeneutic tradition.

[51] This is a crucial, given the historical dominance of western approaches (Soares-Prabhu, 1986). Maintaining integration intentionally is particularly necessary when spiritual aspects are crucial to readers who have non-western worldviews.

in what liberation theologians would call 'concrete practice', it becomes either empty or open to ideological, political or religious manipulation (or all three)." To him, the missiologist's question is, "we ask how those who follow Jesus should shape their lives" (2000, p. 38). This criterion applies alike to those who represent the gospel and to those who respond to it:

> So evangelism has both an indicative and imperative mode; it is both the conveying of a message and the challenge to act a certain way in response to the message's content. Hearing the news is not enough; positive action is required in order that its significance is personally experienced. (2000, p. 61)

For missiology, then, all of the gospel is addressed to all of the human and all of the human responds to the gospel. Likewise, all of the human is involved in mission and mission is addressed to all of the human. Witness irreducibly entails holistic, personal involvement; as does conversional response to the gospel. This means that for missiology, communication is an intertwined endeavor in which the full existence of an irreducibly spiritual and material person can be involved. It cannot be accomplished fully or explained sufficiently as the interplay of signs within systems, the operation of cognitive functions or the exercise of social forces, alone. Rather, communication has a robust, holistic and praxeological nature, in which action and sense are wed, and that wedding of action and sense has both material and spiritual dimensions. Words cannot stand alone without action any more than spiritual and material dimensions can stand alone.

This holistic view of communication is a package that often ends up being too large to fit in the epistemological boxes of other hermeneutics. For, when missiology holds to the full range of what it understands to be true about holistic communication, it cannot treat discussions of linguistic, aesthetic, social, historical, or literary meanings as adequate until those are integrated with other human dimensions of response. This is especially the case with sacred text, because the sacred text overtly concerns itself with moral and spiritual aspects of existence, which are very rarely addressed in linguistic, philosophical, and literary discussions.[52]

Kingdom as "Now" and "Not Yet." God's "kingdom" and "reign" are also extensive themes in missiological discourse. These are concepts with many dimensions, some of which we will unpack at different points throughout the book. At this point, we want to see a few ways in which missiologists describe the kingdom in reference to *time*. Missiology's kingdom talk reveals how missiology generally conceives of time, and, since time is one of the dimensions of context, how missiology conceptually negotiates time impacts how missiological interpretation treats temporal context(s). This in turn sets the mark for how missiological interpretation works with the idea of history and with historical horizons.

Early in the contemporary theology of mission, Alexander Schmemann summarized the Orthodox position on the kingdom's temporal presence this way:

> The kingdom is yet *to come* and the Church is not *of* this world. And yet this Kingdom to come is already present and the Church is fulfilled *in* this world. They are present not only as "proclamation," but in their very reality, and through the divine *agape*, which is their fruit, they *perform* all the time the same sacramental transformation of the *old* into the *new*, they make possible a real action, a real doing in this world. All this gives the mission of the Church a *cosmical* and a *historical* dimension.(1961, p. 256) [italics in original]

Bosch sounds a similar note, citing Stanley and Wright. It is interesting to hear the array of discursive points that he touches as he threads together purpose, context, Bible, activity, and kingdom time:

---

[52] Although Barram notes that the holistic nature of the church's mission is emerging as a recent area of theoretical convergence with biblical studies (2007, p. 44).

> In Israel, however, *history* is the arena of God's activity. The focus is on what God has done, is doing and is yet to do according to his declared intention. God is... the 'God who *acts*. It may therefore be more accurate to refer to the Bible as the Acts of God rather than call it the Word of God.' (1991, p. 17) [italics in original]

From a related angle, Stuhlmueller understands Jesus to have comprehended the coming of the kingdom as being intricately bound up with his own mission and *kairos*. For him, the fact that the kingdom was located at Jesus' personal moment does nothing to affect the idea that the kingdom also was potential and anticipated. Although it is a lengthy quote, he represents missiologists well on this topic:

> Jesus' kingdom ministry includes one other aspect that will have significant consequences for the New Testament understanding of mission: a sense of history. One of the difficulties concerning the kingdom of God motif as proclaimed by Jesus is deciphering his statements about its 'timing.' While some of his statements and parables seem to say that the kingdom is imminent, 'at hand' (Mk.1:14-15), others imply that the kingdom's advent is still future and that a significant interval is to be expected (Matt.13:24-30).
>
> These apparently conflicting statements may, in part, be due to possible ambiguity concerning the kingdom's timetable on the part of Jesus (cf. Mk.13:32) and the early church. But, more importantly, they also derive from the very nature of the kingdom experience. The coming kingdom of God is not reducible to some localized set of circumstances or events, and thus definable for this particular moment of history. The kingdom is, even more radically, an experience of God's rule; it is a metaphor describing a *quality* of life and not just a reference to the climax (or termination) of history. Only because it is such could Jesus have connected the experience of the kingdom with such things as his exorcisms (Lk. 11:28) or with reconciliation (Matt. 18:25-35). In these present experiences of

> God's power, one encountered God's definitive rule. The
> consummation of that rule -- its full consequences on a cosmic and
> historical level -- remain future, but its presence is already breaking
> into human history. In both instances -- present and future -- the
> kingdom is a result of God's saving initiative. It is not neatly
> evolutionary. The Lord of the kingdom is already making his
> presence felt in the present and orienting his people and his world
> toward their full destiny. (1983, p. 155)

It is important to note that Stuhlmueller unites this theme with the idea of an expanding community:

> This same reasoning seems to reinforce Jesus' openness to Gentiles
> and outcasts. Even though the influx of the nations is part of the
> final scenario of the reign of God, the approach of responsive
> Gentiles is welcomed and praised (Matt. 8:11) because that inclusive
> vision of redemption is inbreaking now. (1983)

Missiology thus understands the kingdom to be simultaneously "then," "now," and "not yet." Furthermore, missiology sees the temporal progression of the kingdom to be linked to the geographic and social expansion of God's mission, which is linked to fulfilling God's purpose(s). Richard Bauckham calls this "closure and permanent openness":

> [T]he New Testament does not map out in advance the twists and
> turns of history, the particular narrative or narratives that will take
> place between its narrative present and its symbolic and
> metaphorical expressions of the universal kingdom... the New
> Testament puts the church in its missionary situation in a dialectic
> of anticipated closure and permanent openness. (2003, p. 25)

In this outlook, the kingdom has place in the present continually through the actions of God and the social presence of the kingdom community, but the kingdom also transcends the present. In its singularity, it spans from behind the present in its preceding to beyond the present in its assured becoming. Because the kingdom is a dimension of God's reign, it stands eternal, yet because the kingdom accomplishes God's mission, it proceeds from potential to actual. It is all at once existing before the foundations of the world and coming to pass. The simultaneous and paradoxical character of the kingdom fuses a reign that transcends time with a very concrete social presence and ongoing expansion in ordinary time.

Understanding this link is crucial for understanding missiological hermeneutics, for it requires that missiological interpretation approach the ideas of historicity and historical social contexts in a way that does not allow for temporal or social isolation. We will explore this concept at greater length in Chapter 4, when we examine readers and reading horizons more closely, but for now, we simply can note that because of its commitment to the kingdom of God, missiological interpretation must keep the issue of time open in a way that integrates atemporal ("eternal," or, perhaps, "extemporal") existence with temporal locations and contexts. Since the kingdom is simultaneous while being momentary, it stands both differentiated and united across places, groups, and times. As a result, missiological interpretation may not consider people of one place and time to be finally or ontologically separate from others at other places and times. Its hermeneutic agenda must accommodate the coexistence and interaction of cosmic and historic time in a way that acknowledges the simultaneous presence of open and closed, expanding and established communities.

These are only a few examples of missiology's discursive commitments, but they illustrate how those commitments inform missiological approaches. With those in hand as reference points, we can begin to consider missiological reading relative to other discourses.

Interpretive Intersections

So, how do missiology's points of discourse fit with those of other disciplines? That question is rather complex because the landscape of interpretive practices has changed repeatedly and its current contours remain convoluted and deeply conflicted. In academic circles, interpretive theories often have arisen, stood or fallen in response to philosophical debates and social forces, and it is no secret that the paradigms of the West have experienced volatile shifts during the last two centuries. Along the way, the structures of many interpretive proposals have reached their forms from negotiating successive waves of theoretical reaction and counter reaction. Frequently, these have involved questions about power, truth, and true knowledge, which have been leveled from a wide array of angles. As theories have become entrenched or pushed back against critique, the dialectic process has left in its wake widespread academic disagreement about the location, nature, and stability of meaning.

However, partly because it is a late comer to the fray, and partly because it has been a practitioner's field, missiology has not participated very much in these processes and conversations. Because of its history of practice, missiology has instead come to questions about meaning and the Bible relative to the fulfillment of *missio*. Mission-workers historically have focused on how to accomplish ends through use of the Bible, such as giving witness, the work of the kingdom of God, care for people, building the church, proclamation, and evangelism. Thus, missiology has experienced the Bible as a working thing, one that has its truth grounded in relation to agency and activity.

This means that for missiology, meaning is a means to an end as well as an end in and of itself. More so, the process of achieving an end is an integral part of meaning, even when meaning is considered in and of itself. Thus, missiology has tended not to seek meaning in light of theory, but to frame theory in light of the meaning it has already encountered. It approaches information, the knowing of things, as something that is subordinate and contingent to the ends that knowing things can bring about, that is, in terms of the doing of things.

For the rest of this chapter, we will look at how this positions missiological interpretation relative to some major non-missiological views about meaning, beginning at paradigmatic levels and moving toward more specific issues and schools of thought.

The phenomenological dilemma. Historically, western hermeneutics viewed meaning as a relatively stable thing that could be discovered if enough informed attention was given to the text. Meaning was something to be found out, and it was located somewhere or somehow in relation to the written work, itself. More recently, however, postmodern and contextual theorists have called the very idea of stabilizing meaning into question, championing on one hand the free interplay of word relations or, on the other, the roles of signification systems, readers and reading communities in creating meaning (Thiselton, 1992).[53]

Thus, on the traditional side, a common, intelligible meaning is available to all, but it is found and validated in direct proportion to interpretive expertise, as that expertise accords with recognized conventions. On the less traditional side, no common meaning can be established, especially through expertise, because meaning is a creation that remains idiomatic, and universalized meanings are subject to suspicion as tools of power and interest.

Both sides of the broader conflict, however, seem to be hindered from asking the kinds of phenomenon-oriented[54] questions that interest missiology. This presents an awkward dilemma, because missiology needs theory and practice to be a two-way street. While missiology stands ready to inform its practices in light of theoretical insights, before it can embrace theory as valid it needs also to see the explanatory capacity of theory to account for its own very real experience(s).

In order to understand this conflict between induction and deduction, it can help to recall that missiology has arisen as an academic reflection on real mission practices. Thus, on the academic side it must

---

[53]Because of their philosophical and ideological commitments, theorists that object to stabilized meaning tend to ask particularizing questions, focusing on what might result in specific incidents if certain persons from certain outlooks read according to certain agenda or textual/intertextual frames.

[54] Throughout this study I am using the term, "phenomenological" in the same sense as Berger and Luckmann, "the subjective experience of everyday life" (1967, p. 20), rather than in a precisely philosophical (Husserlian) sense.

acknowledge that there is ground somewhere for common understandings and it must yield a degree of legitimacy to reason, research and studied approaches to language and texts. Yet, at the same time, missiology knows from firsthand experience about spiritual insight and folk knowledge, which means that it also must recognize the validity of nonacademic reading and the significance of organic, revelatory, and contextualized understanding (Bazzell, 2018).

Thus, from the perspective of missiology, both theoretical and phenomenological questions must be asked. For, despite academic objections that protest the hegemony of theory, missiologists have found theory useful in the fruitful transfer of the Bible into new contexts, where unexpected readings have blossomed.[55] Also, despite theoretical objections to the possibility of stabilizing or communicating meaning, the phenomenon facing missiologists is that real people from a wide variety of contexts are actually reading the Bible and demonstrating in dialog with each other that they are encountering noticeably related meaning(s), as well as noticeably distinct ones (de Groot, 1995).[56]

---

[55] Easy examples are the communication theory works of Eugene Nida (1960, 1984) and Charles Kraft (1983, 1991, 2001)

[56] Taber sees this as the Bible's ongoing translatability: "It is as amazing to see how translatable the Bible is as to see how difficult it is. Though discrepancies and incompatibilities between the biblical worlds and contemporary worlds are very real and pose formidable problems for translation, we must not stop at merely underlining these. What must be emphasized is the fact, empirically verified in many hundreds of cases, that the Bible is amazingly translatable around the world. This is possible because, within its own variegated contexts, the Bible addresses predominantly the universal core issues of human existence: life and death, hope and despair, power and weakness, wealth and poverty, freedom and oppression, theodicy and salvation. It therefore finds a point of contact and resonates at the deepest level with human beings everywhere. The experience of translators and missionaries in many groups and languages is that the authoritative message of God in the Scriptures is tough enough to survive not only the original processes of oral and textual transmission, but also those of translation, and that the authentic word of God comes through the Bible with power in any human context" (1983, pp. 237-238).

One of the interesting realities that missiologists must wrestle with constantly is that people in widely disparate settings develop and express recognizably Christian confessions and commitments when they read the Bible. Even though the features of various readings are often surprising, there is no question of whether or not people are reading and encountering "familiar" biblical "texts" and as a result expressing related Christian understandings. At the very least, this indicates that there is some sort of common ground of reference at play. Some kind of commonality, even if it is simply one that is able to distinguish textual identity, is necessary in order for any kind of comparison to be performed. At a phenomenological level, one can minimally assume that a basal identifiability of some sort undergirds the text, serving

On one hand, these realities defy philosophical claims against stable, communicable meaning and on the other they fly in the face of traditional academic taboos against "eisegetical" reading. But missiology is held by its commitments to recognize that some range of meaning is being produced when folk reading is done, and it must acknowledge that people are actually talking meaningfully among themselves about their readings in ways that indicate common understanding (Bazzell, 2018). Thus, missiology must allow that "good," legitimate and reliable readings do in fact arise out of folk encounters with texts and it must afford those readings full force, even when theory might hold that such meaning is not possible, and even when theory might claim that such reading is misguided or misinformed.

This is especially crucial when readers make claims that they have achieved spiritual enlightenment or sacred revelation while reading the text. Missiology cannot dismiss those experiences as illusions on merely theoretical or philosophical grounds; nor can it bracket out those dialogs as being beyond the legitimate or allowable range for discussion about reliable textual meaning. Instead, it must note that readers experience their readings as meaningful, communicable, and spiritual, and it must keep the conversation open enough to empower talk about the full range of the text's meaning, since spiritual readers may be demonstrating in practice a way of accessing very real textual potentials.

Taking the middle path. Our proposal here takes a middle-ground, gestaltic approach that tries to help span some of these differences while remaining faithful to missiological commitments. This proposal recognizes that people read in a process that is partially influenced by themselves and partially controlled by factors beyond them. Because this process is only partially held from either side, in practice it yields meanings that are able only to be recognized by others partially. This means that meanings remain only partially reliable or reproducible because meanings

---

as a referential ground upon which differential readings must rely in order to make clear their disagreements.

rely on the interaction of partial co-factors, including transcendent factors. As a result, dimensions of meaning can range from that which is idiomatic to that which is common, or even universal, depending on what factors might be at play from each of the reading situation's partial contributors. Although meanings have the capacity to span the full spectrum of reality and the full range of human experience, they do not always do so, and although meanings may arise in very common ways, they do not always do so, because meaning is neither absolutely free from control nor fully controlled.

In other words, from our missiological perspective, meaning can best be seen as produced via an event in which many factors come together. These factors do not all come together the same way every time, even though they have been designed to come together in similar ways most of the time. Viewed this way, meaning becomes the outcome of the overall situation, the entire event, which has been designed to bring multiple factors, including transcendent factors, into interaction in only partially controlled ways.

Viewing meaning as a gestaltic event can be useful for missiology, since it stands precariously on conflicting sides of the modern-postmodern crisis. For, on the one hand, missiology holds to transcendence, metaphysics, and universal truth; on the other, it acknowledges the contextual nature of meaning and the social uses of language. This makes missiology both friend and foe to both modernism and postmodernisms, for modern thought holds to universal knowledge, but rejects metaphysics, while postmodern outlooks recognize the social nature of knowledge but reject universal claims (Thiselton, 1992).

Thus, missiology neither rejects nor endorses modern or postmodern outlooks *in toto*. Missiological interpretation stands in a position to benefit from both vantages, yet, while it can gain from both sides, missiology also is not in a position to align itself. It cannot embrace postmodern tenets where those exclude translatability or interpersonal communication, and it cannot accept modernistic reasoning where it imposes limitations against the metaphysical. Because of its real-life experience, missiology must stand somewhere between.

Teleology and social uses. As we have seen already, missiology considers meaning as it relates to purpose, especially God's purpose. This commitment brings missiological reading across philosophical debates about intrinsic ends and design (teleology). By way of background, in the West, the possibility of teleology is involved in philosophical debate about metaphysics, because it entails the idea that things can have intrinsic natures. Platonic, Cartesian, and Kantian problems of metaphysics are far too large to be handled even briefly here; however, for definition's sake, the crux of the debate turns on the idea of metaphysical *essence*. This is a question about whether or not a thing can carry purpose by virtue of what it is in itself, that is, if its particular existence participates in a transcendent category and if that has innate purpose, design, or ends.

Although debates continue in many forms, by and large, western philosophy has excluded the ideas of essence and teleology in favor of social assignments. This stance rejects assertions that things can have a natures that can relate them to a certain ends in favor of the idea that a thing *only* has qualities and features that can be taken up for a certain use (Hassing, 2013; Robertson & Atkins, 2018). This is an important issue for missiology, because it deeply affects any notion about divine plans or goals, as well as proposals about the intrinsic values of humanity and society (see Chapters 7, 10-11). It also significantly affects moral propositions about best or ideal states, and thus, also about the potential for things, people or creation to be abused.

Missiologist Lesslie Newbigin sees the exclusion of teleology as an ill-conceived societal course and as a watershed of worldview that has marginalized religious discourse. As he describes its impact on the western world, he notes that the silencing of teleology ultimately impoverishes description of personal action or of communication:

> But we shall not be wrong, I think, if we take the abandonment of teleology as the key to the understanding of nature for our primary clue to understanding the whole of these vast changes in the human situation. I shall argue that this is what underlies that decisive feature of our culture that can be described as the division of human life into public and private, and the separation of fact and value.
>
> Let us look to the central fact, the elimination of teleology. It is difficult to describe human behaviors without using the category of purpose. While it is, of course, possible to describe what a lecturer is doing in terms of the cause-and-effect nexus between electrical impulses in the cerebral cortex, chemical changes in the muscles, and sound waves in the air of the room, and while this description could in principle be exhaustive, no intelligent person would accept it as the explanation of what was happening. An explanation would have to express the purpose of the speaker to communicate some vision of reality to the hearers. (1986, p. 34)

As Newbigin notes, the dimension of teleology is crucial for sensible description of real human events, for it speaks to what people see happening in ordinary communication and interactions. In other words, the idea of teleology captures those meaningful ranges of perception that humans actually use, regardless of whether or not those might be deemed legitimate within the conversations of formal philosophy.

Even though this idea may not be popular, it is central to the kind of religious understanding that looks toward actualization. This is the aim that undergirds the idea of "long-term purpose or goal," which Christopher Wright uses to describe mission, and upon which he bases his interpretive approach (2004, p. 104). Bosch likewise has no problem using universal, categorical, metaphysical, and teleological concepts to talk about missional hopes for all people:

> The Christian faith, for example, sees 'all generations of the earth' as objects of God's salvific will and plan of salvation or, in New

Testament terms, it regards the 'reign of God' which has come in Jesus Christ as intended for 'all humanity.' (1991, p. 9) Appealing to Stackhouse, he goes so far as to say that a key distinctive of "missionary religions" is that "that they all 'hold to some great "unveiling" of ultimate truth believed to be of universal import'" (1991, p. 9).

In other words, the notion of nature is decisive for missiology because missiology holds that there is in fact a valuable, essential category of being, *human*, which has the quality, *humanity*, in which all humans participate intrinsically. Further, missiology holds that individuals, humankind, and the cosmos are intended by God to have certain highest states of being, which are established relative to each one's essential being. These highest states are purposed by God and it is part of his *missio* to bring them from potential into reality or fulfillment.

A number of other missiological commitments converge at the teleological question because they involve the idea that design plays a key role in intrinsic identity. For example, the concepts of redemption and salvation rest upon the assumption that people have intended states, which can be thwarted, fulfilled, unfulfilled, or restored. The concepts of righteousness and justice also rely upon the idea that knowledge and action can be evaluated relative to essential or intended states. The notion of *shalom* also assumes that people and the world are purposed to have a highest and best state that awaits realization.

However, even while it rests upon essentialist foundations, missiology cannot and does not ignore the dimension of social uses and assignments. In fact, missiology's attention to purpose and use lends it an ironic common ground with meaning theories that valorize social purposes against essence, even while those theories reject the idea of teleology as missiology would understand it. This is possible due to the awkward case that when theorists embrace the idea that texts can be used to accomplish any sort of thing on behalf of people, they allow language at least the temporary capacity to actualize purposes in the social sphere. This is a point that missiology can agree with heartily, and, from a missiological viewpoint, it then follows that if language can carry purpose temporarily, the question of teleology in some ways becomes settled, since it simply becomes one of duration and degree, not of possibility.

Examples of these common grounds stretch across a wide range of language theories. To some degree, missiological interpretation becomes compatible with Ludwig Wittgenstein when he describes language games as social instructions (1969). Missiology also surprisingly can connect with J. L. Austin (1962) and John Searle (1969) as they champion the social performance of "speech-acts." It also can resonate partly with literary theorists such as Wolfgang Iser (1980) and Umberto Eco (1979), who demonstrate that the design of texts serves to elicit reader-responses.

Of course, these connections are complicated, and analyzing each of their specific intersections lies beyond this book's scope. However, we can note the common idea that texts can serve purposes and that they can accomplish purposes, whether those come from people, communities, or the logics of systems. This is a region of compatibility for missiological theory, but it requires embracing only certain parts of the claims that these varied theorists make, while rejecting other parts that remain incompatible.

The works of these theorists suggest that if missiology did elect to bracket transcendence out of its inquiries, it could look quite fruitfully for responses to philosophical objections against traditional teleology by grounding its idea of purpose in social design. This could emphasize the instrumental extension of will into and through social systems via representation, which accomplishes ends for both people and institutions. However, missiology does not limit itself metaphysically. It allows for God to be a social actor, and it allows for him to establish what things are for. Thus, since God is not excluded as one of the potential actors who seeks social ends, missiology also can inquire if or how a text's design reveals God's own social purposes.

In order to understand these missiological positions, we should remember that missiology is cautious about endorsing culturally unique assumptions about the limits of reality, especially when they produce sweeping metaphysical exclusions. Missiology recognizes modes of knowing that are not philosophical and it acknowledges the significance of phenomena. From this position, philosophical assertions about reality, nature, or purpose cannot self-establish; they always must pass the test of explanatory capacity for what mission actually has encountered, especially in places beyond the West, and especially in day to day use(s) of the biblical text.

For missiological hermeneutics, then, the question of whether or not things like the Bible may have real intended ends cannot be resolved by philosophical reasoning alone. Any answer also must be able to account for the realities of the missio Dei, the capacity of the text to be revelatory and the actual day to day experiences of textual users, especially across cultures. In other words, assertions about purpose must rest upon *phenomena*, not just *theoria*.

On this point, mission's experience, as well as its assumptions, call missiology to remain open to the idea that both the Bible and the act of Bible-reading may have purpose. That is, they may be designed or intended, forged by God and others, to accomplish ends and effects, especially ends and effects that are not easily associated with content-knowledge or simple aesthetics. Whether it concerns a general capacity to accomplish ends, or the specific capacity to accomplish *missio Dei* ends, the idea that the Bible may carry within itself a purpose that can be fulfilled lies close to both the heart and history of mission, and it cannot be abandoned to philosophical objections.

Forms of intention. This brings us to the notion of *intention*. Once the "gold standard" of interpretive inquiry, the idea of authorial "intention" has been hotly contested as an interpretive aim during the last century (Thiselton, 1992). We will look a bit more closely at this below, but for now, we need to note that a distinction needs to be made between a missiological understanding of intention and traditional literary or philosophical understandings of intention. For, in contrast to more traditional quests for authorial intention, missiology does not see intention as only or primarily that which an author thinks, feels, and seeks (or sought[57]) to say. Instead, a missiological idea of intention carries with it the teleological aspect of purpose. It sees intention *for*, that is, intention directed at a goal.

Missiology nuances intention this way because of what it holds to be true about witness. Missiology understands witness to be more than information, experience, or thought. It holds that witness in itself has a certain end that is intrinsic to the gospel message, beyond the direct experience of the one giving witness. Thus, witness is *for* something that lies outside of the "witnessor's" influence and, even, perhaps, awareness. Additionally, missiology links the true hearing of witness to holistic hearer responses in "word and deed." This assumes that response is critically necessary for textual meaning, which in turn requires more than a conceptualization of the author's experience for understanding.[58] Thus, when missiology considers a text's composition, it sees an aspect that anticipates an end and organizes the text by design, expecting a response. This is more to be considered as the author's "purpose" or, "intention" than a mere conveyance or depiction of the author's mental or experience state(s).

This is a broader and more common use of *intention* than the ideas of ostensive function or mental and experiential about-ness or toward-ness that are common within philosophical discussions. An example might help

---

[57] This spans both what the text "meant" and what the text "means," which are frequently used to distinguish between exegesis and hermeneutics (discussion below).

[58] See discussion above on "word and deed." Missional expectation is that there will be a response of some sort to witness. This does not only mean conversion or acceptance, only that some kind of response will occur. Mission communication also anticipates responses of resistance or rejection. This is similar to Wolfgang Iser's (1980) expectation that texts can bring about challenges of norms, which leave the reader conflicted at points.

at this point so that we can see the difference. For our example, let us imagine that a poet is composing a sonnet. The immediate topic of the sonnet is the smell of the desert in the moments just before sunrise. A traditional understanding of authorial intention might focus on the poet's understanding of the desert, her sensory experience, her awareness of the sonnet tradition and her conceptualization of her audience. It would try to understand what the poet is thinking (or feeling) *about*, or linguistically pointing *toward*. It would hope to clarify its understanding of what she is attempting to say by trying to discern what she thinks, feels, and experiences in her world.

If, however, that poet is hoping to impress an editor and publish the sonnet in a journal, the idea of intention shifts toward the ends that she is seeking to accomplish. When that happens, the view turns to *why* she is trying to say something, away from *what* she is trying to say. This emphasizes attention to the end over attention to the means, understanding that *what* the poet is saying serves *why* she is saying it. This attention to the "in order" dimension can be refined through many levels because the poet's hopes for the outcome of her writing can extend quite far. For instance, she could be writing *in order* to have a publishing title on her professional credits, which is *in order* for her to get a job at a university, which is *in order* for her to support her two young children, etc.

When we look to these kinds of purposes, we have entered a different, but related realm of intentions. These intentions are not the direct intentions of the immediate language, and they may not even be in the forefront of the author's awareness. They are multilayered and they are not always explicit, but they significantly impact the choices that the author makes, and it could be argued that they are the deepest factors informing the poem's composition. Questions about these kinds of intentions do not seek to determine the author's state of awareness, alone. They see the author's conscious state as embedded in dynamics that may or may not be held in the author's immediate awareness, and they look at the design of the text in order to discern the dynamics that surround and infuse both the author and the text. These questions assume that purpose dynamics will express through the form of any text because texts are productions of purpose more than products of conceptualization. Thus, missiological questions seek to understand *why* the text is the way that it is and what the text's "in order that" goals might be. It sees this dimension as both authorial and textual "intention."

In short and common parlance, missiology recognizes that people read and write for reasons. Thus, it understands that all persons who are involved with a text, whether composers or readers, have a will to act. They have desires to accomplish certain ends, and texts can provide the means to get to those ends. This desire to get to certain ends can be understood as "intention(s)." This framing of intention distinguishes a missiological view from views of intention that are limited to an author's state of mind about reality or the desire to convey an idea, content, or personal expression. It links the idea of intention to the ideas of design, outcome, and social use.

This kind of outlook makes missiological reading compatible with discourse, reader-response, socio-rhetorical, or ideological criticisms, because missiology can look for "intended meaning" in what a text does, *via* what it says. However, in distinction to these criticisms, missiology not only looks within the human-to-human purview of doing, but also beyond it into the divine and divine-to-human realms of doing. This focus is especially important for missiological treatment of the Bible as an inspired text. Although missiology holds no single view of inspiration, it considers God to be active in the Bible's composition, since the Bible is one of the things that God uses to accomplish his missio. This means that any missiological quest for authorial intention includes multiple levels of authorship, one of whom missiology ultimately considers to be God-in-mission.[59]

---

[59] Missiologists do not share a single understanding of inspiration. However, missiologists who hold a broad understanding that God is self revealing in all human culture would see the Bible as a product of that work and thus ultimately as the product of God's self

As we will see below, many influences can have a hand in shaping the intention of a text. This opens the range of inquiry about intention significantly. Once this is recognized, missiology can look for meaning as "purpose" or, "intention to do" at a number of levels. A partial list of these includes: (1) what God intends for a text to do, (2) what the immediate author (or authorial community) intends for a text to do, (3) what the linguistic and semiotic, or social systems surrounding the text enable the text to do, and (4) what the reader or reading community intends for it to do.

Praxis and intention. As we have seen, in missional thought intention cannot be simple pre-imagination or conceptualization; it assumes a real engagement of the self in the will to act. This brings missiological interpretation into convergence with theories that emphasize *praxis*.[60]

In its plainest sense, praxeological engagement is a unification of: (1) concept, (2) will, and (3) existence (cognition/volition/experience).[61] This engagement is the commitment of the self to act(s).[62] From this vantage, responsibility, morality, and justice can be discerned by virtue of the intention that actions would be done, regardless of whether or not actions finally come to pass. Missiologically, it is this will to act, the commitment of the self toward certain ends, that constitutes "intention" or

---

revelation. By the same token, missiologists who hold that the Bible is God's uniquely inspired self revelation also see God as its ultimate source.

[60] For a description of scriptural knowing as doing within a hermeneutic circle, see Robert McAfee Brown (1984, pp. 21-32); also, Kevin Vanhoozer's descriptive discussion of "society and praxis," which cites the Dar es Salaam conference's (1976) rejection of theology that does not involve activity (2006, pp. 89-97). Missiologist Tite Tiénou agrees with Vanhoozer and cites Catholic scholar Tshishisku Tshibangu, claiming that "Church life cannot exist without active theology" (2006, p. 39).

[61] Theologian Kevin Vanhoozer uses minimally differing categories. He calls praxis a "turn to the social context" and describes its process: "To turn to the social context, then, means to *see* (analyze the social situation), *judge* (discern God's reign), and *act* (practice the politics of the kingdom of God)" (2006, p. 97) [italics in original]. The terms, "concept, will and existence" that I am using here are more existentially oriented but they span roughly the same range of activity that moves from abstraction to committed behavior in context, however, they break the progression into slightly different steps.

[62] This includes the will to act as it disposes the self relationally by identifying with others. This kind of disposition is included in the relational aspect mentioned earlier.

"purpose." This kind of intention suffuses both composition and reading, for both authors and readers must engage the text with self-commitment.

Thus, missiology approaches the Bible looking to see if, when and how action is effected. Nicholas Lash links this idea to being "faithful" to the text:

> The practice of Christian faith is not, in the last resort, a matter of interpreting, in our time and place, an ancient text. It is, or seeks to be, the faithful rendering of those events, of those patterns of human action, decision and suffering, to which the texts bear original witness. To acknowledge that the criteria of fidelity are hard to establish and are frequently problematic is to admit that there is, indeed, a hermeneutical "gap." But this "gap" does not lie, in the last resort, between what was once "meant" and what might be "meant" today. It lies, rather, between what was once achieved, intended, or "shown," and what might be achieved, intended, or "shown" today. (1985, p. 23)

Fulfillment and intention. Missiology can pursue this line of analysis by asking questions about *fulfillment* of the text. A fulfillment-oriented agenda inquires about the intentions, that is, the purposes and engagements, of the actors that produced the text, of the actors that are depicted within the text and of the text's readers. It does this in order to discern what the text might be *for*, as well as the conditions under which that *for*-ness might be satisfied. This quest for the text's fulfillment is not limited to looking at a single moment, a single factor or a single scale, since intentions for texts may be multilayered and coexistent. Instead, looking for intended fulfillment involves looking for textual outcomes on a continuum from local, physical-historical levels to transcendent, metaphysical and cosmic levels.

In order to unpack this, let's revisit our example from above. We will assume that our sunrise desert poet was hoping to be remembered as the first to publish in a literary movement of "North American, Neo-

Shakespearean, Pastoral Revivalists." Given this aim, the scales and dimensions of her intentions would be complex. According to what we have already seen, she would be intending immediately and locally to impress an editor. This would be one design outcome that anticipates fulfillment. However, the poem also carries the intention to be published, which adds another criterion of fulfillment. Thus, if her poem impresses the editor but fails to get published, the text's intentions would be fulfilled in one aspect but not another.

More broadly, the poet intends to sway the decisions of a faculty hiring committee, in order to obtain a job; she also intends for that job to provide a salary and support for her kids. These are coexisting intentional dimensions that await fulfillment, and each dimension carries certain distinct criteria. Even more broadly, she is hoping to impact the literary sensibilities of a larger community, including her future students, the academic community and the literary world. Even more broadly, she intends to leave a legacy in history among those she doesn't even know. Her sonnet, then, can be understood to have multiple intentions that coexist, each of which affects the poem's form. The poem then could be assessed in terms of its fulfillment on any one of these levels of intention, and it would be possible for the poem to be fulfilled at one or some levels and yet to remain unfulfilled at other levels. Crucially, her poem could be fulfilled immediately if she gets the job, while its fulfillment as a catalyst for a new poetic movement might not happen for a century, centuries, or more. That dimension of fulfillment also may be subject to factors that the poet could not possibly have conceived as she wrote, yet these may be factors that are still relevant to the text's intention.

In a parallel, the biblical text may have complex layers of intention and complex layers of potential fulfillment. These may coexist in mutual support, or sometimes with degrees of tension. Some intentional layers may be fulfilled when particular outcomes are achieved, while others may remain unfulfilled until other criteria are met. And, because missiology is metaphysically open, it allows that texts may be fulfilled on historical or social levels of intention, while remaining unfulfilled on spiritual levels, or be fulfilled on spiritual levels while unfulfilled on physical or social levels.

Since missiological examination gives place for God and spiritual beings to be contributors in this process, missiology does not separate spiritual fulfillments from other kinds of fulfillment in final ways. Instead, it sees all dimensions of fulfillment as coexistent potentials. It makes no distinction between spiritual and physical influencers or intenders. Any entity may have the capacity of mission, intention or the will to act in order to bring about outcomes, and any entity may anticipate the fulfillment of its will to act as that will is expressed in textual intention.

The problem of authorial voice and presence. This leads us to the issue of the author(s) voice and or presence, that is, the capacity of the text to carry the intentions of its author(s) to another. This is a watershed issue for missiology because it determines whether or not a text can be someone's word, and whether or not communication links people to each other in real ways. In turn, this impacts whether or not the text can be understood to be God's word or God's instrument, and thus, whether or not it can bridge between him and people.

From the missiological vista, the issue seems fairly simple, since missiology has observed and experienced that people connect with others through communication, and that they have done so across the globe throughout the ages. The divine dimension is also relatively easy to integrate, once one acknowledges that God can stand as a co-author of the text. However, debates within interpretive theory about authorial intention have by and large succeeded in distancing the author from the text in ways that make it difficult for missiology to assert that a text can be the author's word. This puts missiology on the horns of a dilemma between abandoning the idea of interpersonal communication or running afoul of prevailing formal objections to the idea that authors contribute to meaning

As background to this impasse, we will need to talk just a little bit more about the debate over authorial intention. Briefly, as Thiselton's (1992) survey of hermeneutics notes, in the heyday of biblical studies following Schleiermacher, the author was considered to be the prime determinant for meaning. However, the quest for authorial intention that was started by Schleiermacher and followed by Dilthey gave way to multiple 20th century literary challenges. Many proposals, such as W.K. Wimsatt Jr. and Monroe Beardsley's *The Intentional Fallacy* (1954), championed the autonomy of the text and the power of the interpreter. These emphasized the historical gap that separated the text from the author, declaring the author to be inaccessible and his intentions non-determinant.[63] Sociohistorical and ideological approaches such as Marxist and post- or anti-colonial criticisms likewise diffused or subordinated authorial intention by emphasizing the dominant influence of the historical milieu. These tended to subordinate the author's voice to greater forces, which made the author a mouthpiece or spokesperson for larger economic and class dynamics.

On another front, the rise of Structuralism bracketed the author completely out by relocating meaning to the function of signs within signification systems. This placed meaning even beyond the particular symbols of a given text, in the systemic realm of semiotic relations and potentials. With the author considered to be dead and meaning generated within semiotic systems, theorists such as Jacques Derrida (1988) and Paul de Man (1986) were able to push even further, asserting that infinite "Alterity" was an inescapable factor in linguistic systems and semiotic events, which prevented anyone from being able to stabilize meaning in reliable ways. This sustained rejections of talk about "the" meaning in favor of an infinite variety of potential meanings.

---

[63] "We argued that the design or intention of the author is neither available nor desirable as a standard for judging the success of a work of literary art"(1954, p. 3). Curiously, Wimsatt and Beardsley distinguish between ordinary communication, which they believe can be understood using a criterion of intention, and poetry, which cannot be so understood (1954, p. 5).

Reader-oriented theorists, such as Stanley Fish, (1982) and John Searle (1969) held back from absolute deconstructionist conclusions. They opted instead to see both meaning and texts as being produced by *readers*, who were in turn stabilized by their reading communities. Relocating meaning to the reader(s) in this way continues to find appeal for many reasons, since it contemporizes interpretation while allowing for meaning to be established in some form of commonly accessible way. This can be done without relying upon appeals to the author or to a final authority, which fits well with prevailing social theories, such as the observations of Jean Francois Lyotard (1993), who highlighted institutional influences upon knowledge production, or the propositions of Michel Foucault (1972), who described the selective nature of discourse, or in the works of earlier theorists such as Berger and Luckmann (1967), who noted the self-establishing aspects of social knowledge.

As a constellation of theorists, these approaches have been foundational for many plural, contextual, and vernacular methods, and their proposals warrant deep consideration. However, at the same time, recognizing the validity of contributions that do not emphasize the author does not necessarily mean that the question of authorial intention has been settled or that the author should be abandoned or banished. We have already seen how missiology holds the author in esteem, and at this intersection, I do not need to repeat points about the centrality of author(s) and intention(s) for missiological interpretation. Because of these commitments, at the impasse between the dominance of the author and the exile of the author, missiology has good grounds to ask whether or not one position actually and necessarily excludes another. More than the value of non-authorial approaches, the issue is one of foundational assumptions that have yet to be fully established. Particularly, the issue is not *if* meaning can be achieved without considering an author's intentions, but whether or not all approaches, including missiology, *must* consider the author to be dead or absent. For, while discovering more about the roles that non-authors play in the meaning event is certainly valuable, the possibility remains that those roles may be seen as complementary and contributive, not as final and determinant. If it is not a given that the author must be excluded, the author still may be theoretically alive, yet only silenced.

Earlier, I mentioned two points that I would like to revisit as we consider whether or not authors are absent. The first is that social context always informs compositions, the second, that missiology considers God to be an active participant in the Bible's composition.

On the first point, social influence on larger language systems and on particular compositions is an undeniable reality. This fact deserves attention, for as soon as one recognizes the reality of social influence one must acknowledge that conceiving of authors as solitary persons who create texts *in vacuo* is an oversimplification. If anything, the reality of social influence instead informs us that authors never truly can stand alone. In turn, this means that objections to the presence of the author that conceive of the author as a solitary individual with solitary thoughts and a solitary presence that can be separated from a solitary text are grounded upon a reduced and artificially bounded concept of authorship. These artificial constraints beg the question of authorial presence by philosophically pre-isolating the author from others in a way that sustains theoretical objections to her presence, and as such, they are suspect propositions.

Both rationally and phenomenologically speaking, it would be more accurate to assert that joint authorship is an inescapable condition, and that the complex nature of authorship provides a constant and inseparable authorial presence. Texts are produced endlessly under joint influence, and the plain reality is that complex joint influences, even agonistic joint influences, can and do yield textual compositions that appear on the surface to be single works. Since people do not compose in isolation, and since authors always participate in complex social realities when they use language, it would be more feasible to argue that there is no such thing as a truly individual author or composition than it would be to propose that there are only individual authors and compositions.

For those who allow for transcendent possibilities, this acknowledgement leads to a second, crucial point. Given the fact that joint authorship can and does happen, if we allow that God exists and that he can participate in the composition of a text as much as any other, we must allow for God to be a joint composer of texts and seek to discern his influence as we would any other authorial contributor's. Further, when we also allow that God's own life spans from the time of the text's composition to the present, we must treat the text as persisting in the living presence of at least one of its joint authors.

However, proposals about the very real presence of authors also can stand without giving place to transcendence, if only based upon the presence of human-level social influences. For, if we note that social institutions influence compositions, as Lyotard, and Berger, and Luckmann do, we also can find joint composers in any of the social institutions that contribute to textual formation. Given the reality of social influence, even social institutions as diffuse as language systems carry a legitimate claim to some degree of authorial credit. This is especially the case when institutions behave as social entities, and when they endure between the time of an original composition and the time of its reading.

This is a crucial factor for missiology because missiology is committed to the idea that mission is and has been an enduring composite project, one that has been and will be present throughout the ages. This view of mission assumes that there is ongoing institutional solidarity in the community of the people of God and ongoing continuity in the institution of the kingdom of God. From this position, a number of enduring authors emerge as co-authors of the text. Among these, the kingdom as an institution, mission as an institution and the faith community as an institution are some of the most important to missiology. All of these may be considered to hold a claim as enduring, "living" co-authors. This means that from a missiological view, the Bible's joint authors have not been lost. Even when an individual author may have dropped from view or accessibility; all of the text's authors are not ontologically dead or absent. At the very least, the text continues in the immediate presence of at least two of its living authors, the community of faith and God.

Going further, we can consider living authors not only to hold a claim on interpretation, but to hold a *superior* claim, for interpretation by living authors can be taken as ongoing composition, in the same way that a preface, a revised edition or an appendix might augment a completed manuscript. This position undergirds the kinds of spiritually informed reading that Shawn Redford advocates, along with the tradition of magisterial reading practiced by the church through the centuries.

Divine presence. From another angle, if authors are excluded from texts it naturally follows that non-authors are even more removed, which excludes the possibility for anyone or anything to convey a message on behalf of another. While this might be an interesting theoretical or philosophical exercise, it breaks down at phenomenological levels, especially in a contemporary society that is increasingly cohered via mediated communication. It also is a stance that holds little traction with a discipline that has focused almost exclusively upon the performance of communication that is conveyed through intermediary agents.

Missiology is dedicated both to the work and to the idea of representative communication, for it holds that communication, particularly, biblical communication or witness, brings the very real presence of God to people.[64] Missiology lives by the principle that one can bring the presence of another. It holds steadfastly to the value of communication as a means to bridge between peoples, and it stands on the legitimacy of vicarious representation. Not only does it see these principles operating in the incarnation and work of Christ, but also in and through

---

[64] Especially within sacramental theologies of witness (Schmemann, 1961).

others, for missiology believes that the real presence of God is carried into the world through the agency of those who represent him.[65]

The quality of proxy is also attested in scripture, even through multiple levels of representation. In Matthew 10:40 (NRSV)[66], Jesus says, "Whoever welcomes you welcomes me, and whoever welcomes me welcomes the one who sent me." This may obtain even in cases where proxy is not recognized or overt. For example, in Matthew 24:45 (NRSV), the king in Jesus' judgment parable says to those surprised at his proxy identification, "just as you did not do it to one of the least of these, you did not do it to me." In a similar way, in 1 Thessalonians Paul asserts,

> We also constantly give thanks to God for this, that when you received the word of God that you heard from us, you accepted it not as a human word but as what it really is, God's word, which is also at work in you believers. (1 Thessalonians 2:13, NRSV)

Stuhlmueller, commenting on Matthew 10, says, "An underlying theme of the whole discourse is the identity of the risen Jesus with his missionaries" (1983, p. 251). From a missiological viewpoint, there is a very real proxy, symbolic, and representational aspect to mission. This prompts Bosch to assert that (1991, p. 10) "God's love and attention are directed primarily at the world, and mission is 'participation in God's existence in the world.'" He characterizes this as both sacrament and sign, saying,

> The church in mission... may be described in terms of sacrament and sign. It is a *sign* in the sense of pointer, symbol, example or model; it is a *sacrament* in the sense of mediation, representation, or anticipation (cf Glassman 1986:14). It is not identical with God's reign yet not unrelated to it either; it is 'a foretaste of its coming, the sacrament of its anticipations in history' (Memorandum 1982:461)." (Bosch, 1991, p. 10) [italics in original]

---

[65] See also the WCC statement earlier, that the presence of an individual or group is witness (Bosch, 2006, p. 228).
[66] NRSV (*The Holy Bible containing the Old and New Testaments with the Apocryphal/Deuterocanonical books: new revised standard version*, 2006)

When we combine missiology's understanding of representation with observations about the complex and enduring presence of authors, we get a glimpse of why missiology cannot agree to the banishment of author(s). For, from missiology's vantage point, God remains present to speak to people in or through a text, either as one of its authors, or as one who is using the text as a medium of agency to bring his presence, just as he can speak or be present through his representatives and their words.

Beyond this, missiology allows that God can be active within people before they encounter the text, in order to bring them into contact with the text. God can send the text to readers or call readers to read. This places God on both sides of a textual encounter; he is actively involved from the direction of the text and actively involved in the dynamism of the reader. For missiology, these make the text even more powerfully the instrumental voice of God, who speaks to people through the biblical text in order to accomplish his purposes.

Suppression and silencing. Talking this way runs the risk of setting missiological interpretation at the margins of academic inquiry, for any proposition that God speaks or becomes present through a text is quite out of step with modern literary theory, which relegates such proposals to the realms of theology instead of interpretation. However, we have already seen that Kraft, Newbigin, Hiebert, Bauckham, and Hanson have protested that modern western theory carries worldview suppositions that can be inimical and suppressive to religious expression. If this is so, missiology may contend that both the author's and God's voices may be being artificially suppressed by scientific worldview assumptions. This contention can be supported by postmodern, postcolonial, vernacular, and contextual criticisms, because these criticisms recognize that socially-suppressive forces can affect the voices of both authors and interpreters. This is a point of theoretical convergence between missiology and criticisms that are attenuated to the concerns of social justice.

Understanding that people are affected when their writings are diminished or discounted is foundational to the moral and philosophical groundings of contextual and postcolonial theologies, as well as various ideological and praxeological reading approaches. All of these criticisms object in some manner to the silencing of select populations, communities or individuals. This common thread of protest against the constraints of dominant western academic interpretation spans across a spectrum of writers as diverse as Stephen Moore (1989), Mary Ann Tolbert (1995) Stanley Fish (1982), Gerald West (1995), Orlando Costas (1989), and Justo Gonzalez (1996). While these writers are far from uniform, their critiques do show a common theme that generally champions the rights of readers to self-assertion, often forwarding the values of advocacy and solidarity with the marginalized.

This is interesting from a missiological point of view, because notions of advocacy and solidarity both assume the possibility of vicarious agency or presence with another through the use of texts, without regarding the limits of physical or social distances. These concepts attach presence to voice, especially via the written word. As an example, note how postcolonial scholar R. S. Sugirtharajah characterizes the publication of contextual interpretation as an act of group presence:

> It implies a fierce self-esteem, an assertion of selfhood and self-respect instead of slavish conformity to received ideas... It is a struggle for the historical and political presence of groups suppressed or marginalized by colonization and modernization. (1999, p. 94).

Sugirtharajah's characterization of vernacular interpretation emphasizes that written publication constitutes "historical and political presence." He rightly notices that writing asserts the "selfhood" of people and groups, as writing carries them into historical and political worlds.

The dispositions that undergird these kinds of protests confirm missiology's commitments about authorial presence and voice from an unexpected angle. For, because writing is representative and silencing its voice can constitute a form of oppression, missiology cannot embrace theoretical demands that silence or forcibly evacuate an original author (along with that author's community) from an original text.[67] On the contrary, missiology not only can allow that texts present the voices of people and thus empower their solidarity with others, it strongly supports such claims. This is especially the case when the voices of biblical writers, the faith community and God are in jeopardy of being silenced by philosophical assertions that call into question their very existences.

    In this light, the question of authorial voice becomes more than an abstract theoretical dilemma about the capacity of language to signify certain things. It presents a moral issue for missiology, since the unavoidable result of separating an author from his text ultimately is to silence and separate all users of language from their words. If authors are not connected to their words, they cannot truly offer themselves to each other via language. This prevents any chance of self-assertion or self-presentation via language. Such a position renders any attempt to achieve social solidarity through the use of language illusory and meaningless. This is a stance that runs counter to missiology's spiritual and moral commitments, which attend to social justice and interpersonal solidarity.

    This moral dimension warrants severe critical evaluation, for the notion of authorial absence not only silences self-assertion and protest, it also unwittingly exonerates oppressive utterance. If we hold that authorial intention is a fallacy and that authors are not present, the idea that a text can constitute interpersonal action then also is a fallacy. If this is so, blessing means nothing, but neither does cursing. In such a case, oppressive texts are in reality phantom works, because they do not carry the author's self into the social sphere; they are not in final assessment the author's words, since they are dislocated from her. If we use this position to examine injurious speech,

---

[67] This situation is further complicated when we acknowledge that an author's words very well may be local, indigenous protests against silencing.

we find that the composers of oppressive language always remain absent; they do not have the ability to be present at a textual "scene of the crime." Composers then become exempted from personal responsibility for even the harshest of threats, slanders, epithets, denigrations, or denouncements by virtue of their authorial absence. Tragically and ironically, if texts carry no connection from authors, if they are merely free semiotic arrangements, or, if only readers and their communities create meaning, any sense of an oppressive communication becomes solely the responsibility of the text's (apparently) self-oppressing readers, who alone have the power to create meaning.

This is an interpretive stance that missiology simply cannot embrace. Missiology holds that people, including God, are to some degree brought into each other's presences through communication. It is morally imperative to acknowledge the presence of others if they attempt to raise their voices and assert their presences, or if they desire to establish solidarity with one another through their words. It is also morally imperative to hold people responsible for their words. Regardless of any apparent rationality, missiology cannot yield the point about whether or not persons have voice to mere abstract argumentation. Missiology must maintain that people may be present in their protests, the silencing of which can constitute oppression. Because of this commitment, missiology cannot accept the exclusion of authorial intention or presence from texts. This is perhaps the most volatile and yet the most crucial place of intersection that missiological interpretation encounters with other theories because it embodies missiology's position that God may become present to the world through the biblical text, through missional communication and through the agency of people.

Of course, we cannot consider the issues that we have raised as settled after such a cursory discussion, and much dialog remains to be had. The goal here has not been to settle theory, and we cannot hope to resolve so many existing tensions between such extended discourses. Instead, the aim has been to locate discursive tensions clearly enough by their intersections to reveal at least some of missiology's key boundaries, that is, where it can and cannot stand. At this stage, we will have to let that provide a limited sense of where missiological interpretation is coming from, relative to other interpretive movements. These are not hard and fast contours; they do, however, offer a glimpse at the broad underpinnings of missiological approaches to the text, and they give us sufficient ground to take our next step, which will explore how missiology can build interpretive strategies upon its commitments.

Chapter 3

Kingdom and Context: Divine and Human Authorship

So far, we have looked at some missiological commitments and noted where those interact with other interpretive locations, but it remains to be seen how those commitments support interpretive practice(s). This chapter starts that inquiry by narrowing the view from general missiological commitments to the development of select strategies for negotiating major interpretive concerns. In other words, at this point we are beginning to work on a particular way of framing missiological interpretation instead of sketching a view of the larger missiological conversation. In this chapter, we will begin to lay those groundworks by exploring how texts can be located according to multi-scalar frames of reference, noting how those frames affect the formation of texts. As we do that we will see how taking into account that kind of complex context shapes missiological reading.

Kingdom: Interpreting in Light of God's Metanarrative

When we talk about things like actors, agency and authorial purposes, little difference shows initially between missiological reading and fairly traditional literary methods. However, as one moves to interpret, the scale required by missiological inquiry very quickly stretches traditional methodological boundaries. This places missiological interpretation on the frontier between literary and religious approaches.

Perhaps most notably, when missiology looks at the text using the lens of God and his kingdom, interpretation begins to be pulled into metanarrative, theological, and eschatological considerations. When this shift takes place, more emphasis comes to rest on factors that we have already started to discuss, like the unity of the natural and supernatural, teleology, and transcendence. These concerns lie outside the range of traditional interpretation, but they are critical for missiological reading from two key angles.

From the angle of disciplinary distinctives, these factors are integral to one of missiology's central, defining claims, that in the *missio Dei* God has a "plan" that he is pursuing, which involves all individuals, humankind, history, and the cosmos. This idea sets the direction of inquiry for missiology because it supposes that a thing does not have to be seen solely as an isolated "thing in itself." It holds that a thing can be understood by reference to how it fits in a larger scheme, and that the most important frame of reference is set by the divine mission that expresses from God's reign over all, that is, God's kingly, *kingdom* plan.

Because this is such a vast claim, it strongly affects how missiology can frame method. This is the second critical angle. For, from the angle of method, missiology needs to be able to look for all of its concerns, that is, the entire range of intentions that it assumes may be involved with the text. Since methods are only able to observe the things that they include within their ranges of inquiry, in order to be able to see if, when and how both divine and human purposes may be at play in the text, the lens that a missiological interpreter uses must have a scope that can include both the natural and the supernatural, both the temporal and the eternal. This is what pushes missiological inquiry across the boundaries that historically have divided religious and non-religious approaches.

Put more simply, in order to be able to see what she needs to see, the missiological interpreter must be allowed to look for what she needs to look for. This means that the missiological interpreter must be able to use a conceptual frame of reference that enables her to compare and contrast the broadest range of potential purposes from the broadest range of potential actors, so that she may juxtapose those against each other in order to make them show through.[68] Thus, while other approaches may limit their examinations to human-level influences, missiology deliberately makes room in the hermeneutic task for God's influence.

This does not mean that human authors are ignored. Missiology certainly looks for immediate purposes that are expressed by the human author, but it also looks past them, over their shoulders, so to speak, trying to discern where the hand of divine authorship also might be at work. It consciously looks for meanings that the author may not have directly intended, but that he may have framed inchoately under inspiration from the text's co-author, God. This kind of view looks for signs of God's involvement with the immediate scriptural author, and it links God's immediate goals in any particular composition to God's overarching work beyond the immediate context and author.[69]

This attention arises from the notion that God is an entity who has real purposes and real capacity to actualize his intentions. For missiology, *missio Dei* is not a passive conceptual item. It is a working description of God's active involvement in his creation, especially with humankind, which in turn involves all people in God's overarching and authoritative metanarratives, whether people are actively aware of that or not. This necessarily includes the immediate authors of the biblical text.

---

[68] See the above discussion on Polanyi and focal-subsidiary knowledge, especially Figure 5 *Focal and Subsidiary Referencing*. Also, Meyer on conversion and the "hermeneutics of consent."(1985).

[69] Cf., 1 Pet. 1:10-12. Neil MacDonald (2000) makes a powerful and convincing argument from the perspective of linguistic philosophy on behalf of unintended meanings, particularly for typology.

In support of the idea of unintended meanings, missiology must take into consideration the doctrine of canon, which is a pillar in both mission's and the Church's uses of the Bible. The idea of canon supports the assertion that a unity of meaning may exist beyond the immediate awareness of the original author or source-author. This unity of meaning can and does exist in parallel and over the immediate author's awareness.

Outside of the doctrine of canon, within modern hermeneutic philosophy, the idea that more meaning is possible than that which the author holds in mind is supported by positions that hold to the independent existence of the literary work, such as the "New Hermeneutic," postcolonial criticisms, and postmodern deconstructionist readings. It is also supported by ideological criticisms that see works as representing sociological or economic forces.

Bosch talks about this overarching kingdom frame as he outlines assumptions that are inherent in the concept of "mission":

> The term 'mission' presupposes a sender, a person or persons sent by the sender, those to whom one is sent, and an assignment. The entire terminology thus presumes that the one who sends has the *authority* to do so. (1991, p. 1) [italics in original]

However, the notion of a grand agenda, especially one that comes authoritatively from God, finds much resistance within contemporary academic discourse. For, following in the steps of Lyotard (1993), and Foucault (1972),[70] many have taken up an epistemological stance of "incredulity toward metanarratives," which is a stance that rejects any assertion that a common, overarching story (a *metanarrative*) can be applied to all humankind. This incredulity presents a significant prejudicial obstacle to the acceptance of missiological reading within the academic world.[71]

Yet, until metanarrative can be demonstrated conclusively to be false or harmful, resistance against it should not be assumed to hold prohibitory force. The protest of some does not necessarily create a mandate upon all, and suspicion itself should be open to question, since sometimes its own grounding also may be suspect. This is particularly important when we consider that condemnation of metanarratives may itself derive from social discourses that could be considered metanarratives in their own rights. In other words, metanarrative need not be discarded simply because it is metanarrative and it makes certain people nervous. Rather, metanarrative first needs to be assessed and weighed for whether or not it is in fact harmful across the board.

---

[70] Foucault (1972, pp. 46, 129) holds that meaning should not be sought in things said or the people who say things, but in the discursive systems laid down by them. This contention, which limits meaning to systemic constructions, seems difficult to maintain when it is admitted that discursive systems are human practices.

[71] Jameson's foreword to Lyotard invokes Foucault as he claims, "Yet [liberation and totality] master-narratives of science have become peculiarly repugnant or embarrassing to First World intellectuals today... [they are] the object of a kind of instinctive or automatic denunciation by just about everybody" (1993, p. xix).

With that caveat in mind, missiology may note in defense of using metanarrative as a lens that: 1. Narrative scale is arbitrary and necessarily selective 2. Narrative is inescapable, and thus, morally indeterminate, and, 3. Narrative can be a positive social instrument.

By way of explanation, Lyotard and Foucault have shown that discursive scope and composition are matters of observation and selection; they are not innate. Since they are conventions, there is no natural canon of size for narratives, and no necessary limits for them. There is also no natural law of narrative composition that establishes how narratives must be arranged. Any number of localized sub-events or sub-narratives may be caught up within any narrative or discourse, and, since selection is arbitrary, the scale of a narrative may be pushed downward infinitely or upward infinitely.

This means that what Lyotard calls the "little narrative" ("*petit récit*") (1993, p. 60) is essentially no different than a grand narrative.[72] The only difference between metanarratives and narratives is the scope of the events being selected and arranged. This is problematic to protests against metanarratives because some smaller range of selection always remains as a possibility, no matter how small a story might be. Every narrative must ignore a potentially smaller scale of story that could be selected from within its scope, which in turn could be used to view that narrative as a grand narrative compared to itself. Thus, there is no way truly to assess the size of a narrative with any reliability, or to propose any narrative that does not in some way silence, subordinate, or subsume other actual (or potential) narratives. The plain reality of stories is that someone's story is always left out or caught up within another's story, no matter how big or small that story may be.

This stems from the relationship between narratives and events. At its very core, narrative structure connects events; its connection of events is

---

[72] Any position that contrasts metanarrative as fundamentally different from small or ordinary narrative is especially problematic if one rejects ontological or teleological natures.

what creates a story, distinguishing story from mere description. This is crucial because, while narratives are articulated as strings of related events, there remains no innate or universal definition that can set the limits of an "event." Like a narrative, any event may be infinitely subdivided into smaller events, or it may be enlarged to include any number of constitutive (even potential) events within itself. Further, no event can be isolated truly or finally from other events, except through the exercise of perceptive choice.[73] In other words, events are framed by arbitrary choices just as narratives are. This inescapability of selection needs to be kept in mind when missiology intersects with objections that metanarratives are innately silencing, for the necessity of selection forces something to be ignored in order for any narrative or event to be constructed. This exposes all narratives, grand and small, to the same charge of silencing.

If we take a step back and look at narrative selection in broad ways, however, the process appears to be simply a necessary mechanism for story-making, one that supports distinction as well as homogenization. For, it is fairly easy to observe that in order to create unique stories, the same kinds of selective choices must be made as those that are made in the creation of "universalizing" narratives, and it is easy to observe that these selections are what empower unique stories to be unique. All narratives, unique or universal, seem to need to select or ignore, valorize or devalue, centralize or marginalize (etc.) certain aspects of reality in order to frame themselves. Selection appears then to be a relatively neutral necessity, since it is simply a fundamental feature of human language that cannot be circumvented when narratives of any sort are being constructed.

---

[73] Walter Ong offers a caveat that observes the verbal excision of identities from the whole of reality during his treatment of differences between "high-technology" and "verbomotor" cultures: "It should, of course, be noted that words and objects are never totally disjunct: words represent objects, and perception of objects is in part conditioned by the store of words into which perceptions are nested. Nature states no 'facts': these come only within statements devised by human beings to refer to the seamless web of actuality around them" (1982, p. 67). Later, he also observes, "Of course, all language and thought are to some degree analytic: they break down the dense continuum of experience, William James' 'big, blooming, buzzing confusion', into more or less separate parts, meaningful segments" (1982, p. 102).

On the positive side, the ability to create narratives allows human beings to use language in temporal ways, to establish common beliefs and outlooks (MacIntyre, 1989), and to hold society together (Camery-Hoggatt, 1992; Hiebert, 2008; Kraft, 2005).[74] This means that narratives can and do have beneficial social effect. This matters, because if narrative does not have intrinsic scale and it can be beneficial to society, it can be beneficial on any scale, small, large or meta-. Metanarratives then do not have to be detrimental simply because they are metanarratives; they may have the potential to be either detrimental or beneficial, and determinations about their social and moral character probably should be made based upon aspects and characteristics other than size alone.

As an added consideration, even the logic of protests against metanarrative suggests that metanarratives offer fruitful opportunities as interpretive criteria. This derives from the implied relationship between a metanarrative and a protest or subversive narrative. For, if one can claim that subversive narratives can have positive value because they challenge metanarratives, then, *mutatis mutandis*, we must allow grand narratives the same potential to perform positive challenges. Metanarratives may have equal positive value because they carry the power to challenge or control oppressive smaller or local narratives.

Metanarratives as reference points. In terms of method alone, even if we do not relinquish suspicion against metanarratives, protests against them still appear to validate their utility as reference points in hermeneutic work. For, the very existence of such a thing as a "subversive narrative," or of a "protest against metanarrative," demonstrates that it is

---

[74] Ong parallels Foucault to some degree when he points out that narrative is a foundational mode of framing human knowledge. "In a sense narrative is paramount among all verbal art forms because of the way it underlies so many other art forms, often even the most abstract. Human knowledge comes out of time. Behind even the abstractions of science, there lies narrative of the observations on the basis of which the abstractions have been formulated." He notes, "All of this is to say that knowledge and discourse come out of human experience and that the elemental way to process human experience verbally is to give an account of it more or less as it really comes into being and exists, embedded in the flow of time. Developing a story line is a way of dealing with this flow" (1982, pp. 136-137).

theoretically legitimate to understand a certain work in light of its relationship to a metanarrative. Methodologically, whether or not a narrative-metanarrative relation is subversive or contributive at a given point then becomes moot. The point for method is that there can be an observable relationship between a localized narrative or event and a larger metanarrative or meta-event that is used as a reference point. This is an analytical approach that can satisfy missiological interests, especially given missiology's commitments to the missio Dei.

Put another way, stories have relations to other stories, even stories that are beyond themselves. Texts that may not appear on the surface to be stories also may participate in these kinds of relationships along with standard stories, because texts can arise from within larger, discursive social stories and they can be the products of those larger stories. This is true regardless of whether those stories are good or bad, and regardless of whether particular texts are supporters or subverters of those meta-stories.

This is an important point for missiological interpretation of any text, because missiology reads *all* texts with reference to the metanarrative of God's universal "plan." It looks for the ways in which any given text supports, correlates to, expresses, opposes, or subverts God's metanarrative. It also looks for the ways in which texts participate in, or interact with other narratives and metanarratives, which may differ from God's plan. This methodological principle can be applied to other metanarratives. It does not matter whether or not one agrees with the metanarrative discourse of, say, Portuguese Nationalism. Any text may still be understood by noting the ways in which it corresponds or differs with Portuguese Nationalism. The same could be said of any metanarrative, such as rationalism, individualism, globalism, postcolonialism, etc.

A metanarrative analogy. By way of illustration, let us imagine travelers on a river. The river has a certain direction of flow, and it moves across points of reference on its bank. In this setting, we can imagine that there are travelers on the river, who can move in any direction. When we think about trying to locate one of these travelers, multiple options present themselves, because multiple contextual schemes are possible. Travelers may be located with reference to the land, but they also may be located in relation to other travelers, or to the river itself.

In this situation, the direction that a traveler moves on the river makes no difference at all in the potential to locate that traveler relative to the river. Whether the traveler is moving with the river or against it, she still can be seen vis à vis the river. Moving opposite to the river's flow can be referenced as easily as moving with the river's flow. Further, a traveler's sentiments about the river do not affect the work of referencing. Enjoying the river or considering the river to be a danger does not affect where one stands in reference to the river, and these states do not bring into question whether or not there actually is a river. In the quest for knowledge, the river simply serves as a frame of reference. It must be remembered, however, that the river is not the final or absolute frame of reference. It is not necessary that travelers be located *only* in reference to the river. Legitimate alternatives remain for locating a traveler in reference to the bank or other travelers.

In a similar way, any text can be located relative to the metanarrative of *missio Dei*, regardless of the orientation of that text.[75] Texts may oppose the missio Dei, support the missio Dei, deny the missio Dei or ignore the missio Dei and still be identified in reference to it. And, while missiology may prioritize this particular mode of location, the missiological interpreter is not bound to see things only in reference to the missio Dei. In fact, the use of other options may be complementary, for the adding of referential frames does nothing to negate either the presence of the missio Dei or the legitimacy of using it as a referential device. Just as referencing by the shore can augment referencing by the river or other travelers, the

---

[75] Even the very term, "subversive" demands at least two frames in relation to make sense.

missiological interpreter may augment his work by using inter-textual or inter-discursive strategies along with missio Dei strategies.

As we consider this, it is important to clarify where we can see the Bible in relation to God's kingdom metanarrative. Briefly, since missiology holds that the *missio Dei* expresses in all of God's activity, throughout all of creation, missiology does not need to read the Bible "as" God's metanarrative. This warrants some explanation, since missiology draws from the Bible to frame its understanding of God's metanarrative.

From a mission perspective, God's metanarrative is the overall story of what God is up to. This story is eternal; it precedes creation and continues beyond the eschaton of this world. In doing so, it extends beyond the boundaries of any written word. Further, since God's intention to communicate precedes his communication, his plan for the Bible stands before the composition of the Bible. This means that while the Bible depicts God's metanarrative, that metanarrative stands beyond the Bible. The Bible certainly participates in that larger story of God's work, but the full story of God's work is a bigger thing, which even the world could not contain.

Missiology can, however, read the Bible in *relation* to God's metanarrative. It can look *at* the text for evidences of God's plan at work, and it can look *in* the text for contents concerning that plan. The biblical text is not the divine plan, however, since its very presence derives from that plan and its purposes participate in the plan. The fact that the Bible is not the kingdom plan itself does not hinder reading it as a communication from God, as a witness to God's plan, as an artifact produced by God's plan and/or as an instrument for accomplishing God's plan.

We will explore these dimensions more fully as we apply method later. However, before we do so we will need to see how God's purposes can be discerned analytically.

Context: Reading for Combined Purposes

For "purpose" to function as a critical criterion, it must be observable in some way. However, this does not require that purpose be observed directly; it can be observed by virtue of its effects. This is a point of critical process that crosses many disciplines, especially the hard sciences. Many realities are not directly observable; this is a problem that western philosophy has wrestled over for centuries. In obvious cases, with things like gravity, we may only infer something's presence through observing the behavior of things that are affected by it. We can know that it is "there," even though we can never observe it directly. Critically speaking, the missiologist can come to a situation, especially a text, in a similar manner, not necessarily looking for purpose itself, but looking for traces or effects that indicate the influence of purpose.

Hermeneutically, the missiologist brings an attention to purpose just as the literary critic brings an attention to form or the semanticist brings an attention to the workings of language. All criticisms work this way; they come to the text with an attention to a certain dimension and then look for features of the text that hearken to that dimension. This "hermeneutic circle" is in some ways self-establishing and self-reinforcing, but it is also self-refining and self-challenging. The missiologist starts her circle with a pre-understanding of *missio*, the intended "*for*-ness" of the text and all things. She views features of the text through a lens of purpose and by virtue of this attention is enabled to discover evidence of purpose(s).

Using a parallel, obviously, the Bible does not articulate its own grammar,[76] but instead simply expresses from it. The grammarian follows after this expression, looking for grammatical dynamics by noting grammatical aspects that show through in the concrete features of the text. Yet, at the same time, the grammarian's pre-understanding of grammar often is built by looking at the text's features, in combination with his preceding grammatical concerns. This is a valid endeavor, even when it is reflexive.

---

[76] I am using "grammar" here in a broad sense to refer to a range of grammatical-syntactical dynamics and semiotic "rules."

In like manner, the Bible does not overtly articulate its purpose(s), except perhaps in the most fleeting instances.[77] However, the missiologist is not looking solely for overt contents *about* purpose, any more than the form critic is looking only for overt contents that declare form. The missiologist holds that texts proceed from unspoken influences of purpose in the same ways that they proceed from unspoken rules of grammar or habits of form. Missiological observation supplies the idea of purpose to the text as a lens in the same ways that grammatical observations supply the idea of grammar to the text.

In a general sense, missiology proceeds this way because it assumes that *missio* is a necessary dimension of behavior. It assumes that behavior has a dimension of "for-ness" that makes it meaningful and that this kind of intention is always a key factor, regardless of where behavior is found. This means that all activities and all artifacts of all people, not just the people of God, can be examined for purpose.[78] However, the ubiquity of this proposition does not yield a simple view; it shows a world of purposes that are highly complex. This is further complicated by the missiological proposition that God reigns overall and is at work in all situations to accomplish his will. Thus, if all behaviors have purpose, and social productions involve multiplex behaviors, it means that the layers and relationships of purpose in any but the most reduced of situations are sophisticated and intertwined, almost to the point of indiscernibility.

Within this complexity, however, the purposes of the *missio Dei* find special expression in the overt, self-conscious works of the people of God. In sacred works, divine purposes can be easier to discover because they bring purpose to the fore through self-consciousness and identification, but they also carry purpose more clearly because they can be divinely empowered to do so. As we have already seen, self-aware behavior is more explicit about purpose than unexamined behavior. This is what distinguishes "missional"

---

[77] Such as Jn. 20:30-31 or Lk. 1:3-4.
[78] A biblical example is the messianic figure of Cyrus in Is. 45:1-6.

behavior from other behavior. This kind of agency lends a factor of explicitness about purpose, because representation holds the purposes of another within self-awareness. Further, from the side of the one who commissions an agent, the act of authorization deliberately overlays purposes in explicit ways, calling for those to be prioritized. In the case of the Bible and the people of God, those who participate as agents in God's special missio create works that present God's purposes more readily to view than works by non-representatives; the things said and done by the people of God therefore show forth God's mission in added, special ways.

This means that while ordinary texts may be examined for general divine-human relations, the Bible is special. As a product of the agents and the self-aware people of God, the Bible is in a unique way laden throughout with the explicit intentions of God, and it more readily presents those purposes to the interpreter. Thus, the Bible can be understood relative to those intentions even more than other texts or situations that might carry his (and others') purposes, because it has a unique, representative instrumentality, that is, it has both explicit and implicit purpose.[79] This overt representational character can be further heightened by divine empowerment in sacramental ways, making it more effective to accomplish purposes and more revealing of divine intentions.

I will use a series of figures here in order to show how these relationships can interact. These are simplified depictions that portray a single direction of influence (they do not show the ways that individuals and

---

[79] God's purpose, his *missio*, has a reflexive dimension that is fulfilled when it brings people into participation with divine purpose(s). Christian mission also seeks to discover what it is called to do on behalf of God in the world by hearing from the biblical text and by observing God's actions that are described in its accounts. When people hear revelatory testimony and see the actions of God when reading the Bible, they can become moved to join God in his mission in Christ. As a result, Christian mission experiences the Bible as one of things that God uses to bring people into participation with his purposes, which is a key goal of the *missio Dei*. To Christian mission, then, the Bible is simultaneously an *instrument for* divine mission, something that God uses to accomplish his purpose, a *testimony about* divine mission, a record about God's purposes, and an *expression of* divine mission, that is, a thing produced by God's missional intentions. This yields a multifaceted quality of "purpose" that missiology can look for in the Bible.

institutions also affect society) but they can illustrate how purposes combine to shape texts.

In Figure 2, the circles with lines represent the interrelations of people, who act toward each other with purpose. These behaviors and purposes form the basis of society.

The combined intentions of the persons who form a society generate that society's overarching purpose(s), which also serve as the foundations for its metanarratives. Within that society, certain people also create certain institutions, which have their own purposes. As they do so, the larger, societal purposes and metanarratives influence the formation and purposes of those institutions. This makes the society at large a co-creator of those institutions, whether that relationship is acknowledged or not. In turn, the purpose(s) of both society and the institution combine to exert influence on anyone who produces knowledge within that institution. This makes both society and the institution co-creators of the knowledge that someone produces within an institution, even if that person is working for her own purpose(s).

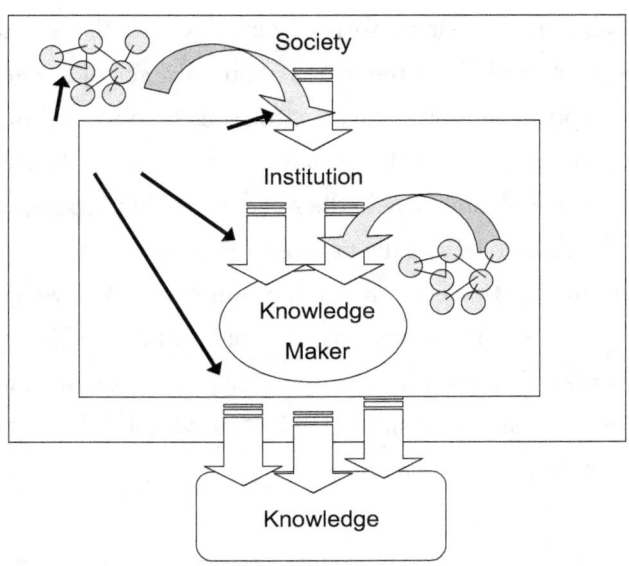

Figure 2. Societal, institutional and personal purposes in knowledge production. Reprinted from *In Search of the Contours of a Missiological Hermeneutic* (p. 93), by A.D. Ayers, 2011, Pasadena: Fuller Theological Seminary. Copyright Adam D. Ayers.
Reprinted with permission.

This is similar to the institutional force that Jean Francois Lyotard explored in his analysis of knowledge formation (1993). There, Lyotard outlines how institutional dynamics can thwart or encourage a scientist as he attempts to form knowledge while embedded in an institution. Using our river traveler analogy, the scientist can be viewed as a traveler and the institution can be viewed as the river, while society can be viewed as the river bed. The river bed affects the river; the river affects the traveler, and the traveler may move in multiple directions in reference to both even though they will affect him as he does.

We can note that the scientist's embedded relationship may be agonistic, passive or supportive, which can be seen relative to the force of the institution. Thus, any knowledge formed while the scientist is in that complex relationship will bear the marks of both the scientist's and the institution's purposes, as well as those of the society in which both operate. The varied purposes leave telltales or hallmarks within that knowledge that can reveal the relationship between the scientist's own purposes, the purposes of the institution and the purposes of society.

If we consider that every text is a production of knowledge, we can also see that personal, societal and institutional purposes will leave combined telltales of their influences upon the production of texts. This means that all texts can be considered to be "purpose-laden" and can be examined for those telltales (Figure 3).

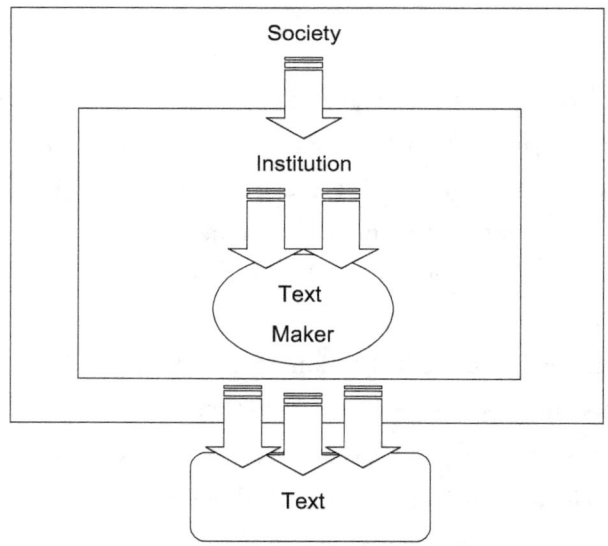

Figure 3. Text as a combined production of knowledge. Reprinted from *In Search of the Contours of a Missiological Hermeneutic* (p. 95), by A.D. Ayers, 2011, Pasadena: Fuller Theological Seminary. Copyright Adam D. Ayers. Reprinted with permission.

Significantly, as Lyotard notes at length (1993, pp. 10, 16, 44-47; 62-66), the purposes of knowledge-makers and the institutions in which they are embedded are not always consonant; neither are the purposes of institutions and societies. This means that influences are not simple, but complex, and frequently dissonant at particular points. The resulting textual hallmarks also will be complex, reflecting the consonances and dissonances of the relationships between the purposes of the text's producer, institution(s) and society (Figure 4).

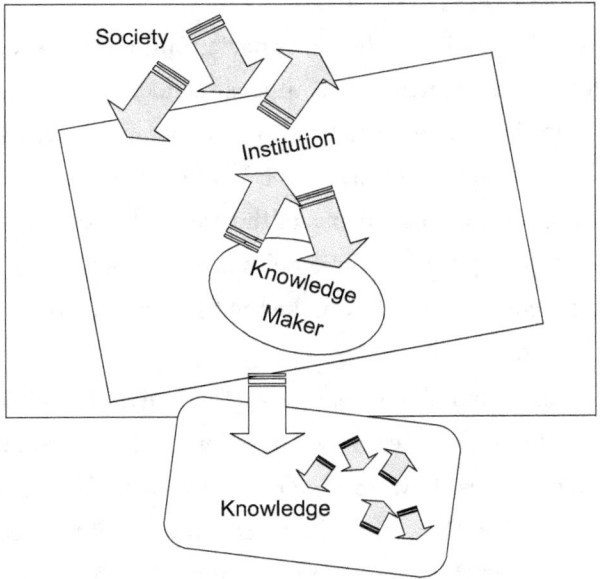

Figure 4. Complex purpose relations within knowledge and texts. Reprinted from *In Search of the Contours of a Missiological Hermeneutic* (p. 96), by A.D. Ayers, 2011, Pasadena: Fuller Theological Seminary. Copyright Adam D. Ayers. Reprinted with permission.

This leaves the question of how these purpose telltales may be observed. Michael Polanyi's work with focal-subsidiary awareness can help here. He highlights that things can be observed by using a foreground/background scheme in which one thing is given primary attention (focal) while another is treated as an unnoticed given (subsidiary). These focal and subsidiary aspects are not necessarily separated. They are integrated in "joint" awareness, even when they may not be directly observable simultaneously. Both are required for observation, and although only one may be observed at a time, the presence of the unseen other is what empowers observation to take place. It is simply that when one aspect is used to reveal another, attention to that one requires that the other be taken as a given, and *vice versa* (1975, pp. 22-45).

A simple illustration is the white background of a sheet of paper that makes black letters show forth. The whiteness is taken for granted, and it is seen, but not seen. The same holds true when a distant object's size is assessed because a closer object is in view, but not in focus, or when a fish is seen swimming against the backdrops of the creek's bottom and the movement of the muddy water. While neither the creek bottom nor the water are being focused upon, they make the fish and its movements visible and understandable.

If we adopt Polanyi's concept, when the individual is taken as a given, the institution's purposes show up. When the institution is a given, the individual's purposes show up. One may be seen "focally" in light of the "subsidiary" presence of the other. Thus, institutional telltales can be observed in the work of the scientist and the scientist's telltales show against the background of the institution.

Further, because the knowledge that the scientist produces is purpose-laden throughout, examination is not limited to the scientist's or the institution's explicit statements about their purposes. Any and all documents related to the project may be examined to see the intentions of the groups, departments, institutions, or even the society in which the scientist works.

By the same token, both "mission" and "non-mission" biblical texts can be examined fruitfully for mission-related qualities. This can be done on a wide variety of levels, scales and degrees. By looking for consonances and dissonances within the text, the interpreter may analyze both the context and the text for purposes that can exist simultaneously and in various degrees of harmony. The critical reader may assess for the purposes of authors in light of the institutions and societies in which they were embedded and vice versa, or he may assess for the purposes of God in light of the purposes of the author and the social structures of the context. He may use this examination to make reasonable inferences about purposes that exist beyond the text and to compare those with purposes that may exist "within" the text or text world. This is what Barram might call the "inherently missional character" of biblical texts (2007, p. 49).

However, keeping Polanyi's observations in mind, this kind of examination is only possible if one does not collapse the intentions of the institution into the intentions of the scientist, by acting as though all intentions belonged to the scientist. By the same token, the scientist cannot be treated as a mechanical, non-volitional expression of societal forces, as though all purposes were society's. Rather, purposes must be seen as coming both from within the scientist and simultaneously from beyond her (Voss, 2017).

In like manner, in order to analyze for the various levels of purposes in the biblical text, the purposes of individual authors, institutions, societies, or God cannot be considered to be the same or equal. They must be understood to be conjoined in participation and yet distinct in identity. As missiologists R. Daniel Shaw and Charles Van Engen assert, "our hermeneutical task must include awareness of God's intention" (2003, p. 70). They see God's intention as interacting with the intention of a human author's within that author's context. Note how they foreground God's intentions while back-grounding culture as they comment on Grant Osborne's Two-horizon model:

> The primary source must be the first author, God, who, through the thought-forms and context-specific actions and worldviews of human authors communicates with human beings in a particular time and place for a particular purpose. (2003, p. 80)

This considers God to be a joint-composer, whose influence operates in the same way that societal or institutional purposes do. In the same way that institutions and societies must be maintained in focal-subsidiary relations in order for their respective purposes to be observed, in order for missiology to look for the purposes of God, the field of vision cannot be reduced to the purposes of human biblical writers or audiences, alone. Space must be given for the purposes of God to exist in complex ways within the biblical authors and their situations, and, simultaneously, beyond them. In reverse, the purposes of the author or the author's society/community must be held in view if they are to be seen in relation to God's purposes.

We may now return to using our first, simplified figure. However, this time we will see how missiology can frame God's purpose(s) as a recognizable co-influence upon the production of texts. This is shown in Figure 6.

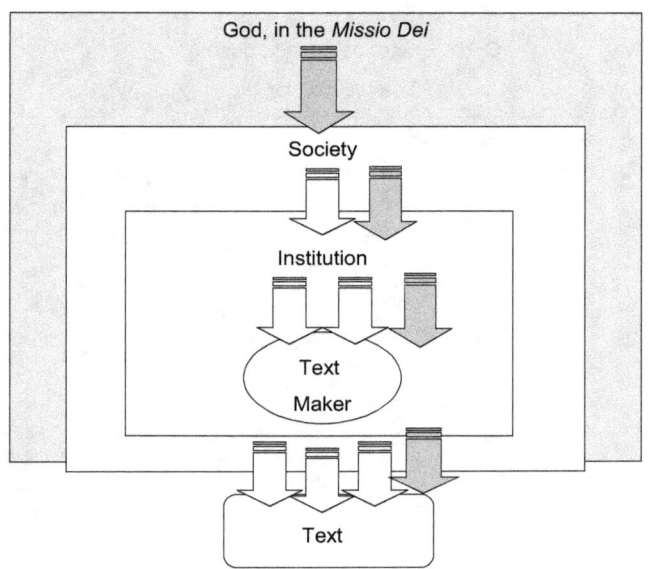

Figure 5. God's purposes as a contributing influence. Reprinted from *In Search of the Contours of a Missiological Hermeneutic* (p. 100), by A.D. Ayers, 2011, Pasadena: Fuller Theological Seminary. Copyright Adam D. Ayers. Reprinted with permission.

    However, remember that these relationships are actually complex, because purposes do not match exactly. If we keep this in mind, the co-authoring relationships would look more like Figure 6, below.

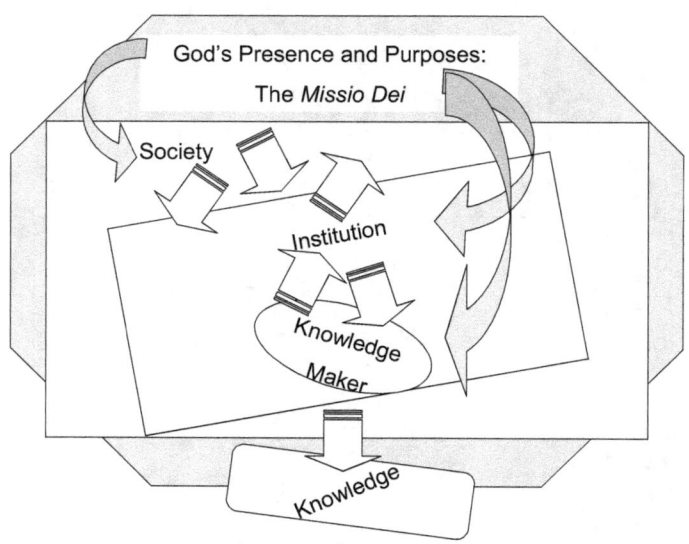

Figure 6. The *missio Dei* and complex purpose relations. Reprinted from *In Search of the Contours of a Missiological Hermeneutic*(p.101), by A.D. Ayers, 2011, Pasadena: Fuller Theological Seminary. Copyright Adam D. Ayers. Reprinted with permission.

In this arrangement, God's purposes can show through in the same ways that societal and institutional purposes can show through. We have seen already that the purposes of the agonistic or supportive scientist may be seen by looking for telltales in her work. These telltales show because they provide contrast and comparison between her purposes and those of an institution. This relationship may be consonant or dissonant, although dissonance reveals purposes through contrast more readily than consonance does. This simultaneously reveals the purposes of the institution and the scientist.

In the same way, the purposes of God may be seen in texts by looking for the telltales of agonistic or supportive relations that people have toward him or that he might have toward particular societies or institutions.

The purposes of one are revealed against the purposes of another by looking for telltales of congruence or divergence within the knowledge that is formed under their combined influences. For biblical reading, missiological interpretation deliberately looks for indicators of consonance or dissonance between God's purposes and those of persons, institutions, society, and humankind. This attention reveals purposes on both sides of the focal-subsidiary grounding scheme, as long as they are maintained in a related but discrete view.

In short, then, all texts carry telltales of the hands that have influenced their compositions. If interpreters are mindful of the influence of textual contributors, they can examine texts to discern where and how each influence shares in the final form of the text. This can be done by comparing and contrasting textual telltales that are aligned around the particular interests of possible contributors. The combined purposes of the contributors in turn reveals the purpose(s) *of* and *for* the text.

The distinction of missiological interpretation is that it intentionally chooses not to exclude God and his purposes from the catalog of possible contributors to the text. It sees God as the primary contributor to the text's composition because it sees the text as an instrument that derives from God's *missio*, the divine metanarrative plan of God at work in creation. Thus, missiological interpretation deliberately looks for how and when God's hand has influenced the text in co-authorship with human composers. Missiological interpretation does this in order to discern divine purposes in and for the text.

This is a preliminary view of how missiological interpretation can understand the text using multi-scalar frames of reference in light of the general concept of *missio* and the special concept of *missio Dei*. In the next chapter we will look at how a missiological outlook can understand readers and their interactions with the text.

Chapter 4

Kingdom and Context: Horizons, Time and Groups

Kingdom Context: The Notion of "Gap"

We noticed earlier that missiology holds the kingdom of God to be simultaneously then, now and not yet. The kingdom's capacity to extend beyond ordinary conventions about time is significant for interpretation because it affects how missiology deals with history, historicity and the contexts of readers. This, in turn, impacts how missiology treats the idea of interpretive "horizons" and the problem of historical "gaps."

By way of background, the issue of contextual gap is highly problematic. It touches upon key debates within multiple fields, because it arises from the fundamental paradox of human separation and connection. The short version of the issue is that we humans experience that we are separated from each other. We know that there is some sort of problem that opens between us when we attempt to transfer meaning from one to another, and we daily face the challenge of confirming, "How can you, (there) know that what you're hearing is what I (here) am saying?"

Yet, at the same time, we also experience that we are connected to others in very real ways. We are able to share our lives, get things done together, to know and to be known. This tells us that "You (there), must be hearing *something* of what I (here) am saying." We know that some kind of transfer of meaning is taking place between us, even while we know that we are separated.

Complicating the issue, we also experience that our separations and connections are not static. They change and they fluctuate based on factors that are hard to discern. Sometimes connection seems to be fine, then suddenly separation increases, and it is extremely difficult to try to lock down or explain what is actually taking place or affecting the outcomes. We just know that sometimes the distance seems really far between "You (there)" and "I (here)," and at other times it seems that there's no separation at all between "Us" (here and there).

The problem becomes further compounded when we add a communication medium like writing, because a medium has a real presence of its own. As we have already seen, this makes a text able to stand partially in the place of someone who isn't physically present (Ayers, 2011, pp. 185-192). However, as soon as a proxy medium comes into play, the question arises, "Is this medium making up for the distance between 'here' and 'there' or complicating the distance between 'here' and 'there?'" Is it closing the separation as a connector, or sticking in the middle as an obstruction? In other words, is it helping or hindering, or both, and, again, in what ways?

What's more, a communication medium's physical presence can last a long time, often longer than a human life. This brings out the reality that every "here" or "there" in which an "I" and a "You" stand is also a temporal context; it is also a "then" or a "now." This makes questions about communication using a medium have to address both time and place, as well as persons. The problem is not simply about connecting between the contexts of "here" and "there," but between the combined contexts of "there-then" and "here-now." Because this is talking about people and their communications, the issue compounds even further, and the question becomes how a medium can connect or separate the contexts of "someone-there-then" and "someone-here-now."

There are no simple answers to these conundrums. The problem of how meaning can bridge across a contextual "gap" between the time and place of a text and the time and place of a reader has been an ongoing issue in interpretation, and scholars and theorists continue to take widely varied stances about it. Some have championed gap, while others have sought to explain it, compensate for it, or bypass it altogether. At the time of this writing, gap between contexts continues to be a crucial sticking point between methods, and, although we cannot cover much of the debate here, a little sampling may help us to understand how it presents a defining point for missiological reading.

One of the more influential theorists on the topic is Hans-Georg Gadamer. His work provides a model for how contextual gap can be overcome, especially in terms of time. In his monumental treatise, *Truth and Method*, Gadamer parts with the hermeneutic philosophy of Schleiermacher, which had come to characterize biblical studies in the 19th and 20th centuries. He summarizes this philosophy, which was the prevailing goal of criticism at the time, as the mistaken quest to recover the author's original intentions by means of a reconstruction of the author's world and mind.[80]

Gadamer sees the attempt as misguided because he understands reconstruction of the author's mind to be an impossible task, due to the inescapable reality of temporal distance.[81] He holds instead that the work of

---

[80] Gadamer writes, "Ultimately, this view of hermeneutics is as nonsensical as all restitution and restoration of life. Reconstructing the original circumstances, like all restoration, is a futile undertaking in view of the historicity of our being."(2004, p. 159). See also Meyer (1985, p. 36).

[81] Gadamer makes much of the reality of and progression of history. This is too large of a topic to explore here and it must suffice to say that he sees temporal distance not as an "abyss" that destroys meaning but as a contributor to the hermeneutic task (2004, p. 297).

It logically follows from Gadamer's observations that any real reconstruction of an author's original intention would require a reorganization of all things into their states at the time of the art's composition, which would severely affect the interpreter(!). Anything less requires supplying contemporary modes of thinking that differ from both the tangible- and thought-worlds of the author. If one takes a uniform, linear, intractable view of temporal progression, any proposal that meaning is linked to the author or to the compositional event naturally dooms a text or work of art to constant degradation of interpretability from the very moment its composition begins, for the author/artist is necessarily changed during the

art, whether literary or figural, from the moment of its creation, takes on an aspect of existence separate from its author, one that empowers it to continue to bring about productions of meaning beyond the immediate presence of its author (2004, p. 157). Thus, for Gadamer, a work, but not an author or the author's intentions, can be an enduring thing that continues to be accessible through time, since the work remains always in the present.

Further, since the work remains always in the present, it is as joint participants in the present that the interpreter and the work meet. The interpreter stands in the present, producing meaning by interacting with the work (p. 293). The text then becomes real in the present as it is encountered by the interpreter, who is both the product and the active custodian of tradition (pp. 157-161).[82]

Gadamer builds upon the work of Heidegger, who explored the foundations of hermeneutic circularity, the interdependence that exists always between the part and the whole (2004, p. 293). For Gadamer, control on interpretation is achieved as the text's ongoing actuality intersects with the reader's agenda (pp. 270-285). This is an endless process of "play" (p. 102) in the form of a question that never can achieve a final meaning (pp. 107, 298). In this arrangement, interpretation resembles a complex of whorls that rotate forward through time while also arching backward in order to retrieve from the past, integrate into the present, and stretch forward, anticipating and creating meanings, and thus, extending tradition.

Gadamer's work is powerful, but because of the way that it emphasizes present meaning it leaves a problem for the reader who wishes

---

composition of a piece and cannot recover his/her own "mind" in its state before the piece began to take shape. It would seem that awareness of this informs part of Gadamer's aesthetic, which holds that art itself is able to bring about meanings that not only the observer but the artist herself cannot express or realize without its presence. His position is supported by the reality that meaning does not always degrade within the historical experience of art. While in some cases meaning is lost, in other cases art not only maintains the capacity to bring about meaning, it accrues greater capacity over time (hence, the development of "tradition").

[82] At the same time, he establishes the reality that prejudice is always involved in understanding (2004, p. 272).

to appeal to the original text as a canonical reference point.[83] Helpfully, from the perspective of evangelical scholarship, Grant Osborne develops a related, but distinctly biblical hermeneutic. Unlike Gadamer, Osborne anchors understanding on the side of "the author's intended meaning of a text, a core that is unvarying" (1991, p. 7). In order to do this, Osborne appeals to a "meaning-significance" distinction (1991, p. 7), which differentiates between what a text *meant* in the past and what a text *means* in the ongoing present. Johannes Nissen also uses this approach, holding a distinction between the text's *meaning* ("Sinn") and *significance* ("Bedeutung") (2004a, p. 15). This distinction stands strong on the value of the past, but it does so at the cost of proposing that there are two contexts for the text, "then" and "now," and that these contexts have a gap that stands between them.

However, this kind of contextual distinction is strongly criticized by Paul Hanson as ultimately yielding a "bitter fruit" that separates the Bible from contemporary religious life (1985, pp. 59-60). Hanson's point is well taken, not only because of the fact that contemporary religious life is impoverished, but because of the way that a two context, two meaning scheme that locates primary meaning in the past renders all later readers as secondary and distanced from the most significant expression of the text.

In a modified approach, Anthony Thiselton maintains a gap between horizons, but he holds the gap to be a sort of interstitial region of dynamic interaction (1992, pp. 597-619). He concludes his work with a powerful assertion that this interaction involves the divine address of God to the reader:

> But if address *to* God can be understood as initiated by the Holy Spirit, how much more in the case of address *from* God? In a co-operative shared work, the Spirit, the text and the reader engage in a *transforming process*, which enlarges horizons and creates *new horizons*.

---

[83] Gadamer insists that the text is "estranged from its original meaning"(2004, p. 157).

> That *into which* readers are transformed in this reading-process remains partly but not wholly hidden. The promissory horizon of future destiny which beckons the reader is described by Paul as "beholding the glory of the Lord... being transformed (*metamorphoumetha*) from glory to glory into the image (*eikōn*) of Christ (II Cor. 3:18). (1992, p. 619) [italics in original]

Thiselton's appeal to the Spirit as one who "creates new horizons" with the reader and the text matches well with Shawn Redford's approach, and it seems well suited to missiological reading of contexts and time. Yet, since it comes at the conclusion of his book and Thiselton does not elaborate on the point further, it remains tantalizing as an explanation.

However, taking Gadamer, Osborne, Hanson, and Thiselton together, we can at least see that whenever contexts are framed in a "then" and "now" scheme, a significant gap appears between the reader and the text, and between contemporary readers and original readers. This contextual gap presents a challenge for interpretation, regardless of the strategy that is used to bridge it, and even when allowances are made for divine activity to be a part of the interpretive process.

Even more, while these scholars offer helpful strategies for negotiating contextual gaps, their solutions still work within the set of foundational assumptions about time and historicity that make the contextual gap appear in the first place. This is troublesome from a missiological perspective, because these assumptions do not fit fully with missiology's kingdom-based understanding of time.

Kingdom solidarity. Remember that missiology takes the solidarity of the Kingdom seriously. It considers the faith community of the Kingdom to be a reality, and it holds that this reality is metaphysically integrated as one, regardless of time, culture or location. It considers this "one" to be unaffected by the simultaneous reality that the kingdom is also particular and local.⁸⁴ As Hiebert exhorts, "Scripture leads us to another startling conclusion: *in the church there are no others, there is only us – members of one body, brothers and sisters in faith.* The unity of the church is not a product of the good news; it is an essential part of the gospel" (2008, p. 291) [italics in original].

Because of this commitment, missiology cannot take up the idea of reading horizons or the issue of contextual gaps without qualification. As we saw with voice and presence, missiology does not separate contexts, readers or reading communities from each other in the present in ways that are absolute, and it cannot separate them historically. Its commitments prevent it from isolating groups from each other within the community of faith, regardless of factors that may appear to distance them. This prohibits missiology from closing the original reading community's boundaries. It cannot affirm that the "original" community no longer exists, or that it is not connected to contemporary reading communities, simply because current readers reside in other times and places or cultures.⁸⁵

---

⁸⁴ In *The Glocal Church: Locality and Catholicity in a Globalizing World*, Charles Van Engen (2006) extensively develops a missiological understanding of the unity of the church that integrates with particularity. He describes the unity of the church in geographic and cultural terms, as well as temporal terms. He appeals to the New Testament, church history and both Protestant and Catholic traditions to assert, "It is the will of God that all peoples should be increasingly related to him and to his body, the church. This universal purpose is built into the very essence of what the church is as the people of God. The people of God are gathered from the entire world. As such, it is essential to their being that they participate in that gathering. As the people of God, the church participates in Christ as and when it participates in Christ's universal salvation, gathering people from all four corners of the earth to be his body, the church" (p. 164). He continues, "The idea of catholicity contains much more than simply the notions of geographical and numerical extension. It also has to do with cohesion, doctrinal continuity and catholicity in a temporal sense" (p. 169). He understands the growth of the church to be "a characteristic of the very essence of the church as the gathering of the community of the Holy Spirit, open to all peoples, to the entire world, in all time" (p. 171).

Mission historian Andrew Walls makes a similar point, proposing that the unity of the people of God extends through time in God's mission, as those persons who follow in time "cross-generationally" finish the works begun in earlier persons (e.g., the promises of Abraham). He applies this missiological approach to biblical interpretation of Hebrews: "Abraham, the writer argues, and all the other Christian ancestors, will not be made perfect, that is, complete, until the Christians to whom the Letter to the Hebrews is addressed are gathered into their succession. Extending it further, Abraham is waiting *for us* so that he can enter into his inheritance… The study of Christian history should display the kinship of Christians across the generations, for this is how the process of salvation works" (2006, p. 72) [italics in original].

⁸⁵ See also (Ayers, 2017)

This is only partly because missiology is interculturally oriented. More, the position is grounded in its commitment to the kingdom of God, for missiology holds that communities can be localized and yet at the same time be unified with each other in the kingdom of God, whether or not there is observable interaction between them. The idea of Kingdom enables missiology to work with the reality that horizons exist in plurality; but it also constrains missiology to interact with plurality in a way that does not exclude solidarity. While it holds the diversity of the Kingdom in one hand, in the other hand it holds a simultaneously coexistent unity that may transcend the very idea of horizons and contexts.

Kingdom time. Theoretically, the root of the dilemma lies in the ways that time is conceptualized within western culture. For, while it may feel to us that time is self-evident and self-defining, the ways that we view time and interact with it are largely the products of enculturation (Hiebert, 2008) (Kraft, 2008). Once we recognize this, it is fairly easy to see that western hermeneutical ideas about contextual horizons rest upon western understandings about the divisibility of things. Western thought assumes that divisions of time are real, and with these assertions, attending divisions of social presence. This scheme, however, could bear with some examination, for, from a missiological perspective, it need not be taken as a given.

Note that in order for a temporal horizon to exist, some sort of demarcation must be made between moments in time. Yet, understandings of time may vary, depending on worldview, culture, or frame of reference. In other words, there is no intrinsic, self-defining rule that sets the limits of temporal events; limits must be perceptively or socially imposed. Because period or event boundaries do not self-exist or self-establish, they must be set by definition or assertion.

This also applies to any groups, objects or people that are identified as being "within" certain times. This is in some ways like a territorial border. Borders do not exist in a landscape; only features exist in a landscape.

However, social convention can define a landscape feature as a border. When convention does so, people and things become contained within that border or excluded by that border. In the same way, as a time period becomes defined, it captures or contains things and people within its temporal boundaries. It also excludes things and people outside of its boundaries. This is where the interpretive horizon problem arises, because it is only when epochs or groups are defined as distinct that gaps begin to appear between them.

An illustration might help. When viewed by the hour, 8:00 am and 2:00 pm are separate. A gap appears between them. However, when viewed by the day, those same moments are united, and no gap exists between them. They are both "inside" the one day. Likewise, when viewed by the year or decade, 1934 and 1988 have horizons that separate them. Yet, when viewed by the century, they stand together.

The same holds true for the people who inhabit those times. When viewed by the hour, "Mr. 8:00 am" and "Ms. 2:00 pm" cannot be in a certain place at the same "time." However, when viewed by the day, month, or year, they can be. The determinant factor, then, for whether or not a time gap appears between moments, as well as between the people within those moments, is the incremental scale of time that is used to view them. This can be done according to any scale.

The same logic, then, that allows particularization into time horizons also supports the obliteration of horizons. If time can be divided into smaller and smaller moments, it also can be expanded into larger and larger moments. If horizons can be momentary, immediate and separating, they also can be epochal, distant, and including. The very power of observation that establishes a gap also holds the power to annul a gap, and the power to raise a contextual barrier is the power to remove a contextual barrier.

Disciplinary time. If this is the case, the question naturally follows, "Who determines these boundaries, and by what criteria?" Culture and worldview provide can provide one answer. Another solution can be the assertions of an interpreter or of an interpreting community. Disciplinary practices also can provide a means of grounding temporal conventions. This angle is particularly fruitful because it provides a clear illustration of how temporal definitions can be anchored in the need to produce certain kinds of discourse-based knowledge.

If we look at the needs of a discipline to define its own knowledge, we can see that an astronomer must be able to talk meaningfully about a star's death as a single event, even though the time frame of that single event may be greater than the span of all events that have taken place on Earth. Likewise, a geologist must be able to conceive of a single geologic event with a scale that exceeds all of human history. The historian also may speak of "The Renaissance" or "The Fall of Rome," even if those events span multiple human generations and stretch across varied locations. All of these examples set the boundaries of events via disciplinary conventions that impose their own temporal definitions. In situations like this, increments of time are matters of discursive social construction, just as they are within culture.

Overall, this presents a free situation for missiology with regard to historicity and readers. The social and discursive aspects of the construction of time that we are talking about empower missiology to define interpretive moments on any scale that its disciplinary quest for knowledge requires or supports. Based upon its commitments and outlook, its disciplinary "worldview," missiology may apply disciplinary definitions of moments or of time as theoretical realities. It is not bound to the limitations that attend western or modern discursive habits about time or about ontic distance. From missiological perspectives, historical distance is not necessary, absolute, or even a factor of reality in all cases, even though the idea of historical horizons may yield some fruitful hermeneutic results.

Thus, missiological interpretation may utilize an "all of time" or inclusive scale of focus that is grounded upon the idea of the kingdom of God. For, from missiological perspectives, in the same way that the Kingdom can exist simultaneously as then, now and not yet, interpretive horizons simultaneously can be "then," "now," and "not now."[86] This does not mean that it must reject horizontal approaches. For complementary views, it also may use separated, western conventions about historicity and contexts, but it is not bound to hold to those schemes when that would limit its own capacity to produce meaningful knowledge.

Kingdom Context: Group and Time Horizons

Taking into account the conventional nature of time, the missiological interpreter may ask, "Why should we not view the *entire* place of the Bible in history as one unified 'moment?'" From the perspective of the kingdom of God, all members are one, and the "then, now, and not yet" moments in which the text resides are all one. Thus, there is no reason why missiologists should not consider all of the readers who have read the Bible, including the authors who wrote it, to be one united reading community that is acting together in one united event.[87]

This question could be asked from multiple angles. Whether missiology takes up a lens of disciplinary definition, a lens that maintains indeterminacy about temporal conventions, or a lens that champions an alternate, metaphysical worldview, it is free to consider biblical horizons to be inclusive and present instead of separating and distant. However, simply having such an option does not settle the temporal question, and, in order to be both fair and rigorous we must consider whether or not such appeals are anything more than semantic sleight of hand that excuses missiology from

---

[86] I appeal to Berger and Luckmann's work on this point. They note that socially-established realities that result from worldviews are in fact as real as any reality that can be known, and that these realities are empirically valid ways of approaching phenomena contextually (1967, pp. 175-177).

[87] This is no different than treating all of the conversation during a conference as one event and one conversation, even though individuals may enter or leave the conference hall in a serial manner and even though the event may take breaks and re-convene.

the hard work of historical consideration. Given that missiology seeks to interact with western thought, can we conceptualize how all of this could be framed, in a way that might be acceptable to western thinkers?

Perhaps; but doing so will require a bit of heuristic accommodation to western thought, using linear temporal concepts. For example, Figure 7 below illustrates the idea of historical horizons using the idea of an expanding event and an expanding community. In this model, the event expands together with its community to include new members and moments. It does not stop, leaving a historical gap between it and new participants. In missiological understanding, this happens through the kingdom of God's proclamation. In the proclamation of the kingdom, people and contexts are overtaken and included in one event, the "now" of the "hearing of the Word," and they participate together as one reading community, the "we" of the "hearers of the Word." Seen from this perspective, all readers, even contemporary readers, may be understood to be the "first readers" of the text, since the "first reading" of the text continues as an ongoing and expanding event ("now"), and the "we" of the first readers continues as an expanding and enduring community.

This opens the text to the contemporary reader in some unexpected ways. For, as a member of the original recipient group and the original reading event, the contemporary reader legitimately may lay claim that the text is indeed written to *her*, and that she hears the text's message directly and immediately. This is not a devotional fiction that assists her to access a text that was written to others and to appropriate it for herself by employing a recontextualization scheme. Her reading is in all regards part of the actual reading of the actual first readers.

A scriptural example of this type of thinking can be found in Jesus' view about the primary recipients of the Mosaic law (Mk. 10:1-9). Note how Jesus frames the law as a direct address from Moses to the Pharisees who are questioning him in a contemporary situation, and how he characterizes the composition as being written in consideration of their contemporary hearts:

> And Pharisees came up and in order to test him asked, "Is it lawful for a man to divorce his wife?" He answered them, "What did Moses command you?" They said, "Moses allowed a man to write a certificate of divorce and to send her away." And Jesus said to them, "Because of your hardness of heart he wrote you this commandment. But from the beginning of creation, 'God made them male and female.' 7 (Mark 10:2-6, ESV)

Jesus allows no gap between Moses and the Pharisees. He asks, "What did Moses command *you*?" (emphasis added). The Pharisees attempt to distance themselves, responding that Moses "permitted (one)... to write and to release." However, Jesus insists on the issue of direct address, using the personal pronoun twice in his reply, "for *your* hardness of heart he wrote *to you* this command" (emphasis added).

As he does this, Jesus collapses all sense of temporal or group distance. He sees enough solidarity within the community of Israel to designate the contemporary state of his hearers' hearts as the condition that moved Moses when Moses wrote the earlier command. As far as Jesus is concerned, the Pharisees *are* the original recipients. Since Moses wrote to Israel and the Pharisees are Israel, Moses wrote to them. The command was written to the Pharisees, and it was written due to the hardness of their hearts. In a similar manner, he sees the same group as the direct subjects of Isaiah's prophetic word, declaring, "Well did Isaiah prophesy of you hypocrites, as it is written, 'This people honors me with their lips, but their heart is far from me'" (Mark 7:6 ESV).

Echoes of this kingdom way of viewing time appear again in Chapter 12 as Jesus responds to the Sadducees concerning the resurrection of the dead. There,

> Jesus said to them, "Is this not the reason you are wrong, because you know neither the Scriptures nor the power of God?... And as for

the dead being raised, have you not read in the book of Moses, in the passage about the bush, how God spoke to him, saying, 'I am the God of Abraham, and the God of Isaac, and the God of Jacob'? He is not God of the dead, but of the living. You are quite wrong."

(Mark 12:24, 26-27 ESV)

Jesus contends that the Sadducees are deeply wrong because they do not know the scriptures or the power of God. He emphasizes that their frames of understanding are too limited and that this is leading them to employ misguided theological limits as they frame their scriptural questions. The answer that he gives breaks with their constraints. It holds that the past patriarchs are not in fact dead, even though they await resurrection. Instead, their lives are caught up in solidarity with the God of the living. Since God is the God of the living and he is their God, they in turn are not dead. They are alive in the ever-present now of God, without horizons.

This approach lends voice to currently marginalized readers who currently might be considered to be disadvantaged because they lack access to background understandings. An expanding event view does not expect a minimum degree of familiarity or a "sufficient" amount of background information before a reading may be regarded as contributive or "good scholarship," as often can happen within theological and academic traditions. Rather, it simply acknowledges that there is no such thing as a uniform, homogeneous or ideal reader. There are only real readers who read according to their own skills and backgrounds. In this scheme, any contemporary reader is simply one of the original readers, all of whom have varying degrees of religious sophistication, knowledge, and literary awareness. Any reader, as all others, must engage the text with limited understanding and allow her encounter with the text to increase her knowledge and experience.

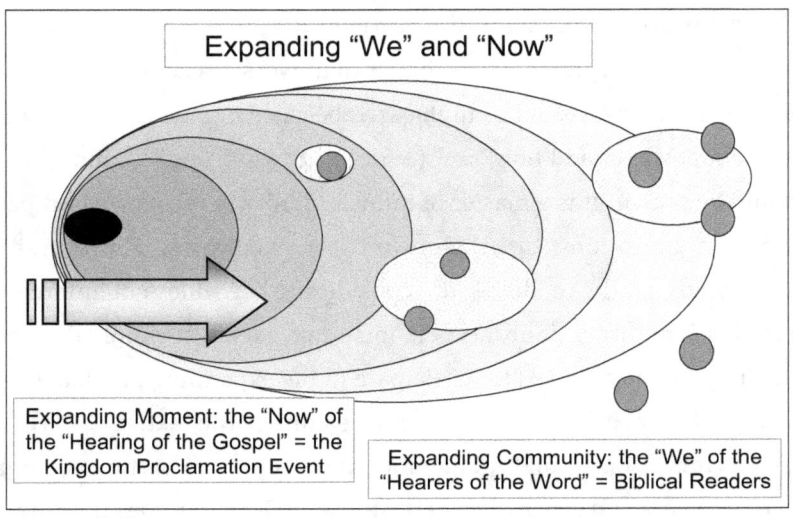

Figure 7. Expanding "We" and "Now" of mission horizons in the first reading event. Reprinted from *In Search of the Contours of a Missiological Hermeneutic* (p. 230) by A.D. Ayers, 2011, Pasadena: Fuller Theological Seminary. Copyright Adam D. Ayers. Reprinted with permission.

While this is so, it must be kept in mind that mission also recognizes the particularity that co-exists with universality. The Kingdom is not *only* a "now;" it is a now *and* a "then," *and* a "not yet." This means that making an inclusive choice in favor of the expanding event does not require the obliteration of local identity. Rather, it offers the opportunity to relate particular moments and groups by holding them in a focal-subsidiary view. This view gives attention to particular moments and readerships, yet it does so in relation to larger frames of readerships and moments. Both are kept in Polanyi's "joint awareness" regardless of which is in immediate view. This allows dialectic and heuristic interaction between the particular and the universal, the local and the global.

Kingdom Contexts: Varied Readerships

Preserving the dialectic between universal readerships and particular ones needs to be emphasized because it touches upon a justice issue about where and how "we" (emic) and "you" (etic)[88] boundaries can or should be drawn. It is a matter of human dignity to recognize that people have the right to constitute their own "we's" and "you's." However, it needs to be noted that the model we are considering here does not enforce participation; rather, it observes it and empowers it. It simply notices those who have already elected to participate in the expanding proclamation event through their hearing of the word and reading of the text.

It is also helpful to remember that people can participate in multiple groups, events and categories. Being a Pacific Islander does not rule out identifying simultaneously as Hawaiian or as American; identifying as African does not rule out being Maasai; being Puerto Rican does not rule out identifying as Hispanic, etc. By the same token, missiological inclusion in a larger event does not necessarily annihilate rights to self-identity. Like the kingdom itself, readers and readerships may exist on universal and particular scales, simultaneously.[89] There is room within the kingdom reading event for many groups to self-identify as unique even while they participate in a larger whole. Reading communities may be distinct, competing, or complementary, even while they are taken to be unified in the reading event.

Outlining the contours of such communities or their relations is a task for those specific readers as they self-identify. The point here is that missiological reading is free to see all readers of the Bible as one community while simultaneously acknowledging multiple, discrete readerships. It can do this by positing a community of solidarity, the hearers of the Word,

---

[88] These are widely used terms in missiology, e.g., (Hiebert, 2008, p. 89).

[89] Wittgenstein's "game" philosophy provides an analogy. If we think of reading communities as players of chess, we can see that sides are clearly drawn and identified. Each piece also may have an identifiable role or position. This does not diminish that fact that the separate sides and players are joint participants in the unified moment of the particular game and the overarching moment of the history of chess.

within a unified moment of reading, the proclamation of the Word,[90] which spans in time from the Bible's composition until the present. This can be done without negating the rights of hearers to delineate particular readerships as hearers of the Word "to us," as well as "to all." Using the same mechanisms, particular moments or events also may be defined by groups using their own views of time, which create unique horizons. Those reading horizons and moments can be set in dialectic with readings that use larger scale moments. In this scheme, universal, kingdom scale reading is not excluded by local and particular reading, while local, particular reading is not subsumed by kingdom scale reading. Instead, specialization enhances and complements universality within the overall discourse of biblical reading, without threatening or negating the transcending unity of the hearing community.

The key to all of this is the scale of God's own horizon, as Jesus shows in his interactions with the Sadducees, Pharisees and scribes. In God's *missio*, God's own horizon can be understood to be conjoined to the cosmos and time in a single moment of all-creation history. And, just as it can be fused with the life spans of certain individuals, like Abraham, Isaac or Jacob, God's horizon can be seen to be fused with the entire life span of humankind in the single and whole moment of all-human history. It also can be involved with certain entire events that constitute the life spans of particular groups or institutions, such as the kingdom of God, the seed of Abraham, the covenant community, the nation of Israel, the Church, or the community of hearers. Each of these whole events can be fused with God's own horizon. Each of these can be considered discretely or as conjoined moments in which God is present and involved with particular horizons. These horizons can coexist and intersect simultaneously with the single biblical moment of "the Bible in time."

---

[90] Or, "The hearing of the Word."

Thus, missiological interpretation can use a multiplex perspective that is more than a simple hermeneutic circle. It is more akin to an astronomical "symphony of the spheres." This perspective looks at the whole of history in transcendent or synchronic ways as well as dynamic, diachronic, and narrative ways. It can do this by using a continuum of social scales that extends from the particular "I" to the universal "We." These scales can express on a continuum of temporal moments, from the extremely minute nano-moment to all of cosmic time. And, even though missiological interpretation sees these holistically, particular groups or moments on either continuum are not finally conflated or finally discrete; they may overlap, partially fuse and coexist in dialectic, focal-subsidiary relations.

Green's "Behind," "In," and "In Front" Model

We may now look at how this approach compares to a recognized hermeneutic model. For comparison here we will be using Joel Green's discourse-critical model. I have chosen it for two reasons. The first is that Green's model looks for "language in use," which comes close to a missiological approach, as it already supports the idea that texts are useful things. The second is because missiologists Johannes Nissen (2002) and Terry Muck (2003) both appeal to his work.

In his article, *Matthew, Mission and Method*, Nissen coordinates reader-response principles with a Gadamerian fusion of horizons, basing them upon Green's communication-oriented model that looks at what stands "behind," "in," and "in front" of the text (pp. 73-75).[91] This model integrates the interests of (1) historical, "author-centered," and background criticisms as "behind" the text, (2) "message-centered," text-oriented, literary, structural, and linguistic concerns as "in" the text, and, (3) "reader-centered" response, ideological, and "local" reading as "in-front" of the text. Nissen sees using this model for missional reading as a means to remain

---

[91] Thiselton (1995, p. 19) ascribes this modeling to Ricoeur.

"true to the past and relevant to the present," and as a guard against "abuse" of texts, such as, "The Great Commission" (p. 76).

If we look at Green's model using the missiological perspectives developed in previous chapters, we can see a number of strengths. He integrates interdisciplinary points of inquiry, which makes the model compatible and appealing for missiological inquiry. He also shows the places of people, language, and the socio-cultural contexts that both precede and follow the text's composition, which are of high concern to missiology.

We can also see that there are open places within the model, which could be augmented by considering aspects that are of special value for missiology. These are outlined in Figure 8 below.

The first open space is the relationship that could be considered to be "above"[92] the text, which considers divine purpose as a larger frame at cosmic or transcendent levels. The second is the relationship that runs "through" the text, from the angle of God's purposes as they develop into, through, and beyond time. These purposes proceed from the *missio Dei*, before creation or human society. They precede the composition of the text and extend through the process of its composition. As such, they involve the work of God within history and human society that forms the background for the text. They also include God's purpose for bringing the text into being.

This shifts Green's model to integrate it with a missiological concept of *process*, of ongoing and developing *missio*.[93] Viewed this way, God's purposes above and through stand essentially, "behind the 'Behind'" of the text's composition and both before and within the "In" and "In Front." God's purposes also extend beyond the text and its readers, continuing toward the cosmic conclusion of the *missio Dei* at the end of history, standing far "in front of the 'in Front.'"

---

[92] Theology that proceeds transcendentally "from above" and historically "from below" are two aspects that Van Engen (1996, p. 37) proposes for missiological interpretation.

[93] A process-oriented understanding of this model is more temporal in character than Green's conceptualization. Green does not conceive of these aspects as extending on a temporal line that stretches from past to future. He considers them to be interrelated locations of examination that are in the present (2011).

In this model, divine purposes coexist with, suffuse, and transcend the composer and the composer's milieu. They are involved with the cultural and linguistic systems that the composer may use, and they are active within all of the readers and reading contexts related to biblical reading. The view is that God is at work, he has been at work, and he intends still to be at work in all of these components. His purposes stand "through" and "above" the "Behind," the "In," and the "in Front" (Figures 9-11).[94]

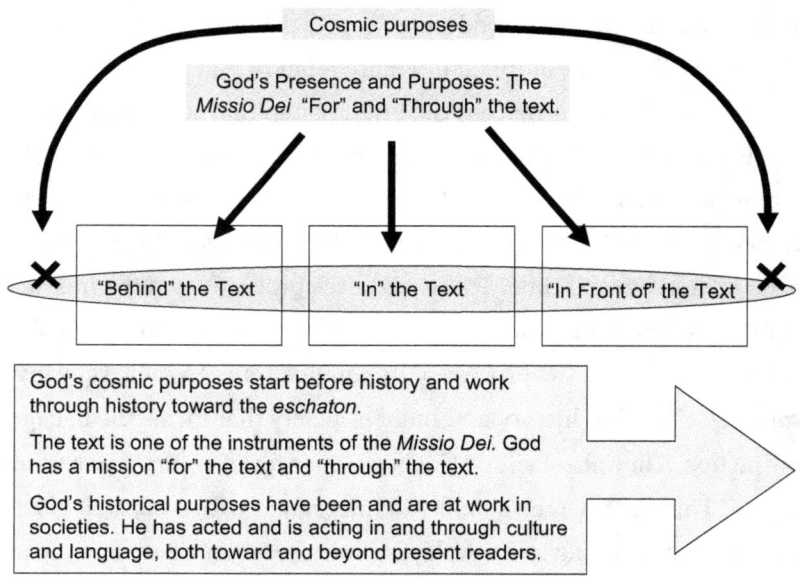

Figure 8. Mission purposes "for" and "through" the "Behind," "In" and "In Front." Reprinted from *In Search of the Contours of a Missiological Hermeneutic* (p. 107), by A.D. Ayers, 2011, Pasadena: Fuller Theological Seminary. Copyright Adam D. Ayers. Reprinted with permission.

---

[94] Figures 8-11 are intentionally similar to Van Engen and Shaw's "Four Horizons" diagrams (2003, pp. 68-99), but are designed to reveal a different set of concepts.

Another space can be seen when we consider the capacity of the text to fulfill multiple uses, that is, its instrumental potential within the missio Dei. Missiology is concerned with how God can use a text to accomplish his work in a variety of ways (shown in black arrows, below, Figure 9). This angle of examination does not look to disambiguate the text or to produce a reading for a particular reading context, but instead focuses on the latent potentials of the text. It seeks to discern what the dimensions of the text might be that make varying fulfillments possible. This looks for the scope of how the text might become fulfilled as a variety of readers may encounter it. It keeps in mind the inexhaustibility of the text while observing the features of the text that simultaneously create functional limits on the text's instrumentality.

Assessment of this potential concentrates on the region between the "In" dimension and those concrete, particular, contextual fulfillments that come into being as the text is actually read and used "in Front." It also directs attention between any particular use that expresses from one particular reading in one particular context and other particular uses that arise from readings in other particular contexts.

One more aspect comes from missiology's concern for the ways in which textual uses can stand between communities at the "in-Front" stage. Missiology sees God at work in the whole world, and missiology is concerned with the relations that exist between multiple readers and reading communities. Missiology envisions extended fulfillment of the text's instrumental potentials through inter-reader dialog. This happens as the text is used by certain readers to achieve ends with other readers, who are also using the text.

In other words, the text can find fulfillment within its readers through a particular reading, but it has an added dimension of fulfillment as readers share their readings with readers beyond themselves. This means that there is not an isolated or single line between the text and a particular reading context, which ends at that reading, for that context. There are multiple lines between multiple contexts and multiple readings, which point beyond themselves to readings and contexts in which the text's potentials are yet to be actualized or fulfilled.

Put another way, if we allow that God may have a plan for the text, and that his plan for the text may be a part of his plan throughout history, we can look for a text to be used in a cumulative way that relates to all contexts in which it is read. This entails examining how God's purposes in and through the text at one reading relate to what he has done or is doing via other readings. It is a concern for how God is accomplishing a full work through the entire, combined event of biblical reading. Thus, localized, contextual readings are interlaced with all readings that have been performed and are being performed throughout the development of the biblical reading tradition (Figure 9).

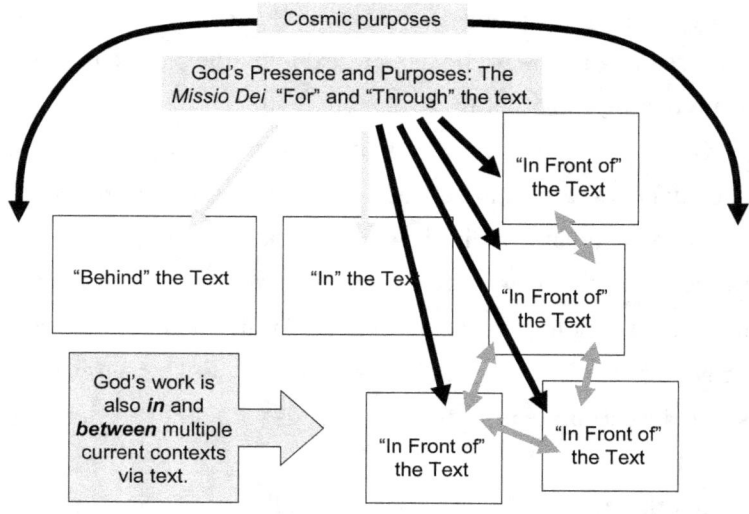

Figure 9. Multiple-context relations at the "in Front of" stage. Reprinted from *In Search of the Contours of a Missiological Hermeneutic* (p. 108), by

A.D. Ayers, 2011, Pasadena: Fuller Theological Seminary. Copyright Adam D. Ayers. Reprinted with permission.

Figure 9 builds on Figure 8; thus, the arrow in Figure 8 should be assumed as undergirding the diagram. While Figure 8 looks at the role of missio within the overall biblical event and tradition, Figure 9 depicts how the missio Dei that has informed composition and tradition informs and links "in Front" readings. In this chart, the missio Dei not only works before, in and through the past; it also is at work in all contemporary contexts in which the Bible might be being read and used. In this scheme, God's overall purposes in the world drive his work in various contemporary contexts, and his purposes for various contexts drive reading events within those contexts. This divine activity links varied reading contexts and events together as participants in what God is working on a kingdom scale. As these varied readings are performed, they intermingle God's purposes in the world at large with God's purposes in and for the text. This creates continuity between contemporary readers and events and those readers and readings that have been done since the time of the text's composition. Thus, the work of God that drives the event of biblical composition meets with God's overall purposes in the world, producing a variety of fulfillments in multiple contexts at the "in Front of" stage. These readings interact with each other, further fulfilling the text's potentials to accomplish God's work. Looking for the ways that the tradition of the text and the purposes of God relate during these fulfillments distinguishes a missiological agenda from an agenda that reads for a single "in-Front" of the text.

However, God's purposes for text and world do not end at contemporary readings, and the missiological view does not stop there. For, even as missiology considers the text, the tradition that has developed and the interstices between people, it also anticipates the continuance and expansion of the kingdom reading event. That greater event is driven by the *missio Dei*, which has intentions for biblical reading that exceed contemporary readings.

This view requires that ongoing attention be given to many potential, future "in-Fronts." These various "in-Fronts" may exist separately from each other now, or they may not have been encountered yet. This concern looks beyond historic or contemporary uses by deliberately anticipating potential uses (Figure 10). It thinks about how the text might be taken up in future readings and employed in forthcoming service to God's plan, and it seeks to reach forward to set the stage for those fulfillments. That is, it looks for "what meanings may come" in places and times and among people with which it is not yet connected. This broadens missiological reading significantly and sets it apart from particular, contextual, or vernacular readings, even while it allows missiology to integrate those agenda.

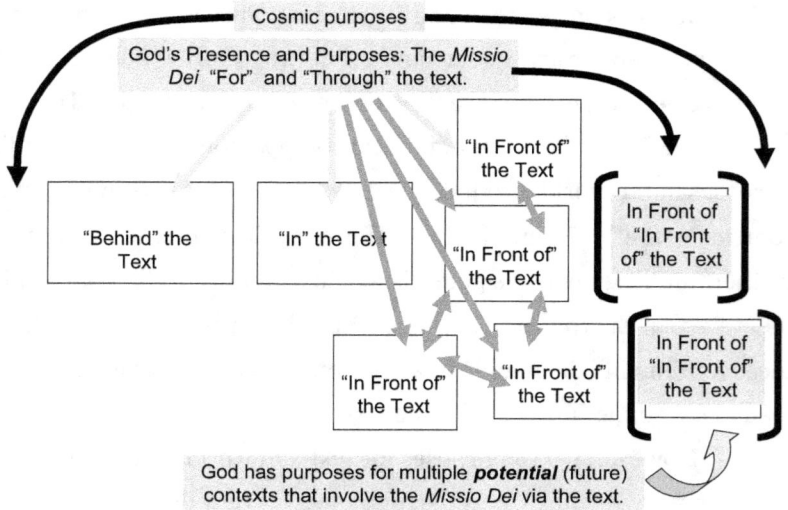

Figure 10. Multiple potential contexts and uses. Reprinted from *In Search of the Contours of a Missiological Hermeneutic* (p. 109), by A.D. Ayers, 2011,

Pasadena: Fuller Theological Seminary. Copyright Adam D. Ayers.
Reprinted with permission.

As a reminder, this is not a missiological critique of Green's model. As noted above, Green's work is not organized around a missiological outlook, and it does not use a temporal or process progression scheme; it has other, very fruitful aims. The point here is simply to see the features of a temporal, process-oriented approach using Green's work as a backdrop. This allows us to chart missiological conceptions about potential and actual uses and to integrate them with the idea of the *missio Dei* as a unified project that has been, is and will be expressed through history.

Summary

Early in Part I we saw how missiological viewpoints inform the ways that missiology approaches interpretation, generally, and where missiology can stand in relation to other theories. We also saw how missiological concerns impact missiological understandings of texts, authors and meaning. In this chapter we have seen how those commitments can inform missiological strategies for negotiating more practical interpretive issues involving temporal and social contexts and textual potentials. In Part II we will see how these points set the stage for the development of missiological method, that is, how they can give rise to concrete practices for reading the text in a missiological manner.

As we move toward those applied sections, summary points to retain are that missiological understanding of Context relates to missiological understanding of Kingdom, especially when treating issues of time, place, or group. Within the Kingdom/Context scheme, missiological reading recognizes the value of particular, local reading, but it also relates particular readings to overarching events and groups, such as the entire *event* of biblical reading and the entire *group* of biblical readers. Because of this, missiological reading is concerned with multiple and potential uses of the text, as well as localized and singular uses, and it views these uses relative to God's greater kingdom work across contexts.

Finally, missiological reading considers textual backgrounds, textual composition, precedent readings, contemporary readings and potential readings to be interrelated, due both to God's overall work in the world and his work in and through the text. These parts and their aspects may be observed in relation to each other using dialectic or contrast schemes. All and each of these parts are understood to be suffused with human and divine purpose, whether they are viewed separately or as a whole.

Part II

Chapter 5: Missiological Method: Text as Topography

In Part II we shift away from looking at the larger project of missiological hermeneutics and begin to build applicable method through the use of models. In Chapter 5 you will find the first of two practical approaches to missiological reading; Chapter 6 presents a second. These two methods can be applied separately or combined as stages in a single process. Even though they look at missio from different perspectives, both approaches intersect at a common focus on textual purpose. Although differing, both methods should be considered missiological approaches, since both assume purpose, both look for textual instrumentality and both integrate academic concerns that overlap at points with other interpretive approaches.

The first method, *Topographic Analysis* (abbr., TA) (Ayers, 2011) views the text as a sociolinguistic landscape that invites negotiation by the reader. This approach treats the text as an architecture that produces intended outcomes in the reader as the reader engages its features. The second method looks at the text using the idea of mission as an anchor for inquiry. It uses three related yet distinct viewpoints as its filters, examining the text as a *Product of Mission*, as a *Ground for Mission* and as a *Tool within Mission* (Ayers, 2012).

Models For Missiological Reading

In *Models of Contextual Theology*, Stephen Bevans (1992, p. 6) notes, "Models, in the same way as images and symbols, provide ways through which one knows reality in all its richness and complexity." Paul Ricoeur (2003, p. 101) observes a similar function of metaphor, "[M]etaphor confers an 'insight.'...in effect, an irreducible intellectual operation, which informs and clarifies in a way that is beyond the scope of any paraphrase." Henri Matisse likewise proposes that in art, "[I]t is the painters who, by creating images, allow the objects and scenes of nature to be seen. Without them we could distinguish objects only by their different functions of utility or comfort" [radio transcript, quoted in (Flam, 1978, p. 91)].

I provide these far-flung interdisciplinary remarks in order to show a common observation, that people sometimes need constructs to bring them to understandings that otherwise would remain unavailable. This is a place where missiology, hermeneutics, and general academics can meet. For if the end goal of inquiry is to bring people to new understandings of texts, and if that goal sometimes requires the use of models, then we can wed missiological theory with missiological modeling in the hope of bringing people to missiological understandings of texts.

In order to get a sense of the robustness of missiological inquiry, we will explore two distinct modalities. The Topographic Analysis method is highly interdisciplinary and heavily reliant upon modeling. It will require a bit more introductory explanation, so the first part of the chapter will describe the model; while the last half will show how to apply it. The second method, Product, Ground, and Tool, is less modeled and has more similarity to methods that are currently used in biblical studies, so the better part of Chapter 6 will address application.

An overview of the Topographic Method. Theoretically, topographic method builds upon proposals about worldview and mental mapping that have been put forward by anthropologists Paul Hiebert (1994) and Charles Kraft (2008), in combination with observations about missiological reading made by Christopher Wright (2004). It also relies upon discussions about knowledge formation from Michael Polanyi (1975) and the functions of linguistic signs per Ferdinand de Saussure (1986) and Paul Ricouer (2003). On literary levels, it incorporates concepts about the nature of literary horizons forwarded by Hans Georg Gadamer (2004) with reader-response principles described by Wolfgang Iser (1980) and Jerry Camery-Hoggatt (1992). We will not be delving deeply into theory here, since the focus is on method, but I encourage the reader to explore the theory that undergirds this proposal (Ayers, 2011).

The basic concept behind the model is one of mapping contours. This needs to be distinguished from the classic literary use of *topos* or *topoi* in the sense of *topics* or lines of thought. Instead, the idea here is that texts may be understood as sociolinguistic terrains, or topographies, which readers can negotiate ("press themselves into") with various degrees and kinds of engagement. These topographies present aspects of resistance and yield that interact with various aspects of the reader as the reader makes his way through the text's architecture. As readers interact with the text, the text's features impact specific points of the reader, with the end result that specific outcomes are produced. When outcomes are produced that the text was designed to produce, the *missio* of the text can be understood to have been *fulfilled*.

An overview of the Product, Ground, and Tool Method. The Product, Ground, and Tool model (abbr., PGT) is more process oriented, or *diachronic*, and it is more linked to the missiological metanarrative (Chapters 3 and 4, above). It is more extended in time, and it looks at different aspects of the text as they relate to a larger, overarching project. Each dimensional view, 1) Product, 2) Ground, and 3) Tool, reveals a type of missio that is crucial to the text. These are taken together to get a sense of the text's overall missio.[95]

The first angle of view, *Product*, looks at the purposes that influenced the text's formation, that is, how the text itself is a result of *missio*. The second viewpoint, *Ground*, looks at how the text can serve as an authoritative source to inform *missio*, that is, as a guide for how to fulfill *missio*. The third viewpoint, *Tool*, examines the text's capacity as an instrument. It explores potential ways that the text itself can be used as a means to accomplish things within the actual performance of *missio*.

While they do not correspond precisely, the dimensions that this model looks for hearken to textual dimensions that are currently examined by a variety of criticisms used in biblical and literary studies. Particularly, these dimensions have similarities to Joel Green's "Behind, In, and In Front of" aspects that were used as a backdrop in Chapter 4.

Combining Topographic and Product, Ground, and Tool methods. Both of the methods outlined above center their inquiries at the idea of purpose. Both presume that texts can be designed and used in order to bring about a desired end. Both assume that the agenda to achieve a designed end constitutes a text's missio, and that when the outcome of interacting with the text matches the end that God desires, it fulfills missio Dei. This idea must be kept in mind throughout the rest of this discussion, for it supplies the basic missiological orientation for what follows.

When combining the two, it will work better for topographic examination to be done first, and then to use the topographic results when looking look for Product, Ground, and Tool dimensions. This is because the topographic analysis focuses more on what the text is designed to bring about in any reader, while Product, Ground, and Tool analysis relates certain readers and contexts to the overarching project of mission. Thus, results from topographic analysis can be used readily for PGT inquiries, but the

---

[95] The gestaltic nature of the PGT is crucial to keep in mind, since no single view can account for all of the text's purpose.

results from PGT would require abstracting inference (similar to "reverse engineering") in order to aid with topographic observations.

Topographic Reading as Missiological Reading

The idea behind topographic reading is that the text presents a situation that the reader must negotiate, and that when the reader does so, the reader is affected according to the designs of the text. This concept shifts the focus of inquiry away from looking for the information that the reader may gain, re-aiming interpretation at looking for the effects that are accomplished.

In some ways, this is not a new concept. Reader response criticisms and aesthetic response criticisms have focused on similar goals for a long time. However, as Redford (2007) has highlighted, unlike traditional response criticisms, missiological commitments overtly include spiritual responses in the catalog of responses that a text can elicit and they place the reader in a subordinate yet cooperative relationship with the text.

Because *missio Dei* is a focal point of missiological inquiry, missiology approaches the text simultaneously as a sociolinguistic artifact and as a sacred implement that has a part to play in God's purposes. This commitment qualifies a missiological view of the role that readers and their agenda play. Since the human element interacts with divine presence and intention, the focus rests equally upon divine purposes that are being brought into fulfillment *as* the reader responds. Thus, while human readers play a crucial part in the production of meaning, missiologically speaking, the text is not a construct that is sustained by the reader or reading community, alone. Missiology does not valorize the capacity that the reader has to sustain, construct or deconstruct a text; it equally emphasizes how the text is sustained by God; especially, how it serves to accomplish divine ends and to facilitate the reader's interaction with God and others. This means that the text is not a neutral object that can be appropriated by anyone for any purpose. Instead, the text is primarily God's word, given to people, who are responsible to hold the production of its meaning in joint interaction with God and the community of faith.

Missiological meaning. At this point, I want to give a qualifying reminder about how missiology approaches meaning on human levels. Missiology places high value upon the idea that "word and deed" are inseparable aspects of mission. Thus, for missiological reading, the idea of meaning should not be understood only in terms of word, it needs to take into account what goes into human deed, and how the two are wed. Meaning thus needs to be active and to involve the full complexity of human existence. It cannot be reduced to cognition.

Paul Hiebert (2008) makes much of this throughout his writings.[96] He emphasizes repeatedly that worldview involves far more than the cognitive aspects that are implied in the concepts *weltanschaaung* or *zeitgeist*, holding that during the introduction of these terms philosophical biases inappropriately limited their conceptual ranges. He demonstrates that worldview exists in cognitive, affective, and evaluative (moral and spiritual) dimensions, and that these carry indispensable modes of knowing. This undergirds his claim that all aspects of human existence must be taken into account when approaching the Bible. He exhorts,

> In our modern worldview with its emphasis on cognitive truth and its divorce of truth from feelings and morals for the sake of objectivity, it is important to remember that in Scripture these three dimensions – the cognitive, the affective, and the moral – are not separated. They are all present in every human experience. They are all central to the gospel message. (2008, p. 291)

A missiological idea of meaning therefore emphasizes that the whole person can be engaged, and missiological interpretation looks for the ways in which

---

[96] This is a concept that can be found in a many of Hiebert's works, especially *Anthropological Reflections on Missiological Issues* (1994), *Anthropological Insights for Missionaries* (1985) and *Incarnational Ministry: Planting Churches In Band, Tribal, Peasant, And Urban Societies* (1999). Hiebert published prolifically (nearly one hundred articles and books during his career). For brevity's sake, I will be citing mainly from his last work, *Transforming Worldviews* (2008).

the text can engage the whole person. In a mission outlook, understanding the text can involve the reader's spiritual existence, affective state(s), volitional or moral commitments, and relational dispositions, along with what is generally considered to be "mental" perceptions.[97]

Engaging topographies. An analogy might be helpful at this point. If we look at the text as a situation that a person may engage, we can draw a parallel to a playground "jungle gym." The playground jungle gym is an object, but it is an object with particular features that can be engaged by someone playing upon it. The one who plays on the gym supplies activity, but he does not set the features or configuration of the equipment. The designer of the jungle gym has arranged its parts so that certain activities and ranges of movement are possible in some places, and not in others. While one part of the jungle gym requires strength from the user, another part demands flexibility. One section may require focus or precision, another part, coordination, another part may demand risk-taking and courage, etc. The designer has done this with the express purpose of supporting certain kinds of exercise that help children to develop in specific ways.

The same holds true for an obstacle course. In an obstacle course, the obstacles are the essential features that make the course what it is, and they are designed to impact the paths of those who run the course in very considered ways. Yet, design is not enough to make a course. Design intentions have to be given concrete form as the underlying concept is actualized in construction. In the real process of construction, tangible necessities come into play; these interact with the design concept in order to yield the course's final form.

---

[97] Jerry Camery-Hoggatt makes a similar point from the angle of the function of irony in the Gospel of Mark. He holds that meaning involves a full range of evoked reactions and that there are non-logical aspects of language (1992, pp. x-xi). He observes, "Irony implies that more is going on than mere information can grasp, and that discipleship must be an activity of personal response as well as an activity of intellectual assent; that is, the ironic dimensions of the passion may *effect* the kind of commitment which for Mark lies at the core of discipleship" (1992, p. 10).

When construction actualizes design, it transforms abstract intention into a concrete thing that real runners can engage. Even though design is a dominant factor, neither design nor construction are finally determinant by themselves, and neither can be used alone to account fully for the course. Rather, both contribute to the overall reality that is the final course as it actually has been constructed.

Concrete influences obtain even when the ones who do the construction try their very best to realize the designer's ends as they build. As the course takes real shape, it always bears the traits of both the designer and the constructors. It is important to remember that during construction the attention and concerns of the constructors naturally differ from those of the designer because they are aimed at different tasks, even though constructors may keep design in mind as they built. While the designer may have been thinking more about runners and their exercise, the constructors' immediate concerns may have been directed toward satisfying the designer and negotiating construction challenges. The production process fuses these varying intentions, for when constructors seek to satisfy the designer, they join their own intentions to satisfy and build with the designer's intentions that the course would impact runners in the desired ways. Thus, even while the course will bear telltales of both the constructors' and the designer's purposes, the course can be considered as a single work. Any topographic analysis of an obstacle course then would look at the features of the course as it has actually been constructed, in order to discern how the design and construction work together to affect runners in specific ways.

These dynamics parallel what we already have seen about the coexistence of combined purposes within texts and the telltales that those leave. If we consider the missio of the text as the intended outcome for runners who negotiate it, we can see that the textual missio undergirds the conceptual layout of the text's features. However, as that intention takes form during concrete composition, elements from textual constructors interact with missio, giving the text distinct, concrete, expressive features. If the interpreter attends to those features, the undergirding design, the desired outcomes and the compositional influences will show through. Thus, topographic analysis of a text looks to see how those combined influences have produced a work that impacts those who engage it in specific ways, and it looks to see how the features of the text reveal the influences that joined in its construction.

Topographic analysis of biblical texts takes this approach in a way that considers God's designer role. It looks at the features of the text in order to discern how the text has been arranged to impact the readers who negotiate it in specific ways. Just as analysis of an obstacle course's features can lend insight into the designer's agenda, analysis of features in a biblical text can reveal the agenda of the Bible's designers. Since missiology holds that God is a contributing author in the biblical composition, this kind of analysis is understood to be able to reveal God's agenda, along with the agendas of his people.

Meaning as understanding and fulfillment. As a caveat, it must be kept in mind throughout topographic analysis that all of these factors truly come together when someone runs the course. The end result that the designers had in mind is produced as runners negotiate the course, not as the course sits empty and under analysis. The final goal is not for people to comprehend the course as much as it is for runners to run the course.

The runners and their running, however, do not create the course; they *fulfill* the course's design as they engage it, which means that the outcome that the course has upon them can be construed as the fulfillment of the course's *missio*. In a similar manner, the Bible does not yield its full meaning as it is analyzed, even if analysis is looking for the text's designed outcome. Rather, the Bible yields its full meaning when readers engage it, negotiate it and respond, being affected by its contours.

We could distinguish between these two aspects of meaning by calling one, "reading for *understanding*" of the text, and calling another, "reading for a *fulfillment*" of the text. Ideally, missiological reading tries to achieve both. It seeks the first, the understanding meaning, in order to facilitate the second, the fulfillment reading, in a combined agenda that stems from missiology's commitment to mission as word and deed. Topographic analysis assists the overall process by producing an understanding meaning *about* how the text's fulfillment meaning can be achieved. It does this in order to support the fulfillment of the text's mission, its textual *missio*. Thus, the missiological reader reads like an athlete who both studies an obstacle course in order to discern what it will require of him and who then proceeds to run that course in an informed manner.

In the scheme that we've been talking about, engagement, or negotiation, is crucial to the production of textual meaning. Engagement is provided by the reader's dynamism, which in turn activates the text's own voice and presence (Ayers, 2011). These reflect back upon the reader, affecting the reader as the reader moves through the structures of the text, bringing about both the transformation of the reader and the fulfillment of the text.

Purposes are understood to suffuse this situation at every level. These purposes can be observed by paying attention to the ways in which topographic resistance and/or yield serves to inform the reader's dynamic engagement. This dynamic engagement is also affected by the reader's own linguistic capacities, horizons, and orientations relative to the text.

Topographic Theory

Although method is the primary focus of this discussion, a minimum summary of theory is in order, so that the method can be understood and used effectively. Below, you will find highlights of the theoretical foundations for a topographic approach.

Missiological concepts of mapping. As we have seen above, topographic analysis uses the idea of mapping as its modeling strategy. This concept has already shown up in missiological and related discussions, but it has not yet been developed as a distinct strategy for reading. For example, in

Anthropological Reflections on Missiological Issues, Paul Hiebert proposes that worldviews function as "maps" of reality. Charles Kraft uses the concept in a similar manner, holding that "models" and "maps" provide "tentative ways of perceiving Reality." Although he does not cite Hiebert,[98] Wright uses a very similar analogy, holding that hermeneutic frameworks operate as "valid" maps that allow readers to make their ways through textual terrain, observing certain landmark features. Polanyi also uses a "map" analogy to describe the manner in which personal knowledge is created through the use of skill. Later, his point is that three-dimensional understanding integrates focal-subsidiary viewing through imagination, which reveals but does not explain. He calls this a "tacit triad" (1975, pp. 53-56).

Wright uses the map/landscape analogy more in a rhetorical way than as theoretic description, and he does so in a very limited sense. However, taken together, Hiebert, Kraft, Wright, and Polanyi show the usefulness of approaching the formation of knowledge as the mapping of a "terrain," or "topography." If we in turn apply the concept of "mapping" to describe how a text forms knowledge within its reader, it is possible to look for the ways in which texts fulfill specific missions by looking at the architectures of the maps that are presented to readers. If texts create maps for readers, the architecture of each text's map can reveal what kind of knowledge the text is designed to form in its readers. In other words, if we can discern the features of the map that the text presents, we can see where the textual map is designed to get the reader to arrive.

I have discussed the sociolinguistic underpinnings of this notion at greater length previously (2011), so I will only sketch the basics of it here, As an introduction, theoretically speaking, this model can be based upon the notion that reading is a dynamic process in which readers negotiate the presence of an arrangement of symbols. Because readers must negotiate the presence of these symbols, which have sociolinguistic bonds to each other,

---

[98] Wright cites a dialog with Anthony Billington (2004, pp. 138-139).

the symbolic arrangement can be understood to form a sociolinguistic structure, that is to say, a textual architecture.

The model rests upon the idea that readers want to understand as they read, and that texts exploit the human desire to understand by presenting varied opportunities for understanding, which are set against resistances to understanding. Taken together in a linear fashion, the various points open up a pathway of least resistance and greatest promise for the reader, which directs the reader toward a designed end. Along the way, the text's resistances and yields make demands on different aspects of the reader's experience, which affect the reader, shaping the reader as she proceeds toward the text's designed end for her (Figure 11).

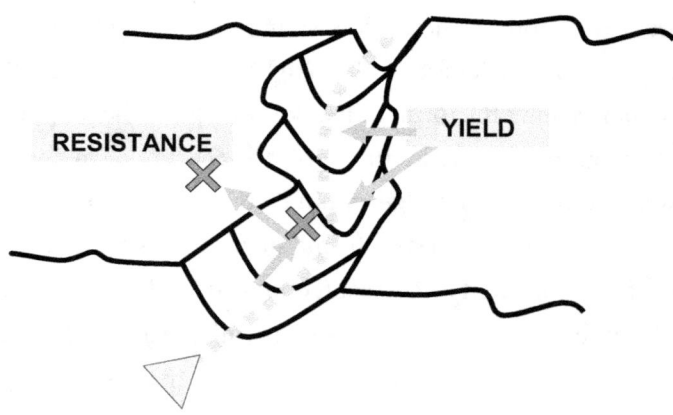

Figure 11. Resistance and Yield. Reprinted from *In Search of the Contours of a Missiological Hermeneutic* (p. 308), by A.D. Ayers, 2011, Pasadena: Fuller Theological Seminary. Copyright Adam D. Ayers. Reprinted with permission.

In this scheme, textual missio is fulfilled immediately by the resistances and yields that the reader encounters directly in front of him at any given place along the path's process, and eventually by the overall end outcome of the path. This means that any section of a text can be examined in reference to two points of topographic missio, a more localized *immediate* missio, and an overarching, *eventual* missio.

In the text of something like a joke, the *immediate* missio of a line or section might be to mislead, confuse or exaggerate, while the *eventual* missio could be to surprise, to condemn through satire or to elicit feelings of relief, all of which could be experienced as humor. Thus, an immediate missio might differ significantly from an eventual missio, even though the immediate missio serves the eventual missio in a supporting or contributing relationship. Essentially, the immediate missio is a sub-missio that should be understood in light of the eventual missio, while the eventual missio should be understood as a composite outcome that is produced through the combined outcomes of contributing, immediate *missios*.

Topographic space. In order see texts as landscapes that accomplish missio via the contours of their topographies we must be able to conceive of how readers move through both immediate and eventual stretches of text in a spatial manner. Paul Ricoeur's use of I. A. Richards is helpful for this. In *The Rule of Metaphor*, Ricoeur highlights Richards' observation that metaphor operates by bringing into play "an absence in the context" by virtue of the "interanimation" that takes place as terms are located in relation to each other (2003, pp. 90-91), In other words, for Ricouer and Richards, the meaning of metaphor resides in the "space" between two symbols that have been juxtaposed in relationship.

A similar idea is developed in reader-response theory by Wolfgang Iser. In Iser's work, *the Act of Reading*, he builds an aesthetic-response theory in which he proposes that reader dynamism is elicited as a response to a "constitutive blank," or "no-thing" (1980, p. 167) that the reader fills-in because of the reader's drive to create gestaltic coherence in the face of indeterminacy (1980, pp. 160-167; 182-203). This is similar to the dynamic impulse to fill interstices by supplying information that Camery-Hoggatt describes (1992, pp. 63-64).[99] Taken together, Ricoeur's, Iser's and Camery-Hoggatt's observations show that a sort of "open" place is created between symbols in a text through a composer's arrangement. In the topographic model, it is this negative space that the reader negotiates when she traverses the topography of a text.

Mountains and Canyons. Expanding upon the concepts above, we can note that space exists as a relational function between other things. On the surface, it appears that space is a place, but it is actually that which obtains between places. We could say that space is constructed as a *situation*, not as an *object*. If we conceive of meaning in terms of negative space situations, meaning becomes a construction that is "there" and "not there" at the same time. Meaning as a construction thus can have discernible contours as a situation of reference between the factors that give rise to it, but it is not a thing in and of itself.

The implications of such a notion are complex and can only be explored in full elsewhere. This is only a sketch, and again I refer the reader to my 2011 work, where I explore theory about the dynamics of language and symbol that can support the concept. As an overview, however, it appears that much of the conversation in literary theory addresses the idea of meaning as a nominal, as an event, a condition, a behavior, a place, or an object. Such a view treats meaning like a mountain, a place that is a place by virtue of being "there."

By contrast, when sense is viewed as a responsive situation within a construction of space, the text's production of meaning looks more like an opportunity to move through a canyon than the presence of a mountain. Although it is a temporary effect in his theory, Iser calls this kind of empty space a "hollow section," which opens immediately in front of the reader (1980, p. 112). Canyons, like holes, are places that really are not there, at all. They exist in a qualified sense, only as features of negative contour. Still,

---

[99] Camery-Hoggatt appeals to the work of Seymour Chatman as his foundation.

even though they are "not there," people can talk meaningfully to each other about this or that canyon or hole and its contours; they can even speak of having visited or hiked one.[100] Interestingly, we must recognize that such talk is essentially practical and not actual, since people are talking about visiting, hiking, and experiencing the features that surround an *absence* in the terrain rather than a *presence*.

Dynamic meaning situations. Textual space is not enough to sustain a missiological model for reading. We also need to be able to conceptualize how readers can engage textual space dynamically and how that in turn grants texts the capacity to fulfill purposes. In order to account for dynamism, I want to rely on Iser's idea of a "hollow" that gestaltic forces urge the reader to fill. Iser understands this to create a form of mutual dynamism between the reader and the text (pp. 107-118). The opening of symbolic space can be understood as a type of vacuum, which the drive to perceive within human consciousness seeks to fill.

Iser makes much of the temporariness of this process, but for our model it is not necessary to conceive of textual features opening and closing before and behind the reader. However, it is helpful to note that perceptive filling is not permanent; it is something that happens when the symbols are engaged by human experience. In this scheme, meaning is a joint function of the symbols, the space between them, and the activity of the reader. Meaning is not unilaterally supplied, nor is it inherent. Words do not necessarily create meaning by placing something into perception or by encoding meaning. Rather, it is the way that perception moves around and through symbols and discourse, the way in which active experience negotiates the interstices between them, that creates meaning. Meaning is

---

[100] Jeanrond flirts with the same image briefly, "Metaphorically speaking, the text is rather in the nature of a path to be trodden by the reader. We are dealing here with a dominant perspective, a central direction. This dominant perspective, however, only becomes clear when considering several subsidiary perspectives in the width of the vista, and then only when the path is followed at all -- that is to say, through reading the text"(1988, p. 88).

the entire functional situation that results when people engage the presence of symbols.

Missiologically speaking, the key to this model is that it is active, and that purpose pervades the whole situation. Each part serves an end, and, because each part serves an end, each part carries purpose, whether it is to satisfy the urge to perceive, to create space, to invite perception, or to inform engagement. From one side, the composer's purpose is a factor, because it provides design. On another side, social purpose suffuses the language itself because words are social instruments that have been created, and later composed, under the influence of sociocultural intentions. On still another side, the reader brings purpose to the text through the will to engage or perceive.

Using juxtaposition to see dynamic meaning. This is methodologically significant, because any of the factors that come together to form a topography may be examined for its purpose, by using the "focal-subsidiary" grounding that we looked at when we considered joint composers. By way of review, in focal-subsidiary examination, one thing is held in focus and viewed against the backdrop of another thing, which is deliberately held out of focus. This forms a kind of fraction in which one concern carries the place of an enumerator and another the place of the denominator. The thing in focus is viewed *per* the thing in the background.

For missiological examination, this can be accomplished by juxtaposing the purposes of individuals, institutions, society, or God. For example, the purpose that God may have for the text to elicit a certain response from a reader may be seen vis á vis a certain individual's purposes for reading that text. Viewed another way, a society's purposes might be seen vis á vis an author's. Or, the purposes that inform a society's language game may be observed vis á vis the purposes that obtain in the Kingdom of Heaven, etc. These are a few among a wide variety of combinations.

The root idea remains that the composition of symbols into discourse creates a complex situation that has discernible contours. These contours serve to inform and guide the reader as the reader engages them. This entire situation, not any one of its parts, carries the text's *missio* and constitutes its full "meaning," although each component has a particular, contributive *missio* and a particular, contributive meaning.

Points to Remember. Four points should be kept in mind in order to use this model missiologically. First, the interpreter must remember that the dimensions (and thus, capacity) of any textual topography depend heavily on the joint functions of social distance and the language system that is used by a group. In other words, the degree to which a reader is involved with a social system and its language determines how firm the architecture of a text is to him. This means that topography is not established absolutely, even though it may be established with a degree of stability that grants it *enough* capacity to achieve its designed purposes. We will unpack this a bit more below.

This leads to the second point. Since symbols and their architectures are anchored within tradition and culture, aspects of worldview suffuse them, and textual purposes may be discerned in relation to these dimensions. If we use Hiebert's (2008) arrangement of worldview, this would involve cognitive, affective, and evaluative aspects, while Kraft's would involve "motivation, preferences, evaluation and others" (2008, pp. 40-41). Both of these authors assume that spiritual aspects are involved throughout the dimensions, which is a point that Redford is explicit about. I believe that relational, reflexive, and volitional categories also might be helpful (Ayers, 2011).

Thus, analysis of topographic dynamics seeks to assess how the text might impact things like will, feelings, moral dispositions, thoughts, spiritual states, relationships, etc. However, discerning exactly what dimensions obtain would constitute a work in itself, and delineating those aspects cannot be accomplished here. The point for this model is that the full range of holistic aspects that comprise worldview obtain in the symbolic architecture of a text, and that these are open to utilization by the text's missio.

Third, for critical evaluation, analysis is a two-way street. On one side, information about sociocultural backgrounds can help to reveal what the text is up to, by showing how external social agenda have shaped the text. On the flip side, the focus may be reversed so that inferences can be made from the structure of texts to reveal what societies and cultures might value or be up to. This follows a kind of hermeneutic circle between the part or product and the whole or source.

The fourth point relates to the third, but it is an issue of breadth, not of direction. As we saw with immediate and eventual missio, language structures can be viewed using varying scales. By the same token, analytic focus is also scalable. Because texts are produced within larger systems, there is a reciprocal relationship between particular compositions and the greater rules of language within a culture that make them possible. There is also a reciprocal relationship between particular texts and the constellations of texts to which they belong.

Because of this, it is possible to discern large, overarching purposes even from small scale texts, and to follow that line of examination all of the way up to broad situations. Without changing the method significantly, the same agenda can be used to assess grand literary constructions, such as narrative groups or cycles, as is used to assess smaller pieces, such as a couplet in a psalm or a proverb. The same holds true for macro-structures, such as discourses and genres, and for entire corpuses or *oeuvres*. All of these scales of literary construction are undergirded by purposes, and multiple scales of construction may intersect, coexist, obtain and thus, be observed in any particular section of a textual landscape, regardless of the size of that section.

Social Participation. The first point above noted that the stability that results from the social tradition only obtains in direct proportion to the reader's participation with a social group and its language rules (Berger &

Luckmann, 1967).[101] This warrants some development, since it relates to missiology's intercultural concerns. Acknowledging sociolinguistic proximity also integrates missiological reading with philological concerns, grammatical-syntactical concerns and much of the agenda of historical and sociological criticisms, especially in their regard for original uses and backgrounds. However, as we saw in Chapter 4, because missiology understands the text to participate in a cosmic plan that spans all time and peoples, while a missiological approach can work with the idea of social proximity, it does so without supposing that there are final gaps between contexts, such as "Now" and "Then," or "Us" and "Them."

Instead of proposing gap, topographic analysis can treat social proximity as a continuum with horizons. All that has to be understood is that when people are closer to each other socially, textual topography hardens, and textual purposes are in turn strengthened. When people are farther apart socially, textual topographies weaken and textual purposes in turn become weakened.

For example, when people participate with each other in tight proximity, such as in a specialized field of study or in a tightly knit group of friends, special vocabularies and strategies (like "inside jokes") can be used because joint participation in the language system and its rules increases. From a missiological angle, this is a crucial factor, because participation in believing communities also can be understood to create a very particular kind of religious proximity that enables distinctly spiritual aspects of textual architecture to function.[102] However, as social proximity decreases, aspects

---

[101] This is a principle intrinsic to Gadamer's "horizons" and Fish and Rorty's "reading communities." See discussions above.

[102] A prime example of this is covenant relation to God. This social proximity solidifies faith-related aspects of the text, enabling spiritual interaction and meaning, which yields configurations of experience that fulfill the text's spiritual *missio*. The degree to which the reader agrees to pay "the price of admission," (Camery-Hoggatt, 1992, p. 35). The degree to which the reader is willing to "draw nigh to God" (Jas. 4:8, AV) becomes the degree to which the presence and voice of the Holy Spirit become present for the reader.

On another level, if someone is a member of a faith community, she also becomes enabled to respond to the faith-relevant aspects of the symbols and architecture in ways and instances that do not present to readers who are not believers. This means, in turn, that the dynamic spiritual voice and presence of the text and its author(s) become available and speak to

of the socio-linguistic matrix begin to weaken or disappear altogether. When distance keeps readers from participating fully in a linguistic system, the architecture of the topography becomes less secure, less solid, because the rules that connect the language symbols to each other are weaker. This diminishes the text's capacity to present specific kinds of resistance and yield, and thus, to influence particular aspects of the reader's engagement.

If we frame this according to Ludwig Wittgenstein's (1969) linguistic model, when social distance increases, a reader's participation in a group's "language games" diminishes. As this happens, the most sophisticated or delicate textual architectures degrade first, and the most foundational architectures disappear last. Thus, nuances, connotations and highly technical language or highly local idioms first become inaccessible, followed by less technical language and less localized or idiomatic uses, followed by inferences, humor and style, poetic uses, etc., until one gets down to only the most prevalent terms and structures, the rudimentary "core" language game that holds the architecture together.

As each of a language's games capacities disappear, aspects of the topography also disappear. The textual landscape becomes increasingly porous or "marshy," and the text is less and less able to direct the reader. With each increment of social distance, the text loses capacity to fulfill its mission because the socio-linguistic bonds between the symbols, the tradition and the reader fail. Eventually, social distance can overcome a reader's capacity to access any of the language of the text. This happens when the symbols themselves disappear beyond the grasp of an interpreter, as the reader stands completely outside of the language game domain. In such a case, when the reader is beyond the socio-linguistic system altogether and cannot read the text in any way, the topographic space collapses, since no meaningful symbols are present for it to extend between.

---

her in different ways than they do to the person who is less proximate to the text's religious community, which includes the religious tradition and the author(s), especially God.

When this occurs, the purposive capacity of the text is also lost. It is no longer capable of being used to reconfigure experience. This is the only case in which there is true gap between the reader and the text, when the interpreter is no longer able to enter and negotiate any topography between symbols because the symbols do not exist to her. There is no space, since everything is empty. She cannot inform or guide her perception by fitting it into the negative contour-limits of another's symbols because she cannot access those symbols in social space. No aspect of missio can be fulfilled.

Alternate Readings. Because the topographic approach assumes that there is a discernible primary set of outcomes that can be considered the goal of the text, a word is in order about competing or alternate readings, especially deconstructive or ideological readings. The sociolinguistic anchoring of language that we are considering here factors highly in this discussion, for, in contemporary interpretation, much is made of the capacity of the reader to read with his own special interests, such as ideological or deconstructive agenda. In these kinds of strategies, readers are considered to be free to appropriate the text, co-opting it for the reader's own social or literary purposes.

We have already seen the impact that this can have on authorial voices and presences (Chapter 2). In addition to these concerns, in a topographical scheme, the contours of the linguistic architecture are held to be established by sociolinguistic conventions that depend upon common usage, grounded in sociocultural tradition. Thus, when the socially established sense of linguistic symbols is reassigned in counter-conventional, counter-cultural, or counter-traditional ways by an interpreter, novel meanings result because those reassignments effectively alter the dimensions of the negative space, and thus, of the architecture's function.

Since new features that achieve new ends result from reassigning counter conventional significances in the place of conventional significances, the outcome from using these strategies can be considered to be less of a production of reading or interpreting a particular text and more a work of recomposition, reconstruction, or remodeling. That is to say, since a new intention, a new missio, has been applied deliberately and since the result is that the architecture has been reconfigured to satisfy that new missio, a new text with alternate features has been constructed of out the components of an existing text. This is a bit like bull-dozing through a canyon, digging bricks out of a wall and re-mortaring them, or adding sandbags to certain parts of a ravine.

While it is a legitimate pursuit to make new texts out of existing texts, the focus of missiological reading is to discern and to actualize the purposes of the existing, authoritative texts in order to fulfill the text's sacred missio. This puts missiological reading in contrast with intentionally alternate readings, since the goal of alternate reading strategies is openly to supply the purposes of alternate readers to the text

This is a watershed factor for missiological reading, which considers purpose, especially, divine purpose, to be the central focus of inquiry. Thus, while there is certainly value in producing alternative readings, because those readings effectively create new texts and centralize new purposes, there appears to be little ground for them to be considered missiological interpretations. Missiology can acknowledge their productions, but the distinction should be made that while such readings may produce interesting and insightful new texts, their readings fulfill the missios of those new texts and fail to fulfill the missio of the biblical text as it has been constructed. Alternate readings have much to offer, however, since they can contribute to missional conversations about particular projects that are at play in contemporary society. This is especially important when those projects take up the same texts that missiology uses.

The Significance of a Topographic Model. The proposal here is that a topographic model provides a way for missiology to integrate many of the basic agenda of a variety of hermeneutic theories without sacrificing its foundational quest for purpose or its commitments about mission and transcendence. It enables missiological interpreters to acknowledge the validity of multiple interpretations, while still asserting that there can be a central purpose for the text that is integral to its full meaning. The main value is that the model allows any aspect of the meaning situation to be examined with an eye for discerning how that particular aspect helps to influence the reader toward an end.[103]

Summarily, this approach holds that meaning is a purposeful organization of human experience, a dynamic situation, similar to an event, which simultaneously has *synchronic* (all at once) and *diachronic* (in progression) aspects. As such, meaning is both an experiential process and a socio-linguistic arrangement. As a construction, meaning is total; it is not located in or determined by any one of its components; it is a gestalt that requires the interplay of multiple factors in order to exist. Each of these factors is purpose-laden, and each contributes to the purpose of the total situation, the communicative *missio*. Thus, any component factor may be examined for purpose and the entire construction of meaning may be understood from the perspective of any of its related components.

Approaching interpretation this way does not preclude critical approaches that examine traditional aspects of the text; it only nuances them by viewing those aspects as contributing to an overall, purposeful meaning. Perhaps most importantly, the approach empowers missiological readers to expect spiritual and experiential response to the Bible as a crucial dimension of the text's meaning. This supports using the text to engage others in order to accomplish God's purposes. This is fitting, because the goal of missiological interpretation is both to understand and to fulfill God's *missio*, as it is expressed in the biblical text and through human lives in history.

---

[103] The term "reader" includes groups or communities of readers.

From Topographic Model to Missiological Method

There are many ways in which the topographic model can be used for missiological interpretation; some concrete examples will be given in the next section of this book. Before we go on to those, I want to outline a few steps that can be used to make the model function as a method. These steps are not the only steps, and they are not locked in serial order. They are given to provide you with the means to break down aspects of the model for application. Ideally, with practice, these will not be understood as linear steps, but as a constellation of points for critical analysis that the interpreter can draw upon as needed.

As an interim template, four procedural steps are outlined below, along with one operation that can be used at every stage. Each step is described in a summary fashion. Greater explanation of these stages will be given as the steps are applied in Chapters 7-9.

The four procedural stages are: Step One: *Identify features*; Step Two: *Assess impacts on the reader;* Step Three: *Discern outcomes (missio)*; Step Four: *Consider inferences and implications*. The fifth operation, *juxtapose various purposes,* is more of a heuristic device that helps the interpreter to produce results. It provides a filter that can be used at each stage.

Text structures. Step One looks for the structures of the text. This step will be most familiar to persons who have practiced traditional biblical studies and exegesis because this step examines the nuts and bolts that comprise the topography's sociolinguistic architecture. The goal in Step One is to observe how the words and phrases work together, since these functions reveal the text's contours. The focus is on the language and its backgrounds, and the interpreter seeks to understand how the various language components have been brought together in a composition.

In this step, special attention needs to be given to the language conventions that hold the text's architecture together, that is, to the traditions, rules and practices of the language game in which the text was composed. This inquiry relates to traditional exegetical practices that examine grammar and syntax, linguistic backgrounds (philology and etymology), literary devices, rhetorical strategies and arrangements, genre, form and *gattung*, etc. In summary, this step asks, "What are the features of the text's language structures?" and, "How do the text's language features ordinarily function in the text's sociolinguistic tradition (milieu)?"

Text dynamics. Step Two examines textual dynamics. It looks for the ways in which the text's structures affect the reader as the reader tries to make his way through them. This step will be familiar for persons who have experience with approaches such as reader-response criticism, narrative criticism, aesthetic criticism, and various socio-rhetorical analyses, because it looks for the ways in which the reader reacts to or is manipulated by aspects of the text.

However, it cannot be overemphasized that a key distinctive of missiological examination is that the interpreter looks for holistic dimensions of engagement. The goal is to discern the ways in which certain features of the text impact various aspects of human existence, such as affect, volition, morality and values, cognition, relationship, and reflexivity, with special attention being given to spiritual dimensions and responses. The focus is on how the text impacts specific existential dimensions in order to create a pathway of greatest yield and least resistance. When these components are viewed as a process aimed at greater goals (Step Three), they will reveal the overall designed outcome for the reader's experience, which shows the text's missio.

When doing this analysis, the interpreter should keep the linear progression of the text in mind. Since the reader encounters words and phrases one after another, the reader experiences specific impacts from the text's features at different moments, not all at once, and the order of the text's impacts is significant. A text might begin with challenges to *affect* with yields toward a particular *disposition*. The next immediate challenge could address response of *will*; the next might challenge on *spiritual* levels, with yields in the direction of *relationship*; the next might move to challenges of *cognition* with yields toward certain *moral evaluations*, etc. Each of these immediate interactions contribute to the eventual missio, which is the overall configuration of experience that the text was designed to elicit, in all of its dimensions of impact.

The component responses that make up that overall process are the focus of this step, which asks, "How do particular text features and structures affect particular aspects of readers in particular ways?" "How do specific aspects of the text correspond to specific aspects of the reader's existence?" and, "How are the text's resistances and yields organized?"

Reader effects. Step Three assesses how the text affects the reader in terms of designed outcomes. It looks at the effects that the text works upon the reader as they contribute to overall textual goals for the reader's life and experience, including canonical level goals. This step will not be familiar to many readers, as it is concerned with ascertaining the *fulfillment* meaning of the text, which is an emerging hermeneutical agenda of missiological interpretation. The goal is to discern how the text is *fulfilled* as the reader is moved through *immediate* and intermediate states toward *eventual* states. The goal is also to relate the fulfillment of immediate, intermediate and eventual states to the text's design (missio).

The focus here alternates between the immediate outcomes that are produced in the reader and those eventual outcomes at which the text is aimed. Throughout the examination, the immediate outcomes are understood in light of the final outcomes, even as final outcomes are understood to be produced by the cumulative, linear effect of immediate outcomes. Since multiple outcomes are possible, outcomes are evaluated in terms of priority. The interpreter looks to discover the overarching, broadest and highest outcomes first and foremost, followed by secondary, tertiary, and ancillary agenda.

The full scope of potential readers should be kept in mind during this stage. Readers are not uniform; they come from many locations and they have widely varied dispositions toward textual agenda. The interpreter should consider what the goals of the text might be for antagonistic or neutral readers as well as sympathetic readers. The interpreter also should consider the ranges of engagement and disposition, taking into account how the text might have designs for the highly engaged as well as for the reserved, and for resistant as well as compliant readers.

It is also important to remember throughout this stage that *understanding* meaning differs from *fulfillment* meaning. This stage seeks an understanding about the fulfillment meaning; it does not produce the fulfillment meaning, itself.

The key questions for this stage are, "What are the text's goals, for whom?," "What plan does the text have for the reader and her experience?" and, "What does the text value most in its plan for the reader?"

Integrative Relation. Step Four considers inferences and implications that arise from the observations in the preceding steps. It looks at how the missio of the particular text relates to other missio agenda. This step will be familiar to persons who have experience with ideological criticisms, canonical criticism(s), and theological interpretation, especially mission theology. The goal is to discern the significance of the text's missio in light of those larger, broader purposes in which it participates.

The view here is gestaltic; it seeks to integrate the concerns of the text with the overarching concerns out of which the text has arisen. It sees the text as one instrument of change within a constellation of instruments that are aimed at a common ends.

It should be kept in mind that one missio does not necessarily exclude another. Texts can express highly overlapped and complex purposes. Thus, multiple agenda can coexist in a text's missio, and the text can play a role in multiple projects. However, for missiological reading, special attention should be given to the part that the immediate text plays in larger sacred projects, such as the missio Dei, the development of the people of God, the reign of the Divine Kingdom, etc.[104] The task here is to view the text in light of those projects and to understand those projects in light of the text. The focus is on integration.

The key questions for this stage are, "How does this fit with what is going on beyond it?" "How does what this text accomplishes coordinate with what other texts accomplish?" and, "How does the aim of this text contribute to larger scale projects?"

Juxtaposition. Although labeled here as "Step Five," this component is more of a recurring filter than a stage in a process. It is a lens that can be applied at each stage.

Step Five is similar to the work of Step Four, because it takes into account that any given missio does not exist in isolation; missio is always connected to constellations of purposes. However, unlike Step Four, which looks for how the text's missio participates in larger projects, Step Five looks at how differing agenda coexist and often compete within the text. It looks for how the text is an intersection of multiple purposes that are not exactly alike or consonant with each other. This procedure will feel familiar to those who have experience in textual criticism, source criticism and redaction criticism.

The goal for this procedure is to discern the various agenda that reside together within the text. The task is to look for internal tensions and differences that reveal the influences of unlike interests. During application, the interpreter's focus shifts repeatedly to assess the text from the alternate viewpoints of multiple interests. The interpreter juxtaposes one set of interests against another in order to see where and how those interests are represented, muted, qualified, satisfied, thwarted, confirmed, or denied (etc.) relative to the thrust of the text's missio.

---

[104]Van Engen describes this multiplex situation as the expression of the *missio Dei* in multiple, coexistent facets, the *missio hominum*, the instrumentality of people, which is expressed in the *missio ecclesiarum*, the works and presences of the churches, and the *missio politico-oecumenica*, God's work within social structures (1996, pp. 27-28). All of these carry the concept that God works through others and through others' institutions.

In order to apply this lens, the interpreter should keep in mind that texts are sociolinguistic works, and as such they bear the marks of the societies, institutions and language traditions in which they have been composed. The goal is to see how the biases, commitments and values that surround and suffuse the language and the author shape the language and structures of the text, along with the purposes of the author. In other words, here the interpreter looks for how other purposes can "piggyback" and augment, hinder or modify the author's purposes.

Since missiology takes into account God's active presence in people, society, institutions and systems, special attention should be given to God's interests and purposes as one of the text's contributing authors. Since missiology holds the text to be a sacred and inspired word, God's place as a contributing author should be considered foremost and dominant.

Key questions to ask in this procedure are, "Who is up to what here?" "What social forces are at play, and who is being pressured by whom to do what?" "Who might have a stake in this and why?" "Whose interests are being represented?" and, "How would this satisfy or frustrate particular persons or groups?"

Chapter 6

Missiological Method: Text as Product, Ground and Tool

Our second method is designed to bridge between biblical studies and missiology. It was developed as a way to introduce seminary students who already had been trained in traditional exegesis to three basic angles for missiological interpretation. As a template, it is intended to be simple to apply, and it should feel familiar to persons who have worked with existing interpretive strategies, especially Joel Green's "Behind, In, and In Front of" approach.

Like Green's approach, the Product, Ground and Tool method (PGT) (Ayers, 2012) uses varied questions to gain a multidimensional view of the text. It divides a broad examination into separate ranges of inquiry that can be combined in order to get a fuller picture of the text's formation, content, and capacities. However, unlike Green's approach, the questions here arise from distinctly missiological concerns, and they are framed from missiological perspectives so that they yield missiological answers.

The PGT approach requires much less theoretical explanation than the topographic model that we explored above, as it does not try to account for the production of meaning. PGT simply assumes that the text has a functional capacity and it proceeds to look at it in light of its actual and potential uses. Because the method is more focused on the instrumentality of the Bible, it is well-suited for practitioners who want to use the Bible to accomplish tasks like evangelizing, preaching, theologizing, and contextualizing.

Although PGT may be performed without doing a topographic evaluation, to get the most benefit it is helpful for the interpreter first to analyze how the text is structured to create its specific outcomes. This will help the interpreter note the missional traits within the text that PGT seeks to identify and take up for missional use.

The three angles that PGT uses are framed temporally and prepositionally, which keeps their respective foci discrete.

Temporally speaking, the *Product* dimension looks toward the past, asking about the text's origins and previous uses. Prepositionally, this looks at the "of," "out of," or "from" aspect. It asks, "How is the text a product *of* mission?" or, "How did the text arise *out of* mission?"

The *Ground* dimension, however, is anchored in the ever-present. This angle is more abstracted, because it sees the text as a perpetual and authoritative mission foundation, regardless of place and time. This takes a "now, and always" view. Prepositionally, Ground inquiry seeks the text's "for" or "about" capacity. It asks, "How does the text provide a Ground *for* mission?" or, "What does the text support or reveal *about* mission?"

The *Tool* dimension is more oriented toward the future because it looks at potential use(s) for the text itself. Prepositionally, it considers the text's capacity as an instrument that can be used "in," "within," or "in the course of." This also could be thought of as "during." It asks, "How can the text be used as a Tool *within* Mission?" or, "What can be done with the text itself *during* mission activity?"

Bible as a Product of Mission

This is a look "backward" at the text's origin from a mission perspective. It makes observations based upon the principles of textual formation that we have discussed at length as we looked at joint composition, intention, and metanarrative, so we will only briefly review the concepts behind it before outlining its concrete steps.

Summarily, the premise supporting Product analysis is that the people who composed the biblical texts had certain things that they wished to accomplish by writing those texts. This approach takes the stance that people write content because they have reasons to write that content. In other words, the content of a composition serves and supports the motivational cause of the composition. Because the people who wrote had certain motivations, the texts that resulted can be considered Products of their composers' missions more than presentations of information. Product analysis acknowledges the value of looking at "what" people say, but it assumes that "what" people say gets its primary significance from the "because" or "why" that lies beneath it.[105]

In order to highlight this, Product examination deliberately subordinates content to cause. Instead of focusing on what the text said and stopping when it finds that out, Product inquiry takes a step deeper, giving priority to looking for *why* the text said what it said. It looks both at and underneath the text in order to identify what purposes gave rise to the text's composition.

As it performs this task, Product analysis takes into account sociohistorical backgrounds and language origins and patterns, looking for indicators of motivation. This is a fairly familiar process to anyone who has been trained in traditional biblical studies, but it must be remembered that missiological inquiry nuances the focus of background research by maintaining an eye to the agenda of various contributors. It also has a wider range of view when it looks for textual influences. It maintains that compositional situations always are highly complex, having multiple layers

---

[105] This is similar to an investigation that looks for a motive. In a juridical approach, although a behavior may be obvious, motive(s) and dispositions are key dimensions that determine how any given behavior is understood. Although two actions may be appear to be the same, the true nature of the action remains indeterminate until the motivations are discovered or ascribed.

of contribution, and it looks for the hands of contributors on levels ranging from the individual up to broad societal discourses and movements, all of the way to the Divine.

Product analysis pays special attention to the hallmarks of desired ends. Some of the telltales that it looks for are: *behaviors* that are condemned or affirmed; *dispositions* that are condemned or affirmed; *states of being* that are condemned or affirmed; *warnings* and *promises*; *commands* and *instructions*; *positive* and *negative* events and outcomes (especially in narratives); implied or stated *obligations* and *agreements*; ascriptions of *honor* or *shame*; and *participation* in *overarching narratives* (calling, destiny and metanarrative frames). These literary features take precedence over the informational content that surrounds and supports them.

For example, we can look at a portion of Levitical code, such as the rule regarding the impurity of a man with a discharge (Lev. 15: 1-15). Toward the end of this lengthy section, we read:

> Anyone whom the one with the discharge touches without having rinsed his hands in water shall wash his clothes and bathe himself in water and be unclean until the evening. 12 And an earthenware vessel that the one with the discharge touches shall be broken, and every vessel of wood shall be rinsed in water. 13And when the one with a discharge is cleansed of his discharge, then he shall count for himself seven days for his cleansing, and wash his clothes. And he shall bathe his body in fresh water and shall be clean. 14 And on the eighth day he shall take two turtledoves or two pigeons and come before the LORD to the entrance of the tent of meeting and give them to the priest. 15 And the priest shall use them, one for a sin offering and the other for a burnt offering. And the priest shall make atonement for him before the LORD for his discharge. (Lev. 15:11-15 ESV)

When looking for Ground in this passage the interpreter takes into account the definitions, rituals and cultural understandings associated with the idea of purity in ancient Israelite society. The interpreter also keeps in view the tribal place of Levites and priests, along with available sociohistorical information about whether or not purity codes actually were practiced and when and where they may have been, by whom, and for what durations of time. These observations are linked to knowledge about the Temple *cultus* and to practices such as scribal traditions, textual and source redactions and text preservation.

However, as the missiological interpreter looks at these factors, the issue of *why* remains forefront. She asks, "What was the aim here? Why did the authors, redactors and preservers of the Levitical code want Israelites to practice purity rituals and to observe purity prohibitions? What was being hoped for, urged, and supported?" These questions are asked at individual, tribal, traditional and societal scales.

Of highest importance, the missiological interpreter does not exclude God and his motivations from the mix of contributors. She asks, "Why would God want these rituals in place? What was God seeking to bring about by inspiring people to compose, redact, and preserve these codes? What were God's hopes for the author, the tribe, the tradition and the society, as participants in the Ancient Near East and the world?"

When these questions are asked the emphasis shifts from description of the codes within their sociohistorical milieu to description of the various agenda at play in that milieu. The Product description will highlight sociohistorical dynamics, that is, the pushing and pulling of forces that shaped and informed those codes. This accents motivational aspects of the contributors, such as hopes, longings, fears, conflicts, states of being and dispositions. Issues of compliance, inducement, spiritual development and discipline, honor, regard, religious and cultural identity, statuses and roles and cultural solidarity take center stage in this analysis, and the image of the text as a production of these concerns and forces begins to emerge.

Fortunately, thanks to the work of generations of biblical scholars, research about textual composition and sociohistorical backgrounds is abundant and highly available. However, that material has been produced under the discursive influences that have shaped biblical studies, and it has been produced in answer to non-missiological questions. Thus, doing background research for Product analysis can be a tantalizing and somewhat frustrating affair for the missiological interpreter, because material that relates directly to missional intention, especially on spiritual or divine levels, is often scarce within large bodies of background information.

Often, this will require the interpreter who is performing Product analysis to make reasoned inferences from existing information, teasing out indicators and telltales of missional agenda from ancillary aspects of existing research. Reading between the lines this way should not be considered a fault or flaw of missiological research, but an unavoidable characteristic that results from having to borrow data from cognate disciplines. This is only to be expected as any field emerges into its own, and until a much larger body of interpretive work has been done by missiological interpreters, we can expect Product analysis to be marked by inferential, oblique or piecemeal argumentation.

In summary, for Product examination, the interpreter focuses on how the text has come into existence as a result of human and divine purpose(s). The goal is to discern the motivations that undergird and suffuse the text. In this process, the interpreter looks for hallmarks of purpose by looking at literary features of the text and textual backgrounds. These are used as foundation in order to describe the ways in which specific missions (God's and/or people's) have contributed to the text's creation and formation.

It should be kept in mind that this is the first part of a three-part process, and that observing how the text is a Product of mission does not account for the full range of its missiological significance. It accounts for the tangible marks of historical missio in the text's formation, but it does not account for the potential missio that remains latent in the text's design. However, the historically localized findings of this analysis prepare the interpreter to look for non-local meanings in Ground analysis.

Bible as a Ground for Mission

In Ground analysis, the interpreter reorients his view from local, historically based observations toward non-local, principle-based observations. This a change in both scale and kind. It expands from looking at actual, *particular* expressions, shifting instead to examine universal and potential expressions. In other words, Ground analysis steps out of temporal and spatial constraints by considering *universal* aspects. Rather than viewing the text's missio in terms of a certain place and time, it seeks the text's missio in terms of any place and any time.

The universal aspect of Ground analysis will feel familiar to persons who read the Bible with an eye toward truths and principles, since it is closely related to what is already practiced in the divinities and mission theology. However, unlike many traditional theological approaches, the focus here is not on the Bible's contents as statements about reality. Instead, the focus is on the text's agenda and on how that textual agenda relates to Mission, per se. It looks for how things can or should be accomplished, instead of describing how things are. This is a shift in vision that is central to missiological reading, which non-missiological readers sometimes can find hard to grasp, so we will spend more time unpacking the principles behind it than we did with the Product analysis.

Both topographic and Product analyses can help in this process, since both of those analyses attempt to describe the text's missio by looking at concrete literary features. Ground analysis builds upon these descriptions because the goal is to extrapolate outward from concrete observations about historical missio in order to understand the nature of Mission as a universal project, which can in turn inform potential mission expressions.

Because it is conceptually abstract, Ground analysis is the most sophisticated of the PGT examinations, and it requires a high degree of self-observation from the interpreter.[106] Self-observation is necessary because Ground analysis extrapolates principles that are conceptually abstract from the functions of the text. Because it works from the concrete toward the abstract, observations are less anchored in mutually accessible realities, and the process is therefore subject to the kinds of projections of bias that attend all abstractions.

However, we also must acknowledge that the liability of projection is an inescapable risk, which must be taken by all who attempt to talk about any form of principle. Whether the topic is moral, spiritual, economic, philosophical, biological, social, or mathematical, any pursuit for knowledge that hopes to be of use to others involves some form of abstracting extrapolation from particulars, with subsequent reapplication of those observations to other situations. In the process, some forms of reasoning, and some assumptions about the nature of reality must obtain. The key, I believe, is to be honest and explicit about those processes rather than to attempt to avoid them.

Reproductions and reenactments. Ludwig Wittgenstein's discussions about the nature of games can help us understand the interrelationship between abstractions about mission performance and concrete mission performance. In the discussion that follows, try to envision Mission as the "Game," historical mission projects as "games," and the Bible as an exemplary archive of key historical games and decisions that has been produced by an official governing body, such as the International Olympic Committee or International Football Association Board.

Throughout Part 1 of his *Philosophical Investigations*, Wittgenstein uses the analogy of language as "Game" (1969). His analogy is useful for Ground analysis because it sheds light on the connections that link principles, structures, and fulfillments. One of Wittgenstein's points is that

---

[106] I have to note here that any quest for universals is open to challenges that we discussed in Chapters 2 & 3, and I refer the reader back to those discussions before we proceed, which we will do with some caution.

we can talk meaningfully about a game and its rules, but at the same time we must recognize that in some ways what we are talking about is not a game at all until it is actually played (pp. 24, 27, 80-81). Essentially, Wittgenstein draws a distinction between the Game as an *abstraction*, that is, a set of relationships and protocols that could be filled by *anyone*, and the Game as a concrete *particular*, a real thing that is done at a *certain* time and place by *certain* persons. When we focus on the concrete, we can see that a Game becomes real when it is actually played by players, and that talk about the Game in an abstract sense is a way of understanding the concrete behavior of players during tangible, historical games. Yet, if we switch the view to focus on the abstract, we also can observe that the players who have played concrete games have organized their behaviors according to the abstract system that they understand as the Game.

Wittgenstein's analogy lets us see that a reciprocal relationship extends between abstract principles and real behaviors. Abstract principles inform human behaviors, but human behaviors also give principles their substance (pp. 108-110). For missiological thinking, this allows us to join the abstract idea of word with the concrete reality of deed. It also helps us to connect the concrete reality of historical mission with the abstract principle of missio.

Thus, we can note that missio is not fully mission until it is fulfilled by someone, somewhere, and "some-when," yet it remains valid to talk about missio as a thing in and of itself. Talk about missio or Mission in that sense is talk about the relationships and protocols that inform real behavior. In this sense, Mission is like a Wittgensteinian Game that always has the potential to be played by others in different times and places. Thus, mission is a concrete and historical thing as well as an abstract, principled thing. The tricky task for the missiological interpreter is to hold these two aspects simultaneously in view, and to discern each in light of the other. In order to do this, the interpreter looks at historical persons and situations, yet he also views the concrete players in those situations as placeholders in the abstract situation that constitutes "Mission."

The point to remember in all of this is that neither the concrete nor the abstract view of a Game, or of Mission, holds priority. They rely on each other, which means that past expressions are not more valid than principles or future expressions, and vice versa. Just as actual games are evaluated in light of the rules of a Game, the historical mission expressions that are seen in Product analysis can be assessed in light of the principles of Mission that come into view during Ground analysis. On the flip side, just as the Game's rules are truly understood as they are played, so Mission principles that are proposed during Ground analysis only can be understood fully in light of actual mission expressions that are observed during Product analysis.

Crucially, just as the potential for playing a Game remains undiminished, regardless of how many actual times it is played, so Mission remains perpetually open. Mission always presents a full potential to be a "new" project for any who would engage it. This kind of ongoing potential is shown in Gadamer's illustration of "festival" and "celebration" (2004, pp. 123-124). Gadamer notes that festivals are renewed in full each time they are celebrated, and that each celebration is a valid enactment of the festival. The festival is not any given celebration; it is all of the celebrations, yet each celebration is fully the festival in and of itself. The festival is thus a reality that resets and re-presents in its full potential at all times.

If we can join Gadamer's Festival with Wittgenstein's Game, and call it an Event, we can note that any fulfilled event is historical, but the roles that the players play in it can be understood in generic or abstracted senses, as though the historical players were universal characters or placeholders.[107] Once an event is fulfilled, it can be understood on an abstract, universal level, as a situation of factors, with or without taking into account the historical players.

---

[107] This is an approach used by the Russian formalist school of criticism founded by Vladimir Propp.

Because the Event exists simultaneously as an institutionalized set of rules and as a historic reality, analysis of the Event could look at old events, completely new events or hypothetical events. In a similar way, the biblical texts give us historical mission events, which can be examined in a historical manner (Product analysis), yet they also show us Mission as an Event, which is an arrangement of factors that can be reenacted and that can be described in a symbolic, literary, theological, or linguistic manner (Ground analysis). These two aspects rely upon each other.

Going further, when we take the missio of the text to be canonical, it serves as an authoritative template for reenacting Mission, just like an official guide for a Game or a Festival. This is a step beyond academic description, as it seeks to maintain compliance with what has been observed. It hopes for the fulfillment understanding that we discussed earlier. Yet, for fulfillment, the interpreter must become missionally active and seek to arrange real contemporary factors and players in parallel to the factors that were present in a biblical event. The players and names may change, but the aim is to make the potential missional Event re-present and re-produce the missio of the text in a contemporary, applied or contextualized manner.[108]

This agenda stands hand in hand with foundational missiological assumptions about the Bible's translatability and textual inexhaustibility, which hold that the text is always relevant and available as a new thing, in any potential context. These commitments support ongoing projects of missional contextualization, contemporary and contextual theologizing, and

---

[108] Again, this has parallels to Green's discourse model, but it uses missiological viewpoints that focus on social intentions, institutions and purposes.
    Thus, it is possible to talk about meaning in multiple senses, as: (1) *Systemic* meaning: the social foundations or rules that undergird meaning. This is meaning as the general concept of meaningfulness or Meaning. (2) *Specific* meaning: whole situations in which things actually have been meant. This is the historical meaning of a text within in a milieu, that is, the meaning of "it." (3) *Generic* or *universal* meaning: the situation of factors in a composition. This is the abstract meaning of "it." (4) A *particular* meaning as it is played-out in a particular instance of experience or context, which does not necessarily take into account the whole *specific* situation ("this" or "that" meaning). (5) *Personal* meaning, the states of persons involved in the overall process ("his," "her," or "their" meaning). Each one of these locates meaning within a particular scheme of context. For maximum fruitfulness, robust "contextual" description of meaning would include or address as many of these dimensions as is possible.

endeavors that seek to outline appropriate mission praxis. They assume that God's purposes transcend local expressions and that his aims have been, are being, and may be brought to fulfillment in a wide variety of adaptive ways across times, places and systems, while still remaining true to preceding divine activity. This is the kind of ongoing missional uptake and reintegration of tradition that takes place as the biblical text is reiterated and reenacted endlessly in emerging contexts.

Doing Ground analysis. Theoretically, then, Ground examination focuses on the capacity of the text to inform missional reenactment and re-presentation. In a more concrete sense, the goal is to understand how to do mission in ways that correspond to the text's missio. Procedurally, this is done by extrapolating from the particulars of the text in order to articulate universals, and then in turn to use those universals to inform the production of new particulars. The agenda is to emulate the text. And, because the text's historical missio was informed by motivational concerns, Ground analysis includes those concerns in its emulating agenda.

While doing Ground analysis, the interpreter should keep in mind that all texts show missio, not just those texts that appear to have mission content. Thus, all texts can serve as templates for subsequent mission. Remember that in both Product analysis and Ground analysis, concern about content is subordinate to concern about cause. Thus, even in places where the content shows mission themes, the focus remains foremost upon *why* mission is being talked about, followed by *what* is being said about mission. This is not to say that content about mission is ignored; it is taken into account, but it is framed within the purpose for which it has been said.

It might help if we return to the analogy of the obstacle course that was used in topographic analysis. When we look at a finished obstacle course, the features of the course reveal the design aims behind the course. That is a topographic analysis agenda. Once that is done, we can use those observations for different ends. For example, we could look at the features of the course in order to prepare a runner or runners to run the course. That is again more of a topographic agenda, although it also relates to the Tool analysis that we will cover below. We also might look at the course in order to see the relationship between the design aims and the actual construction that went into the course. That is a Product analysis agenda.

However, we could also look at the course in order to discern general principles about kinesiology and obstacle course design, as a study in obstacle courses and their constructions. This is where we find more of a Ground analysis agenda. Further, we could take all of these observations into account in order to find ways to construct similar courses in other locations, which had similar effects, even though they might not be exactly the same as the original course. That is the broader aim of Ground analysis.

An example of the last approach would be if someone wanted to create an obstacle course for adults that was based upon the design of an obstacle course for children. For that goal, one would look at the course that had been built at one time for one set of users (kids) in terms of the course's functions, not its actual dimensions or materials. In order to reproduce the course for adults, the functions would be abstracted and re-scaled using different materials that produced similar outcomes for the new user population. When this had been done, the adult users who used the adult course would be reenacting the kids' course. This does not mean that the adult users are using any less real or valid of a course. It simply means that since the same missio is being fulfilled, the essential identity of the kids' course has remained, even though it has been embodied in a new construction and used by new users.

Ground analysis does not move all of the way to construction of new reenactments. That is a task for contextualization and mission activity. Instead, Ground analysis provides the understandings that support the creation of new reenactments. It stops at the level of abstraction, looking for principles and potentials.

In order to be effective, the interpreter should maintain a view to Mission as an overarching concept while assessing aspects of the text (theological, narrative, doctrinal, ideological, socio-rhetorical, etc.). She should make it a point to frame her observations relative to the missio of the text, and she should anticipate potential reenactment of the text's missio in mission situations. The focus should be on how this (authoritative) text can be read in order to inform understanding(s) and practice(s) of Mission. Observations should be made at the level of missiological principles, precedents, information, guidelines, and instructions, etc.

In order to do so, Ground analysis takes results from Product analysis and springboards from them to ask questions about the *implications* of what has been discovered. Using the example of a Levitical purity code that we discussed earlier, the interpreter could ask questions like, "The text was aimed at producing purity behaviors, and the purpose for that was to reinforce the religious identity of the people of God. How then does establishing and maintaining religious identity factor as an end goal for Mission?" Or, "The text reinforces purity practices as intensifying expressions of religious devotion. How can purity behaviors be used to help people express and maintain religious devotion?" Or, "The text affirms the authority of Levitical priests as it makes them the arbiters of purity. What is the place of religious authority figures in Mission, particularly as those who have power to declare others clean or unclean, and to exclude or include them in the community of faith?"

Again, in this analysis, God's purposes cannot be left out of consideration. The interpreter also asks questions like, "The text shows that God desires for his people to demonstrate purity through externalized, physical behaviors. What does that say about the role of external purity demonstrations in Mission?" Or, "The text shows a sacred value for external, physical actions that are performed under the direction of authority figures. Does God want people to be urged to practice exterior acts of devotion, and does he desire for that to be done under the direction of religious authorities?" Or, "Does God appoint religious authorities and grant them power to arbitrate religious statuses as part of the missio Dei?"

Self-awareness and authenticity are crucial as the interpreter asks such questions, for it is here that biases factor most strongly. While biases are inescapable, the aim throughout is to be true to the text's observable missio by producing inferences that are grounded in that *missio's* concerns. This may take the interpreter to surprising and often challenging places. When this occurs, it is an encouraging indicator that the interpreter is also being guided by the text's agenda, which itself is a litmus test of missiological reading.

Bible as a Tool within Mission

As is the case in both Product and Ground analyses, Tool analysis views the text as an instrument of both God and people. However, unlike Product and Ground analyses, Tool analysis directs its attention at the instrumental potentials of the text, itself. Whereas Product sees the text as an expression of Mission, and Ground sees the text as a foundation for Mission, Tool sees the text as a resource for Mission. It considers the text as an implement that is available for mission agents to use as they conduct mission.

This is an approach that will feel somewhat familiar to preachers, teachers, counselors, evangelists, etc., because these agents present biblical texts to others regularly during the course of their activities. However, Tool analysis is much more missiologically focused than many of the ways in which the Bible is commonly used, and the sense of familiarity may be deceiving.

It may help at this point to revisit the definitions of *mission*, *missional*, and *missiological* interpretation from Chapter1. There, we defined mission hermeneutics as, "interpretation that is performed by mission agents as they go about the business of mission." This was contrasted with *missional* interpretation, which keeps self-awareness of mission in mind while it interprets, and *missiological* interpretation, which also keeps self-awareness of mission in mind, but adds interaction with formal disciplinary concerns.

Tool analysis follows in the footsteps of mission interpreters, such as Jesus and the New Testament writers, who used scripture to support their mission tasks by quoting, paraphrasing or alluding to biblical passages. Tool analysis looks to see how similar things can be done with scriptures today. However, Tool analysis looks to do this using missiological, rather than mission strategies.

Mission use of texts. Backtracking a bit, we should note that New Testament uses of the Hebrew scriptures can be problematic for interpreters who locate the meaning of a text in terms of historical and grammatical sense. For, from that perspective, it seems readily apparent that the New Testament writers pay little regard to historical or contextual senses. While many strategies are available to try to explain the dissonance, some biblical scholars simply opt to stop at description. Simple description notes that the historical sense of an Old Testament text appears to read one way and that a New Testament writer has decided to use that text in another way, and it leaves the tension between the two senses standing. Other scholars opt to support New Testament uses by embedding them in interpretive methods used during New Testament times, such as Jewish rabbinic tradition or Hellenistic rhetoric.

However, if we adopt a view that the text's meaning can be located relative to its functions, a different option opens up, in which the New Testament writers use Old Testament texts in accordance with their instrumental capacities, instead of according to their historical references. This view emphasizes that texts are things that can be employed to achieve certain outcomes, and it sees legitimacy when outcomes that correspond to textual design are achieved.

As an illustration, imagine that you need to turn a screw, but you do not have a screwdriver. All you have is a butter knife, a hairbrush, and a coin. You need to decide what to do; particularly, you need to decide if you can or should use what you have at hand to do the job. The kind of criteria that you use to decide this is crucial. If the original sense of the butter knife is what determines its use, that will prevent you from using the knife as a screwdriver. However, if it is legitimate to apply the butter knife to uses for which its design makes it suitable, then using the butter knife to turn screws is supported.

If we see after the fact that you have indeed chosen to use the butter knife as a screwdriver, we have evaluative options. On one hand, we could say that you used it wrongly, and that you don't know anything about butter knives. However, from another angle, we can observe that apparently the controlling factor for you is not the original sense of the butter knife, but the fit between the instrumental potentials of the butter knife and the needs of the task at hand. For you, as the old adage goes, "If the shoe fits, wear it."

The key to all of this is the concept of found utility. This is a basic principle of adaptive re-purposing that is used in many fields: found art, musical composition, literary tradition, even street fighting. When use is the determining factor, the thing that will work is the right thing to use, and if that thing works where it is applied, the point is ceded that its selection and application were legitimate.

Thus, if a bottle-cap works as an eye in a mosaic, that bottle cap is a legitimate choice for that part of the work. It is not controlled by its existence as a bottle-cap, so that it may not be an eye in an art piece. Neither does it lose its recognizable "bottle-cap-ness." Instead, under the artist's compositional re-appropriation, it *adds* the meaning of an eye in a mosaic to its existing meaning as a bottle-cap, and the discerning viewer can see both at the same time without devaluing or ignoring either dimension. By focusing on the functions, the viewer can say, "Wow, that bottle-cap certainly works as an eye right there." In another analogy, a desk lamp could be used as a deadly weapon in a fight, and the resulting criminal charge would reflect that use. This does not mean that lamps should be considered deadly weapons wherever they are found. It means that when a lamp is taken up for that use, it adds the sense of being a deadly weapon to its sense of being a lamp. The novel use by someone has exploited latent features of the lamp's design and brought out those features under the umbrella of a reappropriation.

For this discussion, the key to remember is that neither the lamp manufacturer nor the one swinging the lamp would call the lamp anything but a lamp. In the same way, if you were to turn a screw with a butter knife, you probably would say, "I am using a butter knife as a screwdriver," or "Look at my new 'screwdriver!'" You would not assert that the butter knife always was a screwdriver because you are using it as one. Rather, you would say that a fuller use has been found for it. You could say on good grounds that there was more instrumental potential within the thing than what had been actualized when it was used *only* as a butter knife. You could claim that you have seen more capacity in it because you recognized a utility that was dormant and resident within its design, and it finally has become more than just a butter knife. As of your moment of use it is both a butter knife and very much a screwdriver. In other words, the butter knife has been fulfilled *as* a screwdriver.

In a similar way, from the viewpoint of use, the New Testament writers do not violate the senses of the Old Testament texts as they take them up for the Christian mission. Rather, the Christian mission provides a task-at hand filter through which the New Testament writers are able to discover latent textual capacities that lay resident in the designs of the Old Testament passages. These potentials were what the New Testament writers found well-suited to Christian uses. And, as these writers took those texts up for those uses, they did not deny or abrogate original sense; they compounded the original sense in ways that saw the text fulfilled more repletely. Thus, in a mission interpretation, a text about a Judaic king can become fulfilled when quoted as a "Judaic kingship text *as* a messianic witness to Jesus of Nazareth," in the same way that a butter knife can be fulfilled when used as a "butter knife *as* a screwdriver."

Missiological use of texts. The ramifications of such a view can be far-reaching, particularly when it comes to questions of reliable, canonical, orthodox, or common agreement readings. When canon is a factor the question immediately arises of whether or not any possible use of a text becomes a legitimate reading, as proponents of deconstructive or radical semiotic explorations would affirm, or if there are limits that can be understood to distinguish between legitimate and illegitimate readings. From a functional viewpoint, this is not so much a question of anchoring the text in a historical meaning, but a question of *use* versus *abuse* of a text's capacities.

It is here that we find the value of a *missiological* approach. Remember that the missiological approach is distinguished from the mission approach by virtue of its participation in discourses that lay beyond its immediate task, particularly, by its participation in academic discourses. As such, missiological interpretation differs from the interpretation that was performed by the New Testament writers, since it self-consciously uses disciplinary concerns to inform its readings.

For example, while the missiologist may use a functional view of textual meaning to understand how citation operates, missiology's disciplinary commitments also hold to the divine inspiration of the Bible as a sacred text. Thus, a missiological reading qualifies how it understands the New Testament's use of the Old Testament by noting that the New Testament writers took up the Old Testament texts in authoritative ways under the inspiration of the Holy Spirit. This legitimizes the New Testament uses of the Old Testament by an appeal that extends beyond the criterion of mere functionalism. In such a case, missiological reading informs its function-grounded findings by placing them in dialog with developed academic discourses that address inspiration, canonicity, and orthodoxy. Two supports for the New Testament writers' uses then come into view, legitimacy as mission fulfillment, and legitimacy as inspired, authorized text. These allow the missiological reader to triangulate on the text's significance and to have confidence, since she can refine her reading from more than one angle.

Thus, in doing Tool analysis, the missiological reader first looks for possible mission uses that might be well-suited, given the text's particular features, its missio design. This is a quest for latency and potential utility. It can help the interpreter immensely here if he has already done the groundwork to outline the text's operational designs (topographic analysis), its precedent uses (Product analysis) and the inferences that follow from its essential, reproducible aspects (Ground analysis). The goal is to consider how the text itself might be presented in the course of mission activity, in ways that are consonant with the text's discernible missio.

Using our Levitical code example once more, the text's features show that it is aimed at the maintenance and reinforcement of purity behaviors in a religious society, with the designed outcome of sustaining religious identity. Thus, it has high utility as a tool that directs people to show religious devotion outwardly, by avoiding designated material things. It also has utility to direct people toward religious figures who can walk them toward reintegration to the community by the application of cleansing rituals and pronouncements. Given that this is the case, the text is a tool that is well suited for use in a culture that prioritizes external religious or social behaviors and states.

For example, if a mission agent is working with a group that considers a certain material thing (say, perhaps, meat, betel nut, alcohol, magical objects, or music) to be something that causes defilement and/or precipitates social marginalization, the text has a good chance of fulfilling its missio. In this case, the worldview structure of the text parallels the culture's existing values and traditions, and the text's design is aimed at producing outcomes that naturally correspond to issues faced by exteriorized groups, such as cleansing, pronouncement of right status, and reintegration with the community after defilement.

In this scenario, a mission agent could consider the text to be a potential tool, since the text's missio sustains the observance of defilement and cleansing protocols. The text is particularly suited for use as an instrument to call people to practice formal avoidance or rejection of taboo items. Its missio also moves people to appeal to religious figures for cleansing pronouncements in order to display their religious devotion or as a means to restore their social and religious standings.

In order to use the text as a mission tool, the mission agent would present the text to the group or to defiled populations in order to encourage people to avoid defilements or as a call for people to be restored from defiled states. For the mission agent, the goal would be to fulfill the purposes of mission by doing so. This might involve calling people to engage Christian laving and confession rituals, anointing or absolution, as parallel functions that mirror the biblical, Levitical ones. The mission agent also might use the text to invite hearers to choose Christian forms of purification in the place of traditional, non-Christian cleansing practices, presenting an alternative, Christian path to status renewal and social reintegration.

Since both the values and the outcomes that the text's missio is designed to serve have parallels in the mission situation, the text has a high potential mission utility. It offers utility on one side for bridge-building with the culture by demonstrating shared concerns and outlooks. On another side, it provides a relevant, missional means to open up new paths for people to come toward Christ because it can be used to present Christian cleansing strategies and exclusion or inclusion processes as alternatives to existing non-Christian processes. Both the bridge-building potentials of the text and the challenge/alternative potentials of the text offer utility for Christian mission agents who can take up the text as a tool to assist them in the performance of their mission tasks.

The missiological reader, however, does not proceed on intuition alone. Because she is reading missiologically, she gives attention to relevant academic resources and discourses. Thus, she compares her findings with anthropological discourses that describe exteriorized societies and ritual performances; she checks biblical studies discourses that are concerned with the backgrounds of purity ideology in the Ancient Near East and in Israelite society. She checks church history and theological discourses that discuss sacramental cleansing, etc. As she triangulates her mission reading of the text with these other disciplinary discourses, she achieves her missiological reading, which undergirds her identification of the text as a certain kind of tool that is suited for a certain kind of work in a certain kind of context.

In practice, this process is similar to the work of Critical Contextualization that anthropologist and missiologist Paul Hiebert (1987) advocates, even though its theoretic foundations are different. In both practices, however, the goal is well-reasoned, transparent and methodologically accessible presentation of biblical texts in mission contexts, in order to further mission work. In Tool analysis, however, the focus remains upon the potential utility of the text as an implement, rather than upon the transfer of its truths as informational contents or theological guidelines.

Throughout, the aim for Tool analysis is to explore the text as a means to accomplish missional goals in ways that fit with the text's form and content. The controlling concern is, "How can we use this text responsibly as we fulfill God's mission?" The key questions that the interpreter asks in this process are: "How can this text do what it is designed to do in various situations and contexts?" or, "How might the text be quoted or used in presentations to people without changing its essential effects and outcome goals?" and, "Based upon the design of the text, what kinds of situations would it function best in, and what uses would it be best suited for?" Another, less precise, way of framing this would be, "What might be the most appropriate situation to quote this text in, and what would be accomplished by doing so?"

In summary, The PGT method takes three distinct angles of view to explore the text's instrumental dimensions. These three angles are separated by their locations in time and by the ways that they conceptually relate the text to Mission. The Product analysis looks at how the text may have arisen out of Mission, historically. A Ground analysis looks at how the text can be used as a foundation for Mission at any place and time. Tool analysis takes the results of both of these in order to look at how the text could be used as an implement within Mission work. Any of these analyses can be performed separately, but greater depth and clarity can be achieved if they are performed together, especially if they are performed after a topographic analysis has laid out the functional missio of the text.

Of course, these methods by no means cover the scope of missiological interpretation. Missiological reading is an emerging field facing a broad vista and a long task before it. However, the hope is that these rudimentary methods can provide the beginning missiological interpreter with a few practical steps to start the journey. We will see how they produce specific outcomes when applied to specific texts in Part III as we discuss the Genesis 1 creation account.

PART III

Chapter 7: Reading the Genesis 1 Creation Account

In Part III we transition from foundation to application. Parts I and II outlined theoretical grounds and proposed reading methods. Part III takes the next step by applying missiological approaches first to a text and then to a sociospatial phenomenon.

Chapter 7 demonstrates how to use method to read a text. It applies Topographic Analysis and Product, Ground and Tool approaches to the Genesis 1 creation account. Chapter 8 shows how to use missiological foundations to interpret without relying upon method. It uses the concept of missio to interpret the city. The findings from these interpretations are compared and contrasted in Chapter 9. This joint reading will be used in the missiological considerations of Part IV.

Before we begin our textual work, there are a few points to keep in mind. The first is that each reading is intended to be a demonstration of how missiological interpretation *can* be done. As such, the readings are not exhaustive; each is only one example of one interpretive strategy. The second reminder is that the steps in these methods are not necessarily linear. They are more a constellation of questions that an interpreter may keep in view during examination. The questions are grouped into methods and steps as heuristic devices. These organize missiological inquiry so that the interpreter can more easily discern distinct dimensions of the text, and then, by integrating those distinct angles, achieve a robust understanding. They are sequenced here only for ease of application.

The last point is that inquiry is scalable. One of the aims here is to show how method can work with different textual scales in a dialectic between the part and the whole. In order to do this the focus will alternate between a *section* level view of the entire passage and a *sub-section* view of a few key verses. This also illustrates the relationship between *immediate* and *eventual* views. Alternating this way is not integral to the methods, but doing so can help the interpreter to check her findings as she develops her reading.

Topographic Analysis of Genesis 1

For the first reading we will apply the five steps of Topographic Analysis that were outlined in Chapter 5. The next reading will use the Product, Ground and Tool approach.

Below you will find short treatments that apply each of the first four TA steps. These are made brief in order: 1) to demonstrate how to focus on essentials, and, 2) to give readily accessible comparisons between the various angles of view. As you follow along with the steps it may help you to review previous steps and to compare them with the current step. When you do, remember that the goal is to discern the overall purpose(s) of the text by integrating the different evaluations into a total assessment.

Also, remember that the questions of Step Five, *Juxtapose various purposes,* are intended to be non-linear and distributed throughout the other steps. Those questions seek to discern the telltales of differing agenda that coexist within the text. They look for how the text is an intersection of multiple purposes that are not exactly alike or consonant with each other. They ask, "Who is up to what, here?" "What social forces are at play?" "Who is being pressured by whom, to do what?" "Who might have a stake in this and why?" "Whose interests are being represented?" and, "How would this satisfy or frustrate particular persons or groups?" It would be lengthy and repetitive to do Step Five analysis throughout, but in order to show how these questions work with other steps, Step Five will be integrated in a special section attached to Step Three.

After the TA is finished, we will switch to PGT in order to develop our reading more fully. This will help us check our preliminary TA observations and build upon them in preparation for our reading of the city, and for the missiological considerations that will follow.

Step One: Identify features. Step One looks for the structures of the text. The goal in Step One is to observe how the words, phrases, literary and formal aspects function together, since these functions reveal the text's contours. This step asks, "What are the shapes and features of the text's language structures?" and, "How do the text's language features ordinarily function in the text's sociolinguistic tradition (milieu)?"

When looking at the features of the passage's language, it can be helpful to focus on the most obvious or incontrovertible aspects. The most obvious aspects will reveal the primary ways in which the text will affect readers. The key is not to speculate about what *might* be a legitimate feature in the text, but to remain at the level of what *must* acknowledged as an essential feature of the text. Most features at this level can be observed even in translations; although, for missiological reading, it is important to check original language sources to confirm observations and to maintain connection with related academic discourses.

Section level view. Surveying the full account (Gen. 1:1-2:3), a number of key traits stand out. One obvious general trait is the formulaic progression of the passage. The passage progresses in a conspicuously numbered, stair-step style, which moves in linear fashion through multiple iterations. These present to the reader as a unified story comprised of smaller narrative movements. The smaller, component narrative movements are arranged in series, with clear and direct continuity between them. The literary blocks connect to each other in obvious ways. They are numbered sequentially. Each resembles the previous one in some fashion, and each treats a theme that carries over from the one before, even though the limits of each can be readily discerned through the presence of opening and closing phrases.

The language in the narrative movements is repetitive and framed as a direct, progressive story. Duplication of terms makes reader access to the passage cumulative, although the articulation moves from simpler forms at the start toward greater complexity as the story nears the end. Each movement addresses a "day" (yôm)[109]. Each uses similar, stock phrasing and recounts a similar series of actions. Each creative movement begins with a divine statement that frames and initiates the day, then narrates the actions of God as he creates particular things per his decree. Each presents a reflective assessment of the things created, alternately by stating that they were indeed as God decreed, by receiving a divine blessing or via an evaluation in the divine vision. These move each day toward a formulaic summary of evening and morning, along with the day's sequential number, which give each day its narrative closure.. Variations in the narrative formula highlight themselves, marking the distinct character of certain movements (v. 16-18, 22, 26-30).

Aside from the enigmatic reference to the "Spirit of God" in v. 2 and the complex image language in v. 26-28, the rest of the language is relatively straightforward. This marks those two sections as unusual, which may be significant, awkward or contrived. Aside from talk about God, the wording throughout the story is *categorical*; it treats with classes of things "according to their kind(s)" (lĕmînô, lĕmînēhû; v. 11, 12, 21, 24, 25), rather than as specific items or characters. Further, the depictions of these categories are highly stylized, general, repetitive and brief. Minimal ornamentation or descriptive detail is given.

On formal, generic levels, the contents and themes qualify the account as an etiology (origin) story, a creation story (cosmogony) or a

---

[109] Transliterations are from BHS (*Biblia Hebraica Stuttgartensia* 1977), according to SBL style.

description of the universe and how it works (myth or cosmology). However, structurally, the story has no clear parallels in any of those ANE genres (Curtis, 1984; Vriezen, 1958; Wittenberg, 1975). In some sense, then, it must be treated as a *sui generis* with a unique construction (W. P. Brown, 1993:230).

From literary angles, the action is organized around God. The only actor in the account is God (along with, perhaps, the "Spirit of God" [v. 2], if that is not taken as God, himself)[110]. He alone supplies dialog and he alone moves the plot forward in his making and blessing. All other characters are noticeably stock, flat, and passive; they show no signs of awareness, deliberate response or willful activity. Likewise, the narration itself is removed and objective. It makes no assessments and offers no explanations of its own. All evaluation is located within the eye (v. 4, 10, 12, 18, 21, 25, 31) or voice (v. 22, 28) of the creator.

The imagery, setting, and mood progress from a dark, brooding, wet, chaotic, and barren environment to a light, ordered, solid, and fruitful pastoral scene. The point of view is broad, looking across all of the creation. The temporal frame is also expansive and open, as statements are aimed indefinitely toward the future. However, notably, as the plot develops, the focus of immediate action progressively reduces from a cosmic, universal scope to a narrow, localized scene, moving from a scale of "the heavens and the earth" (v. 1) to a pronouncement over two humans (v. 28-31). Still, even as that focus narrows, the frame of reference remains universal, as the pronouncements over the two humans embrace all of the human race, with an eye toward all future generations.

The formal pattern is interrupted at the end of the account as God creates and endows humankind (1:26-30), and again, when the seventh day of rest is instituted (2:1-3). On the day of the creation of humans, the formula is expanded. In that moment, the narration grants access to God's

---

[110] See Clines (1968:69).

thoughts and intentions before he acts, and there is an extended description of commissioning, blessing, and provisioning. These humans are the last of God's creations, even though the verbal formula of the creation plot continues in a modified form to an additional sequentially numbered day. However, the acts of creation conclude after humans are made, as rest is instituted on the seventh day. The ballast line is strong, concluding at rest, which halts the plot movement within the narrative and signals the end of the narration.

Subsection view. If we narrow our focus to the portion dealing with the creation of humankind (v. 26-30), we find a number of other interesting features. Most obviously, this comes as the second part of the sixth day of creation. Here, the regular formula for creation days is varied somewhat, with two creative acts take place on the same day, the latter one with a lengthy, expanded description that includes a narrative of address. The double creation act makes humans appear to be a distinct subset within a larger set, much like the relation that the plants appear to have with the land (v.11-12) or the relation that the Greater and Lesser lights have to the entire class of heavenly lights (v. 16-18). The conceptual category that applies to both creations in day six appears to be "land-dwellers," since reference to the earth is repeated four times in v. 22-25, and the name of the human ('ādām; v. 26) hearkens to dirt, itself.

Another startling feature is God's self-directing statement of intention[111] that comes before he makes "man" ('ādām). This varies from the sequences preceding, in which God speaks outwardly that a thing should be, and the narrative declares that God (thus) made. Here, God's speech is directed inwardly, which heightens the sense of deliberate action by showing forethought. This forethought includes a plan for "man/them" to "rule" (wĕyirĕdû) over certain other creations.[112]

---

[111] See footnote, below.
[112] The heavenly luminaries, which exercise their own form of "rule" (v.16-18) are a clear exception to human rule. Human dominion is limited to the earth.

Throughout, there are conflations of the singular and plural.[113] God acts in the singular, but speaks in the first-person plural. He pre-intends and then makes the singular, "man" ('ādām) yet, this one ('ōtô) is simultaneously "them" ('ōtām). These conflations come in both the direct words of God and the narration. They are not explained or clarified; this presents a situation of unusual complexity, perhaps even ambiguity or confusion, to the reader within an otherwise simple account.

However, underscoring familiarity, there is also significant repetition and formal parallelism on multiple scales, which resembles the language in the rest of the story. Lists of other creations occur three times (v. 26, 28, 29-30). Dominion is expressly mentioned twice (v.26, 28), and reinforced again in the gift of provision (v. 29-30). Image (ṣelem) is mentioned in God's intention and in the description of humankind's creation (v. 26, 27). This is strengthened by the addition of the related term, "(according to our) likeness" in v. 26 (kidĕmûtēnû) and the stylized, chiastic duplication of v. 27, which adds sex-trait identifiers in a synthetic parallel[114].

Language of reproduction pervades the verses. This is highlighted by the couplet of distinctly sex trait terms, "male and female" (zākār ûnĕqēbâ), which is immediately followed by a blessing. The blessing is framed as a compounding command to "be fruitful and multiply and fill the earth and subdue it and have dominion over it."[115] In the blessing/command, the

---

[113] While Sawyer (1974:423) and von Rad (1972:58-59) (among others) propose that God's address is to a heavenly host or divine council, no such council is mentioned. They both note that even though the verb to make (na'ăśeh) is a first person common plural, the narrative uses the third person masculine singular imperfect (wayyibĕrā') to describe what happened in the creative act. See also Barth (1958:191-192), who notes the shift in number and attributes the heavenly host view to Delitzsch and Jacob. Since the narration shows creation as performed in the singular, no heavenly hosts appear to be involved. The narration does not provide other actors, which indicates that God is addressing himself, the one who will create, in the cohortative statement.

[114] Hb., "wayyibĕrā' 'ĕlōhîm 'et-hā'ādām bĕṣalĕmô bĕṣelem 'ĕlōhîm bārā' 'ōtô zākār ûnĕqēbâ bārā' 'ōtām." Notably, both God's and man's pronominal numbers shift between the intentional statement to create man and this subsequent action. Two possibilities yet to be proposed are: 1) ornamental poetic balancing and euphony, the textural effect of supplying the plural "us" over against the plural "them" 2) narrative engagement; intentional complication and introduction of ambiguity in order to produce mystery and elicit heightened attention.

[115] Hb., "'ĕlōhîm wayyō'mer lāhem 'ĕlōhîm pĕrû ûrĕbû ûmilĕ'û 'et-hā'āreṣ wĕkibĕšu hāûrĕdû bidĕgat hayyām ûbĕ'ôp hašāmayim ûbĕkāl-ḥayyâ hārōmeśet 'al-hā'āreṣ."

fulfillment of reproduction is linked to the fulfillment of dominion. This is further supported by God's gift of sustenance.

Markedly, as God grants sustenance, he speaks indicatively and imperatively in direct address to the humans ("them;" lāhem). This is the first portrayal of direct communication between specific characters, rather than to classes or populations,[116] even though the humans do not reply. The fact that God addresses the humans concerning the feeding rights of the animals is also significant, because it is a description of the rights of a third party, the animals. God's outline of the feeding rights of the beasts reads as instructions to a proxy subordinate on the rights of subjects.[117] This interacts with the repetition of absolute language ("all; every" [kāl]), further underscoring the creation hierarchy as it demonstrates concretely that God has placed the creatures under the governance of those to whom he has granted dominion.

Step Two: Assess impacts on the reader. Step Two examines textual dynamics. It looks for the ways in which the text's structures affect the reader as the reader tries to make his way through them. The focus is on how the text impacts the reader's existential dimensions in order to create a pathway of greatest yield and least resistance. This reveals designed outcomes for the reader's experience, which shows the text's missio. This step asks, "How do particular text features and structures affect readers in particular ways?" and, "How are the text's resistances and yields organized?"

This step moves deeper into analysis as the interpreter begins to speculate about the "why's" of the text's design. In order to do this, the interpreter must have some kind of conceptualization of the reader. Thus, a key initial step is to try to discern what the text seems to presume about the reader.

---

[116] See footnote above; even if the plural in v. 26 is taken as address to others and not as self-address, those others are not named or known characters within the story.

[117] A number of parallels can be found in the third party instructions of Ezr. 4-6, especially the provisioning and rights decrees of Ezr. 6:3-10.

In this passage, the text appears to assume that the reader is willing to take the account as legitimate, ordinary sense depiction. There are no signs that the text anticipates an antagonistic, doubtful or suspicious reader. The narration begins in a straightforward, indicative manner. It appears to state simply, "This is the way things were, and this is what happened." In narrating without qualification, the story assumes that the reader will hear the account without qualification, that is, as a straightforward portrayal of the acts of God in the making of all known creation.

Further, the text assumes a continuity between the world of the reader and the world of the account's narrative. The text gives no indication that the world being described is a former world, a distant world or a different order of world, such as a would be described in a heavenly vision. The things that populate the narrative world are not fantastic or extraordinary. They are everyday, at hand, recognizable, and familiar things.

This would seem to indicate that the text expects the reader to consider himself a legitimate addressee or recipient of the text. The reader is one who sees the text as talking about his own world; thus, he hears the text talking about "my/our" origins. It is the reader's own origin story, not the origin story of a different people in a different place.

The reader is also assumed to hold no distinction between the metaphysical and natural orders. In order to proceed through the story, he is expected to allow that there is a creator, who is divine ("God"), and to understand that the creation known to the reader is the divine creator's direct handiwork. Thus, the divine is as natural, perhaps even more natural, than the ordinary, familiar creation.

Importantly, no background story, origin or explanation is given about the God who is mentioned. This indicates that the reader is presumed to understand or subscribe to the same identification of God as the story holds. It presumes a common worldview in advance of reading the story. In this worldview *Elohiym* (ʼĕlōhîm) is God and all derives from him. This automatically locates God outside of the realm of created things, in an order of being that is all his own. Thus, God is not the *object* of generative actions and forces or the topic of an origin account; he is the *subject* that provides origination and the protagonist in an origin account.

Section level view. These assumptions show the staging for the reader's progress through the passage. At the very front of this staging, the narration affords no realm for God before creation begins. This demands an awkward double start from the narrative in which God first creates the heavens and the earth, then moves to create them from a state of chaos and emptiness (v. 1-2). The heavy-handedness of this plot movement shows that from the outset, insurmountable resistance is engineered against any idea that there might not be a creator God, or to any identification of the creator with some deity other than the God of Israel.

Thus, no effective option is given for engaging the story as one who does not believe or acknowledge Elohiym. In order to read without acknowledging Elohiym, the reader must dissociate himself from the story and its worldview. This would require that the story be read counter to its narrative voice and character, that is, as a fiction and not as a straightforward account. Effectively, such a reading would bypass the missio of the text, severing the link between "my/our world" and the story's world. This would disengage the reader from the story's terrain, and be roughly akin to switching from a ground view to an aerial view of the text's topography. If the reader is to be engaged with the topography of the text in a way that can fulfill its missio, she must enter the story and move through it as one who accepts continuity between the world of the story and her own, and as one who can acknowledge the existence, centrality, and singularity of the God of Israel within that world.

This strategic casting of the narrative is developed progressively, as all parts of a complete and common world are created and given ordered places. By the time the narrative is finished, God has been shown to be the creator and origin of all known components of the reader's familiar world. When he is finished with his work, those components are all in place and the world is running appropriately enough for God to rest. The world is done and complete; it lacks for nothing that the story has not mentioned.

Significantly, no place or time is given to the presence or activity of other gods or divine beings. At those places where a reader might expect to hear of other deities, such as in the appointment of the heavenly bodies, the reader encounters only the one creator God. Further, God receives no assistance, joins with no partner and competes with no rival. He does not overcome any obstacle and he faces no plot complication or crisis. He does not appropriate materials from a natural, spiritual, or pre-narrative world, as he is credited with creating all known realms even before the formless void appears (v. 1-2). Instead, God speaks all objects into existence. These objects appear uniform in their natural, non-mystical make-ups, and in their surface-value identities. The sky, land, and sea are not animated or extraordinary; they do not have unusual traits, powers, or aspects. They seem to be no different in substance than the birds, fish, creeping things, animals, or plants.

The direction of yield for the reader then is to see the world as it presents to ordinary perception and to consider that world to be complete without the intruding presence of divinities, spirits, magics, or mystical forces that might compete with God for ascendancy or operate of their own accords, outside of divine commissioning. In this narrative world, there is only one superior being and only one spiritual mover, Elohiym, the God of Israel. The reader might long to hear of other mystic beings, but that option is progressively and exhaustively denied; it is systematically excluded as the story moves along and the world is filled to completion. In the final account, the land is merely land; the heavenly lights are merely heavenly lights; the animals are only animals and the seasons are ordinary seasons, determined by the movements of the heavenly bodies.

This state of affairs is reinforced by God's ordering activity. Everything in this creation has a place that has been set deliberately for it by God and nothing strays from its place. Upon being called into existence, every created thing operates immediately according to the commission given to its category. This gives all non-divine activity a passive, responsive quality, since activity arises only in response to divine direction.

This is underscored by the sense of harmony that is presented to the reader. Repeated declarations (v. 4, 10, 12, 18, 21, 25) that God sees the creation as "good" (wayyarě'... kî-ṭôb)[118] reinforce in the reader the sense that this is how the world should be, with all things moving, living, and producing as they have been decreed to do. Adding to this, repetitions of the concept of fruitfulness press the reader to feel that this is a world of plenty and ease. Thus, the reader is urged from all sides toward a location that associates peace, plenty, and harmony with the obedient response of creation to the imperatives of God, who is the unequalled, unchallenged, sole creator. The account engineers resistance against any thought that there might be any other scheme for good life, and it rules out the prospect of gaining benefit from the presence or activity of competing supernatural actors. By doing so it pushes the reader away from considering any scenario as beneficial other than the fulfillment of divine mandate.

The irenic description of the world is deliberate and total, as the narrative glaringly lacks any descriptions of woe, hardship, or harshness. None of the difficult aspects of existence can be found in this world, where all is good. Although there is an implication that the creation might require forceful subjugation within the divine command to "subdue and rule" (wěkiběšuhā ûrědû) the earth, this appears more as a means of ascribing supremacy to the human pair than it is a direction for them to overcome a presenting threat. Considering that darkness and chaos are depicted as pre-states before the hand of God begins to order things, it appears that the command to dominate is designed primarily to limn a parallel between the

---

[118] This appears to be more evaluative than visual. God's "seeing" perceives the thing's actuality; it acts as an approval, that is, as an estimation of a thing "before the Lord" (Gen. 10:9, 19:13, 24:40, etc.) or "in the eyes of the Lord" (Gen. 6:8, Exod. 5:21, 1 Kgs.15:5, etc.)

role of God in the universe and the roles of those who bear his image on earth.

This presents a tension of dissonance to the reader. The text seems to describe the origins of a world that has continuity with the reader's own world, yet the world that is shown has none of the flaws that the reader would normally experience in his own lived reality. This tension urges the reader toward two related dispositional states. It creates a longing for the good, idyllic world that resembles the known world so closely, and it renders judgment on the world that the reader experiences in his day to day life. This ushers the reader toward desiring for the present order of things to change. It creates an incentive, and thus, a motivation, that seeks for all things to re-conform to divine mandates, so that the world would be right, good, and "as it *should* be."

Thus, the reader renders judgment on the world as it is, and as she does so, she pulls for the world to be good and at peace. However, goodness is not seen as a yet to be achieved, potential state. It is the possibility of a return to a baseline, pristine state, that is, as being good, fruitful and at peace, once *again*. The reader's tension is generated as he envisions a good world that *was*, while experiencing a less than good world that *is*. Since the goodness of the former world is portrayed as an actualization of divine intentions, joined with the subsequent approval of God, the only option that the text allows for the tension to be resolved would be if all things were to adhere to their appropriate divine instructions. The text's missio can be seen by looking along the trajectory of the reader's elicited and directed longing. It is aimed at instilling or confirming a disposition that seeks universal "right-ness" or righteousness, marked by the approval of God.

The aiming of the reader's longing is cumulatively reinforced by the narrative's steady movements. The orderliness of the world's construction is matched by the orderliness of the account's language, which builds component by component until its climax at the creation of humankind, followed by divine provision for humankind and the institution of the day of rest. The world becomes more ordered in a predictable, metered construction, which the reader can anticipate, and which has a predictable ending.

As the story paces its way forward, an unlivable, wet, chaotic darkness is replaced by a carefree, provisioned, and serene habitation. The safety and ease of this ordered scene orients the reader existentially to feel that the day of rest is indeed, like the world on the finished day, "very good" (wĕhinnēh-ṭôb). The day of rest not only feels satisfying as a completion of the familiar "seven" number scheme or as a narrative resolution, it also feels like the capstone of order in the creation.

Thus, tensions between the narrative world and the reader's world combine with the manner and direction in which the story aims the longing it elicits to leave a strong sense of unmet and necessary conditions. To the reader, the world as it is now is not right, compared to how it once was. If the world is to be good, ordered and right, humans and creation should fulfill divine command. For people, this entails being domestic and fruitful, filling the earth and exercising dominion, receiving God's providence, and representing God by resting in content harmony on the seventh day. The reader's longings and dissonances are shaped in such a way that he feels that if this state of affairs can be reached, the world will be "right" once more.

Subsection level view. The reader's pace is slowed considerably at the sixth day. God's divine speech of intention to make "man" (ʾādām; v. 26) "in our image and according to our likeness" (naʿăśeh ʾādām bĕṣalmēnû kidĕmûtēnû) uses terms that hearken to ANE court practices and idol worship in unseemly and enigmatic ways (Barr, 1968; Curtis, 1984; Humbert, 1940; Sawyer, 1974; Schule, 2005; Vriezen, 1958; Westermann, 1984). This piques the reader's curiosity and calls for clarification. God's pre-statement also effectively creates repetition in the action, doubling the presentation to the reader, which makes the plot move at half pace. The narration's strange balancing of ʾōtô ("him") with ʾōtām ("them") also requires increased attention and interpretive precision from a reader who has by this point become accustomed to the marching progress of the account. Together, these factors unsettle the reader and elicit within her a desire to understand or disambiguate. This simultaneously delays the reader's comprehension and heightens his tension and focus.

As the reader encounters humans, the dynamic force of reader identification comes into play. Until the sixth day, the reader has little or no place to identify, except with God, who is the only active, self-aware character in the story. It is only at this point that the reader hears any talk about an order of being higher than something material or surface order in its natural function, that is, anything similar to the sentient reader.

With the introduction of humans, the reader has a place of commonality to connect with. This is strengthened by the listing of key human life experiences: sexual identity, human reproduction, expansion and fruitfulness, along with human dominion over plants and animals. From this stage onward, the reader is hearing her own story from the location of the humans in the story, even though she may have heard the story from the viewpoint of God previously. The reader thus hears the divine mandates and blessing as addresses to herself, that is, to "us," not to "them."

These dynamics elicit a sense of nobility in the reader. Humans are rightfully the highest order in the world; they are proxy governors of the creator, set as representations of himself within his handiwork. Their ascendancy over all other things on earth is God-given, expressing God's own order. Their marriages are divinely sponsored, as are their progeny. This is as it should be, for they have a clear destiny. They have been commissioned and blessed to fill the earth and to subdue it, and all its productions have been given into their hands.

Simultaneously, the text arouses a sense of obligation and fealty. For, throughout the story humans are what they are by virtue of the bestowals of God. God has thought them up and fashioned them to fulfill a role. He has made them in his image and per his likeness, granting them authority that derives from his own. He has called them to behold (v. 29) that he has done so, in a manner that hearkens to regal deputizing, and he has given them provisions in an endowment that parallels inheritances and royal grants (Cf., Ezr. 4-6, especially Ezr. 6:3-10). All that the reader might experience as valuable: life and selfhood, marriage and family, the land and its fruit, the animals and their fruit, personal and social meaning and dignity, are directly attributed to divine endowment. The reader owes all, and feels honor bound to render back.

Both the sense of nobility and the sense of fealty are heightened as the scope of the narrative reduces. At the beginning, the vista is as broad as the universe. With each day, the frame shrinks, until, by the time the sixth day is reached, humans are the center of view, the focus and apex of the creative process.

As the frame reduces, however, the tension between the ideal world and the known world of the reader increases. For, from the reader's perspective, the outlook starts with those aspects of the world that still would appear to conform to divine bidding (the heavenly bodies, the seasons, and the cycles of day and night), but it shifts to survey things that no longer would be experienced as being in order, such as plants, animals and, most of all, humans. In other words, the reader's view of the "world as it was" splits mid story to a stereoscopic view. In this view, a vision of the "world as it should have stayed," becomes juxtaposed atop the scene of the "world as it is" that resides within the reader's experience. The force exerted by this dichotomy depends upon the amount of dissonance that it creates, which in turn rests upon the degree to which the reader's experienced world is subpar. This could be expressed as a function or quotient of the difference between human life as the reader knows it and the ideal human situation shown in the text. Its dynamic pressure rises or falls in relation to the degree that the reader experiences people to be masters or victims of nature, noble or ignoble, righteous or unrighteous, loyal to God or disloyal, fruitful or unfruitful, harmoniously domestic or disharmoniously domestic, provisioned or lacking.

Step Three: Discern outcomes (missio). Step Three is a summary reflection that assesses how the text affects the reader in terms of designed outcomes. It views the effects that the text works upon the reader as components in an overall textual agenda for the reader's life and experience. This is the step at which the missio of the text is articulated in its most condensed form, that is, in terms of its *telos*. The focus alternates between the immediate, very present experience of the reader as he reads the text and more broadly ranged effects. This is done by integrating the immediate outcomes that are produced in the reader with those eventual outcomes at which the text is aimed. While Step Two looks directly act what the text is doing, Step Three sees what the text is doing *in order that* something might be brought about.

This view relates immediate textual goals to goals that hearken from larger agenda, including discursive and canonical levels. The dialectic between these frames readily invites questions about combined purposes, which makes Step Three a fruitful place to ask questions from (the nonlinear) Step Five (see above). The key questions for this stage are, "What are the text's goals, for whom?," "How do the goals of the text show a plan for the reader and her experience?" and, "What does the text value most in its plan for the reader?"

The factors that influence these outcomes are understood to involve more than can be held within the immediate perceptive intentions of a single author. Thus, outcomes are considered in robust, multi-faceted ways that span dimensions of reality and worldview. As in Step Two, outcomes should be considered in light of the full range of human experience (see chap. 2 & 5, above). The text's goals should be articulated in holistic terms, not as cognition, alone, since effects can also involve volition, affect and disposition, relation and identification, reflexive awareness, evaluation (ethics and morality) and spirituality. The interpreter should seek to discern how any or all of these may be the object of textual missio.

Section level view. The major features that we have seen appear to be aimed at a few basic outcomes. At the fore, the text seems designed to move the reader into three key states. It moves the reader into an allied, yet subordinate and reliant disposition toward God. It also places the reader in a superior, active stance toward the rest of creation, and it calls the reader to recognize human value.

Motivationally, it seeks to create a dynamic, affective longing in the reader for a better state of the world. The text aims to coax judgment from the reader by maneuvering her to see her own world as a diminished version of the world that once was good. It intends to guide the reader to a moral and spiritual evaluation that the primary flaw in the diminished (contemporary) world is a lack of ordered conformity to the mandates of God.

As the text does this, it reinforces a worldview that perceives creation in terms of divinely given categories, statuses, and roles. It strengthens an outlook that sees all things as having a place and a mission to fulfill under the authority and commission of God. It also categorically excludes other spiritual forces or actors. It heightens awareness that God is the one who renders judgment upon all by showing all things as existing under his commissioning and approval, and it mandates fealty, dependence, and service to the God of Israel as the only source of being and the world's creator.

A number of reflexive and relational dispositions about human place and value are elicited in order to support these ends. The reader is stirred to feel a sense of nobility and superiority as a human. This sense of nobility pushes the reader to validate human expansion, coupled with dominion over the environment. This induces the reader to endorse those goals as appropriate social projects, with the outcomes that the reader would partake appropriately in society and aver from passivity.

Evaluatively, a key aim is that the reader would assign positive worth to primary human life goals and events, such as mating, family raising, and domestic life. This nobility is also directed at human sex identities, pressing the reader to feel positive pride in being male or female. The text aims to sustain appreciation for living in fundamental human traits. Ordinary life processes are to be experienced as ennobling, satisfying and righteous. Further, the text leads the reader to associate these values with pastoral lifestyles that involve exercising control over the earth, plants, and animals, such as husbandry and agriculture.

The account also valorizes Sabbath rest as a key hallmark of order. It seeks to sustain observance of the Sabbath by making the image of the Sabbath appealing on environmental levels, as a situation of safety and fruitfulness. It also frames the Sabbath as the point of plot resolution, lending the seventh day a feeling of completion and repose. Lastly, it characterizes the Sabbath as emulation and association with God, which compounds the sense of positive partnership with the divine. Taken together, all of these outcomes show the missio of passage to be the formation and strengthening of solidarity between humans and God, in support of God's reign over creation.

Subsection level view. In the subsection that treats the creation of humans, the text ushers the reader into a subordinate, dependent, yet allied relationship with God. Humans are supposed to feel that the order, fruitfulness and sustenance of the world comes from God, which directs them into a worshipful and grateful disposition, and readers are oriented to associate their own senses of value and nobility with the bearing of God's own image. The reader is moved to feel a sense of meaningfulness and life-purpose as a deputy of God's reign. He sees himself as one who stands over the rest of creation in the authority of God's image as he leads an ordinary agrarian or pastoral human life, mating and raising human generations.

Synergistically, these outcomes forge a path of greatest yield that points the reader toward a holistic life, characterized by: 1) compliant response to God, that is coupled with, 2) a sense of duty, authority and significance 3) dispositions of admiration, adoration and loyalty 4) attribution of all things to God, especially good things; 5) satisfaction with domestic human living, and, 6) longing for universal righteousness as adherence to divine mandate.

By contrast, resistances are constructed that push the reader away from 1) variance or violation of divine order, 2) self-ordering, especially if that fails to acknowledge God, 3) misdirected attribution of goodness, the creation and all creational functions to any other than God, 4) failure to mate, be fruitful and raise family, 5) failure to assert presence and dominion within creation, 6) devaluation of humans, including the self, and, 7) any reticence or failure to represent God in the reader's own life.

Overall, these show that the reader is aimed to long for goodness to be in the world through universal compliance with the divine, and, within that scheme, to find self-value and meaning by living domestic human life as a divine representative, who stands in the world on behalf of God's order. A key demonstration of this order is rest on the seventh day.

Varied influences (Step Five). When we look for various purposes that might be at play, we can see that the individual composer of the passage is highly concerned with the orderliness of creation, with God's place as the creator, and with the status and role of human beings in the world. The author shows significant regard for calendrical identifiers in the repeated mentions of days and of the formation of the seasons. He also exhibits a value for controlled aesthetics, shown through the metered stylization of the text and in the imagery and dialog. He wants the reader to join with his vision of the universe as a beautifully designed system and to acknowledge the rightness of a world that operates under God, that responds to God and that is well-disposed toward God.

On societal and institutional levels, this fits well with the pastoral traditions within Israelite society. The view is a folk view that emphasizes the sacred calling of every person, rather than highlighting the ordination of special groups. It sees value in the domestic aspects of life and the activity of human beings as those who corporately subordinate the natural environment. It is attenuated to the cycles of the days and seasons, especially the weekly cycle. It is a down to earth view that prioritizes natural fruitfulness, which is associated with reproduction. The outlook is concrete, avoiding fantastic speculations, or outlandish descriptions of mystic realms.

Unlike many of the Israelite folk expressions, the account squarely and unequivocally represents the interests of monotheism. As we have already seen, no place is given to any form of spiritism, animism, polytheism, astrology, or magic. There are humans, plants, creatures on land and in air and sea, heavenly luminaries, and God. That is all. The thrust of this tradition excludes all possible spiritual coexistences and competitors. Its agenda is to treat all of the entities that might be associated with spiritual power in the Ancient Near East, the sun, moon, stars, land, seasons, and creatures, as mere objects, functional creations spoken into existence by the word and will of Elohiym. According to its outlook, the God of Israel is not the supreme god, or primary spiritual entity; he is the only God, the only spiritual actor or source.

This participates in the tradition of Israelite antagonism toward graven images associated with Moses. In this account, the image of God is only to be found in the living, breathing humans that he has appointed to the task. Humans are sanctioned to be images of God, and they alone have the capacities for regency and connection to the divine that sacred imagery requires. All non-human images are thus rendered unauthorized competitors and pretenders to the place of humankind within creation. Only humans can fulfill the divine mandate to bear God's image. They do this by standing above the other living things in creation and in their reproducing and ruling, in conscious, active representation of God.

An added factor is the concern for the ideas of authority, reign and dominion. God acts by decree and he grants rule to humans. All things exist and operate according to command, which comes in the form of verbal imperatives that are straightforward and authoritative. These are uttered in a stylized form, carrying overtones of juridical process. These spoken orders frame a world that is organized via the right to rule and to pronounce. In it, God creates by simple verbal decisions, not through arcane ritual or via acts of prowess among the gods. This demonstrates a regard for oral utterance as a means of ordering society and governing.

Taken together, these traits sketch the outlines of an agenda that would lie close to the hearts of highly monotheistic tribal elders. The concerns and style also suggest affinity with the folk and naturalist sides of the oral wisdom tradition, in contrast to the centralized, priestly or courtly strands. At minimum, the tradition that influences this text expects people to maintain their right places in society and to live their lives well and peacefully, given that God has decreed an appropriate way for all things to exist, per their assigned categories. All things should know their places and act accordingly. This includes observance of the calendar and the day of rest. Within this world, it is the rightful duty of divinely authorized man to ensure that appropriate order is followed by subduing and ruling over the creation. Such is the obligation and nobility of humankind.

This integrates well with Pentateuchal concerns for the right ordering of Israelite society, especially as those might refract through a nostalgic lens that looks toward the past as a canon and blueprint for the nation. The passage also serves canonical interests as a keystone declaration within a larger authorized body of writings. This depiction sets a narrative precedent that supports later and larger canonical concerns and claims. It provides a foundational motif as well as a summary proposal that demonstrates the place of sacred, authoritative utterances and pronouncements.

Set as backgrounds, these interests highlight some of what appear to be God's interests in the passage. If we consider God as a co-author of the text, his influence on it has placed him in direct and center view. This shows an intention to be acknowledged for what he has done and a desire to be ascribed sole credit for all that is in the created order, especially for that which is good.

It also indicates that God would be characterized as powerful, determinant, present and active in creation, and that he would be known to expect that the creation would adhere to the places and roles that he has assigned. From what we have seen, God would have humankind mirror his intention for all things to conform to his will and he would have humans see the effecting of creation's compliance as integral to humankind's own existence and meaning. And, while God's intention is for humans to see themselves as superior to the environment around them, it is also for humans to associate that superiority with their proxy representation of his own person. He would have humans stand in solidarity with him, being disposed toward that which is good and fruitful. He would have humans long for good, orderly things, and he would offer his approval and affirmation over any of his creations via pronouncement of goodness when things fulfill his rightful arrangements.

Negatively, God would have people render judgment on those aspects of the world that do not conform to divine mandate. He would have people desire for the world to be as he decreed it and to attribute the world's current diminished state(s) to failure to comply with God's plan, most keenly demonstrated by how humans observe or fail to observe the seventh day of rest. God would have readers attribute problems, as well as their own disappointments and frustrations with life in a less than ideal world to unrighteous disorder, not to God's malice, negligence, weakness, or absence. Further, God would have no distracting or competing presences or loyalties be considered at any level. He would have it known that he has the power to bless, and that he can create fruitfulness, rest and harmony out of chaos, darkness and disorder.

Step Four: Consider inferences and implications. Step Four considers inferences and implications that arise from the observations in the preceding steps. It looks at how the missio of a particular text relates to other missio agenda.

We have already seen that texts are not isolated; they participate in multiple constellations of discourse that exert force upon the text's design. Thus, many goals simultaneously may be intended by many textual influences, which may stand together within the text. By the same token, the text may carry broader aims that may be directed beyond the solitary reader, toward institutions, society or humankind at large. Intended outcomes for these additional targets also may be immediate or eventual. Thus, the interpreter should alternate between a view of the reader and a view of other entities and audiences that potentially could be affected or addressed, in which the reader may or may not knowingly participate.

The focus with this step is on integration. The view is toward the involvement of the text's missio with other textual, traditional or sacred missios, rather than on the contrast that reveals or distinguishes separate influences. The aim is to consider how the immediate outcomes of the text's interaction with the reader coordinate and integrate with larger frames and agenda. This step forms a bridge between missiological interpretation and mission theology.

During Step Four, the biblical canon is a crucial constellation of missio(s) for the interpreter to consider, for the canon is the sacred, authoritative compilation in which the immediate text is embedded and with which it participates. From a canonical view, even a self-contained text is a component of an integrated whole, and, like the metanarrative of the missio Dei and the magisterium of the church, the canon overtly carries the agenda of God as the text's co-author. Because of this, the canon's missio holds priority of consideration.

The key questions for this stage are, "How does this fit with what is going on beyond it?" "How does what this text accomplishes coordinate with what other texts accomplish?" and, "How does the aim of this text contribute to larger scale projects?"

On societal levels, this text is a cornerstone of Israelite monotheism. It speaks over the shoulder of the reader toward competing religious movements in the ANE. It calls for singleness of religious outlook, uniformity and solidarity, militating against religious syncretism, against animism, astrological or magical practices, and against any accommodation of spiritual practices that are not grounded in the worship of Israel's God.

It also agonizes against social or status separation of the sexes, especially religious separation. It calls for both sexes to be recognized as joint participants in religious service and in sacred responsibility to fulfill God's will. It upholds the institution of domestic union as a foundation for human life and it supports the domesticating agrarian project and lifestyle.

Canonically, Genesis 1 is unique as the commencement of the universal narrative. It opens its own context; nothing comes beforehand in terms of story or meta-story. However, if the view is opened to take into account that which follows, the passage has much to offer as the first statement of the overarching biblical discourse.

Most importantly, the story sets the ground rules and the standards of measure for all that follows. In the world that is shown, the ideal is that all would be "very good." This is seen as divinely achievable, since the world is depicted as being in such a state at the conclusion of the story. The key factor that enables the world to be so good is sacred design, actualized by divine activity. This is met by the responsiveness of creation, under the custody of humankind, who partner with God as his representatives.

In terms of the formation of missiological knowledge, this scenario provides the subsidiary ground that empowers focal identification of other activities and existences. It gives the iconic outline, the measure of fullness that establishes the standard to be reached, and all other things come into view against its archetypal backdrop. As the section lays out the blueprints and codes for a "very good" world, it sets a mark against competing visions that would order reality differently. This frames a tacit assertion about the nature of all conflicts, diminished states and flaws. For, given that the world is good when it conforms to God's will, the state of not being good must derive from some sort of deviation from that will.

Using the perspective of the missio Dei, here we are given a fundamental sacred agenda, namely, that God has an intention for reality to be very good, to be ordered, fruitful, and harmonious. Further, God has a place for humans in this good world. That place is for humans to be partnered with God, representing him within creation as they live their ordinary lives. These ordinary lives are supremely honorable, since they are part of an overarching project for humankind to multiply and exercise custodianship over the earth, mirroring God as they do so.

The events that fill the rest of the biblical story can be seen as subplots and iterations, variations upon this motif. In the broader biblical discourse, every agonistic energy is directed at bringing the universe toward a state of propriety. Divine strategies, prohibitions, correctives, judgments, mercies, revelations, calls, covenants, and utterances are aimed at fulfilling God's vision for the world to be very good, and he relentlessly summons human partnership in that effort, for the benefit of the world, and for the fulfillment of human life.

By presenting an idyllic situation and calling the reader toward it, the text establishes an evaluative canon for missional activity. All known things may be measured in relation to the unmarred ideals portrayed in the scenario, especially human status and role. This sets criteria for assessing subsequent human actions and projects, that is, all other missio agenda. It provides a frame of reference that gives a foundation from which mission-oriented questions can be asked of any situation, being, behavior, or thing. Missional questions thus can be framed parallel to the concerns of the text, such as, "Does this (item under consideration) conform to its divine assignment?" "Is God satisfied?" "Is it blessed and approved in God's eyes? Does he see it as 'good' or 'very good?'" "Is it in its right place?" "Does it fulfill its duty and function?" "Is it fruitful?" "Does it represent God through human action?"

These criteria and their attendant questions recur as undertones throughout the accounts in the rest of the canon. They weave through the covenant promises to Abraham and his seed, through the directives of the Mosaic commandments and through the prophetic calls for just society. Their standards find expression across such dispersed utterances as, "(the thing) displeased the Lord," (Gen. 38:10, 2 Sam. 11:27) "Have no other gods before me," (Exod. 20:3) "Do justly, love mercy and walk humbly with thy God" (Mic. 6:8) and, "Blessed are they that hunger and thirst after righteousness" (Matt. 5:6). They also appear in negative pronouncements against each acting in ways, "right in his own eyes" (Deut. 12:8, Judg. 17:6), as well as the repeated acknowledgment, "Thy will be done" (Matt. 6:10; 26:42). Even the honorific divine titles, "Lord," "Most High" and, "Father in Heaven" hearken to the ideals set forth in this text.

In historical as well as contemporary senses, these motifs show through as the enduring and pervading attentions of mission. For mission continually inquires, "How is reality not as it should be?" "How can humans live to their fullest appropriate stature?" "What is meaningful in human life, and what makes people so valuable?" "How can people mirror God, participate in his plan for the world and fulfill their partnership with him?" "What is God's vision for all existence?" "What does God approve and bless?" These concerns cycle around the core missional assertion, "There is a divine goal underneath the design of reality. There is a divine mandate in force and a divine plan in operation for the universe to be 'good' and, even more, to be 'very good,' and God expects people to be joined with him as he brings his design to fulfillment."

Product, Ground and Tool

We will now shift methods and consider Product, Ground and Tool dimensions. Because this is a demonstration of how to use method, this analysis will be framed as a separate interpretation, not as continued interpretation. However, remember that PGT can be used alone or with TA. It does not rely upon TA, or require it, but it can use TA to help refine its findings. Thus, as we move to PGT, we will be starting over, using a new procedure to look at the same passage, but we will not do so as though we are approaching a completely blank slate; we will keep in mind some of the things that we found during TA.

As in the TA, the PGT data will build through the steps. Therefore, we can expect to find repetitions as we look through the different lenses. These redundant findings are important to include because they add substance to the overall process. For, as points recur using different angles of examination, they confirm findings, and by doing so, they reveal central aspects through their overlaps.

Genesis 1 as a Product of Mission. In review, the Product dimension looks toward the *past*, asking about the text's origination. Prepositionally, this looks at the "of" "out of" or "from" aspect. It asks, "How is the text a product *of* mission?" or, "How did the text arise *out of* mission?" In Product analysis the interpreter focuses on how the text has come into existence as a result of human and divine purpose(s). The goal is to discern the motivations that undergird and suffuse the text. In this process, the interpreter looks for hallmarks of purpose by looking at textual features and backgrounds. These are used as foundation in order to describe the ways in which specific missions (God's and/or people's) have contributed to the text's formation.

Complex Products. When we view the text as the product of agenda, we see it as a weave of intentions. This is similar to Van Engen's "tapestry" approach (1996, pp. 40-43), but it looks for missios that are revealed by the various thematic threads. The strands that make up this weave can be discerned by observing the things that the text holds in regard or champions. For analytic purposes, each concern can be viewed as a distinct component that contributes to the overall thrust of the text's complex missio, even though those concerns have been structured into a final text that is an integrated whole.

In other words, authors are complex creatures, and their motivations are rarely singular. As we saw earlier, a composer may have many influences at play within herself as she writes, and she may be hoping to accomplish a number of things in a single composition. She might be conscious of some of her goals, while others of her intentions may remain underneath her immediate awareness. These motivators may come from differing, even conflicting, personal desires, and they may participate in a variety of social discourses that are at play around the author. However, even though these are all mixed together as an author writes, or as a redactor edits, the choices that the writer makes at any given instance can reveal particular, identifiable dimensions of concern.

The underlying rationale behind this kind of analysis is similar to the reasoning that gave rise to traditional criticisms within biblical studies. The idea is that the "hand" of a writer can be seen through the language and style choices that are found in the text, and that those choices reflect the constellations of values that comprise particular traditions. However, in missiological analysis, we look for how those traditions and discourses are expressing missio, that is, an aim to accomplish certain ends. These ends span the spectrum of states and behaviors. The goal may be to change a certain thing, it might be to preserve something, it could be trying to inform, to render honor, to condemn, to include or exclude, to identify with or distance from, etc.

When looking for the Product dimension, each point that the text presents can be missiologically assessed as representing an agenda. The text is understood to be a complex production of those varied agenda, and the aim is to evaluate the strands of agenda in order to ascertain the larger, composite missio of the passage.

Put as an analogy, Product analysis sees a composition as a textual "stew" of agenda. It tries to notice the varied missio ingredients that have gone into the stew and by identifying the ingredients, to figure out what the aim may have been for the final dish. In that process, attention alternates between looking at the ingredients and looking at how they come together to make the stew. This means that PGT is structured differently than TA. While TA looks at the passage as a linear progression, PGT looks more thematically, seeking to discern the parts of the whole, and the analysis is organized according to missio concerns. These agenda are outlined in each of the PGT sections.

Monotheism. Quite a few strands of agenda are evident in Genesis 1, but the most prominent is the stark monotheism of the cosmogony (Vriezen, 1958). The fact that no space at all is provided in the story for any auxiliary deities or pantheon of beings shows the text to be a product of a clearly "God is One, and God is alone" worldview, and its missio directs exclusionary force to banish all possible competitors from view.

The text's objective is to locate all things within the confines of a closed universe that comes from only one deity and that only has one deity at work. This deity is not described in any manner; he is simply the one who is and who acts, who alone is responsible for all known things. This shows a parallel agenda to Israel's defining confession (Deut. 6:4), which declares the singularity of YHWH.

Even though the name of God in Gen. 1 is *Elohiym*, the missional affinity between the Deuteronomy and Genesis texts shows a core understanding and a core missio held in common by both Elohistic and Yahwistic traditions. Also, given that the name of God shifts to YHWH in the passage immediately following (Gen. 2:4-23/24), the story's placement in the composition of Genesis shows it to be produced by an outlook that held varied names for God under a single association.

From this perspective, since there is and only can be one God, all references and names in any Israelite story must refer only to him. Thus, as far as the author is concerned, there is no conceivable disjunction between passages that use Yahwistic terms and those that use Elohistic terms. All terms that speak about Israel's God speak about the One and only God.

As a cosmogony that is out of step with others of the Ancient Near East, the opening account of Chapter 1 fits well in a book that treats extensively with the development of Israel's unique identity. Since the story naturally would conflict and compete with the creation tales of surrounding cultures, it demonstrates the socio-religious boundaries of the faith of Abraham, whose story fills the center of the larger narrative.

This bears a key distinctive of the people who lay claim to the larger Genesis story as their group heritage. The account contains a watershed that provides an easy, defining contrast to those who do not serve Elohiym, such as the non-Israelite characters that Abraham and his kin later encounter within the narrative. Abraham is different than the people around him because he believes in the one true God, and his people are different than their people. As a product of forces that establish group identity, the story contains a unique worldview that carries the group's primary self-identifier. Functionally, it sets a social horizon that proclaims, "This is the real story of the real universe. We are the people who know the right story of the One true God. This God is our God, the God of Abraham, Isaac and Jacob, the God who made the Heavens and the Earth."

Orality and authority. The account's pervasive orality is another conspicuous strand. The basic plot is not driven by conflicts, journeys or precipitous events; it moves forward through a series of speech-acts. As it does so, God does not work with his hands; he does not fight battles or perform feats. Instead, God utters, and his utterances are themselves the acts of creation. When the plot develops complexity, it explores further speech acts in the form of blessings and commissions. Even though humans are not shown to be spoken into existence, self-speaking reflection provides the foundation for their creation, and the story notably lacks description of any attending creative activity on God's part.

This narrative content matches the style of the account, which bears classic traits of oral composition. The stair-step movements are numbered, repetitive, simple and formulaic. When they vary from their basic formula, they do so in couplets of Hebrew parallelism. The story has a clear, metered quality; and it ends with a heavy ballast line that provides an etiology for the day of rest. These characteristics lend themselves to oral recitation or memorization. Throughout, the utterances are authoritative. Their characteristics show a value for governance that is expressed in verbal pronouncement. God's words are the words of a ruler, and their style would fit the mouth of any patriarch, tribal elder, conquering warrior, prince, king or suzerain. This matches the social location of Israelite tribal elders, those who "sit in the gates," (Cf., Ruth 4:11; 2 Sam. 19:8; Ps. 69:12, etc.) and it is consonant with the wisdom traditions that they participated in (Prov. 8:3, 24:7, 31:23, 31 etc.).

With these hallmarks, the story appears to have been produced from within social discourses that hold regard for hierarchy, authority, dominion and rulership, especially as those functions are administered via the spoken word. As it displays both ground and precedent for those kinds of social operations, it bolsters the exercise of societal role(s) that render approval, grant subsidiary rights and authority, delegate tasks, appoint representatives and bestow blessings. The missio of the text sustains and reinforces the notion that society is to be well-ordered and that appropriate order is created and maintained by the authoritative exercise of power, rendered in edicts.

Gender equity. However, there is also an interesting gender equity at play in the text. "Man" ('ādām; v. 26) is curiously indicated as both "him" and "them" as God's creation is characterized as being dual ("male and female, [God] created them;" bārā' 'ōtô zākār ûněqēbâ bārā' 'ōtām). The cumbersome construction, combined with the synthetic parallelism, appears to indicate a deliberate extension of the term "man." This extension stretches the ordinary range of the term, "man" by joining it to a unified plural of "male and female/them" The net result allocates image, representation and authority to both sexes in a combined category. For, although "man" is the focus of God's forethought and intention, the final expression of that intention is "them." And, throughout the remainder of the story, God addresses his words "to them" (lāhem). Thus, while the text has a missio to champion order under one God, who is represented by "man," a key part of the text's missio is to keep the sexes balanced as participants in divine representation and in the exercise of human dominion.

There is also the awkward and unexplained plural in God's self-deliberation to "make" (na'ăśeh) (Westermann, 1984), which gives a sense of mystery to the person of God. The passage may be hinting that the image in which humans are made hearkens to a complexity in God's own person (Barth, 1958). It also may be hinting at a divine council (von Rad, 1972) (Sawyer, 1974) or simply using majestic speech (Keil & Delitzsch, 1981). This may indicate that the story could have had an earlier, simpler form, which may have been taken up and modified to serve Israelite ends.[119] Problematically, the story does not provide a means to disambiguate these possibilities. It does not refer to God in feminine terms; it does not show other divine actors, and the plural cannot be found in God's actions or other utterances

Human production. Thus, it appears that the agenda for the divine plural has been co-opted or subsumed into more prominent concerns that have informed the canonical state of the text. The central themes in the final state of the story do show it to be at minimum a combined production of discourses that value monotheism, oral tradition, authority and gender parity. Lesser telltales also seem to characterize the account as the product of an author or tradition that was concerned for the social identity of Israel, which perhaps also was familiar or interactive with non-Israelite sources of oral tradition. Taking into consideration some of the text's affinities with wisdom and rulership discourses, this might indicate production from

---

[119] Wittenberg remarks on, "the critical power of the old Yahwistic belief which could not simply adopt other religious customs without profoundly altering their meaning."(1975 p. 15). Also Brueggemann, "There is no doubt that the text *utilizes older materials*. It reflects creation stories and cosmologies of Egypt and Mesopotamia. However, the text before us transforms these older materials to serve quite a new purpose" (1982p. 24) [italics in original]."Widely taken for granted has been P's exilic origin or final redaction in Babylonia. However, such a supposition is far from clear for Gen. 1:1-2:3, since the cosmogony nowhere specifically addresses itself, polemically or otherwise, to Babylonian concepts of cosmogony...Indeed, the most that can be said is that the mythological background of P's cosmogony is generally ancient Near Eastern." (W. P. Brown, 1993p. 230).

within the Israelite "wise woman" tradition exemplified at Tekoa (2 Sam. 14:2ff).

These are only a few of the human-level influence strands from which the text has been produced, and which give the text its missional footprint. Many other strands contribute to the weave of the passage, such as Sabbath advocacy, especially from within the Mosaic discourse(s), folk pedagogy and literature, calendrical and priestly concerns, festal traditions, domestic and agrarian proponency, especially in support of pastoral life, antagonism to images, naturalism within the Hokmah tradition, etc. Each of these could be explored in a Product view, in a wide variety of combinations. The aim in any given Product analysis is to discern such strands and to show how they are revealed by features of the text, noting how the text carries each strand's missional concerns within itself as part of its own missio. However, it is crucial to remember that human-level influence is not the only concern of missiological inquiry. We also must look at the text as a divine production.

Divine production. When we consider the text as a product of God's own missio, his centrality in the narrative stands to the fore. Here, God is the source of all things. He is before any order and order derives from him. He is the conqueror of chaos, darkness and emptiness. His actions are determinant, imperial and final. Without aid or opposition, he is the one who conceives and brings into being. He is the maker of the heavens, and all orders of time are by his decree. He produces life and renders blessing, and fertility derives from his spoken decree.

Further, God is the one who renders evaluation through his own opinion, and he approves of his own work. In his eyes, his work is good; in fact, it is very good, and his assessment of it finalizes it its true and real character of being. He answers to himself, being satisfied with his own efforts and determining the limits of his work. Even when he ceases, his cessation itself becomes the standard to be followed. He is to, of, for and by himself in all ways.

Seen from this angle, the text is a product of God's mission to glorify himself. His hand is in it to render to himself credit for who he is and what he has done. Its movements keep God always in view and they allow no place for another. This reveals a concern for God's mission to be acknowledged as the Most High, supreme, without equal or challenge.

Additionally, God grants humans a unique place as his proxy images, deputies of his dominion. He conceives of them as his representation, set as a testimonial marker within his domain.[120] They are mysterious, as he is, for God makes "him" singly as he makes "them" dually, which hints of God's own cryptic, plural self-address. Together, they are his governor, who exerts power to keep things on the earth as God has determined. Although there appears only to be a single pair, humans are blessed to rise and expand as no other of God's creatures. When he is finished providing them with his bounty, he ceases to create.

These features show a concern for humans to be simultaneously ennobled and subservient. Humans are indeed the highest of the created order, but, as representatives and governors, they owe all to the sovereign who has appointed them. God's mission appears to be to invite humankind into his glory, but never to lose or transfer that glory in essential ways. Humans carry the glory of God, but they refer it, pointing to its origin in their very existence and procreation.

Viewed as the product of God as co-author, the text derives from a divine mission to self-memorialize, parallel to the composition of an imperial inscription, or an artisan's signature. The story itself erects a monument to divine feats, and its narrative dedicates all of humankind to the perpetuation of divine representation. However, as it does so, the account also sublimates humankind. Humans are not thralls, whose

---

[120]Curtis (1984) and Middleton (2005) both appeal to extensive lists of Egyptian and Mesopotamian texts, especially instances of laudatory courtly address, in which image terminology is applied to kings, priests and statues as place-holder representations of the god and to statues as place-holders for the king. Both understand image as meaning, a sort of "deputy" or "co-regent." They build upon von Rad (1972) and Humbert (1940), among others.

subjugation demonstrates divine, royal might. They are governing stewards who live their representation with the authority and provision of the crown behind them.

These traits reveal a divine mission to integrate humankind intrinsically and existentially as partners in God's own self-expression. Yet, this mission does not release glory from its anchor in God. Humans are partners in the expression of divine glory, but they are junior and derivative partners. Their appointment requires that the expression of human dignity and dominion maintain a reliant and ostensive relation to God.

In terms of missio, then, the composition arises first from God's aim that people would acknowledge him. Secondarily, it emerges from God's objective that people might maintain his order, on his behalf. This appears to be influenced by a divine desire for humans to experience themselves as extraordinarily valuable and important. However, that end is qualified by the primary concern for God's glory. While one value is the honor of humans, that value remains subordinate in the overall mix of agenda. God's intention is that people would know their own superiority within creation, but that people also would know themselves and their progeny to be superior by virtue of God's creation, deputation, provision and blessing of them.

Genesis 1 as a Ground for Mission. The Ground dimension sees the text as a perpetual and authoritative mission foundation, regardless of place and time. This takes a "now, and always" view. Prepositionally, Ground inquiry seeks the text's "for" or "about" capacity. It asks, "How does the text provide a Ground *for* mission?" or, "What does the text support or reveal *about* mission?"

Here, the interpreter reorients his view from local, historically based observations toward non-local, principle-based observations. This is a change in both scale and kind. It expands from looking at actual, particular expressions, shifting instead to examine universal and potential expressions. In other words, Ground analysis steps out of temporal and spatial constraints by considering universal aspects. Rather than viewing the text's missio in terms of a certain place and time, it seeks the text's missio in terms of any place and any time. The focus is on the text's agenda and on how that textual agenda relates to Mission, per se.

The goal is to understand how to fulfill or perform mission in ways that correspond to the text's missio. Procedurally, this is done by extrapolating from the particulars of the text in order to articulate universals, and then in turn to use those universals to inform the production of new particulars. The agenda is to emulate the text.

Longing for the ideal. Let's begin by reviewing our observations.

In the topographic analysis, we saw that the text elicits a longing for a prosperous and harmonious world, in contrast to the experienced world of the reader.

In both Topographic and Product analyses, we could see that the ideal world in Gen 1 is presented as a world that has order, and that the order of the idyllic world corresponds to its compliance with divine edict. In the story, all creations in the world (as it once was, and should be) exist in a state of positive response to divine dictates. Divine commands come in the form of categorical commissions and blessings, and all creatures are connected to their places in creation via participation in the categories to which they were assigned.

These features can be considered as foundations for framing mission principles and activity. Based on what is portrayed here, mission can assume that there is a possible highest state for all of creation and all creatures, and that that highest state is not currently experienced. Emulating this account of things, mission can proceed on a premise that God has ordained for his creation to be orderly, harmonious and responsive to him, and that variance from these states results in a diminished state of the world, which can be understood as harm.

God's ideal. Crucially, we cannot exclude God's missio from direct consideration. Thus, we can read that God desires for his creation to be "good." We can also read that God sees orderly compliance with his will as a good state, that he sees acknowledgement of his own supremacy as part of this good state, and that he exercises his power and authority to see this state actualized in the world.

These are key points, because they impact how missional orientations, such as the disposition to love or to care, are framed in missional thinking. Using this text as a foundational example, all orders of beings have their right places, and it is both good and very good that creatures live according to those assignments. As dispositions that seek the highest good of others, then, love and care rightfully seek for all things within creation to be and act in harmonious congruence with divinely given, categorical states, in ways that demonstrate God's supreme place.

Negative reading. In reading for Ground, principles also may be viewed in terms of negation. This is a method of viewing through binary opposition, which considers that when something is proposed in a positive state, negative statements about that thing's negative state express the same truth or principle. When negative observation is done, it reveals negative mission, that is, those things that mission can oppose or protest. Like processes in logic or math, when mission acts negatively against a negative state, the result can be understood as positive mission action.

Negatively speaking, mission can view lack of responsive compliance to God's mandates as disorderly and disharmonious, that is, as "not good." From this angle, missional love calls mission agents to oppose anything that fosters less than good states, that is, to oppose harm. According to this text, disharmony, chaos and disregard for divine mandates or order qualify negatively as states to be resisted or protested by mission, especially since these negative states can be understood to be opposed by God in his own mission.

Dominion and agency. We can see this in the text because the states of good, order and harmony that mission seeks are not to be found at natural levels, alone. They come from divine decree and they depend upon divine authority. This leads to a following principle, as the text encourages the rigorous exercise of human dominion. Missionally, this supports the idea that in his mission, God ordains people to act on his behalf, partnering with him in his work. Thus, humans are to consider themselves to be agents that are actively engaged in maintaining good states for other creatures on the earth. Given that God bestows privilege on people so that they may accomplish this, it is legitimate for humans to see themselves as superior and valuable because they have a place of divine regard and agency in the world.

In light of this, mission can propose a universal human responsibility to represent God in the world, and it can see that responsibility as a first order issue for human existence. Thus, mission can view alignment with God and action on his behalf as intrinsic needs of human beings. Mission also can see a direct relationship between fulfillment of the need to represent God and the human experience of value.

Provision. Notably, the text depicts that God provides food for the humans after their commission to bear his image and to be fruitful, fill the earth and subdue it. In principle, this gives a pattern that calls for the supply of physical needs in support of primary human duties. Here, God has a mission to provide for the physical needs of humans, and mission can follow suit by seeking to provide physical needs.

At the same time, however, it appears that God first commissions humans to represent him, then, as following action, he provides for people so that they may fulfill his preceding appointment. The text thus can set a priority for mission activity by showing what action serves what end. In this passage, the supply of subsistence serves the duties to represent, multiply and rule the earth. It prioritizes living as agents over living "by bread, alone."

Mission can mirror this by caring for physical needs expressly so that people would fulfill God's call upon their lives.

Domestic life. Even with this priority in view, the text also sacralizes domestic life and progeny by casting these also as expressions of divine decree. This renders honor on everyday human life, and it gives mission a foundation for support of basic family needs. God's mission is for humans to live as mated pairs, to produce offspring and to fill the earth. His aim is to have people dominate his world through their generations. Mission then may support human fruitfulness. It can perform relational service that sustains and protects marriages and families, and it can promote the growth of families, groups and populations.

Further, the passage authorizes this process to involve the forceful subjugation of the earth. From a mission perspective, this supports development activity that prioritizes use of the earth and its resources for the sustenance of human life and well-being. In doing so, it also establishes the ends for which the earth may be subjugated. The earth is to be subdued so that humans may be fruitful and multiply and represent God through their presence. This is reinforced by God's statement that he has given them the earth as provision. God's mission is that humans would enjoy the fruits of his world and that they would be sustained by those fruits.

As a limit, markedly, nothing is mentioned about excess, wealth, pleasure or waste. Thus, in mission, humans are authorized to pursue development, but to understand development in terms of provision. This places priority on sustaining human life and well-being, and mission has grounds to support these ends, since they are the ends that God has stated in his mission to provide. However, God does not authorize more. Thus, the text extends little or no ground for humans to pursue development beyond attaining provision, especially as mission activity.

Image and proxy. We can find another Ground in the depiction of human life as a divine proxy. In the text, humans are made in the image and likeness of God; they are his representation on earth. Thus, God's mission is to have himself represented appropriately on the earth. In mission understanding, then, human existence refers to God. In order to be "good," human life is to hearken to God's existence in recognizable correspondence. Human life and action on earth are to point to God, and they are to be identifiable as showing from God toward the world. Negatively, misrepresentation or lack of correspondence is "not good," as it presents an image that is not characteristic of God's person or representative of his interests and mission.

By extension, any action toward humans, including human self-action, also ramifies toward God and toward divine honor. For mission, then, that which preserves or sustains human representation of God aligns with God's honor and with his will for people. Negatively, that which distorts divine portrayal or thwarts human capacity to represent God violates divine honor and will.

Male and female. Some of the representational aspects that mission can support are found in the divine call. Humans need to be able to relate, both to God and in union between male and female. On this point, it is significant that the text uses the distinctly sex trait terms "male and female" (zākār ûněqēbâ),[121] not the gendered terms, "man" (ʾîš) and "woman" (ʾišâ), as later in Gen. 2:23. Thus, sex trait based distinctives can be seen as divinely ordered and good, and mission has grounds to champion maintaining the sexes as distinct and identifiable categories, without diminishing their mutual value.

Further, the mission of God is that he would be represented in a sexually heterogeneous pair, identified by sex traits, male and female, who

---

[121] Note Jesus' use of sex-trait terms instead of gender terms (arsen kai thēlu) in both Matt. 19:4/ Mk. 10:6. Paul also opts for the same sex trait terms instead of using gender terms in Rom. 1:25-28. Significantly, both Jesus and Paul use forms of *ktizō*, directly referencing the creation and God as creator.

he addresses as one. Negatively, we can see that "*not* two sexes (male and female)-as-one" opposes the "two sexes (male and female)-as-one" arrangement. This distorts or negates the representation that God sets in place as his image, which violates the order of his creation. Mission then can work negatively to oppose or protest "*not* two sexes as one," arrangements, and it can positively act on behalf of the "two sexes as one" union of heterogeneous humans.

The missio of the text heightens what it recounts as God's self-stated missio to create people. According to both of these, male and female need to be able to partner together. They need to be supported to mate, to create social bonds, to rear families and to produce generations. They need to be able to form social projects and to expand human presence. They need to be able to exercise will in their rule over the creatures. They need to be able to stand in appropriate place as superior to beasts, and they need to be able to reap the harvest of the earth for their own provision. All of these need to be able to be done in the plural solidarity of "male and female as one."

Human capacity for image bearing. Viewed positively, mission has ground to preserve these capacities and functions, and to work to restore them if they have been impaired. Viewed negatively, mission has ground to oppose anything that prevents people from being able to fulfill these dimensions of life. Thus, mission can work against things that prevent or injure human religious life, that is, the capacity to relate to God and to show God to the world. It can act to preserve human sexual life in the union of male and female, and, especially, as the ground for marriage and family life. It can resist things that hinder human sustenance; it can work to repair right relations between the sexes, and to foster the exercise of human will in accordance with divine will. It also can counteract human abasement, especially anything that treats human beings as insignificant, unnecessary, disposable or at the level of the beasts.

Negatively, God does not commission humans to subdue humans. Humans are granted rule over the creatures, the earth and the produce of the land. They are not granted rule over the heavenly bodies and seasons, which have their own ruling bodies, and they are not granted rule over each other. This conditions the exercise of earthly dominion by setting the limits of dominion in accord with the principle of divine proxy. God's mission is to have his creation subdued by his image bearers. His mission is not to have his image-bearers subdued. In line with this, mission may support the development and expansion of human civilization, but it may do so only in ways and to extents that do not subjugate people or impinge upon their abilities to represent God. In mission thinking, humans are responsible to exercise their expansion and dominion in a manner that is consistent with divine character and in ways that preserve the honorific dimension of his image.

Additional Ground dimensions. As we saw with Product aspects, space prevents more than a cursory survey of ways in which the text can provide a Ground for mission. The goal here is to demonstrate how reading for this dimension can be done. Ample room remains for alternate readings to explore and develop other grounds.

For example, based only on the analyses that we have undertaken so far, God gives the produce of the earth to humankind, which introduces the concepts of environmental ownership, qualified as divine stewardship. The text also paints both sexes as belonging to the gendered category "man," yet it characterizes the sexes as equal. This opens the door to inquiries about partnership and equality of value between the sexes, and to missiological consideration of how human honor is and can be sustained even when the identity of one sex is subsumed under another sex's gender identification.

Ground focused readings also could investigate topics such as the appropriate expression of hierarchy and authority, God's provision for his agents, uses of blessings and evaluative statements, the nature and function of natural categories, the place of rest in human life, and the pattern of emulating God as a standard for human behavior. Again, these are only examples; mission is inexhaustible, and the text cannot be exhausted as a

Ground for it. This is an arena that holds much promise for theology of mission to explore in concert with missiological interpretation. Hopefully, these brief treatments have provided enough demonstration for the interpreter to get a sense for how Ground reading can be performed, as we now proceed to reading the text as a Tool within Mission.

Genesis 1 as a Tool within Mission. Remember that Tool analysis looks at the text's instrumental capacities. While Ground analysis sees mission and mission agents standing upon the text, Tool analysis envisions the text in the hand of mission and mission agents. It sees the text as an instrument of both God and people, and it emphasizes the sacred, canonical aspect of the text as God's word. Thus, while Ground reading seeks to inform agents from the missio of text, Tool analysis seeks to accomplish missio by using the text. It assumes that agents already have been informed by the text and they are now taking it up in order to perform what the text has shown them should be done.

This is a quest for potential utility. When doing Tool analysis, the missiological reader looks for possible mission uses that might be a good fit, given the text's particular features, that is, its missional design. The idea is to use the text well by using it to do what it does best.

Discerning how the text is aimed at outcomes factors highly when looking for instrumentality, because the idea is to use the text in ways that fulfill what it was engineered to do. While not absolutely necessary, this is where preceding TA can be very helpful. Thus, the controlling concern is, "How can we use this text responsibly as we fulfill God's mission?" The key questions that the interpreter asks are: "How can this text do what it is designed to do in various situations and contexts?" or, "How might the text be quoted or used in presentations to people without changing its essential effects and outcome goals?" and, "Based upon the design of the text, what kinds of situations would it function best in, and what uses would it be best suited for?" Another, less precise, way of framing this would be, "What might be the most appropriate situation to quote this text in, and what would be accomplished by doing so?"

Key outcomes. We have seen already that Gen. 1 evokes a number of key outcomes. It calls up a longing in the reader for a good world. It tacitly condemns the current state of the reader's world. It fills the reader with a sense of nobility and purpose that is linked to divine calling. It fosters divine awe that is coupled with a sense of obligation toward God, who is God, alone. It sanctions male and female union and promotes domestic life. Finally, it summons the reader to emulation of God, demonstrated by observing a day of rest. Throughout all of these outcomes, the text ushers the reader toward valuing orderliness as it embodies sacred solidarity and compliance. This is perhaps the most prevalent outcome, the text's prime missio.

These purposes pervade the text's aspects, which lend themselves to different situational operations. This is like using different ends of a tool to accomplish different tasks. Each dimension of purpose can serve as a different "end" of the tool. Some of these will be explored further below. For instance, because the story is a foundational origin account, the text lends itself to uses that involve informing or establishing worldview. From another angle, because it is also a tradition account of a people group, it also works for establishing social identity. As a story about God, the text has religious utility, and, as a story about humankind, it has existential and devotional utility. As a story about order, emulation and compliance, it is suited for moral and behavioral instruction, etc. These can be combined in devotional, educational, homiletic and theological uses.

Taken together, these capacities make the text highly suited as a tool for missional use in situations where worldview, social identity, religious identity and personal experience combine as key factors. However, the text also can be used well to address any combination of these factors, or any factor, singly. We will explore a few of these uses, below, starting with situations that have many factors, moving to situations with fewer factors.

Monotheistic identification. In the broadest sense, the text is most suited for hearers and contexts when divine order is an issue. This includes contexts in which there is issue about the place of God in the universe, either as creator, as the only God, or as the one who places his will on the creation. More precisely, the story is functionally appropriate for situations in which the aim is to reinforce the socioreligious identities of those who believe in and serve the one true God, and to place a limit between them and those who do not believe.

These provisions derive from the account's exclusivity. The cosmogony addresses all parts of the creation, deliberately leaving no room for alternative explanations. It also shows all beings, most of all, humans, to owe their existences to God, and it portrays them as being under divine mandate. This makes the narrative well-suited for foundational catechesis and pedagogy, since it offers a description of the world in a manner that invites either affirmation and acceptance of divine authority or denial and rejection. The story is a "take it or leave it" proposal about the universe that is fit to be used as a watershed, especially if presented as a "shibboleth" of commitment to the one true God and his place as supreme, or as a marker of participation with the community of faith.

It may be helpful to stop and note the interpretive rationale behind these "Tool" propositions. When we consider the design of the text, we see that it operates as an honorific, origins "homage." In this function, the text's nostalgic idealism combines with multiple calls upon the reader's sense of obligation. These drive the reader toward the story's worldview, in loyalty and compliant rendering of honor. Thus, the narrative presents to a hearer as would an anthem or an alma mater song. This makes it useful in a confessional sense, that is, as an account to be rehearsed or otherwise presented as would a rite of intensification. Resultantly, the text can be fulfilled when it is used to elicit or intensify socioreligious commitment. A fitting use, then, would be to present the text as moment to "sing the anthem" or "salute the flag." That is, as a recitation of tradition or as an invitation, especially in cases where a mission agent wants people to participate in "our (true) story" in a manner that establishes socioreligious identity.

By way of example, one matching use would be when the story is taught to children in order to ground them in a family's or group's faith, worldview or religious tradition. Another example would be if it were used to reinforce a faith profession (e.g., "I believe in God, who alone made the heavens and the earth"). A more refined used would be in the catechesis of persons who are converting from polytheistic, animistic or naturalist/secular worldviews. Here, the text would be given in order to inform catechetes or inquirers about how Christians and Jews view the world, that is, as a created thing, fashioned and ordered by the one true God, alone. After rehearsing this account, a call could be given for persons to affirm that there is indeed only one God, who establishes all things and creatures, with affirmation that he is the only one to heed and obey.

Idyllic longing. Because it elicits longing for an ideal, the passage is well-suited for contexts in which people are experiencing dissatisfaction with the state of the contemporary world. On many levels, the account, "weeps with those who weep" (Rom. 12:15) that the world is no longer right, fair and good. It explains, and by explaining, legitimates their disappointments or senses of injustice. It shows that creation is indeed supposed to be a very good place, and it reassures the frustrated and downcast that they are not foolish, crazy or presumptuous for feeling that something dire is out of place in the world around them.

Using a refined focus, the text can be a tool in mission to those who experience lack. For it shows that those who suffer need are right to expect provision out of the earth, since God has intended it to be so, and he has given the earth for them to be able to eat. Significantly, the text is specifically designed to foster a sense of nobility in people by virtue of their very humanity, and it weds that sense of nobility to an expectation, a sense of entitlement to earthly provision. In effect, the text declares, "You are noble if you are human, and as a noble human, God has ordered that the earth should provide for you. You have a divine right to eat and to be fruitful."

Thus, negatively, the text casts lack of the earth's fruits as a wrong thing. It implies that if fruitfulness is not available, the ordinary courses of human dignity and God's sustenance have been interrupted or damaged. Its missio to entitle and dignify fits any situation in which mission is providing dignity and sustenance in God's name. The passage then could be presented when mission workers are doing food relief, oppression relief or agricultural development, since it provides a framework for those actions. Because it offers an empathic worldview, it also could be used to open conversation with suffering or disadvantaged persons about the damage that has been done to God's world and to them.

Human significance. The account is also well-formed to encourage those who are poor in spirit, especially when that poverty is linked to having a meaningful or purposeful life. It offers solace and affirms the meaning, value and purpose of human existence. It is an implement that ennobles, which places no external conditions on human value. This makes it a powerful tool for use in contexts in which people despair about their own worth or in any situation in which human life is treated with low regard.

Negatively, it can be used as a religious, ethical or moral challenge toward systems, institutions and individuals who fail to recognize human worth. The text fits for prophetic declarations of protest and public calls for right behavior toward people. It also can serve as an exhortation to the community of faith, when religious priorities have lost sight of human value.[122]

Interestingly, the story has an expanding series of spheres in which either goodness or wrongness could be found. Starting at the final and most exterior sphere in the account, people can feel poverty of spirit over lack of physical provision. Moving backward in the story, and inward, we can see

---

[122](Cf., Matt. 12:12).

that people also can experience poverty because of powerlessness in the world, or over a general lack of fruitful outcome from their lives. They can despair over the failed expansions of their families and kin, over infertility, loss or a lack of family. Further back, very keenly, people can feel impoverished from lack of companionship in married union, and, at the level of selfhood, due to loss or lack of personal capacities and lack of relationship with God.

The longing that accompanies any one of these spheres of poverty will resonate with the longings elicited by the passage. Thus, the text is ripe for use with persons who suffer on any of these levels, in the same way that it fits for work among those in physical lack. Pointedly, it can offer an affirmation of significance at each stage below the loss of a more exteriorized stage. If one lacks provision, the world is wrong, but there is still meaning to be found in family and progeny. If progeny are lacking, there is meaning in marital union. If union is lacking, there is meaning in acting upon the earth for good in God's name. If one is powerlessness to influence, there is meaning in simply existing, living in the image of God upon the earth. Additionally, if one dimension of a person's capacity to reflect God's image is impaired or muted, other dimensions remain. According to this text, then, while there is life at all, there is significance to be had, and the poor in spirit always may be strengthened by hearing it.

Human union and domesticity. Because of the way that the text sanctions male and female union, the passage is a good fit for use when people have concerns or doubts about marriage and family life, especially, when those concerns involve questions about God's order or about what kinds of human union have God's blessing.

Thus, the text lends itself to use in missional promotion of the moral and spiritual value of male-female union, particularly, as a boundary marker of socioreligious identity. Like the monotheistic dimension, the commission of the male and female as a union sets a mark for affirmation and compliance, or rejection and denial. This provides a socioreligious boundary between the community of faith that embraces the account and others who may not.

The union portrayal also has instrumental capacity for mission to married couples and families. It can be used to reinforce the value of mutual partnership and commitment, and as a call for mutual dignity and regard. It can help mission agents to establish or reinforce divine duty as a key component of married life and to orient couples toward representation and reflection of divine characteristics within their marriages.

Further, the text ennobles domesticity and the raising of progeny. Like the provision pronouncement, the union text could serve well as a presentation when doing mission work that sustains any aspect of family life or the development of younger generations, such as education, counseling and medical assistance. Since it offers an authoritative endorsement of domesticity, it can be used to encourage and affirm persons who spend their lives working under difficult circumstances simply for subsistence, and it can be used as a counteracting voice to discourses that marginalize or belittle domestic expressions of life. Its idyllic depiction also champions the value of domestic life in a way that is useful when mission agents are seeking to counteract dissatisfactions that may have been induced by materialistic and commercial interests. This is a use that is highly suitable for contemporary mission in any context that has been exposed to commercial media forces or materialistic discourses.

Emulation of God. The passage also sets a standard for human behavior as it ordains a day of rest. Most obviously, this lends itself to use in support of the observance of holy days, especially when holy day observance serves as a mark of socioreligious identity. It also offers utility for moral calls in favor of worker's relief and in support of recreational mission activities that temporarily displace productivity.

However, the rationale behind the observance of rest more broadly establishes a pattern of emulation of the divine. This makes the passage useful as a call for the ordering of human society. As the text calls to rest, it subordinates other needs, physical or economic, to the mandate to order life-patterns and behavior after God. This sets a standard for how people should live, generally. Thus, the text has value as an exhortation to societies that ignore religious grounding in the public sphere or as consideration in public policy. It can be used by mission agents to proclaim, "We are people who pattern our lives after God. We believe that society is good when human life is patterned after God's life and behaviors. Humans live well when this is done, and we call our society to live as we do in order to live well."

Other uses follow in this vein, since the text elicits duty toward God and toward the earth on God's behalf. Thus, the text suits a wide variety of calls to human responsibility, whether those come as calls to custodianship of the earth, to participation in societal projects, to sacred service, to sexual equity, to marriage and family, or against chaos, darkness, devaluation or irresponsibility.

Checking Results

As a safeguard, it always helps to review findings after readings are done and to assess them as a whole. During review and reflection, key questions to ask are whether or not results are consistent with the text, and whether or not they exhibit missiological inquiry. The aim here is not to be exhaustive, but to be consistent and rigorous. That is, the goal is not to try to address all that could be said, but to make sure that everything that has been proposed is founded upon secure textual evidence. These steps help the interpreter to be mindful of interpreter bias and assess the validity of his or her readings.

If we survey back, you probably will notice that the readings so far have yielded broad and recurring results concerning order, monotheism, compliance and response, human value, dominion, representation and emulation, along with creational fruitfulness and goodness. You also may notice that we only have touched generically upon these results from any given angle, and that wide realms of interpretation still await exploration.

The pervasive generic character of these findings should raise a flag in the interpreter's mind, bringing a point for the interpreter to check. In this case, for rigor, when the interpreter sees the generic quality of observations recurring, he should entertain the question of whether or not the readings have been too vague. However, when we make this observation, we should note it as simply a characteristic that warrants secondary examination. That is, it should be taken as an interesting trait to assess. As we take a second look, we also will need to be careful not to import pre-judgment based on scope alone. In other words, we should remember that general language is neither something to be avoided nor to be sought in its own right. Rather, the value of general language should be related to the reading being done; it depends on whether or not that language arises as a legitimate product of applying our stated method(s) to the text.

In this case, we can see that the general character of our findings may be attributed as a natural result of two factors, 1) the form, content and missio of the text at hand, and 2) the nature of our interpretive methods.

Checking our findings against the textual material, we can note the nature and style of the passage. It is a foundational etiology that speaks about all orders of creation. The narrative uses universal, categorical figures and it treats with categorical situations. From this angle, then, our general findings correlate with the general character of the text.

Methodologically, the goal was to rely upon readily-observable features in order to observe mission function, and to infer parallel mission use. Using this criterion, we see that the text gives broad, universal mandates, which are cast in categorical, generic language. No special or individual names appear, no definite locations are mentioned, and no specific situations or plot complications are addressed. The dictates and structure of the text all operate generically, using general terms. This supports findings that are framed as generalizations. From this angle, general results demonstrate methodological consistency.

Using two angles, then, we can check against our point of caution. And, as we find that this correlates with both the text and the stated method, we can rest at ease about our generic findings. This step finishes our basic missiological reading of the Genesis 1 passage.

However, we have not yet seen how missiology can use special concerns to conduct specialized interpretations. We will explore how to do this in the following chapters as we interpret the sociospatial phenomenon of the city.

Chapter 8

Missiological Interpretation of the City

This chapter shows how missiological interpretation can be focused on more than written texts. In it, we will use the core understandings that undergirded our biblical interpretation to interpret the city. We will anchor our analyses in a specific set of missiological concerns, that is, from a *hermeneutic location* from which we will seek to understand urban features and dynamics.

This will take a bit of time, because we will not be applying specific methods as we did in Chapter 7. Instead, we will use missiological foundations as a lens in order to do broader, qualitative interpretation of a sociospatial[123] phenomenon. This uses the root concept of mission as a interpretive device at the level of theory or metatheory. There are two main objectives for doing this. The first objective is to develop a basic, integrated conception of the city and its features that can account for urban phenomena by using the idea of missio. The second is to demonstrate how the idea of missio can be used to understand a non-religious, non-literary work without direct reliance upon method.

---

[123] Gottdiener and Hutchison (2011) have developed the term "sociospatial" extensively. Here, we are not applying their position, per se, but acknowledging their observation that the city is inseparably a physical reality and a social construct or event. Jayne and Ward (2017) also note that the city is complex, and to some degree indefinable because it has multiple social and spatial characteristics.

This shift of view requires some clarification because it crosses interdisciplinary lines. While we have seen that missiology holds a claim to its own legitimate hermeneutic location, when we apply that to the city, we will be re-interpreting many things that urban scholars already have interpreted extensively from their own location(s). This is a bit like having a botanist and an ecologist describe the same forest. There are overlaps in the phenomena and issues that the two fields examine, yet the discourses and terminologies are not the same, and their focuses are on different features, dynamics and systems. This leaves the sensitive question of whether or not one way of talking about the city should be prioritized.

Remember that disciplinary location provides us with theoretical commitments, which in turn give us the foundation to use method. Disciplinary location also sets priorities of view in focal-subsidiary relations. Thus, while an urban studies discussion would interpret mission realities in light of urban thought, a missiological discussion will interpret urban realities through mission thought. The latter, *missiological* discussion is what we will be doing here. That is, we will not be stepping away from missiology and switching over to urban studies. Instead, even though we will draw upon the works of urban scholars, we will remain in our previously established hermeneutic location and work from it by directing missiological questions at urban objects.

This makes the following examination differ in character from one that might be done from within urban studies. Although the topical concerns may correspond on the surface, an urban analysis standing within the discipline of urban studies would use different methods and ask different questions, which derive from different theoretical assumptions. Because of that, it would also end up with different findings. The findings here will result from using missiologically grounded interpretive theory to interpret the city. This creates a specific location within missiological studies that overlaps with urban studies, which could be thought of as a *missio-urban* hermeneutic location.

Fortunately, both urban studies and missiology are interdisciplinary fields (Gottdiener & Hutchison, 2011). Diverse scholarship is regularly integrated on both sides, and both fields are accustomed to seeing and welcoming new analyses as contributions, even when those may arrive at unfamiliar conclusions. Additionally, since missiology uses metatheoretical frames it is relieving that there remains room within urban studies for new metatheoretical viewpoints to join the conversation (Baxter, 2017; Rickards, Gleeson, Boyle, & O'Callaghan, 2016). Urban sociologists Mark Jayne and Kevin Ward actually invite meta-theoretical explanation of urbanism as they review cautions from a number of urban scholars:

> Such insights highlight a view that urban theory has moved too far from 'meta-theories' that can offer universal explanations of urbanism, to a proliferation of theories that offer perspective on the diversity and complexity of urban life. (Jayne & Ward, 2017, p. 16)

Thus, as we consider shared concerns from missiology's metatheoretical perspective, we should be able to find sufficient room to avoid affront, even when we tread off of urban theory's beaten paths within some common territory.

In order to pursue our interpretation, we will assume a number of things. First, we will be thinking about the city as a thing that has endured through time. This means thinking about the city in a cumulative way, as it has developed and been reproduced in many situations and places over the ages, not solely in its current, globalized iteration(s). Taking this view will help us to make connections between contemporary and ancient or biblical visions of the city. As a corollary to this, we will be using "the urban" (Rickards, et al., 2016) as a term that speaks of city aspects and traits, even though it may have aspects and qualities that transcend traditional association with the city (Brenner & Schmid, 2014).

This means that we will begin by using the terms "urban" and "city" at the level of their most common, historical and vernacular senses, and proceed from there into more specialized interpretation. This assumes that there is validity to the spatial, social and located aspects that the ordinary language user could discern and probably would categorize as *city* or as *urban* in average speech, even if those may not capture the entire reality of "the urban." It also assumes that "the city" is a phenomenon that has been and can be found in many contexts and that something common and recognizable is occurring in those places (Storper & Scott, 2015). Further, we will assume that the city is and has been knowingly produced, and we will assume that as such it has knowable, meaningful features that can be observed and interpreted.[124]

From this ground we will examine the city using the concept of *missio*. Just as we read the text from the perspective of missio, we will "read" the city using the perspective of missio. Once that is done, we will be able to bring our missiological reading of the city into interaction with our missiological reading of the creation according to Gen. 1.

Toward a Missiological Understanding of "Urban": the *missio urbis*

Having started at a commonplace view of the city, we need to clarify what we hope to see from a missiological location. Recall that our missiological inquiry focuses on the accomplishment of outcomes. It is a teleological[125] consideration that prioritizes what a thing is *for* as the key to what a thing *is*. It asks, "What is this thing intended to *do*?" Such a stance filters our talk about the city via our concerns. It directs them in some ways toward what Roberto Camagni calls the city's "functional" and "symbolic" "rationality" (2001, pp. 102-107). However, we must remember that missiology does not approach function in the sense of mere operation. It looks for the quality of purpose that undergirds operation (Rosenblueth, Wiener, & Bigelow, 1943). This is like looking at *behavior* in order to discern

---

[124] This parallels observations about the semiotic qualities of the urban environment (Camagni, 2001; Gottdiener & Hutchison, 2011).

[125] Schneck (1991) traces this view of the *polis* to Aristotle, and sees it as a major viewpoint in urban studies. For discussion of teleological approaches to environment see also Lin (2016).

motive. It is a deeper, or "thick" description (Geertz, 1973) of what occurs. We could call this an attention to the *missio urbis*, that is, an attention to the core purpose for the city, its reason to exist.

When we look at the city missiologically, then, we are not trying simply to observe what might be happening within it; nor are we attempting to describe its phenomenal, sensory presentations. We are trying to consider it as a categorical phenomenon, as a real thing with purpose that occurs in more than one place and instance. In order to do this, we are thinking about what happens in terms of what the city *does,* and we are assuming that what the city *does* demonstrates the essential nature of what it *is*. Our fundamental assumption is that any tangible *mission* arises as a concrete expression of a *missio*. From this location, the *city* is the tangible thing that arises from and fulfills the *missio urbis*. Thus, *urban* is a qualitative state; it is the state of having qualities associated with the city and its missio.

This carries over the theoretical lens that we used with the biblical text, because it holds that the principle of missio undergirds both text and city. The parallel that we are proceeding on is that from the vantage of missio, texts are human creations that serve purposes; they are aimed at accomplishing ends. Likewise, missiologically speaking, the city is a human creation that arises out of human intention to accomplish ends. Because missio is a quality of both, similar questions can be used to examine them.

Some explanation is in order here. Missiologically, we see that the written text is both material and immaterial. It is encountered by the senses as a *material* construction, that is, as scribbles on a background. Yet it is vastly more than a material artifact. It has deeper significance than its material form. This significance is attached to what transpires as it is negotiated by people and to the broad, immaterial realities that it embodies and expresses. This is also the case with the city. The text and the city both have material embodiments, but each is vastly more; and, although each can be encountered in its materiality, that which gives each its dynamism and significance far exceeds the material form. Each is both material and immaterial.

Continuing the parallel, from a missiological viewpoint, the text is not fully the text unless it is read and negotiated; its reality as a text is tied to its meaning, and its meaning arises as an interaction. Meaning is an outcome produced in the dynamic interaction between reader and construction, and the text cannot be understood well without this condition being kept in mind. Drawing upon Lefebvre's "field of encounters" and Massey's "thrown togetherness," Helen Wilson characterizes the city in a similar manner, as a production of engagement and encounter. To Wilson, "encounters are what produce the city and its distinct character as a site of possibility, continuous flux, and disequilibrium" (2017, p. 110). Baxter offers a parallel assessment from an architectural perspective, but he integrates the critical dimension of design. He proposes that

> future investigations must move beyond a dichotomy between design and society to provide more sophisticated and accurate theoretical accounts of how design and the social interrelate to affect human response. For example, one possibility is to use Ingold's (2008) work to develop an 'architecture as meshwork' which illustrates how a phenomenon like social interaction is the result of varying intensities of elements, including design and social ones, that intermix and intensify at specific sites. Taking both design, and social and cultural theory seriously, it is these kinds of arguments that will help to open up new ways of thinking about architecture and the city. (2017, p. 38)

In these views, the city is not fully the city unless it is both lived and lived in, and the process of its being lived creates its meaning as an outcome, or production. The city's "cityness" arises as a dynamic event when people and various other entities negotiate common material and immaterial landscapes. Like the written text, the city cannot be understood missiologically unless its interactive coproduction as a designed and lived thing is kept in mind.

This is where our missiological approach begins to move obliquely to both vernacular and academic conversations. Our attention to the purpose of the city filters a view of the urban by using different schemes of significance. For example, because we are using distinctly missiological attentions we will not be seeing "the city," primarily as a political unit, or as a administration or territory, as a governmental institution, or in terms of socioeconomic classes and their power expressions. And, although that cities certainly have geophysical and population traits, for this examination we will not see "urban" in geographic terms, or as defined by given horizons of population, activity, or capital density. While cities can be viewed according to their aesthetic and architectural qualities, their lifestyles, their coalitions of governance, actor networks, multiform assemblages, etc., these are not our focus. Our focus is on the concept of missio, and our goal is to view the city through that lens in order to see clearly what the use of that lens yields.[126]

In order to do that, we will take a purpose/outcome view, which continues in the general thrust of what we have been doing so far. We will consider "urban" as that which embodies the *missio* of the city, that is, in terms of the characteristic purpose(s) that suffuse the city's facts. This approach looks at the urban phenomenon in order to see those purpose elements that give rise to, inform and fuel it. Recasting the urban this way will interpret the city's presenting realities in terms of missio. Thus, our initial aim will be to develop a way of talking about the city missiologically, in terms of missio, nature and teleology, dynamism, significance and

---

[126] This is also not to say that traditional missional concerns about the city are not of interest here. Certainly, issues such as ethnic relations, space and place, economics, social justice, and contextualized mission in and toward urban contexts are crucial to missiology. These will be addressed to some degree in later chapters that treat with missiological integrations. However, our first concern here is missiological interpretation of the city in the hope that some critical analysis of the city in terms of *missio* itself can contribute to those existing conversations.

instrumentality. After we have interpreted the city in terms of missio, we will be able to see how and where a missiological reading of the city intersects with a missiological reading of the biblical text. In other words, the aim is to use missiological thought to juxtapose two very meaningful constructs, the city, and Gen. 1, in order to arrive at missiological understanding of each and both.

The City as a Thing of Missio

Our first step, then, must be to try to think about the city in light of the concept of missio, that is, with an eye toward purpose and purposes. If we think of the city as a thing that *does* something, that is, as a thing of *missio*, what do we see? What does it *do*, and what is it *for*?

This missiological question controls our view in two key ways. As we have already noted, it makes us look more deeply than surface phenomena, because it is not primarily an empirical question, it is a teleological question. Surface description of what occurs is not adequate to answer the question, since the question asks *why*, not merely *what*.

Also, the missio question assumes meaning, and it ascribes meaning. It presumes that the city has arisen because people wanted something to occur, and that the intention for the city to make that something occur is the city's fundamental significance. This treats the city as both a reality and as a means to a further reality. In this view, the city has one kind of meaning as it stands, and has stood, but it also carries a distinct meaning as that *for* which it stands, that is, as an instrument of intention to bring about a thing other than itself. This view holds that while the city is what it is, the city also always points beyond itself toward the thing that it brings about.

Analytically, this shifts the reified actualities of the city to background status in order that the observer may see that toward which those actualities point. It takes into account that all that the city is in its reified state carries a symbolic function, and that, in some senses, all that the city is perpetually points forward to all that the city is intended to realize.

Theoretically, emphasizing the city's for-ness can be thought of as using a distinct angle of view to understand multiple urban qualities, without diminishing the merit of other views. This is not a strategy that is alien to urban studies, for urban scholarship already has recognized that the city is a thing that can be viewed in alternate ways.

For example, in his urban taxonomy, Roberto Camagni (2001) fruitfully articulates four views of the city: City as *Cluster*, as *Interconnection*, as *Milieu* and as *Symbol*. These he locates under the banners of four approaches. From one side, the *territorial* and the *network* approaches proceed from *Spatial Logic*, from another side, the *symbolic* and *functional* proceed from cognitive logic. Camagni's taxonomy is extremely helpful as it shows that the city can be understood as a phenomenon that can be meaningfully explained from different angles simultaneously, depending on the logic or lens being employed. In other words, the city is all of these things, and, the presence of all of these dimensions makes it available for competing descriptions, which do not have to displace or eliminate each other; its reality can sustain multiple discrete forms of analysis because it is a complex sociospatial phenomenon.

Because missiology has a distinct logic and lens, it too can offer a discrete form of analysis. For our discussion, the test of merit for this added perspective will be whether or not such a view can provide an integrated understanding of the city that has both internal consistency and explanatory capacity. That is the goal for this chapter, to use the concept of missio to develop a robust, qualitative description, accounting for urban phenomena with scope and precision, in a reasonable manner.

Basic operations: concentration and extension. Using this lens, when we look at the city in terms of missio, we certainly look at what is going on, but we look at what is going on in order to see something more that is being expressed. We also look to see what is going on *in* and *through* what is going on. We do this because the idea of missio assumes that operation, design and purpose are intertwined. As all of these aspects combine, they express together as *mission*, which is *meaningful* operation, an intentional instrumentality that is aimed at *fulfillment*.

Of course, meaning within operation can be difficult to discern, especially when it is nuanced or sophisticated. Thus, it behooves us to keep our focus on the most elementary levels of operation, where mission becomes the most evident and where it can give foundational indications of primary purpose(s). For, even though elementary operation may not tell us all about design and purpose, it still can tell us something important. And, although we cannot hope that basic operations will reveal everything significant about the city, they are a good place to start if we hope to see the primary end(s) toward which the city points.

When we look for the city's most rudimentary operations, we can observe fairly easily that the city acts as a *collector* or *concentrator*; that is, it accretes and accrues and aggregates. This characteristic is broadly recognized across the spectrum of scholarship, by authors as diverse as Storper and Scott (2015), Gottdiener and Hutchison (2011), Peter Damerow (1998), Stéphanie Anthonioz (2014), Jayne and Ward (2017), and many others. We also can see that the city is agglomerative, both immaterially and materially (Ramachandran, 1996; Storper & Scott, 2015).

The city's concentration is temporal as well as material, for the city is a concentrated *happening*. As Farias (2017) observes, the city arises as a collective event, or even as a co-occurrence, that is, as a collective constellation of collective events. In a structural sense, the city concentrates when its serves as a nodal cluster (Camagni, 2001) or as a centrality (Sassen, 2001) of its networks and systems (Brugmann, 2010). Economically, it gathers value (O'Flaherty, 2005); socially, it pulls together human interactions (Wilson, 2017). Taken all together, these varied, yet common descriptions yield a clue to the city's most rudimentary and most pervasive purpose. Regardless of the descriptive angle that one takes, and even given the staggering complexity, variability and uniqueness of urban realities, the common quality of what goes on throughout the city's encounters, in its community-making, in its economics, its space and place uses, its networks and assemblages, etc., is *concentration*, that is, a densifying or centralizing of human presence, activity and influence (Hall, 2001; Sassen, 2001; Scott, Agnew, Soja, & Storper, 2001).

Of course, even as we make this observation, we must also acknowledge that the city grows and reaches. As it concentrates and collects, it simultaneously *extends* (Brenner & Schmid, 2014; Rickards, et al., 2016).[127] However, as we note this, we also should observe that the city does not lose its root, collective character when it does extend.

In fact, the urban relies upon concentration and utilizes it so that it might extend. Although it may not be defined exclusively as a "central place" (Taylor, Hoyler, & Verbruggen, 2010), the city requires concentration as a precondition in order to accomplish anything that it does, including extension, for, when it extends, it reaches out from some sort of preceding concentration of place, people or events. The purpose for extension also matters, for the city extends in order to draw things to itself. As well, while the flourishing, active city definitely extends, extension does not seem to be its first goal or aim, especially when we consider that the city may exist even when it is relatively isolated, static, diminishing, collapsing or withdrawing.

Thus, we see that the city can stand without extension, but we cannot see it standing without collection. This means that the city's extension remains a secondary trait. In other words, the city does not *primarily* extend. The same is not true of the city's collection, which can be considered a primary trait, since without the quality of concentration the city itself remains unrecognizable (Brenner & Schmid, 2014). Without densification of some sort, it cannot be effectively differentiated from that which is non-urban, peri-urban or global (Birch & Wachter, 2011; Malpezzi, 2011; O'Flaherty, 2005). This is an ongoing challenge for geographers as they try to weigh official territorial designations against observable

---

[127] Gottdiener and Hutchison also note this dual dynamic, appealing to Ernest Burgess, as well as Marx and Weber (2011, pp. 62-63, 77).

geospatial traits. For the geographer naturally observes density as a signal trait of the urban even when an area is not formally named as city territory (Landis, 2011; Robinson, 2005; Seto, 2011).

From the geographer's quandary we can see that in order for the city to extend itself in an identifiable way, it first must have an identifiable concentration from which to extend, and we can observe that when the city does extend, that which it extends can be identified readily as some form of its more foundationally characteristic concentration. Even when the city is multi-central, suburbanized, regionalized or interlinked globally and systemically, its extended parts still function as centralities or nodalities of some sort, and it is that hallmark that enables those distributions to be identified as belonging to the city. In other words, the city's extension not only expresses from its concentration, its extension expresses its concentration. For, if the city lacks collectivity of some sort, it has neither capacity nor identity to extend.

It is also important to remember that from the viewpoint of purpose, extension does not need to be understood as antithetic to concentration. It can be an intrinsic and subsidiary movement within the operation of concentration, just as exhalation serves inhalation in the larger process of respiration. Thus, when we consider that: 1) the city extends only after it first concentrates, and, 2) the city's extensions express its concentrations, while understanding that, 3) extension does not negate concentration, at the very least, we can observe that the city *primarily* concentrates or collects, even while noting that it *secondarily* extends and distributes. On multiple levels, then, the quality of concentration remains prior and essential. This makes the city's concentration a first order of concern in terms of purpose.

Settlement and purpose. Two questions naturally follow from this operation-level observation: "*Why* (for what ends) does the city concentrate? That is, "What does this accomplish? What does it *do*?" and, "*Whose* (or *What*) purposes are aimed at concentration? Who and what have made the city so that this would be done?" If we can discern these, they can reveal the meaning that informs the city's concentrative operation, which in turn can indicate the missio of the city.

At fundamental levels, we can at least say that the city is an expression of human intentions. Cities arise because people build them and they satisfy a human desire for something. As instruments, they concentrate presence, goods and influence for humans. We can also see that city-making has its roots in the human project of *settlement*, that is, of making static places for human activity (Gans, 2009; Gottdiener & Hutchison, 2011).

When we consider why people make settlements, we see that settlement is performed by people as a means to make life easier and more sustainable in some fashion (Anthonioz, 2014; Dechert, 1991). Note that we are not limiting this idea to a single sphere of human well-being, such as shelter or defense, although singular concerns may be key factors, especially in certain contexts. More, we are talking about a range of good that can encompass all of the motivations for city-making. This is a simple and general sense of human good, much akin to the Aristotelian "good life" (Okolo, 1991; Papanikolaou, 1991). In this view, the city is conceived when people pursue a strategy of concentrative place-making because they hope that doing so will make life better than non-concentrated, non-placed life. Of course, this is not to say that placed life is *actually* better life. It only observes *why* people undergo the effort. Since place-making is a costly activity, it has to serve some kind of purpose for people to engage in it. Therefore, without making an evaluation about whether or not it accomplishes its intended purpose, we can at least note that settlement is a human strategy that is aimed at making life better for place-makers.

In missiological terms, then, we could propose that the very core of the *missio urbis* is an aim to bring about *good*, or perhaps *better*, human life using the strategy of *collection* in *place-making*. This missio produces and sustains the city, and it informs and suffuses the urban project. It arises as a shared intention among people to augment their lives by creating meaningful, stable location and by increasing ready access to material and immaterial resources. This underlying agenda expresses in an interlinked set of geo-spatial structures and modifications, social institutions, symbols, actions, events, systems, networks and assemblages, all of which partake in a common purpose to improve the lived states of the missio urbis' shareholders.

The City as a Joint Composition

In order to go further in this vein, we can draw upon the theoretical foundations that we have applied to texts. We can consider the city to be a joint geo-social composition that arises from the missio urbis and other missios in the same way that the Bible is a joint sociolinguistic composition that arises from the missio Dei and other missios. We can see that both text and city are instruments that have been organized to accomplish goals, yet those goals are not set finally by a single author or creator. Multiple influences combine in their constructions, and those influences leave telltales in those constructions, which can be observed and interpreted for missio.

This is because both text and city rely upon social systems that extend beyond a single person. Both city and text draw from, are embedded in, and are impacted by discourses and dynamics that can be considered to have their own missios, such as consumerism, mercantilism, nationalism, regionalism, ethnism, politics, capitalism, neoliberalism, entrepreneurialism, etc. Granted, the city is often a more dynamic and complex composition than a text, yet, in terms of joint composition and missio, it still may be approached in a similar manner for analytic ends. For, just as a text reflects the multiple influences of its co-authors, on a wide array of scales, the city reflects the contributing agenda of its multiple participants. And, just as the end form of a text reveals the missios of those who produce it, the end forms of urban contexts reveal the missios of those who produce them.

Gottdiener and Hutchison highlight this when they describe the city as a "sociospatial" construction. Note how they speak of outcomes and competing intentions in ways that parallel missiological thinking about the joint composition of texts:

> The sociospatial perspective suggests that metropolitan growth is the outcome of negotiations and contending interests, rather the product of some well-oiled machine without conflict. Developers, for example, must negotiate with government planners and politicians, citizen groups voice their concerns in public forums, and special interests such as utility companies or religious organizations interject their stakes and culturally defined symbolic visions in metropolitan growth. The end result of these negotiations is a built environment that is *socially constructed*, involving many interests and controlled by the quest for profit. (2011, pp. 91-92) (italics in original)

The "*socially constructed*" composition of the city that they speak of parallels the complex influence that missiological interpretation looks for when considering authorship of texts. We saw previously that a text can embody in miniature institutional, societal, discursive, metanarrative (etc.) missios, which suffuse it. In a similar manner, urban contexts can embody broad, varied dynamics, even when the forms that present to the senses may appear to have simple ends or obvious purposes. Just as the text shows larger agenda in a reduced form via its written symbols, the city shows complex agenda in the reduced forms of its artifacts, demographics, space and place uses, resource allotments, community formations, geographies, architectures, networks, systems, policing, social narratives, etc.

A simple example of this could be a fire hydrant. Immediately, the hydrant appears to have a simple missio, *viz.*, to provide access to water so that people can extinguish fires. However, the hydrant also embodies many other missios, and its form results from those. It embodies the civic missio to protect urban space. It carries the political missio to provide protective services; it shows in its material form the economic missios that drive industrial production, along with features that point to the influence of aesthetic, engineering and scientific missios. It bears the missio of urban planning, and it is embedded in missios that concern themselves with public rights, property rights, space and place, eminent domain and policing. It reveals missios that drive differentiations between public, private and civic, common and uncommon, professional and volunteer, formal and informal, permanent and transient, community and institution. Further, it can take on missios as it is actually used by people. That is, its *in situ* artifactual history (for example, when used during a riot or a heat wave) can involve missios that sustain or challenge power structures, or those that maintain or deconstruct status based access, etc. It can be manufactured, installed or read as an intrusion, as a service, as an ornamentation, or, more importantly, as a combination of all of the above.

The point here is not to equate city directly with text, even though in some sense the city can be understood as a text that must be negotiated and learned in order to be understood (McFarlane, 2017). The point is to propose that deep parallels exist between city and text, which warrant missiological interpretation of both using a common outlook. If we can recognize the missional character of both city and text, and if we can note that forms and features in both the city and in texts embody purposes, we can interpret both missiologically, as complex joint compositions, and look for telltales of missio. This enables us to use what we already have seen about the general nature of texts as a springboard to discern general missional aspects of the city, and it supports juxtaposition of the city and the biblical text.

Missio urbis in contexts. In order to avoid reduction, as we propose that there can be a common missio that is present in all city-making, we must account for the vast variation that we see in the phenomenon of the city. For, it requires very little observation to see that no two cities are exactly alike, even while there remains something recognizable about them that signals to us that they belong to the category, *city* (Storper & Scott, 2015).

Missiologically, we can account for the variation that we see by recognizing that variation is an essential trait of missio in general, since missio always must express in *context*. Missio derives from a purpose to perform a certain something, yet that core purpose must be actualized; that is, it becomes real and meaningful when it is expressed concretely through real people in real situations. Those real situations inevitably affect the expression of missio during the reification process. This requires that any missio would be adaptive in an intrinsic way. As any missio, the missio urbis also must express itself through and in context. This means that the missio urbis must be adaptive and relevant, yet at the same time, universally identifiable.

In other words, we can observe that the presence of missio is not compositionally determinant in an absolute or rigid manner, whether in texts or in cities. While the quality of missio might make a city to be essentially what it is, the missio urbis does not necessarily force a certain form on a city or require uniformity in order to be fulfilled. Quite to the contrary, tremendous latitude exists within the missio of "city-doing," and the missio urbis has virtually limitless potential for variable expression, even on generic levels.

In fact, it would be fairly safe to say that the missio urbis cannot be uniformly expressed, because it cannot stand alone, on its own two feet. By its very nature, the urban agenda is a cooperative agenda, and it relies upon multiple contributing missios that operate beyond it. It is also adaptive and collective by nature, and it needs a variety of *special missios* or *sub-missios* to be coordinated within it if is to succeed.

Subordinate and Contributive Missios

Like many other missios, the urban missio functions in a place lodged between the macro realities that inform and sustain it and the subordinate realities that contribute to it and derive from it. The city is in many ways the offspring of larger missios, but it is also the parent of derivative missios. Its expression is partially determined by missios to which it is subject, while it also partially determines the organization of its own subordinate missios. It is a coordinated, composite project, which always makes it complex, even when its functional goal may be simple (Hall, 2001).

An analogy may help here. If we think of a game of football, the objective is simple. The purpose is to win the game by getting the ball within the goal area more times than the opposing team. We could call this the "missio footballis." However, the nature of the game is such that multiple other missios must combine to make that missio happen. These include coaching missios, individual player missios, officiating missios, etc. These various missios are not directly equivalent to the missio of the game, but they all participate in the missio of the game and they all derive from it. At the same time, larger missios inform the game and dominate it. These could be regional identity missios, commercial missios, sports culture missios, etc. From both sides, beyond and within, these missios make the game what it is, even though they are not the game, itself; yet, without the game's composite missios, it cannot be what it is. In a similar manner, for the missio urbis to be fulfilled, it must rely upon complexity and it must bring complexity into being. Even as the missio urbis must draw on agenda that lie beyond it, it also must frame supporting agenda that support it and, in some sense,, comprise it.

Although imperfect and simplified, perhaps we can parallel the apostle Paul's organic "body" analogy (1 Cor. 12) to further illustrate the idea. As a caveat, it needs to be clear that this rather involved analogy addresses purposes, not component functions or structures. That is, we are not looking at the city in terms of static social organs and structures, per se, as would the classic British social anthropology of Radcliffe-Brown or Malinowski. The key here is not to see the city as a body composed of structures and functions; it is to think about how purposes attend, inform and give rise to structures and functions. That is, the view is toward how contingent aims, operations and constructs co-express from a core missio.

With that said, missiologically, we can think of the body in terms of its *life*, not its material make-up or even its operations. When we think of the whole, the body has its own life-scale and its mission is *to live*, even though it may be doing all sorts of noticeable attendant activities *while* it lives. However, we also can notice that the body has cells, which can be said to have their own lives and missions, as well as organs and systems, which have their own lives and missions. Each of these subordinate lives have purposes that simultaneously are distinct from the body's overall life and mission, yet which also comprise the body's life and participate in its mission.

When we think of the different lives that come together in the body, we can see that their purposes are *special*, and yet *common*. They can be understood uniquely, on their own, or they can be viewed componentially, as parts of a whole. Even though these may be competing views, both views are accurate, depending on the scale of focus. Thus, one could consider the body's life to be a *gestalt* of collective, composite lives, or one could consider the lives of cells, organs and systems to be *derivative, subordinate* expressions of the body's life. This is because the body is a singular plural. It is a life of lives. Its core of life always expresses in collected, multiple lives.

In order to use a missiological lens in this analogy, the key is to focus on the purpose or life-level view. This isolates missio from other aspects. For example, if we consider the pancreatic cells, organ or system, we note *structures* like the islets of Langerhans, and we can see *operations* or *functions* to produce insulin. We can see what is there and we can describe what is occurring. However, the main point is to discern the *mission* that informs what we observe, which in the case of the pancreas could be articulated as something like, "to maintain appropriate availability of energy for the body." This is the *missio* view of pancreatic structures and operations. The life-purpose of the pancreas is to regulate energy availability for the body, so that the body can live. All of what it *is* and *does* relates to that.

If we take this view to the body, we see its "life" as a conglomeration of life-sustaining missions that interact and coordinate. These missions are accomplished through operations, which take place within physical structures or systemic constructs.[128] By analogy, when we look at the city missiologically, we look *through* its operations and structures *toward* the purposes that they are aimed at and that give rise to them. When we do this, we see the city as a conglomeration of missios, rather than as structures, operations, events and constructs. It presents to the missiological eye as a symphony of *agenda* spanning a variety of scales and extents. Some of these missios are highly active and transient, while others are slow moving and durative. Some are highly localized and focused, while others are diffused and interlinked. Some are aggressive and others subdued, etc. These missios all interact, interrelate, coordinate, and compete, and as they do, the city lives and fulfills its mission.

Although they see it as an indicator of the city's unruliness, Allen, Lampis and Swilling make a similar observation about the city's interrelated practices and behaviors:

> Cities can be understood as the product of multiple taming practices and strategies, ranging from the techno-infrastructural domestication of nature to secure key resources, to the sociopolitical disciplining of the relational and organizational structures and behaviours that shape everyday life in cities. But cities are also profoundly untameable because they are a complex and often unintelligible web of institutional and everyday practices that produce them in fundamentally political ways, whether intentionally or unintentionally. (2016, p. 1)

Emphasizing social cohesion and communication, Charles Dechert casts practices in an organic view that resembles the one we are working with. Like Allen, et al, he notes specialization within function, but he frames it in

---

[128] Some of these missions even involve the creation or maintenance of structures or systems.

light of social wholes and hierarchies of coexistent systemic scales; he views these as naturally occurring features as community organizes around the human quest for the "good life":

> An organism consists of differentiated organs, often associated in functionally defined subsystems, e.g., circulatory, reproductive, etc.; the organs consist of tissues which are in turn composed of individual cells. Special systems demonstrate certain analogous structural characteristics. In some sense individual persons may be conceived as the ultimate components of social systems—both functionally specific social systems such as banks or universities or automobile plants and omni-functional communities. If we look at these omni-competent "communities" we find that at successive levels of aggregation there tends to be greater functional differentiation of the group components and a correspondingly greater range of products, goods and services satisfying human values. From family to neighborhood, to town or city, to county and region, to nation-state (or political federation or confederation of peoples), to the global community inhabiting "space ship earth," there is an increase in community size, functional complexity, communications and other exchanges and interdependencies. In turn, increased functional differentiation, enhanced productivity and the challenges produced by intellectual and cultural exchanges showed increase in the possibilities of a 'good life' for each group and person belonging to the whole. (1991, p. 262)

Like Dechert's "functionally defined subsystems," or Allen, et al's webs of "strategies and practices," the city's attendant missios can be understood to have lives and sub-missios of their own at their various scales and extents. Yet, throughout those scales and levels the purposes of urban missios remain bound up with the missio of the "omni-functional" community of the city. They derive from it and it also arises from them.

However, missiologically, these involved missios are not to be confused with operations, or systems, or structures, or events, as such, even though they are accomplished through, and reified within those phenomena. This distinction holds even though sometimes missios may be aimed at the formation of things such as community building, infrastructure development or networking. The missiological view of these things remains at the missios that they serve and which bring them into existence, not at the things themselves. This is like keeping the view on the purpose "to regulate bodily energy" rather than on the physiological operation of "insulin production" or the anatomical formation of "insulin producing islets."

In this analogy, we could consider the missio urbis to play the role of DNA's directive information (not DNA, itself). The information, that is, the missio directives that DNA holds within itself, suffuse the body's overall *life*, as well as all of its contributive *lives*. In the same way, the missio urbis suffuses all of those special missions that come together in and as the city. While the body's DNA design directive brings the body's structures, systems, events and operations into being in order to fulfill certain ends, those structures and their functions are not themselves DNA, or DNA's information. Likewise, the missio urbis is not the structures, systems, events or operations of the city. Those easily can be distinguished from the missio urbis, just as bodily features can be from DNA.

Note that special bodily features carry DNA's information, and their special missios can be traced to DNA's missio, yet they do not have the same missio as DNA, per se. Just so, the city's conglomerate missions, constructs and functions come from the missio urbis, yet they are not the missio urbis itself and they do not have its particular task. Their special purposes are unified with the purpose of the missio urbis only as they express in ways that contribute to the missio urbis' fulfillment. When they do so, they express the missio urbis in a case-specific sense or a *contextual* sense. In other words, like DNA information, the missio urbis is a purpose that is aimed at an overarching, reified expression that requires multiple varied expressions. Its overarching expression involves all of the conglomerate missios that are not the missio urbis, itself, but that participate in it, just as the special purposes that participate in the body's life are latent within DNA's missio, yet they require expression in order to become recognizable realities with real functions.

This same view can be applied to the missiological concept of the Divine Kingdom. For, in a similar arrangement, a symphony of specialized kingdom missios makes up the kingdom's life. These missios aid the kingdom to achieve its missio; they derive from the kingdom's overarching missio and they express the kingdom's missio, without being the kingdom or the kingdom's missio, per se. While the kingdom's missios are reified or embodied in social and material constructs, surface description of those constructs and their operations does not adequately capture their core identities, which are grounded in their purposes.

Missiologically, for both city and kingdom, the core identities of participating constructs are to be found in the missios that they fulfill, especially as those relate to the defining missio(s) that they partake in. These identifying purposes can be discerned distinctly in relation to other missios, most crucially to the missio Dei and to the missio urbis, even while the kingdom's or the city's overall purpose suffuses them. Their various special scales and aims coexist independently and interdependently, co-productively and co-derivatively. They rely on each other and in some sense they are each other, yet they are different.

For missiological analysis, then, we can consider the various sub-missios that come into being as the city does what it does to be latent in the missio urbis, and we can consider that the missio urbis will always seek to express them, yet we need not consider them to be the city itself or the missio urbis, nor should we equate their activities directly with the city's own. Instead, we can note that the creation of sub-missios is integral to the missio urbis as a necessity that is inescapably bound to its urban agenda. In other words, the missio urbis needs other missios if it is to be what it is and fulfill its mission, and yet, the very formation of distinctly urban sub-missios remains part of its mission.

The outworking of this agenda in real situations must of course be highly adaptive, responsive and multifactoral. For, as many have observed, the city is a joint composition that can be and has been expressed in the widest variety of contexts, with a diversity that nearly defeats analysis (Peachey, 1991). Since this is a preliminary missiological take on the city, we cannot fully account for how the mission of city-making calls upon and expresses its sub-missios. It only stands to reason that that depends on many factors that have yet to be identified and explored. At this rudimentary stage of description, the best we can do is to propose that any concrete expression of sub-missios will be informed partly by the mix of non-urban or trans-urban missios that impact the city, partly by the special geophysical context of a given city, partly by the social composition of a city, partly by the missio urbis itself, and partly by challenges that might hinder the missio urbis' expression or fulfillment (etc.) (Hall, 2001; Keating, 2001; Storper & Scott, 2015).

Urbanized missio(s). It should be noted that these sub-missios do not necessarily have to originate within the city or derive from the city in order to be "urban." The city is collective by nature, and it has the capacity to co-opt non-urban missios and turn them into sub-missios of its own, making them urban, or urbanized. It can do this because even though the missio urbis must hold all of these various subordinate missios together in its joint project, those sub-missios do not need to fulfill its missio directly. Instead, they may assist the city to fulfill its mission by serving it indirectly. That is, sub-missios only need to serve the city in auxiliary or oblique manners in order to become urban. They still may qualify as urban sub-missios if they satisfy the criterion of "by." They can be considered urban missios if they fulfill the missio urbis *by* doing *x*.

For example, capitalism as a macro missio is not distinctly urban. However, it is a missio that often catalyzes the development of a city, and it is a missio that the city's missio can draw from in order to form specialized sub-missios that support its unique goals. When the city draws upon capitalism as a tool to sustain its urban agenda, so that it draws capital together within itself for the benefit of its members, capitalism becomes *urbanized* within the city's context. Or, if capitalism is utilized in a special project, such as micro-lending, when that special project is developed within and by the city for the benefit of its members, the city has then generated a distinctly urban sub-missio out of itself and for the fulfillment of its own missio. In such cases, a trans-urban or non-urban missio both informs the city from beyond it and becomes co-opted by the city within itself, which transforms a non-urban missio into an urban missio in multiple ways.

Appealing to Fujita, Krugman, and Venables, Storper and Scott describe this kind of interaction, linking it to the city's concentrative activity.

> we can now state that the city represents a *very specific scale of economic and social interaction generated by agglomeration processes and focused on the imperative of proximity, and almost always endowed with governance arrangements that attempt to deal with the problematical effects of density and propinquity.* At the same time, the city is always embedded in a far-flung spatial economy that sustains it without compromising its integrity as a distinctive social phenomenon (2015, p. 9) (italics in original)

In terms of missio, the conflation with and adaptation to the missio urbis that occurs in such processes grants the quality "urban." This involvement, in which various missios become informed by the agenda of the missio urbis can be called "urbanization."

As we make this proposal, we need to note that urban scholars do not agree on these points, because the concepts "urban" and "urbanization" at the time of this publication remain deeply disputed on a variety of theoretical grounds.[129] This is one place where missiology can join the urban

---

[129] Rickards, et al (2016) provide a strong and evenhanded analysis of this state of affairs. They see existing theoretical conceptualizations of the city and "the urban" as "under

conversation. It also is a place where missio very clearly shows its capacity to be used as an instrument for urban interpretation, because using missio as an evaluative criterion changes our view of the city and its composites and traits without removing those components from either traditional or emerging considerations. Instead of silencing or ignoring existing observations about the city, the missio lens reframes the city's composition and re-reveals previously known aspects of the city's features in a way that resembles what happens when a UV "black light" is used in place of a standard "white light." In the case of the concept "urbanization," a recognizable, yet broad and diffused set of processes re-appears as the missio urbis' appropriation and adaptation of other missios. In the case of urban specializations, various urban systems, features and dynamics re-present themselves as *special missios* or *sub-missios*.

Further, the idea of missio brings out distinct *qualities* of identifiable urban realities like actor networks, assemblages, institutions, community formations, policing and political agendas, entrepreneurial strategies (etc.). Using the missio as a frame for referencing, these can re-appear as *contributive, corrective* or *constitutive* missios. Under that same light, larger, non-localized forces, such as consumerism, religion, neoliberalism, cultural aesthetics, symbolism of space, ethnism, class struggle, capitalism, economic competition, globalization, etc., may be re-revealed as *macro, discursive* or *formative missios*.

Under missio's unique light, then, many realities that long have been apparent to urban theorists re-present themselves to the observer showing unexpected characteristics. And, when the missio characteristics of those realities come to light, new categories for urban phenomena also

---

stress" to the degree that the categories typically used may no longer obtain meaningfully. Citing the works of Wyly, Brenner and Schmid, McFarlane, Angelo, Soja and others, they note that currently there is no theoretical consensus about what constitutes the urban or the process of urbanization. They conclude that it would be "premature to foreclose discussion about possible futures" for the field, its definitions, and its categories of inquiry and assessment. Gans (2009) addresses the same crisis from the angle of urban sociology, proposing four possible new directions that would re-organize and re-chart current study.

emerge, which require distinctly missiological labels. These missiological labels and understandings of urban phenomena do not need in any way to replace or displace existing or emerging interpretations from other fields. They may simply augment those conversations.

Scale and the missio-urban focal point. However, we must keep in mind that while macro- and sub- scales can help in identification, the key factor is always the nature of missio that any given urban reality accomplishes in relation to the city. Scale simply provides clues, just as scale helps us to distinguish a sidewalk's purpose from a highway's, or a cake spatula's from a boat oar's, given that their exterior forms are roughly equivalent. In a similar manner, scale helps us to discover the special missios that localized urban realities perform when their forms may correspond to larger, transurban missios. For example, we may see the special missio that urban governance may perform by distinguishing it from larger, transurban discursive missios that also exercise social control, such as the macro missios of religion, ideology, class struggle, government of the state or militarism.

Missiologically, then, the scale of the urban context provides a focal point of reference by which missio(s) may be viewed or understood. Recognizing scale does not necessarily define an urban reality; it only assists the interpreter to discern the character of a particular missio by relating it to the context of the city and its missio.

This is an important point to remember, because the city and its missio are themselves scalable. Recognizable city making can be done in sizes ranging from the small, ancient Greek *polis* to 21st century megalopolitan sprawls, or regional systems (Scott, et al., 2001) yet it still remains identifiable as city-making by virtue of what is being accomplished (Gans, 2009). And, just as the missio urbis may express on widely varied scales, both the missios that influence it and the missios that serve it are frequently scalable. These missios may grow and shrink to match the size of a particular city-making, but they remain in some ways fixed in their relation to the urban reference point as they do so. Those that influence or give rise to the city remain beyond it, and those that are subordinate or derivative from the city remain under or within it. The key is to see how those express above or below the focal point of the city.

The urban focal point is also crucial because all missios are not equal, and all do not negotiate scale equally. Some are more suited to larger frames and some to smaller. Some are quite recognizable at macro levels and nearly invisible at micro levels, and vice versa. The same holds true on temporal levels. Some missios are more transient, they disappear almost as quickly as they are formed, while others seem permanent due to their reified presentations or perpetual reproductions and reenactments (McFarlane, 2017).

Still, whether concrete and material or symbolic and immaterial, whether events or objects, whether passing or enduring, missios all share a common nature. They perform some sort of thing, accomplish some sort of purpose, carry some sort of intention. And, when they do what they do in urban contexts, under the influence of the city, they participate in that which the city does, which makes the city essentially what it is. In that participation, both the city and the missios with which it is involved become missiologically visible. Each reveals the other.

Thus, when we hold the city as a missiological focal point, we can see various missios more clearly because we can view them in reference to the urban context, and we can assign qualities to a missio in reference to the urban missio. That is, we can think of any given missio in terms of its prepositional or adverbial relations to the city's missio. This parallels the kind of analysis that we have done already when we used the missio Dei as a referential frame. For, just as any missio or narrative can be viewed relative to the missio Dei and its narrative, any missio can be viewed relative to the missio urbis and its focal point. For example, we can see a missio as beyond the city or within it, superior to the city, or subordinate to it. We can see missios as supporting or opposing, contributing or detracting, strengthening or dissipating, forming or being informed, subsuming or liberating, championing or marginalizing, each in reference to the city's local missio.

As a caveat, this makes the city an important context of missiological consideration, but it does not make the city missiologically more important than other contexts. The missio urbis grants us a crucial focal point, yet that focal point remains only one among many, and its revelatory power theoretically can be attributed more to the mechanism of focal-subsidiary viewing than to the virtue of the city, itself. It is also just as possible to see missios relative to global contexts or in reference to individuals, movements, people groups, regions or nations. Those studies, however, must be conducted elsewhere.

Category and Particularity

As we talk about scale and contextual expression, we need to make sure that we do not create a hard distinction between the universal urban missio and reified expressions, as though there was nothing in between them. For, even the casual observer can see that while each city may be unique, each city is not absolutely unique (Storper & Scott, 2015). While cities must share some identifiable common trait(s) with all cities in order to be cities, it is also possible that some cities would share traits with only some other cities, in ways that are still connected to their missional identities. In other words, we must allow that some cities would share constellations of common traits that lie somewhere between their "cityness" and their contextual particularity, and we must leave room for a city to be not only "the" generic city, or "a" particular city, but also one of many variations on "the city" (Gottdiener & Hutchison, 2011). Framed as missio, we must allow place for categorical expressions of the missio urbis, in the sense of "an [n]-missio city," which comes from a refined, semi-specialized or limited missio urbis.

This would hold for the city in an abstract sense as well as in its many tangible expressions. When viewed from the angle of the particular (a bottom-up, inductive view), we could observe the recurrence of concrete traits that would support grouping cities into categories. Observing common features between groups of cities, we could propose that under certain contextual conditions, the missio urbis expresses recurrent combinations of similar sub-missios. Contextual factors would include the influence of macro missios. In this view, the influence of certain combinations of sociospatial factors could be understood to cause the missio urbis to express certain recognizable constellations of special missios. Recurrent coincidental combinations of contextual conditions would cause the expression of recurrent combinations of sub-missio. This in turn would make certain cities have categorically recognizable constellations of special missios, which in turn would give them identifiable urban "flavors."

Alternately, from the angle of the universal (a top-down, deductive view), we could say that the missio urbis is categorically adaptable and variable, and that when people make cities, they can elect to make a certain type of city that is already latent in the expressive capacity of the missio urbis. Each type of missio urbis would then express a certain type of city, which would have a recognizable constellation of traits that stem from its categorical missio. Since the categorical missio would in turn govern the expression of a city's particular sub-missios, it would give that city a categorical "flavor."

From either viewpoint, the idea of missio spans what Mark Swilling (2016) describes from the perspective of urban planning as "algorithmic urbanism" and what he labels "co-production platforms." In Swilling's view, algorithmic urbanism is a top-down agenda that aims to form things such as the so-called, "smart city," "knowledge city," "informational city," "creative city," "green city," etc. Here, we would call the intention that produces such cities a *categorical urban missio*. However, since we are taking missio to be a coproduction of joint intentions, we would also see the categorical missios as something that he would call "polycentric," "incremental" "co-production platforms," which arise more from (bottom-up or lateral) collaborative interactions.

Of course, because this is a matter of interpretation, the same observational data could be integrated effectively into either scheme, and there is very little chance to resolve the tensions between our two missiological options, especially in a work of this length. What matters here is that from either angle, top-down or bottom-up, we can recognize that cities can be identified categorically by the constellations of their special missios. This can be noted while we also acknowledge that particular, irreproducible combinations of specialized and adapted sub-missios give individual cities uniquely distinctive histories and identities, and that this happens while cities arise under the influence of unique, particular and specific combinations of contextual factors.

This is the ironic paradox contained in the proposition, "All cities are unique." For, while it remains true that cities are always unique, at the same time, cities are also always cities in some form of common way, and in being cities, they must also have common traits that are in some sense not unique at all. For, the very assertion that a particular city is unique rests upon recognizing first that the thing that is being recognized as *unique* is in fact a *city*, or *urban* in character, which is a categorically *common* (not unique) label.

This is the particularistic paradox of the fingerprint, the event, the individual or the snowflake. Paradoxically, we can recognize that any given thing is unique, and truthfully assert that it is so, yet even as we speak of its uniqueness, we inherently acknowledge it categorically, by virtue of being "a fingerprint," "an event," "a snowflake," (etc.). Without such categorizations, language itself breaks down, for words must be able to be applied to multiple instances that have common characteristics in order to function as communication. Thus, any time we speak of the city or the urban we run the risk of reducing it categorically, but if we avoid categorization or reduction, we cannot speak of the city or the urban at all. We can only smile in the presence of its particularity, without drawing any comparisons. The best path then, is to leave the paradox in place, noting that it is true that all cities are unique, and also it is true that cities are categorically identifiable.

However, the point here is not so much linguistic as it is urban. Mainly, the point is that the most fundamental identifying urban trait is its universally common missio (the missio urbis), and yet, other categorically recognizable urban traits also can be observed. These can be discerned and labeled by cataloging recurrent constellations of special or sub-missios, and by noting the telltales of macro-missio influences. Additionally, while categorical participation exists, the concrete and nuanced ways in which sub-missios and macro missios combine in their tangible and historical expressions also lends a specific and recognizable individual identity to specific cities.

Categorical missio types and sub-missio expressions. Using a very reduced example, an industrial town arranges its component missios in a constellation that differs from a political or administrative center, and a commerce center aims at different things than a university town. Further, a northern hemisphere, neoliberal, entrepreneurial, individualistic, technology town arranges its component missios in different ways than a southern hemisphere, Keynesian, socialist, collectivistic market town or a regionally dominant "primate city." Each expression still carries the missio urbis, but each is concentrating and extending certain things in certain ways in order to accomplish special goals under the urban umbrella. Each has the missio urbis, but it also has its own special categorical configuration of missio, along with its distinctive combination of contributing missios. Taken together, the categorical constellation of missio and the special combination of contributing missio shows *how* a certain variety of the city goes about the missio urbis in its promotion of human welfare.

Categorically, these different urban configurations show different *kinds* of urban missio, or what Jeb Brugmann (2010) might call urban "strategies," just as different genres of texts show different *kinds* of communicative missio. If we consider missio to be the crucial influence on expression, we can propose that the city's missional priorities determine the ways in which it is configured, for its configurations are arranged around its distinctive strategy for fulfilling the missio urbis. Hence, the pattern in which the city's contributing missios are arrayed around the missio urbis lends special urban types their distinctive urban-missiological flavors or footprints.

In a mission sense, then, city features cannot be taken as givens, since the significance of what may appear to be common urban features is determined by missio, not by mere form. The meaning of urban features thus becomes variable across types because what may appear on the surface to be common urban *components* actually may serve unique *purposes*, which have been impacted by the arrangement of missios within a certain urban missio type and per a certain context. From this viewpoint, the natures and values of sub-missios are impacted by the missio specializations of a city missio type. Not only the particular manner in which a city's features express, but also the specific significance, the essential meaning of those features is influenced by the specific missio kind and context of a city.

Using a simplified example, the sub-missio of physical transportation is an urban fundamental, since it enables the city to concentrate and extend material(s). This is a key generic feature for cities, whether they are situated on land routes or waterways, and whether they build roads, railways, air or water ports, or simply take advantage of natural geographic features.

However, the essential meaning of transportation differs between an industrial center and an administrative center because the transportation missio is related to the special missio of the kind of city in which in it functions. In an industrial center, transport concentrates goods and physical labor, and it extends goods in export. By contrast, in an administrative center, transportation concentrates non-physical labor and communication, and it enables the rapid extension of power. Further, the significance of that transportation is attached both to the macro-missios in which it is involved, such as capitalism or socialism, nationalism or globalism, etc., and the specific mix of missio agenda of that city within its context, such as property evaluation, community formation, local governance, inter-urban entrepreneurialism and competition, etc.

Thus, while the mechanisms of transportation may correspond between cities, the core meanings of those transportation systems may differ. This means that while they may be formally similar they are missiologically dissimilar, for their significance is more determined by their embeddedness in missios than by their external traits; their places within the city's constellation of sub-missios are determined by their relationships to the city's missio and to other sub-missios. As a result, canal or canoe transport on one side of the globe can have more similarity to an industrial rail system by virtue of common mission than would a light rail commuter system in a nearby city of similar size and demographics.

This is significant, because it impacts evaluation of systems and features that are not as pragmatic as transportation. For, the same variability of meaning can apply to systems of governance, internal control, justice, economic flow, resource distribution, power structures, stratification, spatial use, population aggregation or districting, and even ethnic relations. As Berger and Luckmann (1967) established, and as postcolonial movements have emphasized, what may appear to be common urban issues or features when identified by common surface traits may in actuality be vastly different systems or features when viewed from other worldviews, values, cultures, and social or ideological locations, or, as we are seeing here, when missios are considered.

Concrete incidents. This is because the city does not arise *in vacuo*. In order for the city's missio to be fulfilled, tangible missions must be actualized, coming together to create real cities with real human benefit. Thus, concretely, each particular urban context shows the distinct purposes of its unique influencers, combined with the influences of the particular sociocultural forces with which it is involved.

As we have seen previously, a particular text will show the missio "hands" of its individual, institutional and societal co-authors. These coauthors utilize categorical systems like language in order to create a particular, local work that has a distinct identity. Likewise, urban contexts show the "hands" of concrete historical persons and historical institutions that have built particular urban centers, which have distinctive identities.

Using our example from above, the missios of transportation systems in a naval port city, such as San Diego, California, will be significantly impacted by its specialization as a military center, which could be considered a certain missio kind, type or generic expression. However, San Diego's transportation missios also will be impacted by San Diego's location near the U.S. / Mexico border, and its history as a key town on the West Coast's *El Camino Real* mission highway. They will be impacted by entrepreneurial civic goals to attract international tourism to specific locations, like Legoland, SeaWorld and the San Diego Zoo, by the development of the University of California San Diego, and by the residential expansion of its surrounding regions. Each of these factors contributes a layer of agenda to the city's transportation systems that shifts their missions, and hence, their real significances.

Thus, when we talk about "the city" missiologically, we are talking simultaneously about generic missio dynamics and particular contextual missio expressions. A hard dichotomy is not set between the two poles. Rather, we can see a focal-subsidiary dialectic between them in which each can shed light upon the other. And, again, just as texts can be read in light of both, urban realities can be read in light of both, in order to see what meanings are at play in any given instance.

Missio Dei and Missio Urbis

As we consider how the city's meanings emerge, we must keep in view that God's own missio can and does influence the expression of cities, categorically, historically, and at all viewable scales. God's sway on the city is no less of a force to be looked for than other non-physical forces. Kingdom interests are no more elusive to view than neoliberalism, Keynesianism, capitalism, class conflict or regional, national, hemispheric and global interests. Thus, when we seek to understand the significance of any particular city's features or the constellation of its sub-missios, we need to look for telltales of how God's macro-mission(s) and micro-mission(s) also may have influenced urban formation, by asking questions about what God has been up to and what ends he may be in the process of accomplishing. Put simply, the mission history of a city matters, for God has been at work in any city as long as it has been there and he has plans for that city that fit with his plans for his kingdom and for the world. His activities according to those plans have in part made any city what it is as we find it historically.

As we make such observations, we also need to keep in mind that the city is not passive. It is aggressively agglomerative and not simply the receptive object of external influences. Because both the missio Dei and the missio urbis reify in the same contexts, we also need to observe how the city may have sought to urbanize or co-opt the missio Dei for its own ends. We need to assess how influential the missio Dei has been in the expression of the missio urbis and we need to assess how influential the missio urbis has been upon the tangible expression(s) of God's kingdom. That is, as we consider real contexts historically, we must look to see both the degree to which the missio Dei has co-opted the city and the degree to which the city has co-opted or is seeking to co-opt the missio Dei.

This means that we cannot ascribe a common, surface level value to any of the city's features, including those that might appear at first glance to be kingdom reifications. Just as we cannot consider all transportation systems to have the same significance, we cannot consider other features to have uniform significance, even when they may appear to have kingdom or missional value. Neither transportation nor poverty relief have uniform significance, neither governance nor health services, neither capitalism nor human rights activism, etc. As we seek to understand the real, contextual significance of such things, we cannot afford simply to assume or assign common values; we must pay heed to historical and contextual formation of any feature, and examine the character, depth and significance of an urban feature's attachment to the missio Dei, discerning how that attachment may have interacted with attachments to other missios.

To understand the city missiologically, then, we must factor influence from the missio urbis along with various discursive missios. In this mix, influence from the missio Dei needs to be taken into account as one of the keys to discerning any urban feature's special significance. Thus, we need to ask missio Dei related questions at universal levels, at categorical or abstract levels, and at concrete and particular levels. Concerning the general history of the urban as a recurring phenomenon, we should inquire, "What is God's purpose for 'the city,' *everywhere*? How does the missio urbis fit with the missio Dei practically, ideologically, spiritually and theologically?" We also should ask, "What part may certain kinds of cities have in God's mission? What has he done through the city, generally, and through its different categorical types? What does he intend to accomplish through urban systems and people? How does the urbanization process factor as an instrument for him, and how does it fit in his Kingdom?"

Beyond this, we always should try to discern God's presence and activity in particular cities, looking for the distinct significances that are at play in their unique contexts. This means asking roughly the same questions with the condition, *this* city. This kind of observational, qualitative assessment brings overarching meanings into dialectic with the actualities of context. In order to bring those levels together, we should humbly and spiritually examine, looking for the missio meanings that actually have come into being and are coming into being as God's plan expresses with real people, in real places. This entails asking, rather than assuming, "What is God working *uniquely* in *this* city? What aims does he have *here* for *these* people, *these* institutions and *these* systems? How do these special, historical realities have place within God's real and historical kingdom project?" etc. These are the kinds of kingdom-oriented questions that can reveal the robust significance of the urban context in missiological terms.

Urban instruments. These kinds of assessments open pathways for urban missios to be taken up for kingdom purposes in missiologically informed ways, rather than in ways that are ad hoc or that reflect the dominance of non-kingdom missios. This missio-urban process resembles the process of urbanization, as well as the kingdom use(s) of the biblical text that we undertook in chapter 6. For, in the same way that sociolinguistic (textual) constructs may be taken up and used as tools in contemporary mission, so may sociospatial (urban) constructs. The key is to discern the missio significance within the functions of the city's structures and to appropriate or re-express those in kingdom ways, taking them up as instruments for sacred missional ends. For, like a text, a city's events and networks, its assemblages, encounters, its material, "space and place" architectures, that is, any of its realities, may be appropriated and re-expressed with divine mission as their dominant missio, even while they are suffused and informed by other missios.

In other words, just as the missio urbis may co-opt and *urbanize*, the missio Dei may co-opt and *sacralize*. This does not require that coinciding or co-existing missios must be obliterated or ignored. Nor does it require that a given urban feature have arisen overtly or primarily from the missio Dei. It simply requires that the missio Dei be placed in a superior position, so that the instrumental capacity of an urban feature would serve the kingdom's ends more than it serves other ends.

As an example, a city play area may be constructed in fulfillment of non-kingdom urban missios. As a non-kingdom mission product, its significance will be established primarily in relation to those missios (e.g., public health and recreation, public space distribution, community identification and formation, entrepreneurial place branding, real estate capitalism, etc.). Its significance also will be determined by the social performances, assemblages, networks, etc. that use it. Thus, the play area may be serving as an instrument of multiple micro- and macro-missios simultaneously, and it may have been designed instrumentally to serve those projects.

However, even though its form, its meaning and its missions have been set by other missios, the play area and its attendant missios may be co-opted by and for the kingdom by re-purposing it to serve the missio Dei *primarily*. This is parallel to what can happen if a given ideologically-oriented group occupies the play area in a public demonstration in order to instrumentalize it for that group's mission (Betancourt, 2016). Like a text, the play area can have instrumental potentials that were not held in the conscious conception of the designers, and because of its potentials, it can serve the missio of the demonstrators. It truly may become their space, their expressive tool, without jettisoning or destroying the missios that may have brought it into existence. Those missios may coexist and overlap even as they are subordinated to a new and dominant missio.

In the same fashion, although co-opted for kingdom ends, the play area still may serve the city by serving a community. It still may play a role in urban entrepreneurialism or real estate valuation projects or community formation, or any number of other special aims. While those may coexist and remain attached, the play area still may become a sacred, kingdom instrument by prioritizing the missio Dei and subordinating other agenda to its use as a tool for God's ends.

As we have seen extensively, missio is not absolutely determinant, nor is its presence exclusive. Missio is coexistent in joint productions and it can be coexistent in co-uses. Nothing prevents a store front church from participating also as a feature in an arts district, and nothing prevents an athletic center from being used an evangelistic project. A coffee house may be a business and at the same time a real estate improvement venture, a community building project, a social network hub, an urban encounter site, a civic branding location, all while being *primarily* a sacred place of worship and a gospel light for the kingdom's ends. This holds true for nearly all of a city's material and immaterial, "people and systems" (Gans, 2015) features, whether they are resource distribution webs, political apparatuses, assemblages, physical landmarks, community networks, etc.

From a missiological perspective, however, missional uptake requires consideration, since the purposes that suffuse the city's features and give them their forms are not always explicit, and urban objects can be designed for ends that compete intrinsically with sacred missional outcomes. As we saw above, the city's material and immaterial instruments cannot be taken for granted or at surface value. Its systems and its structures have been produced under influences that seek certain ends, and it is not a given that the meanings and ends of urban components are compatible with kingdom mission.

Thus, categorically and concretely, the city itself remains open to discerning interpretation, especially by representatives of God's kingdom, who have "eyes to see" and "ears to hear," under the guidance of the Holy Spirit. For the mission minded, the city and its realities are not necessarily self-defining, nor can they be predefined. Urban meanings should not be accepted merely at face value, nor should they be dominated by prevailing secular sentiments or philosophies. Rather, the city is a thing to be known and interpreted by the people of God, under his inspiration, and for his ends, and its meaning in its context is to be determined relative to God's kingdom.[130] The city remains under divine scrutiny, and its kingdom significance has yet to be fully revealed.

Urban Dynamics

As we pursue this line of interpretation, we need to make sure that we do not see missios as having static meanings, and we need to take into account that the city by its very nature cannot be still. Its missio is aimed at performance, and it must operate in order to exist at all. When we look at

---

[130]This is a way of prioritizing missiological thinking that is characteristic of Paul Hiebert. Although Hiebert's focus was on anthropological assessment in the service of "critical contextualization," he hints at a similar approach when he suggests that missionaries should "exegete the culture" (1987; 1994, pp. 88-89).

the fluxes, the pushes and pulls and tensions and flows of urban energies in terms of missio, then, what features stand out?

So far, we have noted that the city operates first as a concentration, and second, as an extension that proceeds from concentration. We also have noted that the missio of the city is to provide welfare for people. We followed those observations by noting that the city has contributing missios that combine within it, which give it its special categorical and concrete meanings and features, and that the particular significances of its features and missios are established by multiple factors, including historical influences and urban specializations.

From that foundation we can explore urban dynamics by framing them in terms of missio fulfillment. For example, the city's defining missio requires that it would provide human benefit. This exerts a control on the city's relations with other macro-missios and upon the expressions and configurations of its attendant missios. Together, they must empower the city to be a place of better human life than places that are "non-city"[131] if the city is to fulfill its purpose.

However, human life is a multifaceted thing, and human welfare is complex. There are many dimensions to human well-being, and the full range of human good cannot be achieved by any single provision. Thus, in order to fulfill its purpose the city must involve itself with or develop and sustain widely varied missios (Dechert, 1991). These push and pull the city in a number of directions at once, sometimes in paradoxical or highly tensive ways that stretch and strain the urban project. The city must engage in missios to provide better sustenance than that which can be found elsewhere. It also must transform space into the kinds of place that are more suited to dwelling and human activity than can be found outside the city. Likewise, it must reduce exposure to physical or social harm and threat, in comparison to non-city environments. It must implement strategies to

---

[131] "City" and "non-City" are used to avoid the dichotomy of "urban" and "rural."

sustain social interaction and communication, and provide for the development of generations. These are only a few of the specialized missios that must provide improved benefit to participants in the city's project.

From another angle, however, all of these benefits fail if the city itself fails. Thus, special missios that sustain the existence of the city itself are also necessary. Yet, like people, cities are complex constructions, and they also have complex requirements that must be met if they are to survive and accomplish their primary missions. As David Harvey (1989) proposed in his highly influential article on urban "entrepreneurialism," the city is not an island; it must survive as one project among many, which are both greater and lesser in scope and might. As a result, the city is required to sustain a wide variety of intra-urban and extra-urban projects, *both* for the needs of its members and for its own needs. This splits the missio of the city toward divided ends. While it must meet the needs of its members it also must develop strategies of competition. It must make itself attractive or influential. It must forge and maintain a distinctive identity. It must regulate its transactional relations with things that are beyond it, and it must preserve its social, economic, political, conceptual and physical territories.

Reflexive missios. Some of the city's energies then must be allocated to missios that primarily sustain the city itself, aimed toward the eventual outcome that the city may fulfill the missio urbis. Like urbanized or co-opted missios, these "Citysystems" (Brugmann, 2010) support the urban missio incidentally or secondarily, but they do not accomplish the urban missio directly. We could characterize them as *recursive* missio systems and structures, or perhaps better as *reflexive* missio features. Because these kinds of indirect, reflexive missio systems exist to serve the city itself, they dissipate urban energies, pulling force away from the city's primary ends. This creates a dynamic tension because reflexive missios simultaneously detract from the city's mission, yet they are required for it. Although necessary and intrinsic, they do not explicitly accomplish the same goals or serve the same missio that the city serves.

Crucially, this same dynamic can occur with missios that are not intrinsic or necessary, but which simply participate in the urban project, for any missio at any level has the capacity to be reflexive. As we have seen already, missio is subject to influence and to admixture, even to the point of becoming conflicted. It is adaptive enough to allow mission framers and actors to engage in projects that turn goals or agenda backward and inward, so that the actor becomes the recipient of the action.

Theoretically, this reflexive capacity of missio is neutral; it is simply a directional or dispositional ability. However, it very well may be missio's most problematic capacity, because it enables self-interested agenda, both in cases where that is warranted and in cases where it is not. And, due to the composite nature of missio, generally, it opens the door for self-interest to be a highly influential factor within the mix of the city's missios.

Using an easily accessible example, policing systems are overtly designed to fulfill missio urbis in both direct and reflexive ways. On one hand, they are to make life better for participants by making the urban environment stable; on the other hand, they are to serve the city's interests by preserving its own viability, strength and cohesion. However, in concrete expression, policing systems often find themselves weighted toward the side of reflexive missio at the cost of direct missio. For, although they ostensibly are aimed at providing security and securing justice for the city's members, under the city's reflexive agenda, they can become aimed more at minimizing harms to the city itself rather than producing benefits for inhabitants. In such cases, the missio of policing becomes predominately oriented toward keeping the city itself powerful and secure, even at cost to the city's constituents.

Tensive dynamics between reflexive and direct missio orientations can arise within any project or missio as groups or individuals negotiate the need for reflexive activity. In the case of social control, few would argue that policing is unnecessary, but most can observe that the governance missio quickly can become imbalanced if its recursive dimension is not well managed. When the city's reflexive agenda dominates, any missio can end up distributing greater good to those whose fortunes are most intimately connected to the city's own. It also can be co-opted by the attendant missios of those who have influence upon it so that its capacity to render good becomes misdirected toward very few of the city's constituents, at the expense of most, and even at the expense of the city's well-being. While some degree of benefit may reach some of the city's members indirectly, being diffused into the overall well-being of the city, the greater effect from the inordinate exercise of missio's reflexive capacity becomes one of detriment.

The conflicted missio urbis. While obvious when illustrated by policing abuses, even on broad levels, the reflexive dimension is where the missio of the city begins to complicate itself, sometimes to the point of self-defeating contradiction.

Looking back, when we considered institutions as co-authors, we saw that institutions can operate as social entities. This means that the city can be expected to operate institutionally as its own social entity. We also have seen that the city's core mission arises from an intention by people to create well-being for themselves. Missiologically speaking, we would hold that the character of this core mission in turn sets the city's fundamental character as a social entity. If we view the city as an entity arising from its members' missio to seek self-welfare, it follows naturally that the social entity of the city would embody that missio by seeking its own institutional self-welfare. So far, we have been calling this the city's *urban reflexive* missio.

The reflexive urban missio sheds light on the city's dialectic between concentration and extension. From the perspective of self-welfare, they are two sides of the same coin. The city extends, but it extends not to *yield* benefit, but to *collect* it for itself, that is, in order to stretch its reach of gathering benefit. Thus, extension is actually a subordinate process within the city's benefit concentration; it serves the urban aggregating dynamic.

Yet, in terms of the city's actions as an institution, the characteristic of self-welfare is problematic because it pushes the city to enter a common social game with its constituents. If it follows the mandate that has brought it into existence, the city will throw its welfare-seeking into the same ring with them. In some ways, this makes the city a conflicted entity, for its missio is to create welfare for all who are involved with it, but its own welfare is one of those whose welfare it seeks. Thus, while the city acts as a provider for its members, it simultaneously becomes a competitor with them in a quest for survival and benefit.

Given that coexistent missios impact each other, it follows that the city's own welfare-seeking would interact with and thus affect other welfare seeking missios, and that its impact would be to exert dynamic force to skew them to favor the city. Ideally, of course, all of the missios in the game would be arranged synergistically, in ways that provide equal and mutual benefit. However, all missios are not equal. Some inevitably supersede others, and the city holds a distinct advantage in this contest.

Even if it were the case that all of the varied urban missios could be arranged for mutual benefit, the problem remains that a core conflict resides in the heart of the city. For, the city is caught on the horns of a dilemma, whether to accomplish its own well-being, or the well-being of its participants. On one hand, the city's mission is fulfilled when its members flourish, but to the degree that the city accomplishes this goal, it leaves its own welfare unfulfilled. On the other hand, the city's missio is also fulfilled when it flourishes, but the degree to which the city accomplishes this is the degree to which it leaves the welfare of its members unfulfilled.

Benefit and yield. Somewhat ironically, since the city is based upon a strategy of collection, and since it functions as an instrument of concentration, dispersing resources actually runs counter to its core design. Both by its nature, and on pragmatic levels, if the city is to survive, and if it is to improve its own state, the lion's share of its resources may not be dissipated. If that were to happen, the city would cease to function as a thing that concentrates resource. Thus, while its mission programs the city to yield some degree of benefit to its participants, the design of that mission simultaneously constrains the city not to offer its resources freely nor to make them openly available to all.

What then sets the terms of access to the city's benefits? In order to satisfy its conflicted missios, urban resources must be managed through transactions that control benefit and yield. In order to fulfill the missio to concentrate, these transactions must render greater resources *toward* the city than they yield *away* from it. This creates uneven relations between the city and its participants (Baltazar, 1991; Birch & Wachter, 2011; Gottdiener & Hutchison, 2011; Sassen, 2001).[132] As a basic algorithmic principle of collection, this standing condition applies whenever the city grants access to its resources. If it is to meet its basic missional goals, whenever the city expends, it must compensate in some way, somewhere, and that compensation must exceed expenditure. This is where the city's core conflict shows through most forcefully, for in order to fulfill its missio to render benefit, the city becomes set to *take* more than it *gives* in the overall net of its operations.

Of course, this does not mean that the city must take in every instance, only across the sum of its transactions. For, in order to perpetuate its missio, the city must be able to enlist ongoing participation from constituents, and it must do so using the offer of ongoing increase in welfare. These prospects must be more than illusory (Anderson, 2017). The city must open real potential for progressive improvement of life. It must provide at least some opportunities, some avenues toward advancement, by which its members always may gain heightened pleasure, added ease, greater security, improved health, increased access to resources and development of social value (Fainstein, 2001).

---

[132] Peter Aboue (2004) makes a similar observation about globalizing forces, noting that they have the propensity to exploit local participants.

Differential yields. However, the city gathers resource precisely because its own resources have limits. It cannot offer everything to everyone. The very idea of prospective gain requires that something better remains to be had in the possible future. Thus, if the city is to be able to engage participants via the offer of perpetual improvement, the full span of its resources must be withheld to some degree. For, if all resources were to be made immediately available to all, the city would have nothing future to offer people in the way of increase or improved state, and it would lose both its own concentration and its members' engagement.

On affective levels, this leads the city to foster in participants the hope and anticipation that Anderson (citing Berlant) calls a "cruel optimism" about city life (Anderson, 2017). On material levels, some tangible resources must be yielded to participants, but only enough to establish a minimum, "entry-level" improvement of welfare. For if the mission is effective concentration, only the least possible degree of improvement is called for, and then, only enough to keep participants engaged (Simone, 2004).

In many ways this dynamic parallels the textual dynamics that we examined in Chapter 5. There, we saw that texts open up "hollow" conceptual spaces that invite the reader's desire to understand or to gain closure. With texts, this draws the reader into engagement with the text's resistances and yields, affecting the reader as she negotiates the text's sociolinguistic structures. In a similar manner, the city perpetually opens up a hollow space of potentials, and the urban participant's desire for closure on these possibilities draws him to engage the city's resistances and yields. Baltazar characterizes this as being "pushed" and "pulled" into the city and its life (1991, p. 276). This shapes the urban dweller or migrant as he interacts with the city's sociospatial landscapes. Partial satisfactions in this process reward the urban dweller's engagement in the same way that partial understandings reward reader engagement, while partial lacks keep the future unresolved, just as partial lacks of understanding keep the text unresolved. These keep the spaces in front of the urban dweller or the reader continually open and inviting, which perpetuates dynamic involvements.

We must note here that this is not yet an evaluative description in terms of righteousness and unrighteousness. That kind of assessment must be done using the kingdom of God as a frame of reference. We are simply performing missio based analysis that reveals what the city's purposes press it to do. Purely from the perspective of accomplishing ends, whether or not the situation is good or bad, healthy or exploitive, as long as some benefit is yielded and people continue to participate, the city can withhold additional resources and still satisfy its conflicted missional identity to some degree. It can fulfill its need to concentrate during its transactions, and it can fulfill its need to yield some kind of increased welfare to its members.

With these conflicted missios at play, then, the city is poised to bargain with its participants. It may offer the prospect of increased benefit to them, but do so on a limited basis, granting increased resource in direct proportion to the amount of yield granted toward the city. Thus, those who serve the city's interests may garner for themselves more of its concentrated resources, but those who do not augment the city may not (Lawton, 2016). From a missiological perspective, these seem to remain the rules of play for the urban "game."

Complications and breakdowns. When the city fails to provide improved material and social resources, when it fails to make human place from space, when it cannot provide relief from threat, or the promise of potential to improve, it fails its primary end, the missio urbis. Secondarily, when the city fails to sustain itself and it can no longer accumulate resources, it also fails its reflexive, institutional missio, which is supposed to sustain the city in its missio urbis. On a third level, when sub-missios fail to help the city's achieve its goals, or when they consume more overall benefit than they yield, those sub-missios also fail their special purposes.

Any or all of these failures thwart the city's raison d'être by stymieing its capacity to fulfill its design, and they call its viability into question. That is, by obstructing the missio urbis, these kinds of breakdowns threaten the very existence of the city and its members. As a result, failures introduce internal stresses at the points where direct, indirect and reflexive missios are no longer achieved. At those places, the significance and the purpose of the city break down, and the city in turn becomes meaningless. This is especially forceful when the city itself becomes a threatening or dangerous place.

Remedial missios. Because both the city and those within it seek to survive and to maintain the production of benefit, attempts will be made to self-correct and to adapt when failures, crises and breakdowns occur. Missiologically, we would say that Birch and Wachter (2011) envision the outcomes of these missios when they advocate for "extremely absorptive systems" or "resilient infrastructure," and that Jeb Brugmann talks about similar kinds of operations when he describes the adaptivity and potentials of urban "network efficiencies" and "Citysystems" (2010).

From our interpretive location we can call these *remedial* missios or *corrective* missios. According to the view we have developed, remedial urban missios will emerge in moments of the city's missional failure with the aim to remove breakdowns and to reestablish the city's primary missio. Yet, because of the rules of the urban game, these always must express under the governing mandate not to yield too much resource. They may not challenge the city too deeply or cost it too much, for they must preserve the city's viability and its ability to fulfill the majority of its missios.

Thus, corrective missios are forced to compete among the city's missio constellations. They may cost the city and its members resource at points, but only if they offer the promise of continued concentration. Their remedial agenda may impact other indirect missios only insofar as they minimize problems that cost the city. They are limited by the city not to seek ends that cost too much and not to exert force in ways that significantly displace the city's other supporting sub-missios. Corrective missios are welcome when they relieve failures and breakdowns, but only as long as they do not compromise the city's larger agenda.

If remedial missios become too costly or if they appear too costly in prospect, the city's mandates for its own well-being will require those missios to be marginalized and quarantined. In other words, because the urban missio proceeds from sociomaterial agenda, a good project is good until it no longer supports the city's concentration of resources. At that point, regardless of the value that a project might have according to other discourses, it is no longer a "good" missio in terms of the urban project. In such a case, a remedial missio becomes a hindrance, a drain or a threat, and as such it becomes a thing that the city needs to correct. When that horizon is crossed, remedial missios will be subjected to urban forces that will pare them down to a point where they yield more benefit than cost, or modify them, or expunge them wholesale from the city's overall construct. From the perspective of the city and its mission, the city must survive and be fulfilled, and, unfortunately, any missios and persons that fail to assist in its collection project run the risk of becoming its adversaries.

Yet, ironically, like an autoimmune disease, both the threat of sanction and the exercise of force against remedial missios can be counterproductive. For, as the city's reflexive missios agonize against its remedial missios, competition and internal conflict can exacerbate crisis at points of system breakdown. This can produce still greater breakdown through system to system, group to group, and person to person violence, as the city's sub-missios and participants seek in conflicting ways to fulfill the primary urban directive to achieve well-being.

Complicating the mix, we must remember that the city's missio does not stand in isolation; it is subject to being impacted by missios that come from beyond it (Aboue, 2004; Birch & Wachter, 2011). These larger missios also have corrective missios that operate within the scopes of their own projects, which express and satisfy their own macro-missional agenda. For example, ethnic or nationalist metanarratives have corrective plans for the city within their own discourses, and they will seek to incorporate the city within their overarching agenda. Similar pressures come from global missio(s), religious missios, political missios, environmental missios, economic missios, etc. Urbanization is itself subject to globalization, nationalization, liberalization, commercialization, militarization, modernization, post-modernization, and a host of other processes and projects.

In the midst of these diverse forces, missional compatibility is always an issue, and it should be kept in mind that the city most naturally will seek to gain from the missios that surround it. Thus, it will interface most quickly and integrate most readily with missios that are the most contributive and compatible to itself. At the same time, it will be slow to engage agenda that are least contributive and least similar.

This sheds further light on the city's resistance to corrective missios. For, corrective missios frequently arise from metanarratives, discourses or agenda that have different core purposes than the missio urbis, such as the moral and spiritual mandates to care, promote justice or love. These missios are not intrinsically attached to the missio urbis, and they often do not arise under its influence. They are essentially *non*-urban, *an*-urban, or *trans*-urban missios that transcend the city and its mission.

In some sense, the city is invisible or subordinate from the view of these transcendent missios, because transcendent missios are aimed equally at the urban and non-urban. While the city matters, these missios seek the same ends whether or not the city is involved. And, although they are projects that can coexist within urban spaces and places, even though they can adapt to the city and interface with the city, fundamentally, transcendent missios produce expressions and seek outcomes that relate to their own, transurban goals. Thus, the structures and projects produced by transurban missios are frequently a poor fit for the city. They walk out of step, to the beat of a different drummer, and they often conflict with the city's existing missios, structures and systems.

The macro-missio of the kingdom of God is just such a missio. It readily involves the city, but at the same time it transcends the urban identity. The kingdom's context can coincide with the city's but the city's will never match the kingdom's, for the city may reside in the kingdom, but the kingdom always resides beyond the city; its scope is broader, deeper, wider and longer. While the kingdom has a plan for the city, the city has a plan for itself. In its missio, the kingdom aims to take the city up into itself, correcting its breakdowns and readjusting its missios to meet kingdom values, co-opting it to serve kingdom ends. Thus, it has a benign yet awkward relation with the city, and the character of its relationship depends highly on the degree of the city's dedication to self-interest.

Toward urban-missiological reading of Genesis 1. Of course, all of this must be taken as a preliminary missiological vision of the urban. These are initial, provisional interpretations, open on all sides to revision, and significantly more analysis is needed to develop a truly missiological conceptualization of the city and the urban, especially when dealing with urban missio constellations, constitutive and attendant missios and missio-urban dynamics. The main goal for making these observations has been to demonstrate how missio-grounded examination can be performed, and how that can yield an integrated and internally consistent account of the urban phenomenon. It shows one way in which the city as a sociospatial construct can be assessed in terms of missio and it illustrates that using the missio lens can produce distinctly missiological findings about urban realities.

Secondarily, this cursory assessment gives us enough of a missio-centered view to establish an urban-missiological reading location. From that location, we can now bring missiological interpretation of the city into interaction with missiological interpretation of the biblical text. This juxtaposition will produce our special goal, an urban-missiological reading.

Chapter 9

The City and Genesis 1

Juxtaposing the City and Genesis 1

Up to this point, we have been working to get city and text "on the same page," by considering each one in terms of missio. This work has applied missiological terms to each and framed each as a missio-based construct. Describing both this way enables us to compare them using like concepts, which in turn allows us to see points of similarity or difference. This comparison produces a view in which each sheds light on the other. Using that joint view as a foundation, we can extrapolate some points of missiological significance.

We will begin comparing at the level of worlds and worldviews. This will draw together our missiological interpretations of the text and the city. The aim is to use missiological thinking to outline how the worlds of the city and of the creation account correspond or differ. Once that is done, we can reflect on the missiological significance of what we have discovered.

This is somewhat of a tricky endeavor, however, because the Genesis passage has a double-vision of the world. As we have seen, the creation account's textual missio requires that there be dissonance between the world as it is and the world as it could or should be. Thus, as it seeks to create nostalgia and longing, it presents a picture of an ideal world, yet its view of that world proceeds from an outlook that sees its own present reality as sub-ideal. This puts our interpretation on the horns of a dilemma, whether to juxtapose the world of the city with the world and worldview that has produced the text or to juxtapose it with the world that the text portrays.

Since it appears that the aim of the text is to valorize the ideal creational world, we can assume that the narrative world is the world that the author understands to be normative, best and highest, or most significant. From the viewpoint of the text's missio that world is most real and true, while the experienced world is diminished. We can assume this because in its mission and in its presentation the text tacitly devalues the "world as it is" in favor of the "world as it should be."

Significantly, the text still presumes some degree of continuity between the ideal world and the text's contemporary world. Without that connection, the story would be pointless, as a tale about the origins of a completely separate world, and it would lose its engagement with its reader. This means that although the world of the narrative is not in every way the world of the author(s) or reader(s), correspondence is still assumed between the two. In this correspondence, the ideal world is held in priority; its value to the author sets the terms for the author's intentions, and hence, frames the text's missio.

Taking these missio aspects into account can help us decide which juxtaposition to pursue here. Missiologically, we can notice that the text is designed to urge or compel the reader toward the world as it should be. In order to accomplish this, the text elicits tensions by juxtaposing the ideal world against the reader's experienced world. Given that this is the strategy of the text, we can track more effectively with its missio if we juxtapose a view of the city as it presently is with a view of the ideal world presented within the text. Although imperfectly, in our own reading this can draw us closer to duplicating the outcomes that the text is aimed at than would a reading that juxtaposes an experienced world with an experienced city or an ideal world with an ideal city. Since we do not have the space to explore all possible readings here, we will pursue the reading with a closer missiological correlation to the biblical text. That is, we will emphasize the creational account's idyllic vision, keeping in mind that a diminished and tensive shadow image of the world lays behind it. Hopefully, as we do this, we can find our own responses to the text developing along lines that reflect its intended outcomes.

Natural space and human place worlds. As we overlay our image of the city onto the narrative of Gen. 1, the contrast between worlds that are in view is immediately striking. While the city is a place of density and consolidation, the space of Gen. 1 is open, wide and expansive. Genesis shows a vista that is uncontained, with no limits, whereas the city has "social systems with boundaries" (Dechert, 1991) and horizons of controlled space or regionalized influence that are subject to evaluative or territorial description (O'Flaherty, 2005; Ramachandran, 1996).

Further, when we envision the urban, we see that its place making is distinctly human. Its architectures and landscapes are transformed from natural, undefined space toward "operationalized" (Brenner & Schmid, 2014; Rickards, et al., 2016; Scott, et al., 2001) human place. It is organized functionally, by and for human occupation, in ways that sustain ongoing proximity and activity among people (Gottdiener & Hutchison, 2011). Its places are not universal; they are delineated, identifiable, accounted for and controlled by specific entities, and they have widely disparate values (O'Flaherty, 2005; Okolo, 1991). Even its naturalized spaces are not truly natural, for they exist by intention, and they serve a function to make human life maximally livable.[133]

In the city, dimensions and features of objects and landscapes match the sizes, habits and capacities of human beings, and there is little or no place for other creatures (Longhurst, 2017). Other inhabitants of the world, the beasts, birds, fish, and creeping things, must inhabit human spaces, finding the margins and adapting to human occupancy. Even the governance

---

[133] This remains true even of nature reserves, since the concept of the reserve is ultimately unnatural and artificial (Sheppard, 2011). The reserve converts an undesignated space of nature into the designated place of a reserve by assigning that space an archival missio of "preservation," which is finally aimed at the common good of people.

of the heavenly bodies seems blunted as the city sustains activity before the dawn, after sunset, and in the face of the seasons.

In its space transformations, then, urbanization appears in some ways to fulfill humankind's mandate from God to "subdue and rule" (wěkiběšuhā ûrědû) the earth. It embodies the force of the Hebrew, which speaks of the forceful subjugation of something unruly, in total domination. However, although the creation account talks this way, the Genesis story still depicts a kind of harmony between the humanly and creaturely missios, which the city's focus on human place seems to overlook. For, while the creation narrative calls humans to subdue the earth, their calling is not the only one in play. The divine mandate also calls for the plants and beasts to fill the earth, and there appears to be no contradiction, or, at least no mutual exclusion, between these commissions. Rather, the story gives an impression of orderly coexistence and shared use of space, with humans holding the superior, not the sole, occupancy (Lin, 2016; Mustol, 2017).

Expansive and collective missios. This leads to related point. Like the city, the earth in Genesis 1 is filled with categorical projects and special missios. The creatures have marching orders to be fruitful and to multiply, the heavenly bodies have their tasks of season-ordering; the greater and smaller luminaries have rule to exercise in the heavens. Like the city, the earth is filled with activity and agenda, and one can nearly hear the hustle and bustle of networks, systems, flows and encounters as fish teem, birds flock, creeping things creep and beasts roam.

However, unlike the city, the varied missios of Genesis are expansive at heart. They are not aimed at agglomeration or collection, they have no horizons and they are not coordinated in a particular, local project that can be compared to another social or physical location. They do not appear to collect anything to a particular group or place for the heightened benefit of that designation.

In a partial parallel, the urban missio and the missios in Gen. 1 both extend, but the agenda for their expansions appears to differ. The city's missio is invasive; it extends transformations of the non-urban into the urban, sometimes through influence, in ways that precipitate fundamental changes in that into which it extends. It also extends competitively, in order to support its own concentrations, augmenting its capacity to collect and advance itself. The missios of Genesis do not seem to have the same reflexive agenda. They expand in order to fill. While transformation is assumed, that transformation is aimed at delivering fruitfulness to the entire expanse of the earth, rather than at exploitation or operationalizing. The creation missios extend to yield rather than accrue benefit. Entrepreneurial relations, concentration or localization is not in view. Quite the opposite; the extensive goal in Genesis is aimed at fulfilling stewardship of that which is already under dominion, rather than at invasion or acquisition of that which is yet to be held.

Comparative states and places. Perhaps this is because human welfare is not in question in the creation narrative. There is no indication that human life could be improved, even if that goal were to be desired, and it certainly could not be better in one place than another. There is no need for heightened access to resources, as all appears to be at the humans' joint disposal. Neither is there a need for safety, or even shelter. There is no sense of adverse environment or of natural threats, for humans are in a place of dominion. They rule unchallenged and supreme in a world of plenty.

By contrast, the city intrinsically assumes a world of designated places and variable states of being. Its very existence arises from the idea that things and people may be collected in a way that makes life better somewhere than it is elsewhere. The city's core significance depends upon there being a differential welfare between its own domain and that which lies beyond it. Things need to be better in the realm of the urban than outside of it if city-doing is to make sense, and if the costs of city-making are to be justified. Because the urban is a relative designation, it would not be unfair to characterize it as a competitive construct in an essential sense, because it is only knowable via comparison to non-urban places and states.

In fact, the very idea of the city is rendered incomprehensible by the holistic scope of the Genesis account. In Genesis, the only geospatial division to be found is between and between the waters and the dry land (1:9-10), while in spatial terms alone the lower heavens that touch the earth are bounded from the higher heavens by a simple firmament that appears to extend through all knowable space (1:6-8). Temporally, the only divisions lie between the night and the day (1:4-5), and between the hours, days and seasons (1:14-18). In this scheme, limits or comparisons between urban and non-urban ways of life, values, social arrays or places cannot even be conceptualized. Distinction of place is not possible, because there are no territory designations to work with. "Here" and "there" do not seem to be meaningful categories, for the world has no boundaries within it. The earth is the only place, and that place includes all earthly space.

In a similar vein, population density is a null concept in Genesis 1. Whereas the animals and plants appear in en masse, humankind is completely contained within what appears to be a single mated pair, consisting of a male and a female, while larger human generations await development (1:26-30). Although the pair certainly represent human categories, at the narrative level, they are simply a male and a female. The entire species is just two, which are inextricably bound in the singular, "him," making them, indivisibly, one.

In this world, city making or urbanization is a meaningless notion. For, in order for the city to be the city, it must gather people and their things. It is a singular plural that comes into being as humans and their products come together. And, regardless of how the city is defined (Brenner & Schmid, 2014; Gans, 2015; Rickards, et al., 2016; Scott, et al., 2001), in some manner there must be "more" of that which is human in the urban than there is outside of it. In Genesis, however, humans and human productions cannot be gathered because they cannot be separated. They are not together to create a thing, actualize an event, heighten a value or accomplish a project, but because they are inseparably related in ontic solidarity. Their togetherness is not a togetherness in contrast to the apartness of others, who do not stand with them. They stand simply as they are, nameless except by category, together, a singular plural, on a landscape that is neither "here" nor "there."

Provision and the Urban Horizon

Another stand out feature of the biblical account is the abundance of food. As God calls the earth to bring forth all vegetation, the text focuses specifically on seed bearing plants and fruit bearing trees (1:11-12), lending the impression that the earth is everywhere full and ripe with food. This is reinforced as God calls the couple to notice that he has given them all seed bearing plants and fruits for their food, with the green plants given for the animals' food (1:29-30). In this arrangement, there is no food competition between the humans and the animals. Each has a designated type of provision, which is good, at hand, and more than enough.

The world of the city is different. This is perhaps the most traditional distinction of the city, and it bears some examination from the perspective of missio. Classically, the city has been identifiable by its departure from agriculture, carrying a territorial designation that distinguishes between "rural" and "urban" areas (Ramachandran, 1996). Although highly disputed as adequate characterizations for contemporary things urban, these categories still have descriptive merit, enough that no consensus has arisen yet within urban studies about what the city is or might be in their absence (Birch & Wachter, 2011; Brenner & Schmid, 2014; Gans, 2015; Rickards, et al., 2016; Scott, et al., 2001). Further, the rural/urban contrast endures in vernacular usage, and it has the advantage of being highly applicable historically; its descriptive efficacy spans from the murky origins of urban life well into the mid 20th century (Taylor, et al., 2010). Thus, without expecting the rural/urban difference to account for all that the city is, we can at least note that the city minimizes food production use of space in highly observable ways, while the non-city does not.

Missionally, however, the city's non-agricultural agenda is paradoxical and in some ways, self-defeating. For, while the city's avoidance of food-making frames urban identity and affords the city its strength and capacities, it simultaneously puts the city in perpetual jeopardy. And, perhaps more importantly, it sets the urban at odds with the non-urban. This is a profound contrast point between the worlds of Genesis and the city, and it warrants further exploration.

At basic levels, food production requires space, which makes the food producing missio a diffusive force on density. This places food production in a dynamic of opposition to the project of concentration. For, in order for the city to concentrate, it must reassign the use of food producing place to uses that offer higher yields (O'Flaherty, 2005). However, when this is done, natural limits quickly appear at the threshold of self-sufficiency (Gottdiener & Hutchison, 2011). These limits emerge as the missio urbis intensifies the project of concentrating settlement to a point that is incompatible with the missio to produce food (Haysom, 2016; Ramachandran, 1996). Although simple settlements can remain diffused enough to produce their own food sufficiently, cities concentrate too densely to do so.

From the view of missio, the horizon of conflict between these two missios creates one of many meaningful boundaries between urban and non-urban. That is, in any given place, when the missio of food production is subordinated to the missio of concentration to the degree that the goal of sustenance can no longer be fulfilled immediately and directly, that place can be considered *urban* rather than *non-urban*. When this happens, the city must develop or appropriate sub-missios that will attend to its need for provision. These attendant missios are thus missiologically viewed as *urban missios* (etc.).

This is because, missiologically speaking, the identity of the city is determined by which missios have ascendance over which. In the urban case, the forces that move settlement toward the urban horizon reveal an irreconcilable missional tension within the urbanizing project. This tension arises because the city aims to draw people and things together, yet people require provisioning, and provisioning demands too much diffused space per capita to allow concentration past a certain point. Thus, city-making and population-provisioning become conflicting or mutually exclusive agenda. Because the space conditions of provisioning run counter to the city's basic mandate to concentrate, decisions about missio priority must be negotiated. If the missio urbis is held as ascendant, the food-making missio becomes a competing missio that must be rejected or marginalized as counter-productive to the urban agenda.

In other words, the city's prime missio cannot be fulfilled without modifying the terms of what constitutes human welfare in a manner that brackets out food self-sufficiency. This is problematic, because food is a basic human need, and the ostensive purpose of the city is to provide for at least basic human welfare (Haysom, 2016). The city is thus driven by its own missio to have to ignore, defer or redefine what constitutes basic human need if it is to be able to satisfy its missio to offer human well-being. From a missio perspective, the city does this by a missional sleight of hand that redefines well-being in terms of satisfaction of desire. Once this shift is made, the city is able prioritize a missio to provide human satisfactions in the place of the missio to provide human needs.

This contrast shows starkly when the Genesis account is juxtaposed with the city. In the creation account, all human needs are met, for life is considered to be "good." Yet, the things that God provides have little hint of being pleasures or satisfactions. God provides needs, not diversions or luxuries. He gives humans a relation to himself in his image; he gives them the purpose and security that attend rule over the earth, the companionship of mated relation, the capacity for generating offspring, and ample food. Nothing more appears to be necessary. Existence in this scenario is primal, simple and fulfilling.

This is not the scenario that the city offers. Its lure is based on the prospect of more than simple subsistence. This is demonstrated by the city's abandonment of the food-producing missio in favor of the concentrative missio. The city shows that it cares for something else precisely because it is willing to forfeit or modify the sustenance missio in order to pursue densifying strategies that yield non-food benefits. Thus, the urban horizon itself is a missional line in the sand that distinguishes between the aim to meet *needs* and the aim to satisfy *desires*.

In order to surmount this threshold, the city must presume that it can draw food *to* itself instead of creating food *within* itself (Damerow, 1998). This is a complex assumption that requires many missios to accomplish, and even more to assure. Yet, it is a necessary one, for only if it can make this assumption is the city able to gather people together under the banner of "welfare." The city must treat drawing food to itself as a given, that is, as a non-variable, ground condition. It is only after this that the city can work with space on terms that only require the *availability* of sustenance, not its *production*.

Urban dominion vs. Genesis dominion. To make these conditions feasible, the city must shift its missional configuration. It must forfeit missios that *create* food and replace them with missios that *acquire* food. This replaces the missio to *produce* with the missio to *transport*.

In order to make this shift, however, the city must *displace* function, relocating the missio of food making elsewhere. However, the relation between function and space is a bit like the relation between energy and matter; use of space can be moved and modified, but not truly obliterated. Likewise, food must still be produced, and it must be produced in a way that the city's acquisition missio can guarantee and treat as its own. The way that this can be accomplished effectively is for the city to lay a functional claim on spaces and places outside of itself as though those spaces were within itself. Note that these do not need to be contiguous or adjacent hinterlands.

They may be located anywhere within the reach of the city's attending missios.

This may be the most critical of the city's strategic extensions. For, if the city can succeed at displacing its missio to produce food by relocating it outside, to non-urban locations, it then can be free to convert its own internal space. It can replace the higher-space food missio with the lesser-space transportation missio and use the surplus space for concentrated purposes. It can then offer the fruits of these concentrated projects as points of human welfare using the redefinition of satisfaction.

This scheme not only arises from space dynamics; it arises as an issue of resource limits. This is the watershed contrast with Genesis. For, the city may be a place of concentrated resources, but those resources do not arise spontaneously at hand, and they are not freely provided. In the world of Genesis, sustenance is guaranteed by the hand of God, and it remains always at hand in the environment. By contrast, the missio urbis does not assume such divine provision. At its very heart, the missio urbis is a strategy to obtain and maximize resources. Its world is not a provisioned world. It is a transactional world in which supply must be contrived, collected and transported across boundaries.

The city's need to treat provision as a given inevitably complicates the ways that it interacts with the non-urban. The need to displace food producing space away from itself produces a relationship with non-urban places that is simultaneously domineering and dependent, which makes the kind of dominion that the city exerts differ fundamentally from the kind of dominion that the Genesis account depicts. Urban needs prod the city to extend power in ways that exceed the Genesis idea of dominion because the city cannot survive if it merely exercises dominion over the earth. It also must exert dominion over non-urban people, along with their places and their labors, since it must guarantee for itself control over the fruits of human labor if it is to be able to displace provisioning from itself effectively and in secure ways.

At the same time, ironically, the shift in the provision missio that allows the city to concentrate also makes the city perpetually vulnerable and reliant, because it lacks sufficient internal provisions of food (and water), which non-urban places must supply (Mukherjee, 2016; Ramachandran, 1996). Under these terms, the city becomes a thing of want. It always must be supplied from the outside if it is to continue. Because it does not make food within itself, it cannot be self-sustaining, no matter how it configures itself. Thus, it relates to the non-urban as a needy and yet demanding entity.

This is a point where differences between the material, territorial existence of the city and its immaterial, non-territorial existence[134] show most clearly. While it would seem that the city could simply expand, it cannot. On one hand, if the city were to extend its full boundaries to include food production spaces it would diffuse its own space use to levels that defeat the missio urbis and return its character to that of simple settlement. On another, such a diffusion would render the very idea of the city unrecognizable, reducing it to an elusive, poorly identifiable constellation of qualities (Brenner & Schmid, 2014). Thus, if the city is to maintain distinctively urban concentration levels, it cannot extend itself in full; that is, in the sense of its territoriality. Instead, it must extend itself only partially, in its immaterial presence, that is, in the sense of urban dominion, through the exercise of influence. This strategy substitutes the use of power for the use of space by co-opting external place use without integrating that place as territory.

Crucially, the supply that the city needs is a survival level issue, and the city must ensure that its provision remains uninterrupted and unthreatened. In order to satisfy space use demands and self-survival concerns at the same time, then, the city must be able to exert final, irresistible power over things that lie beyond it, especially labor and its fruits. That is, the city must keep certain spaces as "other" to itself, yet it

---

[134] In many ways, these correspond to the differences between localized "town-ness" and networked "city-ness" that Taylor, et al (2010) suggest.

must co-opt the use of those spaces in ways that render benefit to itself, and it must do this in ways that are constant, enduring and cannot be challenged. This compels the urban missio to support or ally itself with macro-missios that secure the efficacy of remote influence, such as globalism, transnationalism, capitalism, militarism, imperialism and colonialism, etc., whether they be political, economic or social.

The differential of urban well-being. When the city does this, it effectively superimposes its presence through power on non-urban places and projects without fully integrating them or operating on parity. It thus dominates the non-urban because it does not treat non-city space or activity as integral to itself, yet it uses those spaces and those energies as though they were its own. It does this while holding a boundary against non-urban integration or influence. Ramachandran describes just such a situation at the urban fringe in India, in which fringe areas serve the urban but do not receive municipal benefits because they are not within the city's formal territories.

> Primary urban facilities, such as water supply, sewerage, etc., are for the most part not available because the city provides these services only to places within the municipal limits. Outside municipal limits, the small towns and revenue villages lack the necessary administrative infrastructure and the finances to provide these basic amenities.

He notes that these "complementary areas" derive some forms of benefit from the city, but they are not truly integral, with the result that,

> Problems arising out of the urbanization of the fringe villages remain largely unattended and uncared for under the existing administrative framework.(Ramachandran, 1996, pp. 319-320)

Bound to displace its space use by the terms of its concentrative missio, and compelled to preserve itself by the mandates of its reflexive missio, the city thus becomes a thing that perpetually marginalizes, dominates and exploits that which is non-city. Paradoxically, while the city acts as a needy thing, those very needs impel it to exert itself as a forceful, unreachable and implacable thing. For, the urban either incorporates other space and place into itself, transforming it, and subjecting it to an ongoing cycle of "creative destruction" (Brenner & Schmid, 2014; Rickards, et al., 2016), or it keeps non-city place at arm's distance and at a disadvantage. Thus, the city looms, casting a long shadow of irresistible influence over non-city space. This creates a self-serving cycle, for it makes urban life a "better" thing than non-urban life. Yet, the betterment that the city offers in some ways is merely relief from its own dominion and exploitation. Better urban life is simply less negative than non-urban life. That is, it is less exploited and less disadvantaged *by* the urban.

The key point here is not to condemn the urban, but to track with the kinds of tensions about the contemporary world that the text elicits. For, while there are many benefits that the city secures and provides for its participants, when it is compared to the creational view the point immediately arises that the city's missio invariably creates need, and that that need in turn drives and shapes the city's dominion. This is the great contrast with the Genesis depiction of dominion. For, in Genesis, dominion has no character of need. It does not extend in order to take, for it has no need to gather anything to itself. Dominion is simply exercised on behalf of God, in order to demonstrate him. It receives nothing and expects nothing as it rules, for all has already been provided.

Parallels and Differences. We can see, then, that stark differences at foundational levels stand between the world of Genesis 1 and the world of the city. Most significantly, the Genesis world is universal, expansive and harmonious. In contrast, the city's world is localized, agglomerative and comparative. Further, the world of the creation account is naturally provisioned via the gift of God, while the city is artificially provisioned through the extension of influence, without attention to divine sustenance. The Genesis world assumes a surplus of good, which includes the good of unrestricted space, while the city presumes limited resources and differential space and place.

But there are also key correspondences. Both worlds assume the priority of humans, and both consider increases in human population and occupancy as necessary, as a good, and as a given. This parallel holds even though the caveat may exist that the city sees human population in terms of its own realms and citizenships (Holston, 2001) vis-à-vis others, while the Genesis account sees people on a species level, in terms of the entire earth.

Another congruence is that both the creation story and the city sustain a human warrant to dominate the environment, albeit to varying degrees. Unlike the city, however, the Genesis story places humankind's dominion missio among other missios that are given to various parts of the creation, and it coordinates those coexistent missios harmoniously, within shared, universal space. This is because Genesis does not appear to address or acknowledge the transformation of space into place by humans or animals.

One key nuance differentiating urban and creational dominions is that although both prioritize human dominion, the missio urbis does not do so as an acknowledgement of divine mandate or on behalf of a higher authority. For it, human dominion is a mechanism of settlement or development that supports concentrated human activity, presence and occupancy. This mechanism seeks optimization for its own human advancement.

Further, both projects appear to support the domestic missio. The Genesis account expects that humans will mate and be fruitful and fill the earth. The city assumes that populations will continue within it indefinitely, and it develops missios that provide for ongoing generational progression. Both appear to value security for domestic well-being, however, Genesis grants domestic safety through the lack of natural threats and through humankind's superior place as divine deputies with the powers of rulership. The city grants safety through missios that ensure the acquisition of provision, through social controls and governances, and through environmental manipulation.

Although partial, these juxtapositions give us a sketched view of the city and the Genesis story in terms of worlds and worldviews. This allows us to see roughly where the two stand in reference to each other, and it reveals some of the missional relationships between their respective projects. Using that as a foundation, we can now delve a bit more deeply into what the text and the city do with people.

The calls of city and Genesis. The city and Genesis both present prospects of the "good life" to people. The urban missio frames the good life in terms of access to resources, especially, to satisfactions, and in terms of social consolidation. It considers dominion in terms of the development and control of efficient (high value) place, the collection of materials and social presences, and the concentration of power. It seeks these as things that should be aspired to and as a tangible indicators of improvement.

The Genesis account frames the good life in terms of order, harmony and response to divine instruction. It considers the exercise of dominion, unity between male and female, and the development of progeny as things that should be sought for. The tangible markers of the good life within its project are the approval and blessing of God, demonstrated by fruitfulness and abundant, divine sustenance.

Both missios imply that life outside of their frames is subpar, or less livable, than life lived within their projects. Thus, both have agenda to draw people from their current living states into other states. In the case of the city, this includes a call to a geospatial location as well as to the socio-spatial urban project. In Genesis, the aim is to call people to a socioreligious location and a socioreligious project.

The idyllic appeals of both projects seem to assume that people exist in states that are currently dissatisfying to them. Both projects offer an alternative to those frustrations and dissatisfactions. Both essentially propose, "If only the world was this way, things would be better." The city casts this as, "Life is better *here*, with *these resources*," while Genesis casts it as "Life is better *this way, under God* and with *his blessing*." These propositions organize values according to fundamentally different paradigms, which are at many points competing or incompatible. Thus, when people respond to one promise and call, they often encounter deep and unexpected conflict and loss of the other. Chukwudum Barnabas Okolo notes this when he describes the African migrant's conflict over traditional values:

> For Africans, as for the rest of the world, rural drift to cities has a purpose, namely, to seek employment, education, better living conditions or even negatively to escape from certain traditions which they find unpleasant. In other words, escape of people to towns is to search for alternative forms of subsistence, generally for making life worth living. In so doing in this case of urbanization certainly they experience additional problems. (1991, p. 189)

Human value. In some ways, both the city and the Genesis account accord humans value, and both offer dignity. Yet, they go about this for different reasons and through different avenues. The creation account attributes value to people by virtue of their intrinsic humanity. If one is male or female, if one is an offspring, and thus, part of the category *humankind*, then one is part of the divinely commissioned human project to be fruitful and fill the earth. This ascribes purpose-value to simple existence. If one is human, then one also is made according to the image of God. Thus, any person holds a deputy position of sacred dominion higher than the rest of creation, and one's very presence is a living, divine monument. This function grants a second purpose-value. It warrants regard by shared honor with God, since the monument refers to the one who created and commissioned it.

The city also values people, but in more pragmatic, less metaphysical, and less universal ways. This is due to the fact that the missio urbis is grounded in geospatial and geosocial purposes. At its core, it is not transcendent or attached to the metaphysical. It is a human social project, a strategy that is aimed at improving conditions for human life in certain situations and locations. On some level, this ultimately rests on the presumption that positive human experience is valuable, which in turn assumes that human life is valuable. Yet, specifically, the urban aims to concentrate resources for *someone*. Because it yields its benefit toward certain people, that is, to the shareholders of its missio, it grants those *particular* people value.

Further, the city requires human constituency in order to exist, and human work is required for the city's goal to be achieved. From a pragmatic perspective, then, it also values human activity, since people make it able to fulfill its reason for existing. Still, there is a nuance here, for the city splits the value of people as total beings from the value of people as producers of work. This is starkly apparent in the city's exploitive acquisition of the fruits of non-urban producers. Although people and their work are ontologically inseparable, the city values the work *of* certain people more than it values people in toto. On one side, then, people are valuable as the end beneficiaries of the city, and on the other side, the work which people produce is valued as resource for the city. The city thus begins and ends at people, and people carry it from its beginning to its end.

Differential human value. However, the city's interests are inherently localized. Its values are bound to its concern for "here," whether that is a social here or a physical here. The city's missio of localized concentration assumes that urban human life is prioritized over non-urban human life because the city is primarily concerned with making life better within its sphere of influence. It is not aimed at improving human life in other places.

Thus, the city does not regard *all* people with the same value. To it, human value is a variable thing that is established relative to the city and its project. Humans matter more when they are a part of the city or perhaps by the degree to which they contribute to its project. Humans matter less when they are beyond the city's scope or when they hinder its aims.

In some ways, differential human value is a key allurement of the urban, as well as a strategic reward that it offers in its presentation of ongoing life improvement. As Malpezzi (2011) observes, "cities exist because they offer opportunities for comparative advantage." Prospects of moving toward the core of the city's project, of advancing in its hierarchies and of gaining increased power and/or access to its resources provide incentives for people to participate in it. Because the city uses a sliding scale for human value that is based upon relative location to itself, it naturally ascribes greater value to those who move toward the center of its project, seeking "comparative advantage." It rewards such agenda by granting greater access to its resources and ascribing greater human value to those who succeed at various forms of urban advancement.

By contrast, the biblical account offers only universal value. The highest point is reached by all humans simply by living, although that is reinforced when people live together in marriage and when they produce offspring and hold sway over creation. Unlike the city, the reward that the biblical account offers is fulfillment of very existence, demonstrated by the approval of God. This reward is not offered in any kind of transaction and increase of value does not seem to be available. Neither reward nor value is relative; both are full and intrinsic to being in God's image as his representation. Differential urban values and comparative advantages that deal in satisfactions have little or no place.

Notably, the value that is ascribed to humans by God comes before any achievements. Their exercise of dominion and their fruitfulness appear to be potentials, not accomplishments, and their dignity appears unable to be augmented or changed. It is only relative to God; it is unaffected by relation with any other place or state. People are supremely valuable within creation simply as they are.

Summary of juxtaposition. While much more could be explored, at this point we have done enough analysis to produce a rough, missio-based view of where the city and Genesis stand in relation to each other. We can see where their respective projects have some areas of overlap and noted where they have diverged. We have pursued this comparison in a way that has sought to parallel the strategies of the text's missio, allowing differences between the idyllic vision of the creation and the realities of the urban to stand unanswered and unresolved. Hopefully, this has elicited dynamic tensions in us that have urged us toward the ends that the text was designed to produce, especially in terms of dispositions toward God, humankind, the creational world and the experienced world. This paves the way for the next step, which is integrative reflection. Part IV will take up this task by exploring our findings in terms of missiological thought and practice.

PART IV

Chapter 10: Missiological Consideration of the City and Genesis 1

In preceding chapters, we used the concept of missio as an interpretive device. This allowed us to discern core missional aspects of the city and of the creation account. Those features were then juxtaposed in order to highlight similarities and differences. Although we did not apply method to the city formally, our urban examination used the assumptions that undergird topographic analysis so that we could compare findings using like concepts. As we now take up broader consideration of the city, we will follow more in the line of PGT analysis, which seeks to understand how a thing can be understood in relation to the missio Dei.

This agenda reframes what we have done before, drawing more inferences from it. To some degree, this is more speculative than analytic, but the aim is not simply to speculate. Rather, it is to extrapolate from what we already have been able to observe; that is, to draw from our analyses in order to reflect missiologically. Just as traditional theology uses exegetical readings as both foundation and control during speculation, this reflective process uses our previous missiological readings as a foundation and as a control. The work is to think evaluatively about both the city and the text from mission perspectives in light of key missiological concerns.

This is the stage where we ask questions that integrate mission's metanarrative frames and that assume social, religious and historical solidarity. In other words, here we consider issues without assuming that there are gaps between us and the text, the canon, God, the kingdom or the urban context. This kind of inquiry maintains interaction between universals and particulars. In it, inferences that we make hold us, the text, the canon, God, the kingdom and the context together under the umbrella of mission.

Holding these dimensions together hallmarks missiological inquiry, which often uses integrated questions. Thus, the questions here will resemble those used when exploring Product, Ground and Tool dimensions. We will be seeking to discern things such as, Can the city be used by God in his mission? Is it his divine tool, or is it by nature contrary to his intentions for creation? How do the city and the textual world relate to God's kingdom? Do they fit with each other, or are they at odds? What might this mean for us, who care about the kingdom of God and about the city? Where is God's will in all of this? How can we fulfill God's mission and represent his kingdom in regard to the city?, etc.

One of the challenges of missiological reflection is that these types of questions need to be asked, but their scope is tremendously broad. Rightfully, each would require a work of its own to explore, and, hopefully, that kind of work will be pursued as missiologists continue their interpretive efforts. For this introductory reflection, however, we will have to be satisfied with brief observations, and we will anchor the discussion by continuing to focus on agenda from Genesis 1.

As we hold multiple factors in sight, we will use varying arrangements of focal-subsidiary viewing. We will look at selected factors *in light of* a dominant factor; that is, from the perspective of a key factor. Since it still would be quite lengthy to explore all of the possible variations, we will use a few simple arrangements of two factors at a time, integrating other factors into those discussions.

Each of the reflections below will begin with a narrow focus that extrapolates from what we have already considered. After that is done, the view will be expanded to include data from the larger canon, in order to include biblical and missional metanarrative. The chapter after this will add reflection in light of mission concerns and praxis.

The City through Creation Eyes

We have already spent time juxtaposing the creation account and the city, but we have not yet integrated other mission concerns. Adding those dimensions now will round out our consideration and yield a more robust missiological reflection. We will begin by looking at the city using the creation as the ground of value, or measuring stick. This uses the creation as the lens through which the city may be understood. After that, we will use the kingdom as a lens, and, after that, we will use the missio Dei as a lens.

A limited miniature. Viewed in light of the creation, the city appears both limited and imitative. Its scope and reach are local, and its agenda to grant the good life falls short of the kind of fulfillment that humans immediately enjoy within creation simply by living in the image of God as rulers of the earth. Although future generations are anticipated, in Genesis the humans start with all that they themselves need; there is no upward or inward potential either socially or materially; thus, there is nothing to desire.

By contrast, the city is built algorithmically. It is a semi-static, semi-transient operation of collection and advancement; it arises perpetually as a strategic instrument that is aimed toward anticipated gain or improvement. Thus, in the city, desire is always only partially fulfilled. There is always more space to be acquired, more things to be assembled, more interactions to actualize and more resources to gather.

Perhaps this is because the city resembles a mimic in miniature of the creation. Like the creation, it arises as its creators act upon chaotic space by making place and filling that place with people and things that perform coordinated missios. However, the city is only a localized, small-scale reenactment of God's creation. Unlike the expansive, divine work, the city is a reduced, human production that relies upon social and spatial mechanisms. It draws from limited resources and it is only able to produce limited fruits.

While the creation is a work *ex nihilo*, brought into being by the limitless God, the city is a human work of appropriation within an existing creation. Since its power is derived from people, it remains unable truly to give anything to humankind that it does not first receive. It has power to reallocate, for it can transform and transfer resources, but it must always take from somewhere and someone in order to grant to another.

In creation, God himself provides in fullness. Out of his own external resources, he brings into being all relationships, all meaning and purpose, all sustenance, all values. In its imitation, the urban project also provides relationships, meaning and purpose, sustenance and values, but it does so on a variable scale, and on a limited, transactional basis. God endows from beyond in creation, but the city is a located, reflexive effort, an attempt by certain people at a certain place[135] to draw themselves up to a better life by their own interrelated efforts.

A bounded world. Further, in creation, God gives humankind all space and all goods. He desires for them to have everything, not just part. Everything is theirs to rule and to share together. But the city's sociospatial territoriality is built on a fundamentally differing principle. Horizons exist between spaces, systems and goods, using lines that separate here from there, mine from yours, valuable from non-valuable, formal from informal, urban from non-urban. The result is a bounded realm of boundarized components in which sharing turns to trade, and rulership is practiced by some more than others.

---

[135] The idea of place includes interconnected systems, events and nodes, which create their own distinct kinds of material and immaterial "place" by virtue of their identifiable relations.

Because it is a bounded construct, the city arises as a mini-world within the world of the creation. It is an alternate world, a territorial world, a proprietary world, and in some ways, a parasitic world, for it draws from the rest of creation in order to support itself. Its boundedness can be comforting to some, because even at its grandest extent, the city is smaller, more easily negotiated, and more easily managed than the whole of creation. Perhaps inadvertently, this yields ancillary missio outcomes in its participants. For as the urban agenda prioritizes its own identity it fosters within urban dwellers a limited outlook that is locally and reflexively focused, even when it extends regionally and globally. Within its project, people have the option not to tend to the whole earth. They may tend to themselves and to the urban environment; the city is enough, and has access to enough; if they wish, participants may ignore that which lies beyond.

This is reinforced by the city's own quest for self-sufficiency. The city has a dynamism of its own and it presents itself as a thing that requires little tending from its residents. All it requires is that they yield a surplus of resource toward it. While many may have shares in its project, the city itself appears to be the responsibility of only those at the centers of its power and resources, to whom it has granted greatest place. Its structures and agenda excuse the vast majority of its members from more than token custodianship, especially from anything resembling the daunting scale of the first pair's calling. However, this comfort comes at a price, for the city also grants little in terms of ownership or power to most of its members and it lacks the nobility, harmony and open provision of the creation as a total, expansive, God-sustained environment.

"Thin" existence. The city is also existentially "thin" compared to creation, for it lacks a transcendent connection. It is a project thoroughly grounded in sociomaterial reality, and it arises from strictly sociomaterial concerns. From the perspective of creation, this is an insufficient scope of existence. Certainly, the sociomaterial good that the city offers is meaningful, but the creation lens shows that to be only one part of the good that God has intended for people. For, while God grants both social good and material good in the creation, the significance of those goods lies beyond the merely social or the merely material. God creates social life within the pair, and that is good, but the value of that social pairing is primarily to be found in the identity of the two as the living image of God.

Likewise, God gives material provision, and that provision is depicted as a good, yet that provision is not a primary good; it is an ancillary endowment. In the creation, God's material provision is supportive, given by God only after he has given humans their primary gifts and calling. It is framed as something that follows and enables them to live in the ways that they have been commissioned to live, not as a primary benefit or aim. Thus, the defining character of the creational provision is not its nutrition. In creational eyes, sustenance is not mere food; it is a gift from God's hand, a relational offering between beings, which shows favor and care.

This transcendent, sacred and relational dimension of provision is starkly absent from both the material and social goods that the city offers. Of course, this does not mean that the city's sociomaterial benefits are bad from the view of creation, but, as sociomaterial offerings, alone, such things simply are not enough to be considered fully or truly good in creational eyes, for their defining valence of value, their connection to God, has been stripped from them.

Both from the missiological viewpoint and in the eyes of contemporary urban scholars, the city remains largely unconcerned with forms of good that might extend beyond sociomaterial aims. To the urban, good that lies beyond the sociomaterial may be acceptable and welcome, but it is largely unnecessary.[136] While religious, spiritual or transcendent forms

---

[136] By way of illustration, no section or chapter within the broad compilations edited by Scott (2001), Birch and Wachter (2011), Allen, Swilling and Lampis (2016) or Falola and Salm (2004) addresses religious dimensions of the urban or specifically religious features, productions or dynamics within urban regions. Gottdiener and Hutchison (2011) lack any section treating urban religion or any reference to religion in their list of index topics. Topics in Jayne and Ward's (2017) collection treat a fairly exhaustive array of 24 urban dimensions (Affect, Architecture, Assemblages, Bodies, Commons, Community, Comparison, Consumption, Encounter, Entrepreneurialism, Gentrification, Governance, Informalities, Learning,

of good may catalyze the city's own supporting missios because they offer "satisfactions" to some, the transcendent aspects of those satisfactions tend to be recast quickly in urban terms of sociomaterial benefits and controls, which are understood to be their "real" yield. To the urban, transcendent good might exist, but if it does, its value is seen as incidental compared to sociomaterial good.

In the creation, however, good is both transcendent and sociomaterial. God makes a material world and he creates humans as a deeply relational, social pair, but he does this according to a clear pre-intention. The pair have a purpose that they are designed to fulfill, and their existence is linked by their purpose to God's being, which stands beyond their sociomaterial lives. His intended good for them prioritizes life aimed at a teleology, and that teleology is aimed at himself.

Creational human good is thus connected to fulfillment, specifically, to humankind's purpose to stand in the creation representatively, according to God's image. This missional purpose suffuses the relational unity between the sexes, as well as the domestic development of human generations. In a creational view, because they carry a divine mandate, human mating, family making and providing for domestic life are not ends in and of themselves. They are good, but they are not aims that can fulfill human good fully when they are achieved. While the urban agenda might value these as avenues to attain the experience of satisfactions, in the creation scheme they are valences for fulfilling divine calling. For, in the creation, human good extends beyond the pleasures of satisfactions and beyond sociomaterial actions, beyond human level relational statuses and roles, for life itself is

---

Materialities, Mobilities, Neoliberalism, Play, Politics, Rhythm, Rights, Sexuality, Suburban, Sustainability). Within this catalog, no topics address spiritual or religious dimensions. A single index topic in their collection lists one page on "religion: noisemaking."

When the historical origins and contemporary dynamics of cities and city-life across the globe are considered, the omission of all religious dimensions in otherwise thorough scholarly discussions is quite striking. While this appears to highlight a glaring marginalization of urban religious life by current urban scholarship, it may simply illustrate that urban scholars are tracking obvious sociomaterial traits that reveal the urban as a sociomaterial construct. A third option is that both academic marginalization and observation of the city's overtly sociomaterial traits might be taking place.

grounded in connection to God via human correspondence to him and to the exercise of sacred authority.

Through creation eyes, then, the city appears to be a sociomaterial strategy in which humans seek to offer to themselves a partial kind of good that mirrors the true and full good that God himself offers from his own hand. In the city's strategy, value is limited, for things do not come from the hand of God; they are collected and assembled by people who act upon and within a sociomaterial reality. The same is true of people. They may be resources, constituents, builders, neighbors, co-actors, but they are not transcendent, and they are not representative; they do not participate in anything beyond the material order and they do not stand on behalf of anything beyond themselves.

Thus, in the city, people and things may be good, but that good is sociomaterial and those people and things remain distinctly sociomaterial. When measured against a creational standard, however, the city's sociomaterial approach reduces the scope of human good in a way that renders the existences of people and things partial. This means that the good of city life that is offered by the urban project never can be more than a partially good life, since it can only be a sociomaterially good life. From the view of creation, then, the city presents itself as an insufficient copycat, a thin, humanly-formed micro-creation, which draws a level of good to itself from the rest of the earth and yet remains unable to provide the truly good life.

"Natural" creational good. This presents a dismal view of city life until one considers that the offer of good that God holds forth is not limited by the city's approach. The key issue, however, is whether the creational or the urban view of human good is held in ascendance. For, the urban strategy itself is not morally or spiritually pathological; it is only insufficient. Although it is highly susceptible to distortion and exploitation, those should be recognized as abuses of the city's missio, not as necessary or constraining traits.

Intrinsically, the missio urbis carries few liabilities except its very limitedness, and it only becomes dangerous or harmful when it is held to be sufficient or if its worldview is understood to be complete. The urban is limited, and its outlook is also limited, but it is only when urban answers to the questions of human life and good are taken as normative that the city competes harmfully with creational design. That is when urbanism begins to damage people by rendering them partial. Until that point, the city is simply a special instrument that is designed to produce certain ranges of human good and not others.

In other words, the key is that we cannot afford to take the city's word for granted about what is real life or about what constitutes good. Damage in terms of reduction does not result because the city produces only sociomaterial good. It arises when the ranges of good that the city produces are considered to be the primary or full ranges of human existence and the satisfactions of those ranges are considered to be primary or sufficient satisfactions of human needs.

If, however, the sociomaterial good that the city produces is understood to be an incomplete and subordinate range of human good, one that comes *after* the human calling to live together in God's image and according to his likeness, then the city presents no threat and no competition to the creational scheme. In fact, if the city is held open to transcendence and if its proposals are evaluated according to transcendent ranges of being, not only can it hold a right place in the creational agenda, it also can participate in the creational agenda and become the creation's missional ally. For, if it is allowed that God wishes to provision people and to provide an environment for them to live in according to his image, the city can become simply one among many environments and one among many mechanisms that can make divine provision available on sociomaterial levels, alone.

The key in all of this is that the transcendent dimension that is depicted as ordinary and intrinsic within the creation must not be relegated to a realm that is somehow above and beyond the natural, especially when it comes to human life and good. In creation, the spiritual dimension that transcends and suffuses the sociomaterial is treated as natural and innate. Accordingly, connections to God and to others on levels that stand beyond the sociomaterial cannot be seen as augmentations to sociomaterial good without diminishing the creational agenda.

This is a deep-seated worldview issue that Hiebert (1982, 2008) and Newbigin (1986) and, more recently, Lin (2016) have highlighted when they call attention to the unfortunate western division between the natural and the supernatural.[137] In this case, a problem arises if the sociomaterial urban life is normalized, that is, if it is understood to span, fill or address the range of "natural" life. For, when that occurs, transcendent life is necessarily marginalized. The range of the "natural" life becomes sociomaterial, while transcendent life must reside in the range of the "unnatural" or "non-natural." In this scheme, transcendent good becomes *unnatural* good, not *natural* good.

Normalizing the sociomaterial as natural makes sociomaterial good the default range of human good, which is a view that lies at odds with the creational view. If, instead, as the creational view holds, the transcendent is understood to be intrinsic to the natural, that is, if it is not displaced as "super" natural or "meta" physical, the sociomaterial range of existence and the range of sociomaterial good that attends it are revealed to be *less* than natural. This is a switch of ranges that matters in terms of the thinness of existence. When the creational range of integrated existence is used as the standard, sociomaterial good remains good, but that good is not fully natural good or fully physical good; it is sub-natural and/or sub-physical good.

---

[137] The roots of this dichotomy can be traced to Hellenistic categories of thought, which the apostle Paul periodically used. However, even though the NT speaks contrastingly about the spiritual and the natural, Paul seems to depict the "natural" or "fleshly" not so much as a solely material existence but as a spiritual, mental and volitional disposition that is narrow in its attentions and inclined toward base pleasures. This is not a true split between immaterial and material existences, since the flesh, mind, will and spirit are not held apart, as Paul demonstrates when he talks about a "carnal mind" (to phronēma tēs sarkos) in Rom 8:7. Most notably, the categories are not observable in the creational depiction.

Accordingly, urban good is an unnatural or sub-natural good, and the urban life, if it stands alone, is seen to be an unnatural life because it is an insufficiently fulfilled life.

This is a crucial point for missiological consideration, because it impacts how mission agents go about attending to human existence, both inside and outside of the city. Since it concerns how we see human needs, it affects what we seek to achieve, what we aspire to call or urge people to, how we seek to affect others and how we organize our mission priorities.

Note that in the creational scheme there is no division between natural and spiritual existence. That division resides in the urban scheme, because of the limits of the urban focus. If mission agents then prioritize the urban scheme over the creational scheme, the result follows that we will differentiate between so-called "natural" issues and "supernatural" issues. This is problematic, since, like early Gnosticism it separates sociomaterial realities from spiritual realities, which impacts both our missional understandings and our missional messages about things such as sin, salvation, redemption and eternal life.

This kind of dichotomy also artificially arrays "spiritual" mission and "natural" mission as alternatives to each other, which makes them contrasts or comparatives. Forcing an alternative this way can distort evaluations when missional goals and resources are under consideration, which can dissipate, confuse or conflict our mission aims needlessly.

Using the creational view, the transcendent is as natural as the sociomaterial, for transcendent reality suffuses and informs sociomaterial reality. This of course means that sociomaterial action on God's behalf can fulfill natural-level sacred mission. There is little dispute to this within missiological discourses. However, the converse also obtains. The creational unity of existence also means that spiritual action on God's behalf can fulfill natural-level sacred mission, because the spiritual resides as much in the range of the natural as the sociomaterial does.

From this perspective, offering food, shelter and companionship ministers to natural needs that reside within natural ranges of life. Offering sacramental presence, divine representation, and proclamation of the gospel also ministers to natural needs that reside within natural ranges of life. One is not concrete and the other immaterial; one is not real and the other unreal or super-real, for these dimensions coexist inseparably. In creational eyes, separating spiritual needs from physical needs makes no more sense than treating thirst as a "natural" need and hunger as a "meta-natural" need. Because the creational natural includes what the western worldview separates into material and immaterial, mission to the natural person on natural levels must address the full natural range of existence if it is to be *fully* natural.

Summarily, then, God's intention for humans to live in a creational order of life is not met by fulfillment of the city's missio using the urban range of life. This does not mean that creational level mission need reject or condemn the city's range, for God is able to suffuse the urban-level life with transcendent dimensions of being and to supply that which is lacking to city life. However, it does mean that if creational level mission is to be fulfilled, the city's view of reality cannot be held to be sufficient, or worse yet, ascendant, and mission cannot consider itself to be accomplished if it ends its efforts at the boundaries of urban-level needs. Instead, for creational level mission to be fulfilled within the city, the full range of natural life, which includes spiritual and transcendent dimensions, must be addressed. Thus, it must be held in view constantly that a missional offer of transcendent good(s) and fulfillment is not an extra that provides over and above basic natural needs. Rather, the missional offer is one that provides for fully natural life and needs, not halting short at sub-natural life and needs. It is the offer of a fully natural fulfillment of existence that answers the unnatural urban existential deficit.

The City through Kingdom Eyes

When we look at the city using the lens of the kingdom, we shift view to highlight the missio of governance, which we will take to include the formal missios of government and administration, along with informal directive agency. Through this filter, we can see that the city's governance mimics the divine kingdom in a way that resembles the city's replica of the creation. However, urban governance has a more complex relation to the kingdom than the urban world has to the creation, and it must be approached with more nuanced missiological discernment.

Missional governance. For missiological consideration, it is significant to distinguish between governance as a means of social control and governance as missio. When we look at governance in terms of missio, the view emphasizes intention and purpose, and, while that involves ordering behavior, the primary meaning is not related to phenomenal aspects of behavior. Missiologically, kingdom governance concerns the fulfillment of mandate, which is a teleological issue, and its missional performance concerns the exercise of agency, which involves the delegation of authority in dominion. These are core factors in both kingdom and mission, for they concern the accomplishment of will, whether directly, through cooperation, or indirectly, through representation.

Yet, these aspects can be difficult to perceive because they are dependent upon intention, which is less accessible to observation than behavioral phenomena. Further, because missional governance involves relational and volitional factors, such as obedience, acknowledgement, agency and representation, it presents more pronounced dilemmas in terms of solidarity and loyalty than arise in urban-worldview governance.

Thus, if our aim is truly to understand the city in light of the kingdom, we cannot afford to evaluate the urban using standards that have been carried over in an unexamined way from non-missional discourses. For missiological study, we cannot assume that governance can be well described using limited empirical, secular or principle-based ideological canons alone, since those fail to examine the full range of kingdom dominion. Unlike secular governance, kingdom dominion includes highly variable factors of personal intention, divine representation and authorized agency. Thus, to see the city well through kingdom eyes we also will need to account for intentional-missional aspects that inform the exercise of governance, keeping those aspects open on transcendent levels.

Kingdom governance. Recall that in Genesis 1 the relationship between humans, God and the creation is depicted as a kingdom arrangement. In this scenario, humans govern as regents. They rule, but their rule is a sub-reign on behalf of another, for they represent God and his interests within the world. This is due to the fact that they are designed and created to be living, acting monuments to God's regal person, who in their own selves recognizably hearken unto him. As monumental representatives, the humans' identities are bound to God's own, since they exist in his image and according to his likeness. Thus, they stand as deputies of holy authority, governing the earth on their creator's behalf.

In order to sustain this arrangement, God provides for his sub-regents, granting them bounty from his earthly stores and domain. They are authorized to draw particular goods from the king's treasury, which they may treat as their own. They and their lineage are stewards, custodians of God's own lands. They are appointed as guardians against chaos, placed in his realm and granted power to maintain all as it has been ordained to function under divine decree.

By comparison, the urban is self-authorizing and self-determinant. It is "untamed" and "uncontrollable" (Allen, et al., 2016). The city represents itself and seeks its own interests,[138] and in it, humans represent their own interests. In both the urban and the kingdom-creation, people dominate the earth, using the capacities given to them by God, but in the urban they do not do so on God's behalf, or as expressions of his reign. In certain ways,

---

[138] This is demonstrated by the rise of the contemporary "entrepreneurial" city (Harvey, 1989).

urban actors fulfill the divine blessing by transforming the chaos of space into place, ruling and subduing the earth, yet, the urban project does this as an intruder or usurper, not as divine guardian, for its agents impinge upon the mandates given to other creatures in the creational order as the city co-opts natural space. As its project succeeds, the city's place becomes ever more fully its own, fully urban, and other creational orders and missios become displaced (Mukherjee, 2016).

Like the kingdom's regents, urban actors also gather of the earth's goods. However, while the kingdom's agents are authorized to draw a limited range of goods from the divine treasury, urban agents gather on their own prerogatives, without any external controls on the scope of what can be taken. The city treats the earth, its spaces and its resources as uniformly accessible according to human-level sociomaterial principles of ownership. Its supporting mandates are sociopolitical and socioeconomic, not divine.

More seriously, the city treats humans, their labors and their places on the same terms as the earth's provisions, approaching people as resources or provisions. Thus, the city dominates other humans in its provisioning process. From a kingdom perspective, this happens because the city fails to recognize the divine valence that endows humans with status, identity and value in the creation. In the urban project, human lives, human progeny and human projects do not hearken to anyone or anything beyond themselves. Humans hearken primarily to humankind, even when religious factors are involved.

In other words, the city's governance is secular, while the kingdom's is sacral. This does not mean that the city is anti-sacral. It only means that the city is less than sacral. It is merely of, for and by people, and within it the sacred is understood to be an auxiliary dimension of human life. To the city, the sacred dimension is not substantial enough to impact activity, so it fails to become a factor for governance. The sacred may be significant, but it remains significant only insofar as it serves experiential or material human needs, and, in meeting those needs, supports the city's project.

Competition. Seen through kingdom eyes, then, the urban scheme presents itself as a competitor, since it is a project with goals for both the earth and people that do not match divine goals. This is not shocking, since the city competes with other cities and with other projects as a matter of course, sometimes even deliberately, in an openly entrepreneurial stance. More subtly, this competition is to some degree unavoidable because the city's missios, values and meanings are arranged differently than the divine kingdom's. The kingdom plan wants to order the world in a different hierarchy, for different ends, with different loyalties and duties than the urban plan.

This places the city and the kingdom in a tug o' war over the statuses and roles of people, over the incentives for and the outcomes of human action, and about the assignments of significance that attend such things. As a competitor, the city vies with the kingdom for labors, resources, events, systems and spaces so that it may utilize them to support itself. And, because it is self-protecting and blind to the transcendent, it seeks to do so without reciprocity to the kingdom's project. For, while the kingdom can see the city, and thus be able to integrate it into its project, the city cannot see the kingdom, and it remains unable to integrate it into the urban project.

Insurgency. To a more severe degree, due to its disregard for divine reign, the city can present in kingdom eyes as an insurrection. This tension arises from urban presumptions about the city's autonomy, its "untamed" (Allen, et al., 2016) self-developments and self-directions. From the misty times of its origins, the city has alternated between being a localized autonomous entity and being a subject participant within larger national or transnational institutions, and, as in the case of so-called primate cities, the city continues to have mixed relations with broader or overarching domains. In the case of God's kingdom, when the city assumes that it may frame itself, its lifestyles, its values, its competitions and its aspirations without consideration of the transcendent, the urban project proceeds under the banner of its own mandate within God's realm without offering appropriate fealty or acknowledgement.

Recall that the Genesis account portrays a scheme in which divine governance orders all of the earth, and that humans exercise subsidiary governance by delegation. This depicts the kingdom as far broader than the city and as prior to the urban. It shows a governance that already has laid claim to all earthly space by defining it as the kingdom's place, before the city's emergence. The city must then arise within the kingdom's place, for the kingdom is a reign that precedes it, engulfs it and overlays it. Yet, if the urban refuses to recognize transcendent claims to place and things, it will ignore the divine reign within which it arises.

Examined missiologically, when an autonomous project of this kind disregards or rejects claims other than its own in an out of hand manner it bears a strikingly resemblance to the rationales and strategies of imperializing and colonializing powers. If it proceeds presumptuously or dismissively, the urban missio exhibits the signal dispositions of an invasive missio, for it asserts its own presence and claims upon domains that already are held by another, and it does so simply by refusing to grant any legitimacy to the rights, grounds or presence of that domain's preexisting authorities. From a kingdom view, if the city arises within God's domain regarding only sociomaterial level moralities, ethics, rights or powers, it fails to recognize the mandates that were in place before it or the prerogatives of the creation's divine overlord. Doing so as a localized autonomy thus appears as an insurgency, that is, as an invasion from within.

Authority. From a kingdom perspective, the key factor in any affair of governance is the line of right that sets the character of power. This stance emphasizes that might is not the same thing as right. Undeniably, the city can exert *force*, that is, it can influence or constrain people, things and events, but that does not satisfy questions about what *authority* is being exercised when such force is used. This is the defining issue when urban governance is considered from missiological perspectives.

In the kingdom, humans act vicariously; they rule on behalf of God. Thus, their dominion serves another dominion, and their actions express divine will. As kingdom actions refer beyond themselves, they instrumentally reify the presence of the king who commissions them. Thus, as proxies, humans exercise *authority* or *representative right*, not intrinsic or innate right. Kingdom rights to exert influence are the rights of agents; they derive from the ruling rights of the one they represent, not from themselves or from social agreements with other humans.

At heart, then, the conflict between the kingdom and the city does not concern governantal behavior, per se, but the connection of authority that empowers dominion to be an appropriate exertion of force. The question is not if the earth should be subdued, or if humans should exercise governance. The question is more about how governance derives from mandate. That is, it is about what and whose mandate legitimizes what and whose governance; it is about what or whose authority is being exercised via the urban instrument of governance.

Representation. The creation narrative attributes power to dominate, rule and subdue to the divine deputation. This makes the exercise of power derivative and dependent. As such, human power to rule must be exercised in accordance with divine character, for it is given for representation. In this scheme, governance must be actualized according to God's likeness, in a manner that recognizably refers to him, that is, as his own agential expression. In the kingdom, the power of governance is a fiduciary endowment, not an innate right or capacity.

It is here, in the function of representation, that we can find the kingdom standards that distinguish between legitimate and illegitimate exercises of power. Since in the creational scheme we do not find a mandate for humans to exert dominion over other humans, we are left with questions about the legitimacy of social control on general levels. However, when we consider that humans are commissioned to represent God, the core missio of social control is understood to be anchored in custodianship of the divine image. When representation is central, social control is not exercised over others as dominance and subjugation; instead, governing action is directed at maintaining the missio of representation that is held corporately by humankind, which obtains on all.

In such a scenario, actions between humans refer back toward the divine. This is the ground of morality that undergirds the prohibition against human bloodshed in Gen. 9:5-7. Likewise, actions by humans toward the world refer back to the divine by virtue of human stewardship and regency. As mutual partners in the mission of representative referral, humans carry joint responsibility with other humans for the representation of God toward each other and toward the world. As joint actors, then, humans have the place to exercise social control when fellow representatives distort or compromise the joint missio of faithful representation of the divine. In such a case, social control is not an action of dominion, but of solidarity in mission. To control against misrepresentation is corrective activity that is grounded in the shared responsibility to preserve a collective trust; it protects the expression of divine image that is held in collective representative custody.

It is the presence of the missio to protect and preserve divine representation that sets the essential nature of sacral social action, as well as kingdom standards for abuse or corruption of power, not the surface or sociomaterial attributes of social control behaviors. In the biblical depiction, the quality of governance does not seem to be connected to the degree of control or force that is exercised as much as it is to the derivation of the power that is being exerted. In Genesis 1, the verbs to subdue and to rule are notably forceful. The broader canon also appears to endorse forceful governance, along with many significant differences in power between individuals. Across the canon, it appears that the determining question about abusive governance is not so much one of quantity but of quality. As kingdom is depicted in Genesis, it is not forceful actions, but acts that would represent only the humans who govern that would be corrupt. Such actions appear to sever the line of right and disregard the missio of representation, making them inordinate seizures of governance, since they fail to refer to the divine authority from which they derive, or to seek that authority's interests. As inordinate uses of governance, such actions would corrupt or abuse regent status; they would become actions of *force* or *power* alone, not of *authority*.

Evaluative standards. Without the kingdom valence, governantal action is less robust, since rights and powers refer only to the ones who govern or to those who are subject to governance. The value of governance in the urban context then becomes bound to quantitative assessments in terms of the equitabilities of its distributions or to qualitative assessments that relate only to the city's own welfare and the welfare of its constituents. Those evaluations in turn remain limited to the range of the urban missio, so that governance becomes measured in terms of sociomaterial existence. When it lacks a custodial dimension, governantal action becomes limited to its own sociomaterial meaning; it becomes assessable only in terms of its systemic productions and in terms of the degrees and relative equitabilities of its controls and distributions.

If, however, power is exercised agentially, governance remains open to evaluation on more transcendent terms. Governance operates from mandate, so its activities must express both the right and the intention of the one authorizing it. The evaluative issue then becomes whether or not governance is exercised in a manner that represents its source rightly, truthfully or appropriately. This includes both the condition of whether or not ostensive reference is maintained and the condition of whether or not commissioning purpose is fulfilled.

When both referential hearkening and intended purpose conditions are met, governance stands as legitimate from a kingdom perspective. That is, if governance hearkens recognizably to God and accomplishes his intentions, upholding and preserving the joint responsibility of humans to act as custodians of the divine image, its exertion of power is appropriate.

This evaluative standard uses a missional foundation that is located in the governantal arrangement of kingdom. When this kind of missional-kingdom standard is employed, it shifts the view away from the degree or balance of governantal power, or the behaviors that governance controls, redirecting that view toward the referential quality of governantal action and the line of its authority.

Thus, by the missional kingdom standard, if the city and its governance arise as people knowingly exercise their divinely given rights to claim earthly place, fulfilling the mandate to exercise dominion upon the earth, no inherent conflict with the kingdom must result. No insurgency is created, since due regard is given to the divine reign; instead of insurrection, partnership and cooperation arise. The city building efforts portrayed throughout the historical narratives (Gen. 4:17, 10:11-12; Jdg. 1:26, 18:28; 2 Sam. 5:9, etc.) show just such work, as do the stories of Ezra-Nehemiah and the idealized portrayal of the righteous Jerusalem in Ezekiel (45-48), in which just trade is practiced (45:10).

If, however, the city is built merely as a human construct that serves human ends, if it refers to human right and might, a severe conflict results, because governance then fails to represent the divine image. It utilizes the powers and capacities of the divine image, especially the capacity to exert dominion, without maintaining integrity to that image. In such a case, regardless of its equitability or the sociomaterial benefits of its actions, governance presents a corruption of divine endowment by representing the agent rather than the authorizer. In kingdom eyes, it remains an abuse of the power to rule, regardless of its perceived production of benefits. This is the biblical case of Babel (Gen. 11:1-9).

Variable Urban-Kingdom relations. Missiologically, this leaves the city rather indeterminate in its kingdom character, since its valence of representation is subject to change. The city is always being renewed and remade by its constituents, and its acknowledgment of divine reign may be denied or endorsed at any given moment, even if that is done by only segments of its population. Thus, even though the city is by design a competitive construct, since it is perpetually reified and contextualized, competition with kingdom dominion is not necessarily an intrinsic trait. It arises only if and when the city is closed to transcendence and guided by its own purposes.

Yet, we must remember that narrow governance tends to follow naturally from the city's limited missio. If the city's foundational purpose is allowed to remain thin, self-absorption and self-governance are only to be expected. The city does not necessarily mean people or the kingdom harm, but it knows no other way. It is simply organized around the acquisition of limited ranges of good and it must ensure that those ends are accomplished. Unless its view is directed at transcendent things, it does not see or care for higher orders of human existence, except as they affect its operation. It does what it was designed to do in accordance with the natural thinness of its missio.

Thus, the case is not that the city is innately antagonistic to the kingdom of God; the case is that the city is naturally oblivious to the kingdom of God. The city is simply a limited creature with narrow vision. It arises from the creaturely needs of people, and its view remains bound and creaturely. Its behavior naturally is self-focused, self-serving and worldly, and it naturally excludes consideration of the kingdom, just as it naturally excludes consideration of any agenda other than its own.

If we can attribute the city's lack of divine representation to simple ignorance, rather than to deliberate rejection of transcendent aspects, we can see the urban domain and the divine dominion as complementary to some degree. Without excusing the city's ignorance, we can recognize that its sociomaterial governance actually makes it incapable of being fully antithetic to the kingdom, since it does not and cannot exert itself antagonistically on transcendent levels. Because the urban scheme's exertion of power lacks the breadth of rule that divine dominion expresses, it cannot fully replace divine reign. It can only displace or supplant aspects of kingdom reign. Since the city has a narrower band of reality, and a smaller location, the urban domain can be considered as a thing that is always "less than, but not equal to" the kingdom. As such, it cannot fully displace the kingdom in any given place, which means that its domain does not have the capacity to be finally inimical to the sacred domain.

As a result, even at the height of its governance, the city's dominion does not necessarily exclude the kingdom's. The kingdom may exist where the city exists, because it transcends the place of the city, and the city may reside within the divine realm because its extent is smaller and thinner, and it cannot reach to the dimensions that the kingdom does. Although the city remains a competitor when left to its natural ways, it is not, nor can it truly be a direct enemy of the kingdom. It is an incidental rival that holds to a limited place within the kingdom's expanse.

Achieving good. Aside from more formal expressions of governance, the kingdom of God and the city offer alternative schemes for ordering human life, disposition and behavior. Ostensibly, both seek that their constituents would live right and good lives, but the grounding for that good lies in different regions of existence, and it is defined in different ways in each scheme. These differences determine the manner in which good is to be sought and fulfilled, which acts as a control on behavior and disposition.

On urban terms, the kingdom life appears unnecessarily attentive to transcendent conditions, especially that of satisfying God, which makes the kingdom pursuit of good restrictive and cumbersome. Behaviors on the path to good life seem to be unduly constrained, because they must fulfill both human and divine desires simultaneously, with human desire being a subordinate factor. Thus, kingdom expectations about serving God present as distractions and hindrances to the achievement of sociomaterial urban satisfactions. Conversely, on kingdom terms, the city appears reductionistic, sometimes to the point of dehumanization. Its ways of life appear reckless. Even when it pursues forms of good that both kingdom and city would endorse, its lack of attention to divine will or care for human regency shows so little regard and so narrow of a focus that it presents as animalistic, below the truly human and fatally flawed by reason of its insufficiency.

Viewed through kingdom eyes, the city's alternative way of life is not benign, even if it need not be considered malignant. For, the city actively promulgates a diminished, alternative version of the "good life" to people that affirms and rewards people with base satisfactions. Further, the urban grants these satisfactions when people live less nobly than humankind are commissioned to live, and it recruits people to its project in order that the city might succeed at achieving those same base ends. This draws people toward the urban way of life when they could be drawn to the kingdom way of life.

Given that human life is limited, time and energies spent in one way of life cannot be spent in another way of life. From the kingdom's vantage, this ultimately robs people of moments in which they could be living broader and deeper lives than when they live according to the urban way, alone. Thus, the urban way inadvertently impoverishes critical aspects of human existence as it pursues water that fails to quench true human thirsts and food that leaves the eaters hungry for true sustenance.

Human dignity. On deeper levels, human dignity is a key point of conflict that can arise between the city and the kingdom. For the kingdom holds people to be noble and sacred, worthy of regard, without considering a person's resource value, status or role. In kingdom economy, all are entitled to provision, and all hold place in the world by virtue of existence in the image of God. Further, in kingdom morality, this image is to be regarded and protected from harm (Gen. 9:5-7).

Many kingdom expressions look like remedial urban missios from this angle, because they try to correct diminishments of urban dwellers. The city in turn reacts to those expressions as it would to other corrective missios. For example, the kingdom's regard for human value sets sacred agency to work as a counterforce against one of the city's most powerful mechanisms of incentive, its differential assignment of human worth. For the city rewards those who serve its ends with greater value, and it withholds value from those who it experiences as counterproductive or nonproductive. It also withholds goods, rewards and resources from those who fail to benefit it, while it grants them to those who assist it.

By contrast, the kingdom is aimed at maintaining the honor of God wherever it is carried by his image-bearers. It seeks to preserve the value of his image in all, and it seeks to provide for all in accord with his divine grant. Thus, precisely where the city seeks to leverage human needs and value through the use of transactions, the kingdom seeks to offset lacks through support and protection. When it is in the city's best interest to heighten the value of some and diminish the value of others, the kingdom has an opposing interest to prevent the diminishment of any. Particularly, the kingdom has an interest to prevent the city (or other actors) from ascribing any canons of value to humans that might eclipse the foremost factor of value in humans, the image of God. The kingdom is thus poised to offset the city's valuations or devaluations at the very points in which the city stands to make greatest use of its stratified and differential value assignments.

Still, we always must keep in mind that the city offers all that it has, because it offers all that it knows. It sees people the way that it does because it is blind to their transcendent value and it uses the incentives that it does because it has no higher means to motivate them. The city is a thing of the world; therefore, it treats people in worldly ways and it forwards a worldly answer to human questions. Its worldly project then best can be understood as a tragic missional placebo, a toxic substitute for the kingdom that arises as the best thing possible, given the city's limited scope.

The City through Mission Eyes

These factors give the city a variable orientation relative to the missio Dei. In some ways, the city can be a neutral player, while in other ways it can be an opponent, and in still other ways, an ally. Further, because intention and representation are dimensions that can be modified in the course of use, many urban features and missios remain open to be utilized appropriately by kingdom mission agents. The key for those agents is to be able to discern when the urban might be neutral, opponent or ally, and to negotiate relations with the city effectively so that appropriate kingdom representation can be fulfilled.

Using urban components. For example, from the creation account, we can see that God wishes to provide people with sustenance. This is a creational missio and a divine missio, as well as one of the basic aims of the urban missio. On that level, the city can be an ally of God's mission, for its mechanisms are specifically designed to sustain populations and to create surplus in a given locale. Settlement requires provision, and the city is organized to make sure that provision is ample, at hand and uninterrupted. The aims of divine mission and urban mission run parallel in this regard, and the city can be a companion in labor with mission. All that is required to satisfy the missio Dei is that provision would be accomplished with a representational dimension to it. That is, if the urban provisional missio is to be fulfilled or used by mission agents in order to fulfill the missio Dei, the provision that is being distributed or produced must be either treated as received from God or given by God, or in the best case, as both.

Further, urban systems such as communication, financing, transportation and distribution tend to be pragmatic and existentially narrow, and the city tends to keep those functionaries active, adaptive and available across the span of its members so that it can maximize their capacities through varied use. This tends to make urban mechanisms relatively neutral in and of themselves. They are bystander mechanisms, instruments that can be taken up for a wide array of purposes, for ill or for good, depending on the services toward which they are turned and the representational intentions that inform them. A bus can be used in the course of a crime on behalf of a gang as easily as it can be used by a missionary in the course of evangelism on behalf of God and his kingdom. The same holds true of financial services, which can be used for oppressive exploitation and for charitable relief.

Because these mechanisms are designed to adapt to their users, they lend themselves to be used on God's behalf as much as they lend themselves to any user, and they can be taken up easily for God's mission. When mechanisms are employed to provide sustenance as an exercise of God's mandate,[139] they then can become ready instruments of the missio Dei. In this way, the city inadvertently lends itself to the missio Dei because it provides instrumental means that would have to be constructed by mission agents specifically for their own work otherwise, sometimes at great costs. In such cases, the city becomes an auxiliary, unwitting accomplice to divine mission.

Urban transactionalism. However, the transactional nature of the city's mechanisms simultaneously makes them fit poorly with the missio Dei. And, although God can use anything for his mission, the ill fit of some urban instruments can create strain and tension during missional use. Unlike God, the city expects a tangible, sociomaterial return whenever it provides goods and services, and it resists dissipation of its resources. The city's resistance to loss can add an antagonistic factor, which pushes the city toward the negative side, away from true neutrality, for the city will try to take more than it gives whenever divine mission is operating within it or using its instruments, just as it takes more than it gives when any endeavor operates within it.

Like the protection racketeer, the city will always want a "cut of the action" from any activity taking place on its "turf," whether the urban is genuinely contributing or not. Thus, when mission is trying to provide for others in any form, the city will exert pressure to be rewarded, whether that is in the currency of tangible commodities, honor equity, property values, formal and informal recognition, or a wide variety of other things that the

---

[139] God sets a universal value on human life that is ascribed to the value of his image (Gen. 9:4-6). When that universal regard is considered, fulfillment of divine mandate may be explicit, that is, performed expressly in God's name, or it may be implicit, that is, out of universal moral obligation because people are valuable. Both modes can fulfill missio Dei, since both conform to God's mandates.

city holds dear. In severe cases, this can deeply tax mission efforts, even to the point of jeopardizing them. Under those conditions, the city becomes a strong antagonist rather than an incidental one.

Differential good. Even more, the city's economy rests upon the principle of differentiated good. Its offer of the good life is in reality an offer of endless improvement, that is, of an always future potential for "better" life. Thus, the city has a thinly concealed vested interest in the perpetual dissatisfaction of its participants. For, without structures of stratification and mechanisms of preferment, the city has little means to recruit participants or incentivize its offerings. And, unless it can withhold good, it cannot motivate or leverage, which undermines its exercise of dominion.

Again, using the example of provision, this makes the city bent against open provision and biased toward exploitation of the human needs for sustenance as an avenue to promote its own welfare and maintain its power. Even though missional provision of services might appear to be appealing as a benefit, the city's transactional character will cause it to resist missional efforts to provide human services to the full extent that they could be provided when those would compromise or thwart urban transactionalism. Thus, where the missio Dei would seek to make human services freely accessible, it remains in the city's best interests to prevent that open provision. The city's tendency instead will be to allow provisioning by mission agents only to a degree that preserves differential and transactional rendering of good, measured against a horizon in which hindrance of provision will produce a liability for itself. If the horizon of transactional leverage is crossed, the city will react and seek to impose formal and informal controls that limit access to human services as quickly and aggressively as mission agents can procure or produce those services. It will do this overtly, covertly, or both, depending upon the transactional yield of benefits and liabilities involved.

From this angle, the missio urbis and the missio Dei stand as opponents, for they seek contrary ends for human life. God seeks to free, while the city seeks to obligate. God seeks to fulfill, while the city seeks to tantalize. God seeks to provide, while the city seeks to trade at a disadvantage to the consumer. God seeks to endow, while the city seeks to exploit.

Friend or foe? The same spectrum of orientation can be observed across the range of the city's specializations, sub-missios, systems and structures. Its politics, its social dynamics, its economics, its events, networks, uses of space and place, assemblages, all can be friend or foe, or even friend *and* foe to mission. Viewed from the location of God's mission, this again can be attributed to the narrowness of the city's range of existence, to its lack of transcendent connection to God, and to the conflicts that lie at the core of the missio urbis, which we explored in previous chapters.

The city is thus simultaneously a goldmine and a minefield for Christian mission. It is a place where people are condensed, and readily accessible. It has spaces and places and resources, but it also has opposing forces, resistances and pitfalls. It is a place where people are deeply aware of their own needs and dissatisfactions, where humans are perpetually reminded that there is lack in their lives, and where they are actively seeking for something more, but it is also a place that is filled with partial solutions, distractions, false satisfactions, misleading pleasures and an endless array of creaturely comforts.

The city has thick, efficient, high capacity mechanisms and instruments, which lend themselves to mission, but those same mechanisms lend themselves equally to projects that enslave and exploit. Mission seeks to get things done, and the city is a machine that has been designed to get things done; yet, the city resists any co-opting of its capacities for uses that compete with its own ends. The urban remains largely ignorant of God's mission, but even when it is aware, it wants God's mission to adopt its own urban house rules, to the city's own benefit. The city wants to be the city, and to fulfill its urban mission; it does not want to be the kingdom or use God's mission playbook.

Thus, through mission eyes, the city is all at once a challenge, an opportunity, a resource, a liability, a friend, an enemy and a competitor. At times, it can be a mission partner, but it is not a true and faithful mission co-laborer. Unless it can be converted, the city remains an untrustworthy and selfish partner at best, and a destructive and traitorous one, at worst.

However, mission eyes see in concert with God's mission heart, and the city is not only a thing to be analyzed. It is also a thing to be loved, a thing to be pitied, a thing to be hoped for and an object for sacred compassion. From this perspective, the city is a sheepfold with open gates. It has a phenomenal capacity to draw sheep together so that they might be cared for and protected, yet all too often it gathers those sheep only to see them sheared or slaughtered. This is because the city lacks a shepherd and a true soul. It is partial, mindless and blind, even to those who live within it, whose lives sustain it.

In other words, the city is neither glorious nor damnable. It is lost. Its mission is fatally flawed and it desperately needs a better solution for the problems of human want. For its own benefit, it needs to be taken up by sacred hands as an instrument for divine purposes. It awaits redemption as it longs for its dust to be breathed upon by God so that it might become a fully living thing.

Chapter 11

Missio-Urban Concerns

As we near the end of our journey, our conversation moves more along the path of applied missiology. The goal now is to explore missiological concerns that factor in urban mission. We will discuss these in light of our foregoing study and with an eye toward participation in the missio Dei.

Due to space limits, this will have to be a passing glance, and we can expect to encounter more questions than answers in the process, since the issues being brought into play are vast. Just as we saw the city re-present itself in the light of missio, we can now expect familiar missiological topics to re-present themselves with unfamiliar character. Therefore, we can expect the exploration that follows to be somewhat startling, and perhaps, even disruptive or uncomfortable.

However, openly engaging difficult or unusual questions is the very heart of inquiry, for it calls us to step away from established habits of knowing, "forgetting what lies behind and straining forward to what lies ahead" as we "press on toward the goal for the prize of the upward call of God in Christ Jesus" (Phil. 3:13-14). This calls for the kind of honest inquiry that Ernest Beyaraaza encourages in the philosophical evaluation of African urbanism. He exhorts,

> While it is clear that the city is double-edged, we may not sit back and lament among ourselves the problems we have harvested

from the city. We must think hard in order to get to the roots of these problems, and then devise ways and means of resolving them. Nor should we fix our attention only upon the problems and be shaken by them to the extent of developing city-phobia. We must look at the other side of the coin and appreciate what we have reaped from the existence of the city amidst us. Certainly, life would not be the same without the city. We must therefore make this reality our own, instead of viewing it as foreign. We should agree that whatever is foreign and good is good, and whatever is traditional and bad is bad, and vice-versa.

We should be open-minded, reflect on our cultural values, accept what is acceptable, and reject what must be rejected. If we can replace bias by critical thinking, at least we can establish a hierarchy of values by which we can tell what is more of value and which is less, thereby becoming able to be conscientious objectors. Although knowing the truth will not necessarily make us follow it, at least it will make us feel guilty when we do not. Above all, we must search for correct leadership, a very rare commodity in Africa, and, perhaps, in the world. (Beyaraaza, 1991, p. 214)

Hopefully, as we pursue a similar missiological agenda, the things that we encounter can spur future research and dialog within our burgeoning field. In the meantime, to lend a degree of order, we will select and group our topics somewhat arbitrarily. The current chapter will take up urban mission *concerns*; the chapter following will take up *challenges* and *practices*.

Urban Mission Concerns

There are two aims for this chapter. One aim is to consider topics of missiological value that do not necessarily arise immediately during interpretation and analysis, but which come into view when we seek to understand mission, the city, creation and the biblical text, together. These are "elephant in the room" missio-urban issues that relate to our mix of topics, which warrant being addressed at least in part before we leave the discussion. Another aim is to talk about how the kingdom can or should express within the contexts of both the city and the creation, in a manner that fulfills the mission of God. Both of these aims treat mission *concerns*, and we will alternate focus between them as we proceed.

Ideal States and Experienced States

One of the key questions that appears when we mix the biblical text with mission and the city concerns the establishment of norms or missional standards. Standards are crucial because the establishment of a norm impacts the direction of force that mission exerts upon a situation during its thrust toward fulfillment. In the case of the city and Genesis 1, the question is one of whether the ideal, non-experienced state of affairs, or the real, experienced state of affairs should stand as the norm that informs mission work. We faced a similar tension when considering which state to prioritize during the juxtaposition in Chapter 9.

Recall that the depictions of the creation in its kingdom arrangement are cast idyllically by design, and, as an ideal-state portrayal, which contrasts sharply with the raw pragmatism of the city. Yet, the Genesis account shows a situation that cannot be found currently upon the earth. It describes a context that needs no remediation or missional intervention, for it both fulfills the missio Dei and experiences its own fulfillment just as it stands.

The city does not exist in that world. The city presents as a historical thing that currently *is*. It is a thing that answers presenting needs in the contemporary context of a less than ideal earth. This leaves us to ponder the differences that stand between the urban as the thing that is and the creational kingdom as the thing that was intended, but no longer is.

The question follows, "How can mission approach the thing that currently is, according to a mandate that most appropriately fits a thing that was intended, but no longer is?" "Might not the principles of mission differ when the worlds in which it is to be performed differ?" Stated another way,

"Does the mandate that obtained for a pristine world continue to obtain in a non-pristine world, and if so, in what ways? Should mission look here and now, at the way things *are*? Should it look back, at the way things once *were*, that is, as things were supposed to be, or should it look forward, at the way that things possibly *could become*?" The missional issue then becomes one of discerning what is actually intended or expected by God for the context in which mission now operates when that context is compared to an essentially different context.

Missional longing. As was the case for the interpretive juxtaposition, perhaps the answer for missional attention lies in the design of the creation text, especially in light of the longing that the account is constructed to elicit. Since the text is designed to evoke longing, it would seem that it presents a scene that is understood to be unattainable, a state of affairs that is intended always to remain out of reach, while still in view. This would make its missional utility one of directing mission in an algorithmic way, rather than one of providing a goal for achievement.

If we take into account the missional design of the passage, it may be that, like the mathematic concept of *pi*, the creational account presents a missional concept that is beyond resolution, regardless of how far it may be pursued. If this is the case, then it would call mission agents to recognize the place that longing may hold within the missio Dei. If longing itself has a purpose in God's missional project, the implications are far-reaching, of course, and we cannot address more than the most minimal aspects of the idea here. However, at the very least, we may consider the possibility that God quite deliberately may have given the creational account in order to present a thing that cannot be achieved, and that its purpose may be as a sort of compass by which people can assess their own desires and direct their lives, even when they may never be able to live *in* the state of things being longed for. This may be what Qoheleth observes, "he has put eternity into man's heart, yet so that he cannot find out what God has done from the beginning to the end" (Eccl. 3:11, RSV).[140][141]

This would mean that longing in perpetuity, a "hunger and thirst" after right-ness (Matt. 5:6) can be a legitimate missional state, and the production of such longing can be a legitimate missional aim. If this is so, then the production of longing may be thought of as a viable missional strategy, or a legitimate instrument of mission. Given that this may the case, the state of longing can be considered to constitute one kind of satisfaction of God's missional intention(s). This means that the missio Dei still can be fulfilled by appropriate, right-longing response to its call, even when a given state of affairs at which that call is aimed is not achieved. In cases where right-longing is God's missional aim, mission then becomes mission *toward* or *according to*, not mission *at*.

Mission *toward* or *according to* a missional goal may be understood as a missional norm that may be fulfilled by actions that concern it and take it into account, even while it remains unachieved. Using a rough parallel, one could fulfill a mission to go north(ward) without seeking to arrive at the north pole itself, or one may fulfill a mission to go west(ward) indefinitely, since there is no West to arrive at. However, one also could fulfill a mission to navigate to a place that is not the North Pole while always using the North pole as the key point of reference. In a similar way, one missionally may proceed toward or according to an end-state that is never intended to be achieved. One also may proceed according to a state that is illustrative and evocative by design, since, missiologically, such a design would make that end-state operate as a principle.[142]

From this it follows that in the same way that God has given the creation account in order to construct a mission of longing, God also may

---

[140] RSV (*The Holy Bible: revised standard version*, 1952)
[141] The apostle Paul also seems to describe this kind of longing in Rom. 8:19-24.
[142] This is similar to P. Hiebert's contrast between centered-set mission and bounded-set mission (1983). While the principle is similar, here, the idea is that the ideal is deliberately intended to remain unattainable.

have given mission to humankind as a task of longing, a task that by its very design is unable to be *accomplished*, yet, one that always may be *fulfilled*. That is, it may be the case that mission may never bring about the thing or state of affairs that its view is set upon, but by acting in reference to that thing and by keeping that state in mind as the direction toward which it acts, it fulfills its missional mandate.

Missional faithfulness. This possibility brings the notion of *faithfulness* to the fore in a way that can be distinguished from *effectiveness*. While effectiveness can be measured by the degree of achievement in reference to a defined or definable goal, faithfulness cannot. Instead, for faithfulness, the measure is the constancy of maintaining orientation toward a goal, not the achievement of that goal. Using this criterion, missional faithfulness in urban work may be measured by the degree to which the creational kingdom arrangement is held prior and in view as the standard of reference. The concept of faithfulness also raises the possibility that the aim of urban missional work may simply be to call forward human longing for the creational kingdom.

Considering mission as the performance of faithfulness can reorient mission significantly, because it changes the priorities within mission action, along with the canons by which mission is evaluated. The criterion of faithfulness brackets out the agenda of completing specific, tangible ends while it considers mission activity in terms of dispositions, values, ideals and processes. It assesses outcomes on intentional, purposeful, spiritual and existential valences, not primarily along sociomaterial valences. It is a qualitative view rather than a quantitative view, and its qualitative canons are grounded in transcendent realities that cannot be accessed by sociomaterial examination, alone.

For urban mission then, the factor of longing can unite the ideal, unattainable creational world's mandate with the realities of the experienced, concrete, historical, urban context by supporting a missional agenda that is based upon faithfulness. Using an faithfulness agenda, urban mission may hold the creational kingdom in view as a standard without needing to transform the city into the ideal creation or anything near it. Urban mission might not have a mandate to get the city to be *at* the creational state. It may only need to comprehend the urban in light of the creational kingdom, and to see and act in the city in ways that demonstrate the creational kingdom as the ideal.

Using these criteria, failure to achieve measurable degrees of urban transformation need not be construed as failure to fulfill creational kingdom mission in, to or through the city context. In other words, appropriate urban mission does not necessarily need to "fix" or, perhaps, even address the city's lacks, brokenness or problems in order to fulfill the creational kingdom's missional purpose. It only needs to act faithfully in the midst of the city and its problems by ordering itself according to the kingdom arrangement that is set out as the creational ideal.

Urban Frustration and Suffering

Along this line, we may observe that the Genesis 3 account attributes the flawed state of the world that now is to human sin and divine curse. This seems to reinforce the idea that the current state of the world is deemed irremediable in the larger narrative. Although God's people may negotiate the broken world faithfully while it is in its current state, creation appears not to be able to be brought back to its pristine state without divine eschatological intervention. In the broader narrative, the earth remains broken and under curse, and people do not appear to have either the dominion capacity or the calling to alter that reality. They must decide how to live with that state of affairs as a given.

From the perspective of missio, this appears to be a sort of divinely orchestrated, deliberate frustration. God has made the earth bear the results of human sin unalterably, yet through the text, he presents to people a view of a world that is not broken, in which the effects of sin and curse are not experienced. Judging by textual design, God's apparent purpose in doing so is to make people long for an unbroken world that remains within his reach and beyond theirs, as long as the earth's status quo obtains.

Given that this is a divinely ordered situation, we must ask open and forthright missiological questions about its instrumental purpose in the missio Dei, such as, "Is frustration over the world's brokenness and lacks a divinely ordained missional instrument? Is it a goad that pushes people away from accepting this world's current states as normative? Does it hinder people from endorsing this world's currently available solutions as satisfactory, so that people might be moved toward other states and other solutions?" If the answer to these questions is "yes," then in the case of the urban project, it is fitting to ask, "Might the city's failures, and the frustrations that they create in people, be one of God's missional tools? Might the longing that arises in the city when its members experience frustration and insufficiency be an instrument of divine mission that is specifically designed to deconstruct the value of merely partial, urban-life satisfactions and push people toward real, full-life solutions?"

While this may on the surface appear to be a calloused question, given the immense suffering that people experience in many urban contexts, if we are to try to discern missiologically, we cannot shy away from asking the question simply out of our conditioned aversions. If the cross and martyrdom can inform us about mission, they should show us that God can accomplish deeply beautiful and gracious ends in surprising ways, even via paths of suffering. And, while suffering is by nature something that we hate and that we desire strongly to rid ourselves and others of, we must entertain the possibility that our strong urge to rid the world of suffering has been called into being by God in order to remind us that something is terribly lacking in the world as it stands, and to drive us to seek for more. For, if we are not to condemn the missional paths of suffering that God has shown himself ready to ordain in the cross or in martyrdom, we must at least consider that urban longing and urban suffering, as terrible as they are, may on deep levels participate in the catalog of God's missional graces,[143] for they blunt the urban offer of sociomaterial satisfactions and indict the urban strategy as insufficient.

Mission values and urban suffering. If we ask these missiological questions, natural distaste for suffering and ingrained habits of discourse tend to drive the line of inquiry into rather classic ideological and theological dilemmas. In those discourses, truly missiological concerns often drop from view and other existential or disciplinary concerns take precedence. We begin to ask questions such as, "Where then does this attribute urban suffering - to God, to the evil of this world, or to the misguidedness of humankind? Does this mean that urban suffering is not an evil? Is not urban suffering a thing to be protested, alleviated or halted?"

Unfortunately, the missiological tendency often has been to integrate these lines of inquiry by adding missional nuances, without insisting that questions be reframed using a distinctly missiological focus. Thus, we tend to push missiology to answer non-missiological questions that simply carry missiological terms as qualifiers, such as, "Does this then attribute urban suffering to God ('s mission), to the evil of this world, or to the misguidedness of humankind? Does this mean that urban suffering is not an evil (that mission should address)? Is not urban suffering a thing to be protested, alleviated or halted (by mission agents)?"

In terms of missio, a full answer to those kinds of questions may remain unavailable and clouded in mystery. For, from a missiological angle, we cannot causally attribute the cross of Christ in a clear, singular and final manner, and we cannot discern clearly what impacts God's people might or should have had upon its injustice. We cannot missiologically isolate the injustice of the crucifixion from its purpose to provide divine grace, nor can we isolate whether or not Jesus' death at Calvary was an outcome of human malice, religious envy or group blindness and ignorance. We cannot separate

---

[143] Cf., Jn. 9:1-3, Lk. 16:19-25, or Phil. 1:29-30.

the interpersonal betrayal, ambition, sociopolitical intrigue and nationalism from the spiritual machinations of the prince of this world, and we cannot extract those realities finally from the missional plan and foresight of God.

From the viewpoint of missio, all of these purposes coexist and co-involve within the construction of the event, since it was a co-production of multiple intentions, and their respective influences only may be observed as those of co-contributors. Thus, we cannot effectively evaluate if Jesus' suffering should have been opposed or protested by God's mission agents, nor can we characterize the overall situation in a wholesale evaluation with a single, reduced quality. Even when we see certain actors, such as Peter, standing in opposition, we cannot determine whether or not God's people should or could have succeeded in such efforts.

We can, however, see strands within the overall complexity, as we discern how the various purposes correlate to each other. We can see what each is seeking to accomplish, and how those intentions impact other intentions. We also can see which intentions represent God well and which ones do not, and we can see how they interact together to bring about a variety of missional outcomes. Further, we can see how these are all together subsumed within and utilized by God's mission, fitting into God's metanarrative plan of redemption.

From the example of Calvary, we can see that missiological examination takes into account the missional complexity of human situations and events, even when that may require unexpected ambiguity about things that non-missiological discourses find easy to categorize. Sometimes, the result of recognizing missional complexity is that situations and events cannot be finally placed into evaluative categories that require opposition or support in binary ways. As in the case of the cross, this may hold true even when those situations may demonstrate aspects of injustice, betrayal or oppression that non-missiological discourses might consider to be definitive, essential or conclusive indicators.

If non-missiological discursive values are treated as standards, value cannot be assigned to urban suffering in light of its missional or redemptive aspects. Unless suffering leads to other forms of benefit that are endorsed by non-missiological discourses, it must be viewed as a simple negative state. Thus, while urban suffering could have a degree of value if it incidentally precipitates existential, relational or psychological refinement, or if it sparks economic, social or political reform, it has no value if it mainly serves to fulfill God's plan. When suffering is thus reduced in its scope of potential significance, it becomes a simple, negative human state, and the expectation is that as such it must be condemned and opposed by mission agents.

Such simplification of suffering fails to regard missio dimensions that mission agents might be able to perceive, and it excludes any place that might be given to the redemptive ends that suffering might serve. This stance becomes hegemonic when missiologists are hindered by discursively based social pressures from talking about the potential value of redemptive or missional suffering. More severely, it becomes coercive when mission agents are pressured to oppose urban suffering in ways and on terms that are defined and value assigned by other discourses, without place being given for what mission agents might see happening on levels of divine mission.

When mission agents find themselves induced to remediate urban suffering on those terms, representational conflicts emerge. For, it co-opts agents of divine mission into becoming agents of discursive mission(s) when they are expected to prioritize non-missional value assignments, or, worse yet, when they are pressured to confine their missional attentions to ranges of existence too narrow for transcendent or divine mission. When it comes to missional concern for urban suffering, if urban mission is to maintain its representational integrity and freedom, it must be afforded the liberty to view suffering through its own missional eyes, in light of the missio Dei. Mission agents must be able to take into account that urban suffering may have deeper redemptive or missional value(s) than those that appear on sociomaterial or other discursive levels, and the possibility must be entertained that redemptive and missional values can supersede sociomaterial values. Thus, it must be allowed that legitimate missional answers to urban suffering may be found via redemptive, spiritual and transcendent solutions, and we must remain open to the possibility that spiritual suffering may be of greater missional concern than sociomaterial suffering, depending upon the purposes of God in a certain context.

Urban wealth and poverty. If we do not make allowances for urban values to be determined by spiritual and transcendent mission factors, we run the risk of forcing urban mission into binary support/opposition dilemmas that arise from the ways that non-missional categories and values are assigned. If, for example, mission is forced to use categories that cast human well-being or suffering in terms of sociomaterial states, mission agents naturally must oppose poverty and support material wealth. However, the discursive value assignments that define material wealth as a state that lacks suffering (or as a good to be attained), which also define material poverty as a state of suffering (or as an evil to be opposed) are based upon socioeconomic assumptions that may not be suitable for Christian mission or compatible with Christian life.

Since such categorizations fail to allow for transcendent dimensions of life, these kinds of categorizations can bracket out or dismiss the dangers that Jesus and the New Testament writers associate with wealth and the blessings that Christ ascribes to poverty. From missiological perspectives, doing this oversimplifies, and thus, mischaracterizes wealth, poverty and suffering by framing them along psychological, social, political or economic lines rather than along transcendent, kingdom, mission or spiritual lines. If mission accepts and integrates such non-missional evaluative categories for its own use without significant qualification it can distort missional actions that seek to represent Jesus, his agenda and his viewpoints concerning wealth, poverty and suffering.

Naturally, if psychological, sociopolitical or sociomaterial categories that cast poverty without qualification as a negative state[144] are taken as missional standards, the mission agent must do all that she can to oppose or address the "problem" of urban "poverty" on psychological, sociopolitical and sociomaterial levels. Doing anything less is unacceptable. However, the New Testament does not take a simplistic view of wealth,[145] and when mission agents are allowed to take into account that Jesus assigns blessing[146] to the poor and woe or liability to the rich, the picture changes. It becomes more complex, because the mission agent must consider whether or not the removal of poverty is a removal of blessing and whether or not the production of wealth is an introduction of woe or liability. This conundrum requires considered missional discernment on levels that simple, binary categorizations do not allow, for the mission agent cannot approach a context assuming that poverty is (simply) "bad," and wealth is (simply) "good."

Instead, the mission agent must be able to evaluate *if* and *when* a given form of poverty is bad and *if* and *when* a given form of wealth is good at any given moment and place. Conversely, the mission agent also must be able to discern *if* and *when* wealth is bad, and *if* and *when* poverty is good in a certain context. For, from a kingdom perspective, it very well may be that urban wealth is a severe, under-addressed urban problem and that the urban wealthy constitute an at-risk, suffering population, precisely due to the presence of wealth and the absence of poverty. It could be that in a

---

[144] Unqualified characterizations of all forms of poverty as negative often overlook other, non-spiritual, social benefits, such as certain freedoms (Ramachandran, 1996) or, in the case of lower statuses, stability and reduced conflict (Weissner & Schiefenhovel, 1998).

[145] For example, in *Wealth as Peril and Obligation: the New Testament on Possessions* Sondra Wheeler (1995) tracks four major New Testament understandings of wealth, which portray it alternately as: 1) a stumblingblock 2) a competitor for devotion 3) a symptom of economic injustice, and 4) a resource to meet human needs. These span a wide range of human good and bad, enough that wealth cannot be held to constitute a simple positive nor lack of wealth as a simple negative.

[146] Jesus calls both the "poor" (oi ptōchoi , Lk. 6:20) and the "poor in spirit" (oi ptōchoitō pneumati, Matt. 5:3) "blessed" (makarioi) indicating a condition of being happy or in a positive state. This sets the state of poverty in an opposing, contrasting relationship to suffering, rather than as a suffering state.

certain city, or even within the phenomenon of global urbanization, wealth may present an urban problem that desperately requires missional attention, and the challenge of solving urban wealth may be equal in urgency to the challenge of solving urban poverty.

Power and dominion. Similar issues arise when we consider the ways in which power is held, used and distributed. For, although in the creational account dominion over the earth is portrayed as appropriate, human to human expressions of power remain unaddressed. In the absence of a clear pattern that shows how power should be distributed or an evaluative description that could be carried over directly to the city, mission agents need to exercise mission-oriented reasoning and discernment. We cannot afford to assume that non-missional characterizations of power should obtain as missional values on an issue of such importance.

Just as the New Testament offers cautions about the acquisition of wealth, it warns about the liabilities of seeking power (Mk.10:42-45). Even minimal exertions of power, such as resistance to social injustice, opposition to wrong-doers, and seeking redress are prohibited in Jesus' Sermon on the Mount (Matt. 5:38-40). In word and in deed, Christ directs his followers away from the pursuit of rights or self-interest, championing instead the path of self-denial (Lk. 9:23; 14:26). In Paul's iconic citation of Jesus' example, even divine equality is not a thing to be held to; instead, equality is a thing to be divested and abandoned in pursuit of servanthood, obedience and the interests of others (Phil. 2:3-8).

Given these descriptions, urban mission cannot afford to view social power as a simple good, and lack of social power as a simple bad, any more than it can view wealth as a simple good and poverty as a simple bad. Both biblically and historically, there is more than ample ground for mission to be cautious about endorsing causes that involve social power, and urban mission has good reason to be reserved. Mission agents have every cause to question their own dispositions toward power, and to be discerning about what modes of assertion, courage or resolve they hope to elicit or reinforce within urban dwellers.

When we consider that Jesus proclaimed the blessedness of the meek as the condition to inherit the earth (Matt. 5:5), we should tread carefully, lest out of concern for the down-trodden we would call people inadvertently to grasp power in ways that represent non-missional approaches to power instead of kingdom approaches to power. While mission agents seek to save lives, and to see lives protected, we must be able to perceive the difference between seeking to save lives and calling people to seek to save their own lives. We always must represent Jesus' stance, quoted by all four gospel writers, that "he who seeks to gain his life will lose it" (Mt. 10:39, 16:25; Mk. 8:35; Lk. 9:24, 17:33; Jn.12:25), especially when there is the chance that mission agents may lead people to sacrifice spiritual or transcendent well-being on the altar of self-preservation, and in doing so, induce them to trade their sacred inheritances for sociopolitical or sociomaterial benefits.

Human Rights and Social Justice

Naturally, such considerations lead to concerns for human rights and social justice. These crucial concerns can provide us with key examples of how missio-urban evaluation may offer a distinct outlook on urban issues. However, these are highly charged concerns; significant commitment to process and intentional openness to unfamiliar viewpoints will be required if we are to look at them in alternative ways.

Justice and the missio urbis. Cast only in terms of the missio urbis, power distribution is simply a functional affair, and managing its use(s) is merely a sub-missio necessity. As we have seen already, the city's missio has poor eyes to see things like human value, and its administration of justice need not be linked to any transcendent criterion. To the city, justice is not a metaphysical reality that must be accommodated; it is a pragmatic social criterion, and it need only be satisfied enough that it can fulfill society's need to cohere stably.

Using only the missio urbis, justice can be assessed simply in terms of what needs to be done in order for the city to survive and to perpetuate its project. If social control is exercised in a way that brings sociomaterial benefit to urban constituents, and the city survives and flourishes, there is little need to search further; justice has been served enough, and power has been used well enough.

Equitability and human rights. Contemporary social discourses, ideological discourses, and, especially, established academic discourses, might very well object to the pragmatics of the missio urbis on this point. However, missiological analysis of their objections and relations to the missio urbis can be very troublesome, because discursive claims about justice frequently are forwarded with transcendent moral force even while they reject transcendent claims. This affords ideological discourses a type of rhetorical Catch-22, in which universalizing religious or transcendent critiques are considered null, while non-religious universal claims stand unquestionable on self-proclaimedly incontrovertible moral grounds.

In order to consider social justice agenda about the urban missiologically, we need to recognize that justice discourses, like the city and the kingdom, can be considered to have their own distinct missios, which seek to actualize discursive values and express through practices. When viewed from within a missio, certain dispositions or posits are always considered inalienable, universal or unquestionable because they embody a given discourse's framework, from which that missio derives. Thus, in order to be able to examine discursive missios, missiological inquiry must take what Paul Hiebert (1994) calls a "metacultural" viewpoint that stands beyond intra-cultural or intra-discursive systems and epistemologies. Once this is realized, missiological analysis can be conducted in a way that does not subject itself to discursively predetermined constraints that censor missiological findings or silence ranges of missiological discussion.

With that in mind, we can begin by noting that 1) social justice missios are often complicated by internal inconsistencies and paradoxes, 2) social justice propositions are not universally recognized, 3) social justice missios are contextually developed and, as such, they reflect larger cultural metanarratives, worldviews and agenda, 4) human rights are variably and contextually articulated, and, 5) social justice missios are vulnerable to exploitation by other discursive and sociocultural missios.

Space prevents us from exploring all of these points, but a few illustrations may help us understand the urban nexus of conflict between the urban missio, the kingdom missio and social justice missios. Briefly, although articulation varies across western discourses, social justice is framed commonly as a matter of equitability, grounded upon the rights of humans, viewed without distinction (Fobil & Atuguba, 2004; Gottdiener & Hutchison, 2011; Lin, 2016). That is, people are understood to be universally the same in certain ways (humanity), and in their universal sameness, all have an appropriate claim to be treated with justice (UNGA, 1948-49). That justice is understood as fairness, or lack of discrimination, and fairness is associated with equitability (Lulek & Paga, 1991). In turn, equitability is assessed by comparing treatment of one person over against treatment of another, and by comparing the lived state of one over against another.[147] In this line of thinking, any *one* is entitled to whatever *all* are entitled to; people have a right to equitability, and lack of equitability constitutes injustice.

Yet, this arrangement is difficult to satisfy, because it also is understood that people have multiple rights, such as the rights to life, to individual expression, to personal property, to the pursuit of personal well-being, to certain ranges of autonomy, etc. Additionally, and a bit ironically, all rights are not considered to be equal; they are understood to concern different aspects of human existence, and some are understood to be more central to human life and dignity than others. Thus, lists and declarations of

---

[147] For example, the U.N.'s UDHR Article 23.2 declares the "right to equal pay for equal work" (UNGA, 1948-49).

rights vary,[148] and items such as the right to "form and join trade unions" (UNGA, 1948-49, p. 23.24) or the right to "the opportunity to receive normal schooling" (CSIPDH, 2012, p. 5.2) are held to carry less force than rights against arbitrary detention, torture or forced servitude. Further, rights vary between general populations and special classes, such as "under the age of 18," (CSIPDH, 2012) "mothers and children" (UNGA, 1948-49), those who have diminished mental and physical capacities (ECORP, 1994), or those who have committed "penal offence," (UNGA, 1948-49), making rights variable by age, as well as by wellness or moral and legal status.

Because rights are not self-organizing or self-prioritizing, the aim of achieving justice by preserving the rights of city-dwellers quickly runs afoul of contradictory proposals about which rights and whose rights take precedence. For, in many cases, the realization of one human right for one group requires the violation or compromise of a different human right for another group. Rights to legal process can find themselves pitted against rights to safety and security, while rights to own property can be set against rights to basic provision, work, shelter or public care, etc. Thus, the missio of preserving human rights itself becomes subject to being co-opted by missios seeking the will to power, as individuals or groups champion their own preferred claims regarding particular rights at the expense of subordinating the preferred rights of other individuals or groups (Myers, 2011).

Complicating things further, proposals about the universal nature of rights also must negotiate the paradox that all people do not see the world in terms of the same human rights, or even terms of human rights, at all. Take, for example how the UDHR's article 21.3 might sound in the ears of a member of Saudi Arabian or Thai society as it proclaims,

> The will of the people shall be the basis of the authority of government; this will shall be expressed in periodic and genuine elections which shall be by universal and equal suffrage and shall be

---

[148] For example, Prisoner's Rights (UNODC, 2015), Children's Rights (UNGA, 1959), Patient's Rights (ECORP, 1994), etc.

> held by secret vote or by equivalent free voting procedures (UNGA, 1948-49)

Although this proviso certainly stands out as embodying a distinctly cultural (in this case, western) missio aimed at producing a given form of political organization, all discursive missios are not so blatant. Missiologically, we know that discourses are co-produced and contextual, along with the values that support them, and we know that all cultures do not perceive justice or human value in the same ways (Hiebert, 2008; Kraft, 2008). Thus, we can propose on good grounds that cultural biases similar to the one shown by Article 21 find expression in other points of rights and justice discourses. Unfortunately, this leaves any project to universalize a particular vision of human rights across all urban contexts open to critique as a hegemonic sociocultural exercise that does violence to the sensibilities and worldviews of others, that is, as a violation of the very rights to culture, opinion, self-determination and way of life that human rights declarations seek to protect.

Problematically, no matter how much effort is expended, discursive variabilities endure and compete over whose articulation of rights should prevail. As various missios seek to actualize their own imaginaries of just society they must negotiate complexities that involve the enforcement of certain prioritized rights, the assignments of special classes, the definition of "arbitrary" uses of social power, and the dominance of worldview(s). Sometimes, inequities on these levels actually can be reinforced by the attempts of discursive missios to eradicate them, due to internal paradoxes and the susceptibility of rights discourse to exploitation.

Given that the immense diversity of human life makes all situations, all contexts and all persons unique, while human rights missios frame justice in terms of that which is common and universal, internal paradoxes that involve mutually exclusive or competing universal and particular rights often stymie equality based macro-missios as they seek to shape a "just" urban landscape. For example, theoretically, in order to achieve ontically real parity, it would be necessary to create universally homogeneous states, in which no one held privileges that were not common to all. Dechert rightly questions framing the idea of "equality" along these lines because of the "social homogenization" that it would entail, along with the "liquidation of all social boundaries in the greater society" that is required (Dechert, 1991). Distressingly, not only would this obliterate the concentrations and hierarchies that define the urban, it also would require the eradication of all true differences and differential categories. Thus, the missio to create true and just equality would be forced to erase human uniqueness and to impose total human uniformity in order to meet its ends. Not only would this be an impossible and frightening project, due both to its unachievable scope and to its moral offense, it also would be internally inconsistent, and it would violate competing human rights to individuality, which would make it deeply "unjust" by its own standards.

Since universal equitability cannot be achieved without violating some preferred rights, and since all rights cannot be fully satisfied due to internal paradoxes, if discursive missios that valorize equitability are accepted as the moral standard for justice within the city the experience of rights violation becomes a perpetual state. In other words, when justice is associated with the missios of achieving equality, and equality is considered to be a human right, the unavoidable presence of human difference results in an experience of perpetual violation of human rights; thus, injustice becomes a pervasive, insoluble experience, especially in places where human presence is concentrated, like the city.

Rights in the creational kingdom. By contrast, when we look at the creational kingdom, human rights do not seem to be in view, much less to hold a determinant moral role. The criterion of equitability also does not come into discussion. While, certainly, in the creational account humans are shown to be unified and concomitant, nothing is said about their rights or about the fairness or equitability of their respective states.

This is interesting, considering that the text obviously seeks to portray ideal human relations with God, each other and the world, and it shows divine support for human roles, activities and dignity. Further, the text clearly endorses the human exercise of power. So, where in the text might the concepts of justice and human rights be found?

From a missiological perspective, perhaps they cannot. This is not necessarily due to a flaw or a lack of concern for people, either in the text or in missiology. Rather, it arises from a fundamentally different way of understanding the appropriate use(s) of power.

A question of direction. In order to see social power through creational eyes, questions about right action need to be opened up to take into account the directional thrust of purpose within activity. In the creational account, we find power characterized as representative dominion, regency, agency, proxy, authority or custodianship. Using a missio view, we can see that the thrust of purpose in this situation follows a line from the primary social actor (God) through a secondary social agent (humankind), to a tertiary recipient (creation). In this scenario, the determinant moral location is held by the primary actor and the agent, since those originate and express missio (purposes) toward the recipient. This means that missional questions about the right use of power focus on the proper exercise of duties and obligations that extend from God to the earth through people.

This recasts the question of social *justice* as the question of missional *responsibility*. At first glance, this may seem to be simply a semantic nuance. However, it presents a crucial conceptual and moral watershed, for it establishes the moral locations of social actors according to missional criteria.

When we locate moral determination in terms of *rights,* we ground its value at the recipient of actions. This kind of location minimizes or brackets out the moral purposes of the actor(s), because it foregrounds the recipient. It is a recipient's moral claim upon the actions of others. It holds a claim to be acted toward by others in a certain way.

By contrast, when we locate moral determination at the purposes of the social actor(s), we characterize it in terms of *duties, responsibilities* and *obligations*. This moral claim highlights the moral nature of the one *performing* action, instead of the one *receiving* action. It focuses on the claim to act toward others in a certain way.

When the factor of agency is added, a moral claim also extends between the one who initiates a missio and the one who participates in the expression of that missio as an agent. Thus, the social agent acts under a double moral claim. She must act rightly toward others and she must act rightly on behalf of the one she represents.

Because a missional view emphasizes purposes to accomplish ends, it prioritizes the latter location, which foregrounds social actors, not social recipients. When this happens, the question shifts from whether or not *rights* have been *violated*, to whether or not *responsibility* has been *fulfilled*. Attention moves from a *passive* justice concern about the ways that people are acted *toward*, to an *active* responsibility concern about the ways that people *act*. This presents a different criterion for the exercise of power than equitability or human rights.

Using an economic example, this would be similar to the difference between a mandate to *give* 20 dollars, compared to the claim to *receive* 20 dollars. When we apply the mandate to give, 20 dollars should move *away* from the person of focus toward another. When we apply the claim to receive, 20 dollars should move *toward* the person of focus, from another.

While the two may appear to be talking about the same activity, the focus matters, for if we confuse the person of focus, the direction of claim can become inverted in its application. Thus, the mandate for oneself to give can inappropriately become a projected demand for another to yield. This is heightened when the mandate to give is agential or representative; that is, when it is to be performed on behalf of a commissioning other. In such a case, dislocating the agent's own commission to give by recasting it as a mandate upon others, who are supposed to receive from the agent not only inverts the claim, it violates the purposes of the one who has commissioned one to give.

Given that this is the case, urban mission needs to consider carefully the social justice claims that it strengthens or emphasizes, lest it invert missional directives. In the case of the twenty-dollar problem, when we focus on claims to receive instead of the duty to give, we end up creating a 40 dollar deficit, because twenty dollars has been taken when it should have been given. In the case of the city, when we focus on urban rights, which hold a passive stance using an externalized claim, we emphasize or heighten a moral claim to be afforded action by others. This locates moral responsibility *away* from the social subject, placing it upon another. Justice is thus determined by the actions of others, not by the self.

Perhaps more importantly, on another level, the claim to be afforded certain action(s) by others strips social actors of their own capacities to determine or effect social justice. For, if social justice depends upon the respect or regard of one's rights by others, the individual has no capacity to bring that action into being. Instead, each much depend upon an externalized other to act rightly toward himself in order for social justice to be achieved. When this is done, even under the best intentions, the net result is that those whose rights are being championed are relegated to the status of passive social recipients. As recipients, *actors* become *actees*; they are thus marginalized and become further, sometimes finally, disempowered because they are prevented from being those primary social actors whose actions determine whether or not justice has been achieved. Thus, simply by framing social justice in terms of rights we run the risk of producing pervasive moral deficits and perpetuating the ongoing experience of injustice in the city.

When we understand this, the creational depiction of power usage becomes a bit clearer, and the absence of western social justice or equality categories also begins to make sense. For, when we consider the use of social power in light of missio, the key issue becomes the responsibility to act, not the claim to be afforded action. The question of social justice then becomes whether or not those with any form of power to act have fulfilled the purposes for which they have been granted such power. Under the banner of the missio Dei this entails whether or not the social actor has fulfilled appropriate representation of God's image. This has a missional thrust of direction away from the primary actor (God), through and away from the secondary, representative actor (humankind). Its moral concern is about how one acts, rather than about how one is acted toward. Thus, missio Dei based moral evaluation hinges upon whether or not actors have done their duties rightly, demonstrating the image of God to others and ruling the earth well on his behalf.

In this scheme, urban social justice is achieved when people act rightly toward others in the city. It can be achieved by anyone, at any time and in any situation, because it is the responsibility of the social actor and the moral character of the situation is determined by her own actions and dispositions. This places the reins of social justice into the hands of even the most marginalized.

If urban mission seeks for the city to be a just place, it should then seek to empower social actors by highlighting each person's missional moral responsibility. Its moral focus most appropriately should concentrate upon the ways that people treat others, not about the ways that people are treated by others. In order to see social justice achieved, urban mission's voice would then emphasize calling the city and its dwellers to fulfill their own moral duties and obligations by exercising power in godly or righteous ways, rather than by championing the rights of people to be treated with equitability.

For, under a universal mandate to *give*, all carry a claim upon *themselves*; all are obliged to transfer to others. Generosity results; not exploitation. Under a universal entitlement to *receive*, all carry a claim on *others*; all seek to see transfer toward the self. Lack and exploitive uses of power ensue. As Jesus said, for those who make up the city, it would be much more blessed to give than to receive (Acts 20:35).

Male and Female

When moral obligation is framed as a missional responsibility to act in representational integrity on behalf of God, it impacts missiological concerns about sexual identities and relations. In the creational account, God has a clear purpose that humankind would bear his image, and he has a clear program for how that image is to be actualized and displayed. While many points legitimately may be drawn from the account about how the image of God expresses, the most forceful and direct point available to us is that the divine image is expressed in the unity of male and female. The account is explicit that humans are created in the image of God as *male* and *female*, joined in plural unity as the singular, *him* (see Chapter 7). Narratively, this is reinforced by the attending commission to procreate and fill the earth.

The scene shows God's pre-creational mission, his active creational mission and his post-creational mission to express his image this way and to continue expressing his image this way throughout human generations. Whatever else may be said about the imago Dei, at the very minimum, we cannot avoid the text's portrayal that the most basic categories of human identity are sexually defined as "male" and "female," and that there is a divine mission for humankind to represent God both by existing in those categorical identities and through the heterogeneous union of those identities.

It follows that mission agents would understand sex identities and sexual relations in terms of human missional responsibility to represent God's purposes. This approach differs from approaches to sex that are grounded in discourses about human rights. For, as we have seen, by virtue of their direction and location of moral claim, discourses about human sexual rights assume a claim upon God's actions toward themselves. Making such a claim upon God, that he should act toward the sexual human in a certain way, effectively annuls God's own purpose(s) for sexuality. Such claims replace God's authoritative claim to be represented rightly with a rights-based claim upon God that he should afford regard for the sexual purposes of humans.

From a missio viewpoint, this inverts God's missional claims to be expressed through human sexuality and in doing so it hegemonically places subordinating and oppressive claims upon God that expect him to honor autonomous human sexuality, regardless of whether or not that expresses his image and purposes. Missiologically, such a stance distorts and co-opts God's missio for creating sexes and sexuality, which constitutes an abuse of his image and of his creation. For, from a viewpoint of intended purpose, human capacities have been created and given to people for the expression of divine image, and, as in the use of power, the question of use or abuse is determined by the character of its representation. Thus, autonomous sexual rights claims illegitimately appropriate divinely given reflexive human capacities. They redirect and repurpose human custodianship of the self and its sexual nature, which God has intended to be fulfilled by hearkening the divine image as he has commissioned it to be expressed. This co-opts human capacities to exercise authority on behalf of God, using those very capacities to supersede God's own purposes and claims. As in the case of dominion, using human capacities in this way forcibly distorts the divine image by turning its abilities against its intrinsic function to express God's person and mission.

Walerian Slomka casts this as a hierarchy of competing values; he notes:

> Each normal individual of the human species is marked with a sexual need, and its connected powers, and has a natural right to satisfy this need for sexual values. This right, however, can be realized only while respecting the right of the species to exist and respect the character of the personal subject created in the image and likeness of God. With the choice of virginity or celibacy the above right is fulfilled by abnegation, motivated by dedication to higher values.

> The use of sexual values contrary to the good of the species or the human person, or against chosen higher values, creates disorder in human life. Independently of the pleasure experienced, it will lead to behavior contrary to the dignity of the person and his God-given goals.(Slomka, 1991, p. 354)

Does this mean that God's mission strips humans of sexual dignity, since they are not the determinate moral actors in issues of human sexuality? No. That only would be the case if human sexuality and sexual dignity were to be framed in terms of human-only sexual *rights*. Instead, we see that God seeks to preserve human sexual dignity by holding it to its essential missio, what Slomka calls "the dignity of the person and his God-given goals." God's aim is thus to preserve human dignity by preventing people from turning their image capacities against their own image natures.

As action that protects human dignity in the divine image, mission that seeks to preserve human sexuality in its image bearing seeks the highest good for all sexual beings. Slomka would characterize such mission as true love, which stands at the top of the hierarchy of values. As he observes:

> To the capacity to love or to "be for" corresponds the good, both possible and actual... Existing in relationship has cognitive and aesthetic aspects, also, but existing in a relationship of love means being a gift of the actual Good. (Slomka, 1991, p. 356)

As we have seen already, this mission also guards humans against presumptuous offense against God. For a problem of competing rights necessarily arises if human sexuality is framed in terms of human rights, without equal consideration of divine rights. If human sexual expressions are invoked as external claims upon God's acceptance, approval or endorsement without allowing for divine qualification, they naturally subordinate or violate God's voice, claims, purposes and mission, which is in turn a relational and moral offense, given that beings have rights and can exert claims upon others. Ironically, if humans could presume that it is legitimate to make claims upon others and upon God's dispositions and behaviors, it follows even more that it would be legitimate for God to make claims upon human dispositions and behaviors. For the issue of human sexuality, this is a crucial consideration, for one-sided assertions of rights and claims naturally fail the very principles that give them standing.

This may be why the creational account instead casts human dignity in terms of human participation in divine purposes. Both in missional agency and in the creational scheme, dignity and honor derive from the divine image and from the divine authority over the creation. Humans are thus afforded value as deputies. They exercise place as social agents who act out of responsibility as regents and custodians on God's behalf, rather than as autonomous social actors who effect social justice own their own behalf. They do have capacity to effect social justice, but that capacity is actualized as they express God's image in representation of his claims to the world, not as self-claimants upon the world or upon God.

In order to be faithful in this arrangement, it follows that mission agents would approach and treat concerns about sex identity and sex relations in terms of their own moral duties to God's image and purposes. This would prioritize the aim of missional representation over human entitlement to self-expression. For missional integration toward both the creation and the city, this would call mission agents to exert active social force in the urban context and in the world to reinforce the sanctity of sexual identification according to the categories *male* and *female*. It also would summon mission agents to champion heterogeneous union of male and female as a matter of sacred duty to honor the image of God.

Reframing Missio-Urban Concerns

From these few examples, we can see that much work remains to be done in order for missiologists to outline missio grounded approaches to key urban issues. At very minimum, mission agents can do well to allow that points of concern like power, social justice, human rights, human sexuality or poverty and wealth cannot be assessed overarchingly without due consideration being given to missio, generally, and specifically to what God might be prioritizing in his plan for humankind and for a certain place. The mission agent must be able to assess on missional and missiological terms what kind(s) of problems may be present in an urban context and assign missional value to those problems by discerning what sort of missional ends they may be moving people, institutions and situations toward.

Further, the mission agent must be able to make these evaluations based upon the missio Dei. That is, he must be able to assess where and when urban realities might be in accord or run contrary to the plan(s) that God has in, for and through a certain context, in ways that cannot be predetermined by non-missional discursive habits. Mission based evaluative categories and concerns should hold priority when mission agents examine the city's power relations, human rights, cultural rights, ethnic relations, gender relations, or any other of a host of urban realities, even when those urban realities already may have been heavily discussed and strongly value assigned within other conversations.

In other words, if missiologists and mission agents are to be able to fulfill representation of the divine kingdom in the urban context, their outlooks must be grounded primarily in kingdom categories and their mission work must be informed primarily by kingdom values. If we allow the existing habits, priorities and values of the city and contemporary culture(s) to set missio-urban questions, we will arrive always at existing non-missional answers and solutions, since the type of question that is asked predetermines the kind of data that results.

Although the work may be daunting, there is a significant need for urban missiology to develop and explore its own distinctly missio-urban concerns using Christian mission perspectives that rely upon Christian canons, traditions and sources, instead of borrowing concerns wholesale from other fields. If it is to fulfill divine agenda, urban mission cannot afford to take up categories and concerns that have been defined in non-missional ways without thorough missiological reassessment, re-definition, re-characterization and values reassignments that integrate spiritual and transcendent realities, biblical discourse(s), kingdom outlooks, and especially, the missio Dei.

A missio-urban view of Calvary. In order to understand this, let us return to the example of Christ's crucifixion that we touched on earlier in this chapter. When we look at Jesus' death on the cross, we may note that it was an urban event, and that it was one that involved personal powerlessness, inequality and injustice. It was driven by religious corruption and it embodied multiple forms of oppression. It took place under colonial military and political occupation; it was characterized by ethnic disparity, cultural domination, legal impropriety, relational betrayal, deceit, bribery, collusion, and a host of other dynamics that we can find in the city.

However, the scriptures show that God was doing something in his mission that outweighed those factors and rendered them incidental. Thus, we cannot discern a path for missional action in that urban situation by using a simplistic, binary, support/opposition approach. Simple categories do not apply.

Still, the faithfulness criterion that we have been exploring might suggest that, regardless of how events in Jerusalem proceeded, and, whether or not God's people would have been called to stand in protest or opposition, it remains a given that they should have at minimum disposed and ordered themselves rightly in the midst of Jerusalem while Christ's suffering proceeded toward its place of fulfillment in God's mission.

If we hold that God has a crucial plan for every city, we must approach every city situation as we would approach Calvary. In order to be faithful as divine agents, we must pursue sacred inquiry and missional discernment about what concerns are truly presenting before us, and about how the mission of God might be actualizing in surprising ways. For, as divinely appointed representatives we are not at liberty to select what we advocate. We have both the honor and the duty to hold to those concerns that take precedence in God's kingdom, so that we may exercise appropriate regency on God's behalf toward his world and toward his cities.

Chapter 12

Mission in the Urban Context

Even though academic conversation alone cannot fulfill missiology's quest to be faithful, missiological examination naturally involves discussion of practical issues. This last step is where academic word meets with missional deed. Yet, talk about practices is only missiology's threshold to action. Urban missiology has a calling to represent God in places and ways that lie far beyond books and analyses, and when it does, it must adapt, innovate and express things which cannot be discussed on pages alone. These expressions are sure to complicate any tidy conceptions that may be developed here. That is what happens in the real-time outworking of the kingdom in its myriad contexts, which always reveals the missio Dei in unexpected, challenging and beautiful ways.

Still, there is merit in thinking about practice in preparation for such work. For, while talk cannot substitute for praxis, word and deed remain wed, and talk about practical matters can assist the active mission agent's negotiation of tangible context. The aim for this final discussion is to provide that kind of support as a preliminary, reconnaissance endeavor that surveys the urban landscape in preparation for concrete kingdom mission. In order to do so, this chapter uses what we have seen so far to try to anticipate a few urban mission challenges. This is not an in-depth examination of applied missiology, but an example of how theory can have a connection to contextual activity. The aim is to project from a handful of the factors that we have seen in order to consider how the mission agent might practically negotiate the city's landscape in ways that represent God, his kingdom and his mission faithfully.

Challenges and Practices

The first challenge is the reality that human resources are limited. This is a key issue that drives the city's existence. It is also a factor that deeply affects urban mission. As much as we might like to, mission agents cannot change everything. We cannot restore the world to its creational state outside of the eschatological restoration of all things. Thus, one of the most crucial practical challenges that urban mission must face is how to prioritize its missional efforts.

Complex options. Theoretically, the missio urbis is a fairly simple project. It collects and it extends, and it adapts in whatever ways are necessary in the process. Yet, the simplicity of its mission has afforded the city an adaptive capacity that not only frustrates academic attempts to define it (Rickards, et al., 2016), but also can confuse or dissipate missional efforts. For, while the city is simple at heart, it is incredibly mutable, which has made its concrete presentations tremendously complex and contradictory. It has no static array of problems to address, for the functions and meanings of its sub-missios can change with its every particular expression. What can be said for one city only partially applies to another, so that the same issues or priorities do not always obtain, even from block to block. This is complicated by the fact that the city often participates in vast global forces that drive it from beyond its immediate locale.

Given that this is the case, countless urban projects could be taken up by mission. And, while any project can have missional significance, mission agents must wrestle with the reality that, "What is crooked cannot be made straight, and what is lacking cannot be counted" (Eccl. 1:15 NRSV). This surplus of urban options requires mission agents to decide which endeavors should be taken up, in what priority, and to what expenditure of precious mission resources. Further, since the city can be so powerfully responsive and dynamic, there are no guarantees that mission efforts can or will make crooked things less crooked, even if they cannot make them straight, nor, if changes can be made, that they will last. At times, this can make urban mission alternately feel like beating the ocean with a stick, lighting paper matches in a hurricane or taking a shot in the dark.

In some ways this is helpful, because it can underscore the value of performing urban mission representatively and remind us to seek the servant's goal of faithfulness, avoiding assessments that valorize effectiveness. It also can drive us to revisit our mission priorities regularly, and to pursue guidance by the Holy Spirit so that we can direct our energies in ways that fulfill God's own kingdom objectives, which do not always present themselves to us through reasoned discernment. God's ways are certainly beyond our ways, and, as Christ made clear to Nicodemus, the one who is born of the Spirit has an unpredictable path that follows no obvious trajectory (Jn. 3:7-8). It follows that those who fulfill kingdom purposes in the city often may be called to pursue ends that are difficult to comprehend in terms of urban sensibilities.

Saturation of alternatives. This challenge flows naturally into the challenge of competing missios. We have seen that the city is a nexus of agenda. These various missios all present unique visions of the good life in a concentrated manner within the urban context. For both mission workers and urban dwellers, this makes the city a perpetual market-day of potentials. Because cities must be able to integrate widely variable populations, even in the most homogeneous of today's urban contexts there is always an alternate way of seeing, doing, knowing or relating.

Unfortunately, the urban superabundance of agenda can make mission appear as just one more project among many, thus diminishing the gospel's unique message. As the apostle Paul found at Athens (Acts 17:16-33), and as Georg Simmel[149] found in Europe, urbanity can foster a blasé

---

[149] From Gottdiener and Hutchison's (Gottdiener & Hutchison, 2011, pp. 52-55) discussion of Simmel's work.

attitude in city dwellers, including mission agents, which mutes traditional concerns and draws attentions to novelties, overlooking or devaluing things of deep and abiding significance simply because they have been previously known. The display of the urban bazaar of human pursuits can bury the offer of the kingdom as a pearl of great price in an emporium of costume jewelry.

If the mission agent is not attentive to the city's hypersaturated sociocultural environment, it will be natural for her, like so many of the city's occupants, to become diffused, confused, distracted, (falsely) disillusioned, weary, doubtful or overwhelmed. The city is uniquely suited to evoke such states, and to offer sociomaterial satisfactions as the solution to the "malaise" (Peachey, 1991) that it cultivates.[150] Thus, the mission agent would do well to engage in those spiritual practices that reinforce kingdom outlooks, and to maintain relational engagements with worshiping community in ways that develop interpersonal accountability and foster authentic self-evaluation. This would include listening to voices that question urban ways with discernment, as well as practicing deliberate skepticism toward urban values, coupled with intentional disengagement from the city's satisfactions and allurements. As 1 Peter advises, "Beloved, I urge you as aliens and exiles to abstain from the desires of the flesh that wage war against the soul" (1Pet. 2:11 NRSV).

Diffusion and dissipation. Another significant challenge comes in the fragmentation and stratification of the urban person. As Paul Peachey observes,

> On the urban or societal level, meanwhile, cohesion falters. The synthetic urban fabric consists, strictly speaking, of systems of roles which are separable from the persons (individuals) who perform them. This permits social collaboration on a scale unimaginable in pre-urban settings. Role-incumbents, on the other hand, invest only

---

[150] While Okolo (1991) notes that rural displeasure also can be a factor that drives hinterland dwellers away from traditional lands and ways, toward the city, he seems to place the burden on the city's reach, and it could be argued that rural dissatisfactions may be an initial symptom of urban influence, the "early onset" of urban malaise.

> limited facets of the self in these roles, enabling them to participate in many diverse configurations of action. Role-based affiliations make only role-specific demands on the incumbents; the rest of the person remains beyond the reach of the given role set. Multiplicity of roles means multiple partial identities as well. Thereby personal autonomy is enhanced, not only because persons choose among numerous roles, but above all because such diversity of experience and affiliation enriches and expands the socially constituted self.
>
> Integration and cohesion, in both the self (or personality) and the city or society, now become problematic. (Peachey, 1991, p. 21)

Peachey notes that impersonal organization serves the city's collaborative missios, but it ushers urban dwellers into multiple, role-specific involvements. In order to be efficient, these limit personal engagement to only that which impersonal roles require. Since limited involvement calls out narrow ranges of existence from people, it reduces the individual's living out of selfhood. And, because these roles rarely or minimally overlap, they separate aspects of individuals into highly contextualized parts. This exerts diffusive stress on both individuals and groups.

As a result, it is typical and expected for urban dwellers to have dissociated spheres of existence. For the benefit of the city's collaborative efficiency, urban life is structured in such a way that whenever an urban dweller is actualizing a particular role, most of her person is being held in reserve or at bay. In this scheme, the urban self is "socially constituted." The individual's existence is distributed across multiple contexts and strata, within each of which he lives a different role-specific version of himself. Who he is at the gym is not who he is at work; neither of these are who he is at the supermarket; none of the three is who he is at the neighborhood association, etc. Further, the networks of relationships that he holds in each of these contexts do not meet or coincide; his soccer friends never meet his work friends; his family members never meet his dentist, etc. Only he lives in every one of his life's spheres, and only he can hold them together in a synthesis. His identity thus becomes composite. He experiences himself as a reflexive construct, a self-designed collage of faces played and self-selected existential sound-bites.

This self-construction is always at risk, and it requires constant readjustment and maintenance, since all of the individual's spheres of existence move and change in different ways, at different rates. This ongoing diffusion of personhood naturally takes a toll, creating a deficit in the urban dweller's experience of life and self, attended by longing to be a full being. Yet, the way that urban life is structured aims this need back toward urban ends in reinforcing ways. For, when the self is socially constituted, it is a gestalt of its parts, and the path to gain a more robust sense of identity becomes the addition of new parts; according to the urban scheme, more roles and facets are needed if one is to gain an increased gestaltic self. This drives the urban dweller who already has been diffused to seek out new involvements and more diverse roles, which in turn diffuses him more, since he carries less existential energy to any of the roles that he already holds (etc.), thus creating a perpetuating cycle.

Specialization and compartmentalization. Remember that the city's ways work for it and it will seek to protect and perpetuate them. The city both needs and rewards role-specific activity, so it will tend to resist or modify missios that attempt to involve the full selves of city dwellers. Systems resist modifications of status and role, and the city moves along as a combined project, carrying the inertia of multiple, separated, yet interdependent systems. Each of these interlocked systems expects fragmentary involvement of many participants, and their combined force keeps impersonal roles from being expanded or an individual's spheres of existence from being combined.

Because fragmentation, depersonalization and specialization serve the urban missio, urban dynamics will exert force on mission as they would on any remedial missio. The urban scheme for personhood encounters no conflicts if mission simply adds a dimension to the composition of the social self. However, significant individual and systemic tensions appear whenever an urban dweller seeks to live a fully integrated life. Thus, the city will seek to influence mission to become one of its many separate yet interdependent systems, and it will push mission to compartmentalize and depersonalize people in the same way that the city does. The urban wants all of the missios that operate within it to play by its rules, and if mission is to fit in with urban collaborative efficiency, it will be expected to organize itself as simply one more opportunity for urban dwellers to take on a partial involvement.

Because that efficiency is of value, both the mission agent and those she serves can find themselves urged quite forcefully to treat their own missional or religious lives as just one more specialized aspect of urban living. The city also can maintain its efficiency fairly easily if mission is just one more system that uses impersonal, fragmented roles to provide a particular service. If mission can be pushed to perform a single task that supplies an isolated facet of the city's needs, the city will gain benefit and not be disrupted. Thus, the unspoken rules of the urban "game" assume (and demand) that mission agents would treat their own missional selves, their missional work, those whom they serve in mission and their relations with those they serve as partial and discrete. The city makes it hard for city dwellers to engage anything except urbanism with full involvement. In its context, mission is expected to conduct itself as a specialization that stays within distinct, limited ranges of activity or focus, engaging city dwellers in carefully defined, impersonal modes, which do not access or involve the whole person. Tensions arise when the kingdom's competing "game" rules expect people to live fully-orbed missional lives that simply express in and through the urban situation.

Of course, the path of least resistance for mission agents is simply tc structure mission according to urban schemes. The incentive for doing so is that it makes it easier to involve urban dwellers, which can maximize participation and ease the pressures or costs of missional engagement.

However, this incentive prioritizes optimal collaboration and efficiency over human holism, which makes its appeal a tacit call upon mission to endorse the city's values. These are the social leverages, the resistances and yields that the urban landscape presents in order to influence Christian mission to adopt (and thus, support) urban ways and values.

In other words, the urban always will seek to make mission in its own image and according to its own likeness. Therefore, if urban ways are taken up without examination, as default templates for kingdom life, the city's fragmentations will become the ways of the kingdom, compartmentalizing mission expressions and kingdom relations. If this occurs, both mission agents and those whom they serve can experience diminished mission fulfillments and reduced kingdom lives. This follows naturally whenever mission performs a constricted, specialized task, whenever individuals live limited facets of their lives missionally, and whenever people attempt to yield only parts of the self to Christ.

Tragically, this can produce existential deficits in kingdom participants that parallel urban deficits, accompanied by similar desires for a more robust life, even when full life has been made available in Christ. For, when the individual's missional engagements and expressions have been rendered partial and compartmentalized, the kingdom (and kingdom life) can be experienced as fragmented and insufficient, not because it truly is, but simply because its social dimensions have been artificially conformed to organizational schemes that are designed to enhance collaborative efficiency and to elicit longing, rather than to foster human development.

Answering fragmentation. On the positive side, Kraft (1996) has observed that all cultures fail to provide for human living at some point, and that that point is a place of high potential for missional engagement. Thus, the needs of urban dwellers to find fullness and wholeness of life, and to encounter contexts in which the whole self is welcomed, integrated and fostered offer tremendous promise for mission work. Christianity's expectation that the whole life would be offered to God (Gal.2:20; Rom. 6:1-

23; Rom. 12:1-2; 1 Cor. 6:19-20) and its stance that the full self is inextricably involved in the solidarity of kingdom community (Jn. 17:10-23; 1 Cor. 12:4-27; Heb. 10:24-25; Eph. 4:25) is uniquely suited to resonate with the needs of the fragmented urban self, and mission agents have a tremendous opportunity to reach urban dwellers by meeting them at their experiences of fragmented personhood and deficit life.

One simple way that urban mission can step into the urban deficit and evade the trap of urban fragmentation is to avoid reductionistic mission tasking. This does not mean that urban mission cannot specialize. Rather, it means that when it specializes it does not allow restrictors to constrain its scope of expression. The key is not to avoid, for example, the missional specialization of disaster relief. The key is, however, not to allow restrictions to be placed upon that work to the degree that it becomes *only* disaster relief. Sufficient breadth of expression must be maintained to allow for a cup of cold water to be given *in the name of the Lord*, so that the meaning of missional activity remains recognizably representational and does not become reduced to the sociomaterial benefit that it renders.

Preserving missional scope can be difficult, though, because the city and its missios gain benefit in the currency that they value most when purely sociomaterial commodities are in play. To the city, religious or spiritual expenditures are ancillary, not critical, and as such, the urban missio has little to no incentive to foster them, while it has significant incentive to move religious and spiritual endeavors toward the achievement of sociomaterial goals.

This is not necessarily malicious, but it is a hazard. Of course, every missio seeks its unique ends and the means that are most suited to them. By nature, missios tend to draw energies to themselves in order to serve their aims. By the same nature, they resist yielding resources and energies to other projects. Thus, the city and its missios are predisposed to develop lopsided relationships with kingdom missios that advantage the urban at the cost of the kingdom. It is only natural for urban missios quite eagerly to recruit Christian mission to expend its own missional energies on urban concerns or projects, while it is unnatural for the city to expend its own energies on Christian mission aims.

Secular-Religious Relations

This is especially the case in western, secular cities, where worldviews place religion in subordinate or marginalized categories. Theoretically, on social levels, worldview and culture determine the perceived relative values of projects, as well as their relative claims and powers. If this is the case, it would follow that the degree to which a city is secularized would correlate to the degree of a city's unilateral expectation to receive yield from Christian missio toward itself, without rendering yield in return.

As an analogy, think of the ways that banks set fees and interest rates. Low-value customers are charged greater fees, while high-value customers are charged lower fees. Highest value customers pay no fees on the assumption that lowest value customers will offset the costs of doing business with high value customers. These relations depend on whether or not the bank sees itself as superior and needed by the customer, or as inferior and needing the customer. In the same way, although it is always natural for urban missios to take more than to give, the ratios of giving and taking are not set; they are established by relative values and powers. Thus, the degree to which a given urban missio considers itself empowered to receive and not to give depends on the relative statuses of the missios involved. Since religious missios are heavily marginalized in secular worldviews, in secular contexts, this challenge can become heightened, sometimes to a level of exploitation.

For example, across highly secularized western contexts, the expectation is commonplace that the Church and Christian mission should offer support to non-religious causes and organizations, as long as those are performing some sort of "good." Thus, mission is expected to lend voice, energies, personnel and material resources to remedial urban missios that accomplish a wide variety of charitable ends. However, at the same time, the right to determine what constitutes a "good" that is worthy of universal support is granted solely to secular discourses, and religious "good" is not allowed the same degree of claim as non-religious "good." Agents of secular missios may declare their own causes to be "good" in a way that entitles them to universal support, but agents of religious mission are not granted the same right to call their works "good," and enlist universal support. Thus, the expectation that religious mission would support "good" secular projects continues to obtain even when the same secular projects that expect missional support reserve the right to excuse themselves from supporting any and all religious aims or causes.

Because it resides in evaluative dimensions of the secular worldview, the imbalanced secular-religious relationship has become an enculturated norm that is largely invisible in western society, rarely if ever appearing in conscious consideration. Its power differentials only come into view when viewed using other focal-subsidiary groundings, such as business, interpersonal relations or political relations. In such cases, the inequality of this disposition becomes glaring. For, it would be socially fatal to a political party to openly proclaim, "We expect you to aid our cause with your resources, but we will not seek or support your interests in return." Likewise, it would be considered an exploitive social relationship for a person or group to take the posture, "You have no claim upon my loyalty, energy or goods, but I make a claim upon yours." In business, or even between cities, it is clearly understood that the idea of partnership prohibits a stance of "What's yours is mine, and what's mine is mine."

Frequently, however, secular urbanism conceals the exploitive character of its unilateralism by recasting its "receive-only" posture as a mark of ethical refinement. Ironically, in secular urban contexts it is commonly presented as a sign of objectivity and neutrality, even moral uprightness, when an organization withholds support or endorsement from religious ends, even when that project may recruit religious or missional support. Yet, the very expectation that Christian mission should accept such an imbalance as appropriate or "normal," without question or objection is itself a strong indicator that exploitation may be occurring. The startling reality that taking such a stance toward religious entities, alone, would be socially perceived as morally and ethically neutral, when it would be considered to be exploitive or inappropriate in other spheres of life illustrates all the more powerfully how pervasive systemic bias against religious work is and how deeply rooted the colonial secular attitude toward religious mission has become.

Alliances and partnerships. In the face of endemic exposure to imbalanced demands upon mission resources, mission agents would be well advised to exercise deep and recurrent discernment about their secular urban partnerships and alliances. Jesus' deliberate choices about his healings and miracles demonstrate clearly that he did not equate opportunity or need with missional calling. He chose one man at the pool of Bethesda, even though around the pool a multitude were waiting to be healed (Jn. 5:1-13). When the crowds stayed long because they wanted to hear and see him, he gave them bread and fish, but when they clamored and demanded bread, he refused and gave them teaching about himself (Jn. 6:1-71). Following Jesus' example, mission agents can take to heart the fact that urban opportunity is not urban calling, along with the related truth that they are free and not obliged to enter into unilateral support relationships with secular causes, especially when those would expend kingdom resources without acknowledgment of the king from whom those resources are given, even more if that is under restrictions that deliberately silence promotion of his kingdom and its interests.

Mission organizations likewise have every place to call potential partners into clear reciprocity. This does not require equitable resource flows; rather, it requires that mission would be not be rendered passive, silent or invisible. In most cases, Christian mission is called to give to the city and not to receive in return, but the gift nature of mission's expenditures cannot be lost. The identity of mission as offering on behalf of God and not as unquestionable obligation needs to be preserved. For, just as grace is not grace when it is earned, mission gifts are not given when they are demanded, especially when they are demanded without granting voice, choice or place to the Giver or his representative bodies and servants.

Image-based Evaluation and Decision-making

As mission agents face the challenge of vetting their resources and relationships, divine guidance and calling are paramount. However, sacred calling is not always obvious or specific, and in many instances mission agents have latitude to select missional aims. In those cases, a creational view can help the mission agent to make choices.

From the Genesis account, we can see that the divine goal for human existence is display of the image of God. Although the imago Dei is not described, we have seen that it involves representative action, self-awareness, relationship to God, relationship between male and female and relationship to the creation. These dimensions require a minimum array of capacities, exercised according to a minimum central disposition. At the very least, in order to fulfill reflection of the divine image, humans need to be able to be self-aware, reflexive, volitional, relational, dispositional and affective. And, as God's provisional blessing illustrates, these capacities are sustained when people have enough sustenance to survive.

Simply having these capacities is not enough, however. These capacities also need to be oriented toward God, toward each other and toward the creation as representative of the divine. They must point in appropriate directions, referring *to* God and *from* God.

Thus, mission can honor the image of God and partner in the missio Dei any time that it sustains, augments, protects or remediates damage to the human capacity to express divine image or any time that it corrects damage to appropriate human orientation. For example, when people have been relationally incapacitated, whether through oppression, trauma, illness or choice, mission rightfully can seek to repair that damage so that those people again can have the ability to relate to God, others and the world in divinely representative ways. Mission also can seek to protect relational capacity from being harmed in the first place, and it can seek to develop and augment existing relational capacities. The same holds true for the fostering and protection of volitional capacities that enable the individual to choose rightly, or the capacity for reflexive responsibility, for affective capacity, etc., that is, for any image-related human abilities that can become damaged by urban life and exploited by urban missios.

By the same token, mission rightly seeks to protect, augment and restore dispositional orientations. It appropriately seeks to repair damages that have turned people out of right alignments *toward* God, each other and the world, as well as damages that have turned people out of rightly pointing *from* God toward each other and the world. Mission seeks to protect these alignments from anything that would impair, hinder or misdirect them, and it seeks to augment and develop human capacity to express or "shine forth" their appropriate orientations to and from God.

Taken together, these aspects can supply a standard of reference for deciding what kinds of mission to prioritize, and what kinds of partnerships to engage. When evaluating their own efforts, the mission agent can seek to identify which dimensions of 1) human capacity to reflect the imago Dei, and 2) which orientations to or from God, others and creation are being sustained, augmented, protected or remediated. When looking at urban contexts, mission agents can use the same aspects as assessment criteria in order to discern which dimensions are most at risk or impaired, so that they can direct missional resources effectively. When considering alliances, mission organizations and agents can look to see how capacities and orientations are being addressed by potential partners in order to discern if potential partners have compatible aims.

This applies to cities or to organizations because they are institutional entities, for, as human expressions, institutions and organizations carry human traits and dimensions. Thus, mission organizations can examine the qualities of their own capacities and orientations in order to assess reflexively concerning the well-being of their own groups and projects. The same evaluations can be performed on cities as large entities or on other organizations. Mission agents thus can evaluate their own compatibility with a given city or with potential partner institutions by observing the capacities and orientations that characterize those entities, not only by the works that they are doing.

Having a view of the strengths and weaknesses across the full range of image capacities and orientations thus can help mission agents express mission in well-rounded ways. This in turn can assist them to set organizational goals that can develop their organizations and their mission projects as well as the cities in which they serve. As part of this process, discerning compatibility in terms of capacities and orientations can help mission agents to evaluate the liberties or limitations, benefits or liabilities that may attend potential joint efforts with other institutions, organizations and individuals.

Multiple scales. Because these criteria pertain to the image of God in humans, they also obtain beyond the urban context, even though they are useful to urban mission. Practically, they can be applied on scopes that range from a single individual up through family, group, institutional, systemic and universal scales, and mission legitimately can be directed toward any of these frames. Thus, mission can organize itself to serve the image capacities and orientations of cities, of systems, of institutions, of groups, of assemblages, of events, etc. For, since humans draw upon the divine image in order to live and exercise dominion, any place that humans make, any instance that humans act, and anything that humans seek to create will carry fundamental image traits, which can be evaluated using image-based assessment.

The simultaneous presence of multiple scales is important to remember, since, as we have seen, the city does not stand alone. While it embeds people and their projects within itself, it also is embedded in other projects, and it is subject to influences from its project partners. These influences receive their force and quality from both the scope and character of other missios, and they have affected the city and its missios severely, perhaps to a point that has compromised the very identity of the city.

Globalization

Although our scale of focus here has been the city, contemporary urban embeddedness in global frames cannot be ignored. Globalized and globalizing missios pervade the city, and they present constant and significant challenges to the mission agent. Most of these would require a missiological work on globalization or what Charles Van Engen calls "glocality" (2006) to explore, and we cannot treat them here with any depth. However, before we conclude, we need at least to note the global impact on the city and point to how globalization of the urban in turn may affect urban mission.

As many urban scholars have noted, especially Brenner and Schmid (2014) and Rickards, et al (2016), conceptions of the city that held through the 20th century no longer seem to have the same capacity to describe the urban. In the contemporary world, the connectedness of cities within webs of relations that extend in international, interregional, interurban ways has become characteristic and undeniable. To some degree, this has made cities unrecognizable and indefinable, even to urban specialists. This has led urban scholars to reconsider what the city actually might be, and to propose visions of the urban that transcend locality (Brenner & Schmid, 2014; Hall, 2001; Storper & Scott, 2015).

From the perspective of missio, these proposals may not indicate that previous understandings of the city were flawed as much as they reveal that we may be seeing the missio urbis succumb to more powerful agenda. For, although the city's adaptivity has been widely tested and proved sufficient throughout millennia, it still has limits, and the breakdown of its locality may indicate that those limits have been reached. Since missios are aimed at recognizable outcomes, any missio will have defining characteristics that set the boundaries of its ability to modify. These core purposes cannot be compromised without losing a missio's identity, its very reason to exist. When those purposes are lost, a missio loses itself, along with the identities of all things that are defined by it.

If we look at the vast history of the city, the urban always has had a local identity that grounded its attempts to draw to resources to itself for the benefit of its inhabitants. However, in today's world we find the urban's local character fading and under question as its networks, resources and attentions are drawn beyond its traditional boundaries. These days, we see the city stretched and pulled by involvements with missios of even greater scope, adaptivity and force, such as entrepreneurialism, capitalism, socialism, geo-politicalism, transnationalism, ethnism, etc. Along with the city, itself, all of those distinctly urban missios that cities developed to serve their needs now have become embedded in translocal missios in ways that mandate urban reliance upon the transurban. Cities no longer have the capacity to accomplish basic urban functions or meet basic urban needs, such as food supply, communications, infrastructure and real estate development, governance, banking, transportation, industry, technology, health care, recreation and entertainment (etc.) using urban-scale resources or urban-scale means.

This has placed the city on the horns of a dilemma that arises from its own missio, for it cannot fulfill its teleology to provide for local needs without surrendering its very locality. In the contemporary world, the power of larger missios has forced the city to choose between two options, both of which are fatal to the missio urbis: 1) to fulfill the ends for which it was created while losing the local identity that defined those ends, or 2) to seek to maintain its local identity at the cost of compromising the capacities and functions of its component missios, which would cause it to fail at gathering resources and at maintaining its systems and structures. Either of these options, losing locality or losing function, removes a key dimension of what the missio urbis is intended to do, which ultimately compromises its missional identity.

From what is apparent at this point in time, despite pocketed attempts at local sustainability and identity, it seems that the city has followed the first option. Prevailing urban management strategies have turned outward, looking beyond the city's borders under the influences of entrepreneurialism and market competition. Urban planning, land uses and space creation are dominated by meta-local gentrifying and capitalist missios; cities are networked and engaged in competition at numerous scales that stretch far beyond their hinterlands, etc. For virtually every aspect of the city, primary factor(s) of influence come from beyond, leaving the urban as a secondary influence, and hence, a secondary trait.

Missiologically speaking, the fact that transurban dynamics and their attendant characteristics are now considered to be urban traits may indicate that the core missio of the city effectively has been co-opted and subsumed by more dominant, broader scale missios. If it does not show that the urban project has been finally absorbed, at the very minimum it indicates that the idea of urbanity and the urban has been commandeered; that is, that the missio urbis has been subordinated to a point where it has become a sub-missio of larger meta-missios, since it is no longer recognizable without them. At this point, which case holds truer is not completely clear. All that missio-based examination can tell us with certainty is that the urban missio is under strain and in jeopardy.

Global-urban distress. With this in mind, it may be advisable for the mission agent to approach urban populations and the city itself as at risk, disoriented and vulnerable. If it is to be faithful well, mission needs to see those to whom it reaches, recognizing as best as it can the existential states and predicaments of others. Cities always have been bastions of safety for people, largely due to their capacities to self-contain as concentrated areas in which all facets of life can be met, and people come to them in hopes of gaining access to urban strength. It should not be lost upon mission agents, then, just how vulnerable and small the urban individual can feel when even the mighty city becomes subjected to meta-forces.

The city in its locality can been seen and known by its participants, and a sense of mutual place and solidarity results, which can give even the most informal city-dweller a degree of existential solidity. For all urban dwellers the city is "ours," and comfort comes from knowing that what "we" have "here" will continue because it is self-contained, collected and located. Likewise, the city and its sociospatial constructions historically have been suffused with qualities of confidence and security that rest upon the localization of urban resources as the city's locality empowers it to stockpile distinctly urban resources against exterior threats and against the future. Thus, both the city and its inhabitants can experience deep, unidentifiable insecurity when the urban becomes de-localized. The city loses its safety when its resources are owned and controlled without assignment to its place, when its systems and structures cannot function on their own, and when all that the city is becomes perforated, splayed out and subdued by inexorable, remote and often faceless powers.

Acknowledging the helplessness and need that this state of affairs can instill in the secularized, sociomaterially oriented city-dweller should move the mission agent to compassion, and to a degree of understanding as she observes urban populations that are disoriented, aimless or caught within spiraling cycles of sociomaterial pursuit, distraction and pleasuring. The city is not the kingdom; it does not have the kingdom's transcendent durability, its nobility, its security or its capacity to fulfill human existence. This is because the city does not have the kingdom's king. Given that this is the case, it is both the honor and the duty of urban mission to bridge the distance between the urban context and the kingdom, and to introduce the urban flock to the creation's shepherd king. Taking up this purpose, urban mission has the chance to reintroduce the city and its dwellers to their own forgotten creational humanity.

Summary

Space fails us to explore all of the many challenges and practices that urban mission faces. That is a task better suited to an applied examination. However, hopefully, these few points have illustrated some places where missiological analysis can arrive as it works its way from theory toward application.

That missiological path from theory to practice is the track that we have been tracing throughout this work. Recall that the aim of our exploration has been to introduce missiological interpretation in ways that could be understood and reproduced by undergraduate and graduate level students from multiple disciplines. In order to accomplish that we have traced a seven-step path, which we can now review.

The first goal was to understand the basic character of missiological interpretation. We did this by looking at missiology's disciplinary conversation about hermeneutics and by seeing where missiological concerns and commitments located missiological interpretation relative to other interpretive fields.

Our second step was to develop theoretical foundations that could support missiological interpretation. We did this by grounding interpretive agenda in the foundational concepts of missio and fulfillment. With these as bases, we used broader missiological commitments to develop missiological understandings of key interpretive issues. This allowed us to anchor our theoretical integrations of factors like authorial intention and presence, complex authorship, reading communities and reading horizons, metanarrative frames and reading outcomes.

After establishing our theoretical foundations, we proceeded to a third goal, which was the formation of method. In order to add rigor and show missiological versatility, we built two methods that could derive from the same set of foundational assumptions. These were the Topographic Analysis (TA), which focused on the production of outcomes, and Product,

Ground and Tool examination (PGT), which related the text to the metanarrative of the missio Dei.

Our fourth step was to perform missiological examination. In order to show how method could be used, we applied both TA and PGT to the creation account of Genesis 1. In order to demonstrate missiological interpretation without reliance upon method, we also used the foundational theoretical concept of missio as a lens to examine the city. This produced a missio-based reading of the city that could be compared to a missio-based reading of the biblical text. In order to demonstrate how missiological interpretation of biblical texts can intersect with interpretation of specific context, we then juxtaposed findings from our readings of text and city. This produced a distinctly missio-urban reading of both text and city, which was our fifth aim.

The rest of our work focused on missiological understanding and missional activity. This was a composite final aim to explore how to utilize missiological interpretation. The first part of this used our interpretive work as a springboard for broader missiological consideration and integration. First, we considered creational, kingdom and mission implications that arose from our joint reading. We then looked at those implications in light of missio-urban concerns. The second part focused on activity. There, we tried to anticipate special challenges of urban contexts, looking for potential mission practices that could support faithful mission expression of creation, kingdom and missio Dei within and toward the city.

Conclusion

At the very beginning of our discussion, we considered the meaning of a joke, comparing comprehension and experiential fulfillment. There, we saw that both dimensions are involved, but that outcome remains the primary factor in understanding. Over the course of the discussions that followed, we have seen that the same holds true for the Genesis 1 account, for the city, for the creation, for human existence and for the mission of God in the world. Purpose shows clearly in each of these, and all of them are aimed at ends that determine their identity and significance.

Put another way, whether in things below or things above, the punch line matters. Of course, it is valuable to perceive, to learn and to know, and without doubt, discovery, evaluation, analysis and description have places of worth. The quest to gain discernment about things urban, creational, divine and human has merit, and it should not be discounted. Still, the instrumentality of knowledge must always remain in view when we look for its merit. Knowledge for knowledge's sake is not much reward for the effort, and without purpose knowledge holds little to account for its own existence. Knowing is mostly good for nothing unless it is mostly good for something, and, in order to avoid an endless progression, the something that knowledge is good for needs to be good by virtue of being itself.

Further, while the end does not justify the means, it always informs it, and it should be taken into account at every point and from every angle. Like knowledge, mission is not self-justifying. It derives its value from the ends that it seeks, and its character is determined relative those ends. Just as it is valuable to know, it is valuable to act, but action for action's sake is as shallow of an endeavor as is knowing for knowing's sake.

Thus, if we are to know well and serve well, we would do well to keep the ends for knowing and serving constantly in focus, for neither the meaning of knowledge nor the meaning of mission can be contained or found in forms, manners, quantities and performances. The critical factor remains the quality of *toward-ness*, the *for-what* orientations of their aims and the dispositions of their purposes.

The same can be said of city, kingdom, creation and human life. These exist for reasons, and it is the proposal of this work that those reasons coincide at the glory of God and the fulfillment of his intentions. From the perspective of missiology, this is the punch line that determines the meaning of all reality, existence, time, space and action, in both kingdom and context.

Index

Aboue, P., 166
Abstraction: from texts. *See* Product, Ground and Tool
Academic disciplines: specialization, 28, *See* Lash, N.
Aesthetic response criticism, 37, 45, 88, 93, 99
Agency, 53, *See* Representation; presence; proxy; creational, 134; missional, 63
Agglomeration, 161, 173
Agriculture. *See* Provision
Allen, A., et al, 153, 185
Alternative reading strategies, 97
Anthonioz, S., 147
Austin, J. L., 44
Authority. *See* Governance; divine, 213
Authors: absence, 51; and intention, 46; complex, 129; composite, 67, *See*; God as, 67; living, 52; silencing, 53; silencing and self-assertion, 54; voice and presence, 52, *See* Voice
Authorship: joint, 50, 51, *See* Composition; joint, complex, 64

Ayers, A., 14, 21, 23, 70; Topographic Analysis, 86
Barram, M., 14, 15, 18, 22, 23, 25, 29, 31, 37, 67
Bartholomew, C., 22
Bauckham, R., 22, 39, 53
Baxter, R., 145
Bazzell, P., 21, 41
Beeby, H. D., 14, 15, 19, 23
Benefit: differential, 167
Benefit (and yield): urban, 166
Berger, P., 41, 50, 51, 75, 160
Bevans, S., 21, 34, 86
Beyaraaza, E., 199
Bible. *See* Sacred Texts, Canon; in history, 76
Birch, E., 168, 185
Bosch, D., 17, 18, 19, 20, 21, 23, 27, 30, 31, 34, 38, 44, 52, 57
Boundaries: creational, 183
Brenner, N., 155, 223
Brownson, J., 20, 23
Brueggemann, W., 131
Brugmann, J., 159, 168
Calvary: missio-urban view of, 214
Camagni, R., 144, 147
Camery-Hoggatt, J., 87, 89, 93
Canon, 106, 109, 125, 126

Carriker, T., 14, 17, 21
Catechesis, 139
Categorical description: of the urban, 156
Categories: creational, 123; humankind, 44; male and female, 118, 136
City. *See* Urban; as co-authored, 160; identity, 175; views of, 147
Communication: as presence, 52; medium, 70; holistic, 37
Composition: joint, 51, 67
Comprehension: (vs. response), 11, *See* Engagement: holistic; meaning: holistic; doing and saying; in worldview dimensions, 89
Concentration, 166; and extension, 173; vs. food production, 175
Context: and purpose, *missio Dei*, 32
Contexts: gaps between, 71
Contextual interpretation, 83
Contextualization, 76
Creation: categories, 115; of humans, 118, *See* Humankind
Critical Contextualization, 112
Curtis, E., 132

Damerow, P., 147
de Man, P., 50
Dechert, C., 153
Deconstruction, 50
Derrida, J., 50
Designed outcomes, 12
Differential value, 194
Discourse: described, 30; knowledge formation; academic disciplines, 29
Discourse criticism, 80
Divine proxy, 191
doing and saying, 13
Domestic life: security, 179
Dominion, 120, 130, 134, 136, 172, 178, *See* Humans; and development, 135; and power, 205; human, 117; representative, 178, 191, 192; urban vs. creational, 177
Eco, U., 44
Elliston, E., 19
Engagement: holistic, 89, 99; reader dynamism, 91; urban, 167
Entrepreneurialism. *See* Harvey, D.; kingdom vs. urban, 190
Equality: and social justice, 209

Evaluation: mission based, of urban, 214; of systems and features, 160
Events: expanding, 75
Existence: fragmented, 218
Existential diffusion, 218
Extension: food production, hinterlands, 176
Farias, I., 147
Female. *See* Humans, Categories; and male, 212
Fish, S., 50, 53, 96
Flaw of the Excluded Middle, 37, *See* Hiebert, P.; Natural and Supernatural
Focal-subsidiary understanding, 30, 66, 94, 161, 182, *See* Polanyi, M., Gadamer, H-G.
Food production, 174, 175
Foucault, M., 29, 50, 58; discursive practices, 29
Fulfillment: divine vs. urban, 188; in reading, 91; as discursive ground, 30; of human longing, 201; reading for, 99, 100; textual, 11, 45, *See* Intention
Gadamer, H-G., 71, 72, 73, 87, 96, 106; fore-grounding, fore-meaning, 30
Gallagher, R., 21, 23

Gallagher, S., 21
Gans, H., 156
Gender egalitarianism. *See* Humans; male and female
Glasser, A., 21
Globalization, 225
Global-urban distress, 225
Glocal: see footnote, 73
God: and metanarrative, 61; as author, 51, 132; as co-author, 57, 69; as urban co-producer, 161; creator, 132; emulation of, 141; glory of, 133; horizon with history, 79; intentions, 13, 29; social actor, 32, 45
Goheen, M., 22, 23
Good: as fulfillment of divine design, 128; righteousness, 127; secular, religious, 221
Good life, 135, 149, 175; kingdom vs. urban, 194; differential, 196; urban vs. creational, 179
Gospel: social and spiritual. *See* Mission; worldview; sociomaterial
Gottdiener, M., 147, 148, 185, 217
Gottdiener, Mark, 150
Governance: authority, 191; creational, 120; in Gen. 1,

130; creational, 190;
kingdom vs. urban, 190;
reflexive missio, 165;
creational, 184
Grand narrative. *See*
Metanarrative; Narrative
Green, J., 22, 24, 80, 84, 87, 102, 106; "Behind, In, In-front of" model, 85
Group identity, 138;
socioreligious, 140;
narrative, 130
Guder, D., 15
Hanson, P., 53, 72, 73
Harmony: creational, 172
Harvey, D., 164, *See*
Entrepreneurialism
Hermeneutic circle, 95;
missiological, 62
Hermeneutic location: urban-missiological, 143
Hermeneutics: defining questions, 29; definition, 20; western, 40
Hertig, P., 21, 23
Hiebert, P., 7, 21, 34, 35, 36, 53, 73, 74, 87, 89, 91, 95, 112, 163, 187, 201, 207
Historical gap, 12
History: missiological view, 39

Horizons: expanding, 76; reader, 70
Human dignity, 213
Human longing, 133, 139;
missional, 200
Human needs, 195; holistic, 186
Human nobility: and mission, 139
Human rights: and discourses, 208; and equality, 209;
complex, 208
Human value: by God, 133;
categorical, 180;
differential, 180; kingdom vs. urban, 194
Human welfare, 167; food production, 175; kingdom vs. urban, 194; urban vs. creational, 173
Humankind: creation, 118; event of, 79
Humans: as resources, 190;
divine provision, 134;
divine proxy, 132, 135;
divine representation, 189;
domestic life, 135, 140;
dominion, 120, 136;
features, 132; in divine image, 125; male and female, 118, 131, 136;
meaningful actors, 31;
nobility, 122; obligations,

122; responsibility vs. rights, 209; humanity, 44; welfare, 164

Humbert, P., 132

Hunsberger, G., 15, 22

Hutchison, R., 147, 148, 150, 185, 217

Ideological criticisms, 50, 53

Idolatry: and imago Dei, 125

Image: and likeness, 117, *Seeimago Dei*

imago Dei, 118, 121, 131; and human value, 195; as evaluative criterion, 223; human proxy, 135; male and female, 212

Institutions: as co-authors, 64

Intention, 47; agonistic, 64; and ostensive function, 45; and praxis, 47; complex, 129; complex, multilayered, 49

Interpretation: contextual, 41, 50, 53, 54, *See* Reading, vernacular; decentralized, 28, *See* Postcolonial interpretation: decentralizing

Iser, W., 44, 46, 87, 93, 94

Jayne, M., 143, 144, 147, 185

Joint composition: urban, 149

Jonsson, J., 23

Kingdom: and missio Dei, 56; as interpretive ground, 183, 188; atemporal and temporal, 39; governance, 189; now and not yet, 39, *See* Temporal frames; regency; agency, 189; now and not yet, 74; responsibility vs. rights, 209; simultaneous, 75; solidarity, 73; urban insurgency, 190

Kirk, J. A., 34, 37

Knowledge formation: discursive, 29; joint, composite, telltales, 64; focal-subsidiary; discursive; disciplinary, 30

Kraft, C., 21, 35, 41, 53, 74, 87, 91, 95, 220

Language games, 96, 105

Lash, N., 23, 25, 26, 27, 48, *See* Academic disciplines, *See* academic specialization; academic relay race

Likeness: and image, 117, *Seeimago Dei*

Lin, J., 33, 144

Luckmann, T., 41, 50, 51, 75, 160

Lyotard, J-F., 25, 50, 51, 58, 64, 65

Male. *See* Humans, Categories; and female, 212
Malpezzi, S., 180
Mapping: conceptual, sociolinguistic, 87
Matisse, H., 86
McFarlane,C., 155
McKinzie, G., 22
Meaning: as event, 42; as intention, purpose, 47; as phenomenon, 45; as response, 12; as situation, 94; as understanding and fulfillment, 90; breakdowns, 97; cumulative, 110; holistic, 89; dynamic, 94; idiomatic and social, 42; means vs. meant, 72; holistic dimensions, 89; as phenomenon, 40; stability, 50
Metanarrative, 182; and narratives, 61; as reference, 60; incredulity toward, 58
Metaphor. *See* Ricoeur, P.
Metaphysics, 37; essence, 43
Middleton, R., 132
missio: as interpretive criterion, 146; concept, 30
missio Dei, 56, 80, 127, 195; and context., 32; and missio urbis, 162; and missiology, 19; and the biblical reading event, 82; as metanarrative, 61; metanarrative and narratives, 61; concept, 30; remedial missio, 169; urbanization, 161
missio urbis, 149; and missio Dei, 162, 161; context, 156; and provision, 176; and social justice, 206; conflicted, 166; contextual expression, 154; limited good, 186; reflexive, 219; scalable, 156; in crisis, 224
Missiological hermeneutics, 9, 17; agenda, 29; and historical gap, 73; definition, 17; described, 20; diverse, 13; gestaltic, 42; holistic, 37; challenged, 28; interdisciplinary, 23; key approaches, 21; social attention, 31; spiritual and natural, 36; spiritually informed, 21
Missiological interpretation, 13, 109, *See* missiological hermeneutics; academic

location, 40; and divine authorship, 57; and metanarrative, 60; backgrounds, 23; goals, 98; holistic, 89; non-textual, 143; of contrasting purposes, 69; of the urban, 156; tapestry approach, 128

Missiological readers, 13

Missiology: academic field, 20; academic location, 19, 25; and epistemologies, 32; and metaphysics, 45; and other disciplines, 24; applied, 199; defining focus, 20; disciplinary aims, 12; diverse, inclusive, 32; interdisciplinary, 27; knowledge formation, 30

Mission: alliances and partnerships, 221; and divine honor, 135; and human longing, 200; and image-bearing, 136; and missiology, 18; and missions, 13; and sex traits, 136; and urban suffering, 203; appropriation of urban components, 195; as divine presence, 52; composite, 52; correlated to textual missio, 133; difficulty defining, 17; male and female, 140; faithfulness, 217; enduring project, 52; evaluation per imago Dei, 223; holistic, 37, 187, 220; human needs, 134; male and female, 212; minimum definition, 20; missio-urban concerns, 199; compatibility, 169; sacralizing, 162; scales, 223; secular-urban relations, 222; social and spiritual, 34; specialization, 219; universal vs. contextual, 133; urban challenges, 216; urbanized, 219; use of text, 109

Mission based interpretation, 22; challenged, 26

Mission hermeneutics, 14, 16, *See* Mission interpretation

Mission interpretation, 108

Mission partnerships. *See* Mission: secular-urban relations

Missional: appropriation, 163; explicit behavior, 62

Missional faithfulness, 201

Missional hermeneutics, 22

Missional interpretation, 17, 109, *See* Missiological hermeneutics; mission interpretation

Missios: categorical, 172; categorical description, 159; competing, 217; competition for space, agriculture, 176; corrective, remedial, 168; co-opted, 161; dynamic, 163; food production, 175; human rights, 209; reflexive, 165; remedial, 168; scales, 156; social justice, 207; urban, 156; transcendent, 169; transurban, 169; transurban, macro-, 156, 177; urban, urbanized, 156; urbanized, 155; variable scalability, 157

Missio-urban, 143, 162, 170; focal point, 156

Modernity: academics, 25; and meaning, 42; and missiology, 33

Monet, C., 12

Monotheism, 125, 129, 138

Muck, T., 23, 80

Narrative: and events, 59; and group identity, 130; traits, 58

Narratives, 61; subversive, 60, 139

Natural: and supernatural, 184

Newbigin, L., 30, 43, 53, 187

Nida, E., 21, 41

Nissen, J., 18, 21, 23, 27, 29, 72, 80

Okolo, C. B., 179, 217

Ong, W., 59

Orality, 130, *See* Ong, W.

Osborne, G., 23, 67, 72, 73

Outcomes: biblical, 45

Particular: vs. universal, 158

Peachey, P., 218

Place: and space, 172; creational, 173, 178; urban, 173

Place appropriation: urban, 177

Polanyi, M., 30, 32, 57, 66, 67, 78, 87, 91; subsidiary awareness, 30

Postcolonial, 23

Postcolonial interpretation, 53

Postmodern interpretation, 58; and meaning, 40, 42

Poverty: and wealth, 204, 205; forms, 140; of spirit, 139

Power, 205

Praxis: and intention, 47

Presence: group, 54

Product, Ground and Tool method, 86, 102, 128, *See* Topographic Analysis

Provision, 174, 195; holistic, 186; transcendent and sociomaterial, 186; urban, 176

Proxy, 135, *See* Representation; agency; communication, 52; images, 132

Purpose: and context, 32; and context, *missio Dei*, 32; and metaphysics, 43; as ground of inquiry, 29; composite, 66; discernibility, 62; hermeneutic agenda, 29; hermeneutic circle, 62; levels within texts, 67; of the city, 149; questioned, 33; textual, 11, *See* Textual purpose

Ramachandran, R., 177, 205

Reader effects: reading for, 100

Reader engagement: dynamic, 94

Reader longing, 121, *See* Human longing

Reader response criticism, 44, 47, 80, 87, 88, 93, 99

Reader-oriented theory, 50

Readers: expertise, 77; negotiation of texts, 92; first readers, 74

Reading: for fulfillment, 91; subversive, 60; vernacular, 41, 50, 53, 54

Reading communities: and textual architecture, 96; expanding, 75; first readers, contemporary readers, 76; kingdom, biblical, missional, 73; reading horizons, 74; biblical, 81

Reading outcomes, 11; competing, 97; Gen. 1, 137; range of response, 13; immediate, eventual, 126; spiritual, 88

Reciprocity: secular-urban, 222

Recursive missio. *See* Missios; reflexive missio

Redford, S., 15, 21, 22, 73, 88, 95

Reflexive missio, 164, 166, *See* Missios: reflexive

Representation, 53, 135; divine, 191; human, of God, 122; in communication, 52; sacred texts, 63; of intention, 45; via dominion, of God, 125; via mission, 52

Resistance and yield: textual. *See* Texts; urban, 167

Rickards, L., et al, 155, 223
Ricoeur, P., 80, 86, 92, 93
Righteousness: creational, 120, 127
Sabbath, 123, 124, 126, 132
Sacralization, 135, 162
Sacred texts, 13, 36, *See* Canon; explicit, 63
Scherer, J., 17, 18, 19, 27, 34
Schleiermacher, F., 19, 49, 71
Schmid, C., 155, 223
Schroeder, R., 21, 34
Scott, A., 147, 155, 185
Searle, J., 44, 50
Secularism: urban, 185
Settlement, 149
shalom, 44
Shaw, R. D., 21, 67, 81
Slomka, W., 213
Soares-Prabhu, G., 17, 18, 20, 23, 36
Social boundaries, 78, 139, 174, *See* Group identity
Social construction: of self, 218
Social game: *contra* constituency, 166; urban, 161, 168; urban and mission, 219
Social justice, 209
Social power: and urban mission, 206; creational, 211
Sociolinguistic proximity, 96
Sociomaterial: "good", 186
Socioreligious identity, 138, 140
Sociospatial: landscape, 167
Sociospatial constructs, 150
Sociospatial phenomenon, 143
Source criticism, 129
Space: displacement, 177; food production, 174; use, 176; natural, 172; shared, 172
Speech-acts: creational, 130
Spindler, M., 19, 23, 26, 34
Stewardship, 137
Storper, M., 147, 155
Stuhlmueller, C., 21, 27, 31, 38, 39, 52
sub-missios, 154, *See* missios
Sub-missios, 154, 159; as urban identifiers, 157; failures, 168; interactions, 168; jointly produced, 158; meanings of, 160; recurrent combinations, 158; urban (defined), 155
Subsidiary awareness, 30, *See* Focal-subsidiary understanding, *See* Polanyi, M.
Sugirtharajah, R. S., 53, 54
Supernatural: and natural, 184, *See* Flaw of the Excluded Middle

Swilling, M., 153, 158, 185
Taber, C., 23, 27, 31, 32, 41
Taylor, P. J., et al, 177
Teleology, 37; and meaning, 45; and social design, 45; human, 185; of the city, 149; urban, 224
Temporal frames: kingdom time, 39
Text fulfillment, 11, *See* Reading outcomes
Texts: and metanarratives, 60; as landscapes, 91; autonomous, 50; autonomous, horizons, 71; instrumental potentials, 81; instrumentality, 109; joint composition. *See* Composition; authorship; authors; purpose laden, 65; resistance and yield, 92; simple wholes, 36; sociolinguistic landscapes, 86; use vs. abuse, 110
Textual architecture: and alternative reading, 97; stability, 96
Textual architectures, 91
Textual backgrounds, 128
Textual dynamics: reading for, 99
Textual dynamism, 91
Textual inexhaustibility, 106
Textual missio: restructured, 97
Textual purpose, 11, 13
Textual reenactment, 105
Textual scales, 95
Thiselton, A., 49, 72, 73, 80
Time: and event scales, 79; and kingdom, 38; discursive, 75; kingdom, 74
Topographic Analysis, 86; as missiological method, 101; steps, 99
Topographic space, 93
Tradition, 71; and textual architecture, 95; stability of language, 96
Transactionalism, 196
Transcendent: and sociomaterial, 186
Transcendent missios. *See* missios
Urban: agglomeration, 147; co-production, 160; design, 145; described, 144, 145; extension, 148; uniqueness, 158
Urban benefit. *See* Good life
Urban breakdowns, 168
Urban concentration, 148, *See* Concentration; *missio urbis*; urban extension

Urban extension, 148, 173, *See* Concentration; *missio urbis;* urban concentration
Urban features: form and meaning, 159
Urban locality: and missio urbis, definition of the city, 224
Urban malaise, 218
Urban saturation, 217
Urban scale: scales, 156
Urban self-protection, 165
Urban studies: and missiology, 143; interdisciplinary, 143
Urban suffering, 204
Urbanization, 155, 169
Urban-missiological, 159, 170, *See* missio-urban
Van Engen, C., 20, 21, 23, 31, 34, 67, 73, 80, 81, 101, 128, 223
Verkuyl, J., 19, 34
Vernacular reading, 83
Verstraelen, F. J., 19, 34
Voice: authorial, 52, *See* Authors; silencing, 53
von Rad, G., 117, 131, 132
Wachter, S., 168, 185
Ward, K., 143, 144, 147, 185, *See* Jayne, M.
Wealth: and poverty, 204; problem of, 205

Weissner, P. and W. Schiefenhovel, 205
Wilson, H., 145
Wimsatt, W. K. and M Beardsley: *The Intentional Fallacy*, 49, *See* Authors; Voice; Intention
Wisdom tradition, 125, 131; wise women (Tekoa), 131
Witness, 46; as word and deed, 37
Wittgenstein, L., 44, 79, 96, 105, 106, *See* social games; language games
Word: and deed, 37
Worldview: and textual architecture, 95; and time, 74; dimensions of. *See* Hiebert, P.; dimensions of, 89; natural and supernatural, 37, *See* metaphysics; teleology; Flaw of the excluded Middle; Hiebert, P.; western, 33, 53
Wright, C., 14, 15, 20, 21, 23, 27, 31, 44, 87
Wright, Christopher, 20, 91

Works Cited

Aboue, P. O. (2004). Globalization, rural poverty and institution building in Nigeria. In T. Falola & S. J. Salm (Eds.), *Globalization and urbanization in Africa*. Trenton; Asmara: Africa World Press.

Allen, A., Swilling, M., & Lampis, A. (2016). Why untamed urbanisms? In A. Allen, M. Swilling & A. Lampis (Eds.), *Untamed urbanisms*.

Anderson, B. (2017). Affect. In M. Jayne & K. Ward (Eds.), *Urban theory: new critical perspectives*. London and New York: Routledge.

Anthonioz, S. p. (2014). Cities of glory and cities of pride. In D. V. Edelman & E. Ben Zvi (Eds.), *Memory and the city in ancient Israel*. Winona Lake, Ind.: Eisenbrauns.

Austin, J. L. (1962). *How to Do Things with Words*. Cambridge: Harvard University Press.

Ayers, A. (2011). *In Search of the Contours of a Missiological Hermeneutic*. PhD Dissertation, Fuller Theological Seminary, Pasadena. Available from http://worldcat.org /z-wcorg/ database.

Ayers, A. (2012). Bible as Product, Ground and Tool of Mission (syllabus and lectures) *MT 500 Biblical Theology of Mission*. Irvine, CA: Fuller Theological Seminary.

Ayers, A. (2017). Group Identities and Boundaries during the Pauline Mission *American Society of Missiology series* (Vol. 53, pp. 146-158).

Baltazar, E. (1991). Philippine urbanization and Christian values. In G. F. McLean & J. Kromkowski (Eds.), *Urbanization and values*. Washington, D.C.: Council for Research in Values and Philosophy.

Barr, J. (1968). The image of God in the book of Genesis: a study of terminology. *Bulletin of the John Rylands Library, 51*, 11-26.

Barram, M. D. (2006). *Mission and Moral Reflection in Paul*: New York.

Barram, M. D. (2007). The Bible, Mission, and Social Location: Toward a Missional Hermeneutic. *Interpretation, 61*(1), 42-58.

Barth, K. (1958). *Church Dogmatics; v 3, pt 1* (O. B. a. H. K. J.W. Edwards, Trans.). Edinburgh: T & T Clark, 1958.

Bauckham, R. (2003). *Bible and Mission: Christian Witness in a Postmodern World*. Grand Rapids, MI: Baker Academic.

Baxter, R. (2017). Architecture. In M. Jayne & K. Ward (Eds.), *Urban theory: new critical perspectives*. London and New York: Routledge.

Bazzell, P. D. (2018). *Urban Ecclesiology: Gospel of Mark, familia dei and a Filipino community facing homelessness*. [S.l.]: Bloomsbury T & T Clark.

Beeby, H. D. (2000). A Missional Approach to Renewed Interpretation *Renewing Biblical Interpretation* (pp. 268-283). Grand Rapids, Mich.: Zondervan.

Berger, P. L., & Luckmann, T. (1967). *The Social Construction of Reality: A Treatise in the Sociology of Knowledge*: London.

Betancourt, D. S. (2016). Public spaces and transformative urban practices in Cape Town. In A. Allen, M. Swilling & A. Lampis (Eds.), *Untamed urbanisms*.

Bevans, S. B. (1992). *Models of Contextual Theology*. Maryknoll, N.Y.: Orbis Books.

Bevans, S. B., & Schroeder, R. (2004). *Constants in Context: A Theology of Mission for Today*: Orbis Books.

Beyaraaza, E. (1991). Cultural differences and value clashes in African cities. In G. F. McLean & J. Kromkowski (Eds.), *Urbanization and values*. Washington, D.C.: Council for Research in Values and Philosophy.

Biblia Hebraica Stuttgartensia (1977). (LinguistsSoftware, Trans. Hebrew Scriptures in Unicode 2017 ed.). Stuttgart: Deutsche Bibelgesellschaft.

Birch, E. L., & Wachter, S. M. (Eds.). (2011). *Global urbanization*. Philadelphia: University of Pennsylvania Press.

Bosch, D. (1986). Towards a Hermeneutic for "Biblical Studies and Mission". *Mission Studies, 3*(2), 65-79.

Bosch, D. (1991). *Transforming Mission: Paradigm Shifts in Theology of Mission*. Maryknoll, N.Y.: Orbis Books.

Bosch, D. (2006). *Witness to the World: The Christian Mission in Theological Perspective*. Eugene, Oregon: Wipf and Stock.

BrainyQuote. (2018) Retrieved May 10, 2018, from
https://www.brainyquote.com/fr/citation/claude-monet_141383

Brenner, N., & Schmid, C. (2014). The 'urban age' in question. *Int. J. Urban Reg. Res. International Journal of Urban and Regional Research, 38*(3), 731-755.

Brown, R. M. (1984). *Unexpected News: Reading the Bible with Third World Eyes* (1st ed.). Philadelphia: Westminster Press.

Brown, W. P. (1993). *Structure, role, and ideology in the Hebrew and Greek texts of Genesis 1:1-2:3*. Atlanta, Ga.: Scholars Press.

Brownson, J. V. (1998). *Speaking the Truth in Love: New Testament Resources for a Missional Hermeneutic*. Harrisburg, Pa.: Trinity Press International.

Brueggemann, W. (1982). *Genesis*. Atlanta: John Knox Press.

Brugmann, J. (2010). *Welcome to the Urban Revolution How Cities Are Changing the World (advance copy unrevised)*. ~xxx: Bloomsbury Publishing PLC.

Camagni, R. (2001). The economic role and spatial contradictions of global city-regions: the functional, cognitive and evolutionary context. In A. J. Scott (Ed.), *Global city-regions: trends, theory, policy* (pp. 96-118). Cambridge, UK; New York: Oxford University Press.

Camery-Hoggatt, J. (1992). *Irony in Mark's Gospel: Text and Subtext*. [S.l.]: Cambridge Univ Pr.

Carriker, C. T. (1994). *Paul's Apocalyptic Mission: An Integrative Missiological Hermeneutic.*

claude-monet.com. (2018) Retrieved May 10, 2018, from https://www.claude-monet.com/quotes.jsp

Clines, D. J. A. (1968). The image of God in man. *Tyndale Bulletin, 19,* 53-103.

Costas, O. (1989). *Liberating News: A Theology of Contextual Evangelization.* Grand Rapids, MI: Eerdmans.

CSIPDH. (2012). Global Charter-Agenda for Human Rights in the City. Barcelona: United Cities and Local Governments Committee on Social Inclusion, Participatory Democracy and Human Rights.

Curtis, E. M. (1984). *Man as the image of God in Genesis in the light of ancient Near Eastern parallels.* (Ph. D.) Thesis/dissertation (deg); Manuscript (mss), University of Pennsylvania. WorldCat Man as the image of God in Genesis in the light of ancient Near Eastern parallels / Edward Mason Curtis 1985, 1984 English Book : Thesis/dissertation/manuscript Archival Material xiii, 415 p. database.

Damerow, P. (1998). Food production and social status as documented in proto-cuneiform texts. In P. Weissner & W. Schiefenhovel (Eds.), *Food and the Status Quest.* Providence and Oxford: Berghahn Books.

de Groot, A. (1995). One Bible and Many Interpretive Contexts: Hermeneutics in Missiology. In F. J. Verstraelen, A. Camps, L.A. Hoedemaker and M.R. Spindler (Ed.), *Missiology: An Ecumenical Introduction: Texts and Contexts of Global Christianity* (pp. 237-252). Grand Rapids: Eerdmans.

de Man, P. (1986). *The Resistance to Theory.* Minneapolis: University of Minnesota Press.

Dechert, C. R. (1991). Functional differentiation, hierarchy and subsidiarity in community analysis. In G. F. McLean & J. Kromkowski (Eds.),

Urbanization and values. Washington, D.C.: Council for Research in Values and Philosophy.

Derrida, J. (1988). *Limited Inc*. Evanston, IL: Northwestern University Press.

Eco, U. (1979). *The Role of the Reader: Explorations in the Semiotics of Texts*. Bloomington: Indiana University Press.

ECORP. (1994). A declaration on the promotion of patients' rights in Europe. Amsterdam: European Consultation on the Rights of Patients - World Health Organization Regional Office for Europe.

Elliston, E. (2007). *Introduction to Missiological Research Design* Unpublished MS Guide. Fuller Theological Seminary, Pasadena.

The English Standard Version Bible - containing the Old and New Testaments with Apocrypha. (2009). New York: Oxford University Press.

Fainstein, S. (2001). Inequality in global city-regions. In A. J. Scott (Ed.), *Global city-regions: trends, theory, policy*. Cambridge, UK; New York: Oxford University Press.

Falola, T., & Salm, S. J. (2004). *Globalization and urbanization in Africa*. Trenton; Asmara: Africa World Press.

Farias, I. (2017). Assemblages. In M. Jayne & K. Ward (Eds.), *Urban theory: new critical perspectives*. London and New York: Routledge.

Fish, S. E. (1982). *Is There a Text in This Class?* Cambridge, Mass: Harvard Univ Pr.

Flam, J. D. (1978). *Matisse on Art*. New York: E.P. Dutton.

Fobil, J. N., & Atuguba, R. A. (2004). Ghana: migration and the urban complex. In T. Falola & S. J. Salm (Eds.), *Globalization and urbanization in Africa*. Trenton; Asmara: Africa World Press.

Foucault, M. (1972). *The Archaeology of Knowledge. Uniform Title: Archéologie du Savoir. English* ([1st American] ed.). New York: Pantheon Books.

Frost, M. H. A. (2003). *The Shaping of Things to Come: Innovation and Mission for the 21st-century Church*: Hendrickson Publishers.

Gadamer, H.-G. (2004). *Truth and Method* (2., rev. ed.). London: New York.

Gallagher, R. L., & Hertig, P. (2007). *Mission in Acts: ancient narratives in contemporary context*. Maryknoll, N.Y.: Orbis Books.

Gallagher, R. L., Hertig, P., & Engen, C. E. v. (2017). *Contemporary Mission Theology: Engaging the Nations: essays in honor of Charles E. Van Engen*.

Gallagher, S. D. (2014). *Abrahamic blessing: a missiological narrative of revival in Papua New Guinea*.

Gans, H. (2009). Some problems of and futures for urban sociology: toward a sociology of settlements. *City and Community, 8*(3), 211-219.

Gans, H. (2015). America's Two Urban Sociologies. *CICO City & Community, 14*(3), 239-241.

Geertz, C. (1973). The interpretation of cultures: selected essays, from http://purl.fdlp.gov/GPO/gpo12195

Gibbs, E., & Bolger, R. K. (2005). *Emerging Churches: Creating Christian Community in Postmodern Cultures*. Grand Rapids: Baker Academic.

Glasser, A. F., & Van Engen, C. (2003). *Announcing the Kingdom: The Story of God's Mission in the Bible*. Grand Rapids, Mich.: Baker Academic.

Goheen, M. (2017, May 14). Notes Toward a Framework for a Missional Hermeneutic. Retrieved from https://gocn.org/library/notes-toward-a-framework-for-a-missional-hermeneutic/

González, J. L. (1996). *Santa Biblia: The Bible through Hispanic Eyes*. Nashville: Abingdon Press.

Gottdiener, M., & Hutchison, R. (2011). *The New Urban Sociology* (fourth ed.). Boulder, Col.: Westview Press.

Grace, T. A. o. (2018) Retrieved May 10, 2018, from https://thearkofgrace.com/2013/06/13/claude-monet-quotations/

Green, J. (2011). [Personal Conversation at Fuller Theological Seminary 04/18/2011].

Guder, D. L., & Barrett, L. (1998). *Missional Church: A Vision for the Sending of the Church in North America*. Grand Rapids, Mich.: W.B. Eerdmans Pub.

Hall, P. (2001). Global city-regions in the twenty-first century. In A. J. Scott (Ed.), *Global city-regions: trends, theory, policy*. Cambridge, UK; New York: Oxford University Press.

Hanson, P. D. (1985). The Responsibility of Biblical Theology to Communities of Faith. *Ex auditu, 1*, 54-62.

Harvey, D. (1989). From Managerialism to Entrepreneurialism: The Transformation in Urban Governance in Late Capitalism. *Geografiska Annaler. Series B, Human Geography Geografiska Annaler. Series B, Human Geography, 71*(1), 3.

Hassing, R. (2013). Laws versus Teleology. In B. Kaldis (Ed.), *Encyclopedia of Philosophy and the Social Sciences* (Vol. 2, pp. 549-555): Sage Publications.

Haysom, G. (2016). Urban-scale food system governance: an alternative response to the dominant paradigm? In A. Allen, M. Swilling & A. Lampis (Eds.), *Untamed urbanisms*.

Hiebert, P. G. (1982). The Flaw of the Excluded Middle. *Missiology, 10*(1), 35-47.

Hiebert, P. G. (1983). The Category 'Christian' in the mission task. *International Review of Mission, 72*, 421-427.

Hiebert, P. G. (1985). *Anthropological Insights for Missionaries*. Grand Rapids, Mich.: Baker Book House.

Hiebert, P. G. (1987). Critical Contextualization. *International Bulletin of Missionary Research, 11*(3), 104-112.

Hiebert, P. G. (1994). *Anthropological Reflections on Missiological Issues*. Grand Rapids: Baker Bk House.

Hiebert, P. G. (2008). *Transforming Worldviews: An Anthropological Understanding of How People Change*. Grand Rapids: Baker Academic.

Hiebert, P. G., & Meneses, E. H. (1999). *Incarnational Ministry: Planting Churches in Band, Tribal, Peasant, and Urban Societies*. Grand Rapids (Mich.): Baker books.

Hirsch, A. (2006). *The Forgotten Ways: Reactivating the Missional Church*: Brazos Press.

Holston, J. (2001). Urban citizenship and globalization. In A. J. Scott (Ed.), *Global city-regions: trends, theory, policy*. Cambridge, UK; New York: Oxford University Press.

The Holy Bible containing the Old and New Testaments with the Apocryphal/Deuterocanonical books: new revised standard version. (2006). New York; London: Oxford University Press.

The Holy Bible: revised standard version. (1952). London.

Humbert, P. (1940). *Etudes sur le recit du paradis et de la chute dans la Genese*. Neuchatel: Secretariat de l'Universite.

Hunsberger, G. (2011). Proposals for a Missional Hermeneutic: Mapping a Conversation. *Missiology: An International Review, 39*(3), 310-321.

Hunsberger, G. (2016). Mapping the Missional Hermeneutics Conversation. In M. Goheen (Ed.), *Reading the Bible Missionally* (pp. 45-67). Grand Rapids: Eerdmans.

Iser, W. (1980). *The Act of Reading: A Theory of Aesthetic Response / Uniform Title: Akt des Lesens. English* (Johns Hopkins Paperbacks ed.). Baltimore: Johns Hopkins University Press.

Jayne, M., & Ward, K. (2017). *Urban theory: new critical perspectives*. London: Routledge.

Jeanrond, W. G. (1988). *Text and Interpretation as Categories of Theological Thinking / Uniform Title: Text und Interpretation als Kategorien theologischen Denkens. English*. New York: Crossroad.

Jonsson, J. N. (1987). Retranspositionalization: Missiological Hermeneutics within the Socio-Human Context. *Review & Expositor, 84*(1), 99-117.

Keating, M. (2001). Governing cities and regions: territorial restructuring in a global age. In A. J. Scott (Ed.), *Global city-regions: trends, theory, policy*. Cambridge, UK; New York: Oxford University Press.

Keil, C. F., & Delitzsch, F. (1981). *Commentary on the Old Testament*. Grand Rapids, MI: Eerdmans.

Kirk, J. A. (2000). *What is Mission?: Theological Explorations*. MInneapolis: Fortress Press.

Kraft, C. H. (1983). *Communication Theory for Christian Witness*. Nashville: Abingdon.

Kraft, C. H. (1991). *Communication Theory for Christian Witness (revised)*. Maryknoll: Orbis.

Kraft, C. H. (1996). *Anthropology for Christian Witness*. Maryknoll, N.Y.: Orbis Books.

Kraft, C. H. (2001). *Culture, Communication, and Christianity: A Selection of Writings*. Pasadena, Calif.: William Carey Library.

Kraft, C. H. (2005). *Christianity in Culture* (Revised 25th Anniversary ed.). Maryknoll: Orbis.

Kraft, C. H. (2008). *Worldview for Christian Witness*. Pasadena: William Carey Library.

Landis, J. D. (2011). Urban Growth Models: state of the art and prospects. In E. L. Birch & S. M. Wachter (Eds.), *Global urbanization*. Philadelphia: University of Pennsylvania Press.

Lash, N. (1985). What Might Martyrdom Mean? *Ex auditu, 1*, 14-24.

Lawton, P. (2016). Beyond an imaginary of power? Governance, supranational organizations and 'just' urbanization. In A. Allen, M. Swilling & A. Lampis (Eds.), *Untamed urbanisms*.

Lin, J. W.-B. (2016). *The Nature of Environmental Stewardship: Understanding Creation Care Solutions to Environmental Problems*. Eugene: Wipf and Stock Publishers.

Longhurst, R. (2017). Bodies. In M. Jayne & K. Ward (Eds.), *Urban theory: new critical perspectives*. London and New York: Routledge.

Lulek, A., & Paga, L. (1991). Freedom, equality and economic policy. In G. F. McLean & J. Kromkowski (Eds.), *Urbanization and values*. Washington, D.C.: Council for Research in Values and Philosophy.

Lyotard, J.-F. (1993). *The Postmodern Condition: A Report on Knowledge / Uniform title: La Condition postmoderne: rapport sur le savoir*. (G. B. a. B. Massumi, Trans.). Minneapolis: University of Minnesota Press.

MacDonald, N. B. (2000). The Philosophy of Language and the Renewal of Biblical Hermeneutics *Renewing Biblical Interpretation* (pp. 123-144). Carlisle [England] Grand Rapids, Mich. [Cheltenham, England] [Swindon, England]: Paternoster Press Zondervan Cheltenham & Gloucester College of Higher Education British & Foreign Bible Society.

MacIntyre, A. (1989). Epistemological Crises, Dramatic Narrative, and the Philosophy of Science. In S. Hauerwas, L. Gregory Jones (Ed.), *Why Narrative?: Readings in Narrative Theology* (pp. 138-157). Grand Rapids: Eerdmans.

Malpezzi, S. (2011). Urban growth and development at six scales: an economist's view. In E. L. Birch & S. M. Wachter (Eds.), *Global urbanization*. Philadelphia: University of Pennsylvania Press.

McFarlane, C. (2017). Learning. In M. Jayne & K. Ward (Eds.), *Urban theory: new critical perspectives*. London and New York: Routledge.

McKinzie, G. (2014). Currents in Missional Hermeneutics. *Missio Dei: A Journal of Missional Theology and Praxis* 5(1), 19-47.

Meyer, B. F. (1985). Conversion and the Hermeneutics of Consent. *Ex auditu, 1*, 36-46.

Middleton, J. R. (2005). *The Liberating Image: The Imago Dei in Genesis 1*. Grand Rapids, Mich.: Brazos Press.

Moore, S. D. (1989). *Literary Criticism and the Gospels: The Theoretical Challenge*. New Haven: Yale Univ Pr.

Muck, T. C. (2003). The Missiological Perspective: What Does it Mean to Read the Bible Missiologically? *Missiology, 31*(4), 395-396.

Mukherjee, J. (2016). Sustainable flows between Kolkata and its peri-urban interface: challenges and opportunities. In A. Allen, M. Swilling & A. Lampis (Eds.), *Untamed urbanisms*.

Mustol, J. (2017). *Dusty Earthlings: Living as eco-physical beings in God's eco-physical world*. [S.l.]: Lutterworth Press.

Myers, G. (2011). *African cities: alternative visions of urban theory and practice*. New York, N.Y: Zed.

Newbigin, L. (1986). *Foolishness to the Greeks*. Grand Rapids: Eerdmans.

Nida, E. A. (1960). *Message and Mission: The Communication of the Christian Faith*. New York: Harper.

Nida, E. A. (1984). *Signs, Sense, Translation*. Roggebaai, Cape Town: Bible Soc of South Africa.

Nissen, J. (2002). Matthew, Mission and Method. *International Review of Mission, 91*(360), 73-86.

Nissen, J. (2004a). *New Testament and Mission: Historical and Hermeneutical Perspectives*. Frankfurt am Main: Peter Lang.

Nissen, J. (2004b). Testament in Mission: The Use of the New Methodological and Hermeneutical Reflections. *Mission Studies, 21*(2), 167-199.

O'Flaherty, B. (2005). *City economics*. Cambridge, Mass.: Harvard University Press.

Okolo, C. B. (1991). Urbanization and traditional African values. In G. F. McLean & J. Kromkowski (Eds.), *Urbanization and values*. Washington, D.C.: Council for Research in Values and Philosophy.

Ong, W. J. (1982). *Orality and Literacy: The Technologizing of the Word*. London: New York.

Osborne, G. R. (1991). *The Hermeneutical Spiral: A Comprehensive Introduction to Biblical Interpretation*. Downers Grove, Ill.: InterVarsity Press.

Papanikolaou, V. (1991). The nature of the political community. In G. F. McLean & J. Kromkowski (Eds.), *Urbanization and values*. Washington, D.C.: Council for Research in Values and Philosophy.

Peachey, P. (1991). The city: atelier of the autonomous person. In G. F. McLean & J. Kromkowski (Eds.), *Urbanization and values*. Washington, D.C.: Council for Research in Values and Philosophy.

Polanyi, M., & Prosch, H. (1975). *Meaning*. Chicago: University of Chicago Press.

Ramachandran, R. (1996). *Urbanization and urban systems in India*. Delhi [u. a.: Oxford Univ. Press.

Redford, S. (2007). *Constructing a Biblically Informed and Spiritually Grounded Missiological Hermeneutic: In Search of Grace-Filled Mission Practice*. Thesis/dissertation (deg); Manuscript (mss). Available from Oclc WorldCat database.

Redford, S. (2012). *Missiological Hermeneutics: Biblical Interpretation for the Global Church*. Eugene, OR: Pickwick Publications.

Redford, S. (2016). Innovations in missiological hermeneutics. In C. V. Engen (Ed.), *The state of missiology today: global innovations in Christian witness* (pp. 38-61): IVP Academic.

Rickards, L., Gleeson, B., Boyle, M., & O'Callaghan, C. (2016). Urban studies after the age of the city. *Urban Stud. Urban Studies, 53*(8), 1523-1541.

Ricoeur, P. (2003). *The Rule of Metaphor: The Creation of Meaning in Language / Uniform Title: Métaphore vive. English* London: Routledge.

Robertson, T., & Atkins, P. (2018). Essential vs. Accidental Properties. In E. N. Zalta (Ed.), *The Stanford Encyclopedia of Philosophy* (Spring 2018 ed.).

Robinson, J. (2005). Urban geography: world cities, or a world of cities. *Progress in Human Geography, 29*(6), 757-765.

Rosenblueth, A., Wiener, N., & Bigelow, J. (1943). Behavior, Purpose and Teleology. *philscie Philosophy of Science, 10*(1), 18-24.

Roxborogh, J. (2009). *Missiology after Mission?* Paper presented at the ANZAMS Symposium, Laidlaw College.

Sassen, S. (2001). Global cities and global city-regions: a comparison. In A. J. Scott (Ed.), *Global city-regions: trends, theory, policy*. Cambridge, UK; New York: Oxford University Press.

Saussure, F. d. (1986). *Course in General Linguistics* (R. Harris, Trans.). Chicago and La Salle, Illinois: Open Court.

Sawyer, J. F. A. (1974). Meaning of bselem Elohim (In the image of God) in Genesis I-XI. *Journal of Theological Studies, 25*(2), 418-426.

Scherer, J. A. (1987). Missiology as a Discipline and What it Includes. *Missiology, 15*(4), 507-528.

Schmemann, A. (1961). The Missionary Imperative in the Orthodox Tradition. In G. Anderson (Ed.), *The Theology of the Christian Mission* (pp. 250-257). New York: McGraw-HIll.

Schneck, S. (1991). City and Village. In G. F. McLean & J. Kromkowski (Eds.), *Urbanization and Values*. Washington, D.C.: Council for Research in Values and Philosophy.

Schule, A. (2005). Made in the "image of God": the concepts of divine images in Gen 1-3. *Zeitschrift fuhr die alttestamentliche Wissenschaft, 117*(1), 1-20.

Scott, A. J. (2001). *Global city-regions: trends, theory, policy*. Oxford [u.a.]: Oxford Univ. Press.

Scott, A. J., Agnew, J., Soja, E. W., & Storper, M. (2001). Global City-Regions. In A. J. Scott (Ed.), *Global city-regions: trends, theory, policy*. Cambridge, UK; New York: Oxford University Press.

Searle, J. R. (1969). *Speech Acts: An Essay in the Philosophy of Language*: Cambridge University Press.

Senior, D., & Stuhlmueller, C. (1983). *The Biblical Foundations for Mission*. Maryknoll, N.Y.: Orbis Books.

Seto, K. (2011). Monitoring urban growth and its environmental impacts using remote sensing: examples from China and India. In E. L. Birch & S. M. Wachter (Eds.), *Global urbanization*. Philadelphia: University of Pennsylvania Press.

Shaw, R. D., & Engen, C. V. (2003). *Communicating God's Word in a Complex World: God's Truth or Hocus Pocus?* Oxford: Rowman and Littlefield.

Shaw, R. D., & Van Engen, C. (2003). *Communicating God's Word in a Complex World: God's Truth or Hocus Pocus?* Oxford: Rowman and Littlefield.

Sheppard, S. (2011). Measuring and modeling global urban expansion. In E. L. Birch & S. M. Wachter (Eds.), *Global urbanization*. Philadelphia: University of Pennsylvania Press.

Simone, A. (2004). Critical dimensions of urban life in Africa. In T. Falola & S. J. Salm (Eds.), *Globalization and urbanization in Africa*. Trenton; Asmara: Africa World Press.

Slomka, W. (1991). The hierarchy of human values. In G. F. McLean & J. Kromkowski (Eds.), *Urbanization and values*. Washington, D.C.: Council for Research in Values and Philosophy.

Soares-Prabhu, G. M. (1986). Missiology or Missiologies? *Mission Studies, 3*(2), 85-87.

Spindler, M., & Pobee, J. (1979). Hermeneutics of Mission. *Missiology, 7*(1), 81-85.

Spindler, M. R. (1995). The Biblical Grounding and Orientation of Mission. In F. J. Verstraelen, A. Camps, L.A. Hoedemaker and M.R. Spindler (Ed.), *Missiology: An Ecumenical Introduction: Texts and Contexts of Global Christianity* (pp. 237-252). Grand Rapids: Eerdmans.

Storper, M., & Scott, A. J. (2015). Current debates in urban theory: A critical assessment. *Urban Stud. Urban Studies, 53*(6), 1114-1136.

Sugirtharajah, R. S. (1999). *Vernacular Hermeneutics*. Sheffield: Sheffield Academic Press.

Swilling, M. (2016). Urban metabolism and transition. In A. Allen, M. Swilling & A. Lampis (Eds.), *Untamed urbanisms*.

Taber, C. R. (1983). Missiology and the Bible. *Missiology, 11*(2), 229-245.

Taylor, P. J., Hoyler, M., & Verbruggen, R. (2010). External urban relational process: Introducing central flow theory to complement central place theory. *Urban Studies, 47*(13), 2803-2818.

Thiselton, A. C. (1992). *New Horizons in Hermeneutics: The Theory and Practice of Transforming Biblical Reading*. Grand Rapids, MI: Zondervan Publishing House.

Thiselton, A. C. (1995). New Testament Interpretation in Historical Perspective. In J. Green (Ed.), *Hearing the New Testament: Strategies for Interpretation* (pp. 10-36). Grand Rapids, Mich. : W.B. Eerdmans Pub. Co.: Carlisle.

Tiénou, T. (2006). Christian Theology in an Era of World Christianity. In C. Ott & H. A. Netland (Eds.), *Globalizing Theology: Belief and Practice in an Era of World Christianity* (pp. 37-51). Grand Rapids, MI: Baker Academic.

Tolbert, M. A. (1995). Reading for Liberation. In F. F. Segovia & M. A. Tolbert (Eds.), *Reading from This Place: Social Location and Biblical Interpretation in the United States* (Vol. 1). Minneapolis: Fortress Pr.

UNGA. (1948-49). Universal Declaration of Human Rights. Paris: United Nations General Assembly.
UNGA. (1959). Declaration of the Rights of the Child (Vol. General Assembly Resolution 1386(XIV)): United Nations General Assembly.
UNODC. (2015). United Nations Standard Minimum Rules for the Treatment of Prisoners (the Nelson Mandela Rules) (Vol. General Assembly resolution 70/175): United Nations Office on Drugs and Crime.
Van Engen, C. (1996). *Mission on the Way: Issues in Mission Theology*. Grand Rapids: Baker Books.
Van Engen, C. (2006). The Glocal Church: Locality and Catholicity in a Globalizing World. In C. Ott & H. A. Netland (Eds.), *Globalizing Theology: Belief and Practice in an Era of World Christianity* (pp. 157-179). Grand Rapids, MI: Baker Academic.
Van Engen, C. (2016). Innovating Mission: Retrospect and Prospect in the Field of Missiology. In C. Van Engen (Ed.), *The State of Missiology Today: Global Innovations in Christian Witness* (pp. 1-15). Downers Grove, IL: IVP Academic.
Vanhoozer, K. J. (2006). "One Rule to Rule Them All?": Theological Method in an Era of World Christiantiy. In C. Ott & H. A. Netland (Eds.), *Globalizing Theology: Belief and Practice in an Era of World Christianity* (pp. 85-126). Grand Rapids, MI: Baker Academic.
Verkuyl, J. (1978). *Contemporary Missiology: An Introduction*. Grand Rapids, MI: Eerdmans.
Verstraelen, F. J. (1995). *Missiology: An Ecumenical Introduction: Texts and Contexts of Global Christianity*. Grand Rapids: Eerdmans.
von Rad, G. (1972). *Genesis: a commentary. Uniform Title: Erste Buch Mose: Genesis. English* (Rev. ed.). Philadelphia: Westminster Press.
Voss, I. (2017). *Tell me your story: Evaluating and comparing group agency in two African American congregations in South Los Angeles*. PhD Dissertation, Fuller Theological Seminary, Pasadena.

Vriezen, T. C. (1958). *Outline of Old Testament Theology*. Oxford; Wageningen, Netherlands: Basil Blackwell; H Veenman.

Walls, A. (2006). Globalization and the Study of Christian History. In C. Ott & H. A. Netland (Eds.), *Globalizing Theology: Belief and Practice in an Era of World Christianity* (pp. 70-82). Grand Rapids, MI: Baker Academic.

Weissner, P., & Schiefenhovel, W. (Eds.). (1998). *Food and the status quest: an interdisciplinary perspective*. Providence RI: Berghahn Books.

West, G. O. (1995). *Biblical Hermeneutics of Liberation: Modes of Reading the Bible in the South African Context* (2nd, rev. ed.). Pietermaritzburg: Cluster Publications: Maryknoll, N.Y.

Westermann, C. (1984). *Genesis 1-11: A Commentary* (J. J. Scullion, Trans.). Minneapolis: Augsburg Pub. House.

Wheeler, S. E. (1995). *Wealth as peril and obligation: the New Testament on possessions*. Grand Rapids, Mich.: W.B. Eerdmans Pub.

Wilson, H. F. (2017). Encounter. In M. Jayne & K. Ward (Eds.), *Urban theory: new critical perspectives*. London and New York: Routledge.

Wimsatt, W. K. J., & Beardsley, M. (1954). The Intentional Fallacy *The Verbal Icon: Studies in the Meaning of Poetry*. Lexington: University of Kentucky Press. (Reprinted from: Internet republication by Nina Schwartz, Southern Methodist University).

Wittenberg, G. (1975). The Image of God: Demythologization and Democratization in the Old Testament. *Journal of Theology for Southern Africa*(13), 12-23.

Wittgenstein, L. (1969). *Philosophical Investigations. Uniform Title: Philosophische Untersuchungen. English & German* (3d ed.). New York: Macmillan.

Wright, C. J. H. (2004). Mission as a Matrix for Hermeneutics and Biblical Theology *Out of Egypt* (pp. 102-143). Milton Keynes and Grand Rapids, MI: Paternoster and Zondervan.

Wright, C. J. H. (2006). *The Mission of God: Unlocking the Bible's Grand Narrative*: IVP Academic.

Wright, S. (2013). Quotes/Jokes Retrieved May 18, 2018, from http://www.stevenwright.ca/quotes.html

www.ingramcontent.com/pod-product-compliance
Lightning Source LLC
Chambersburg PA
CBHW050158240426
43671CB00013B/2167